AMERICA'S
BYWAYS™

Mobil ✰✰
Travel Guide

AMERICA'S BYWAYS™ OF THE
MOUNTAIN
REGION

come
CLOSER *to* the heart and soul of
your AMERICA

We gratefully acknowledge our inspection team for their efficient and perceptive evaluations of the establishments listed in this book and the establishments for their cooperation in showing their facilities and providing information about them. Thanks also go to the National Scenic Byways Program and the coordinators of the individual Byways for all their help and support in the coordination of this project.

VICE PRESIDENT, PUBLICATIONS: **Kevin Bristow**
MANAGING EDITOR: **Pam Mourouzis**
MANAGER OF PUBLISHING PRODUCTION SERVICES: **Ellen Tobler**
CONCEPT AND COVER DESIGN: **ABS Graphics, Inc. Design Group**
EDITOR: **Tere Drenth**
PRINTING ACKNOWLEDGEMENT: **North American Corporation of Illinois**

ISBN: 0-9727-0229-6

Manufactured in the United States of America.

10 9 8 7 6 5 4 3 2 1

America's Byways of the Mountain Region

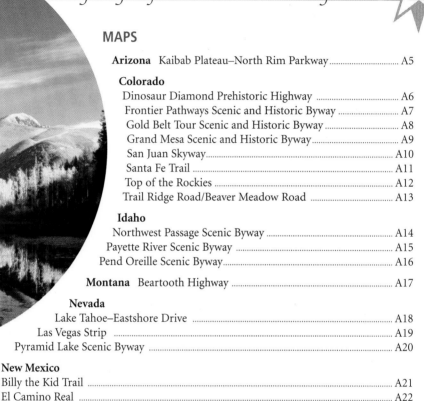

continued on next page

America's Byways Series | MOBIL TRAVEL GUIDE

Table of Contents

Kanab

89 UTAH

ARIZONA

GLEN CANYON N.R.A.

KAIBAB IND. RES.

389 Fredonia

ALT 89

Pipe Spring Natl. Mon.

Kanab Cr.

KAIBAB

Marble Canyon

Jacob Lake Inn

Kaibab Plateau Vis. Ctr.

Jacob Lake

ALT 89

89 US

Bitter Springs

KAIBAB NATL. FOR.

PLATEAU

89

67

Kaibab Lodge

East Rim Vista

Colorado

N

GRAND CANYON

NATL. PARK

▲ Pt. Imperial 8,803

NAVAJO IND. RES.

HAVASUPAI IND. RES.

North Rim

Grand Canyon Lodge

Bright Angel Point

Cape Royal

Desert View

South Rim Vis. Ctr.

Grand Canyon

Tusayan

64

64

0   10 mi

0   10 km

© MapQuest.com, Inc.

WYOMING

43 Manila

80

Coalville

150 WASATCH - CACHE
NATL. FOR.

Oakley

Kamas

44

191

BROWNS
PARK N.W.R.

318

Maybell

ASHLEY
NATL. FOR.

Steinaker
S.P.

Red Fleet S.P.

Dinosaur Quarry

Heber
City

CLOSED IN
WINTER

Maeser

DINOSAUR

40

Altamont

121

40
191

Vernal

Jensen

NATL. MON.

40 Fruitland

35

87

Roosevelt

Dinosaur

UINTA
NATL.
FOR.

Strawberry

Duchesne

Ouray

OURAY
N.W.R.

White

64

Rangely

64

191

6

Colton

Scofield

Helper

Bonanza

UINTAH AND
OURAY
IND. RES.

COLORADO   UTAH

139

0   25 mi

0   25 km

Price

Wellington

MANTI-LA SAL

Huntington   Cleveland

East Carbon

COLORADO
CANYONS
N.C.A.

70

6

NATL.

10

Cleveland
Lloyd
Dinosaur
Quarry

6
191

Green
River

N

Crescent
Junction

6
50

Fruita

Ferron

FOR.

Emery

70   50

24

ARCHES
N.P.

191

Cisco

128

COLORADO
N.M.

**Grand
Junction**

141   50

Fremont
Junction

CANYONLANDS
NATL. PARK

Moab

Fisher Towers

Castle   Gateway
Valley

Delta

Hanksville

Upheaval
Dome

Colorado

MANTI-LA SAL
NATL. FOR.

UNCOMPAHGRE

141   NATL.

24

CAPITOL
REEF N.P.

95

Grand
View Pt.

La Sal
Junction

La
Sal

Bedrock

FOR.

© MapQuest.com, Inc.

© MapQuest.com, Inc.

N

⑨ 9

Parkdale

Royal Gorge

Cañon City

115

FORT CARSON MIL. RES.

I-25

85 87

50

Colo. Terr. Prison Mus.

Penrose

Florence

Arkansas

50

Pueblo West

67

Lake Pueblo S.P.

96

Pueblo

BUS 50

Wetmore

Greenwood

69

96

HARDSCRABBLE CANYON

78

Westcliffe

Silver Cliff

165

WET MTN. VALLEY

Humboldt Pk. 14,064

▲
▲Crestone Pk. 14,294

SAN ISABEL NATL. FOR.

WET MTS.

GREENHORN HWY.

San Isabel

Rye

Cuerño Verde Vis. Ctr.

I-25

85 87

Colorado City

SANGRE DE CRISTO RA.

RIO GRANDE NATL. FOR.

Great Sand Dunes Natl. Mon.

Gardner

69

0 ————— 20 mi
0 ————— 20 km

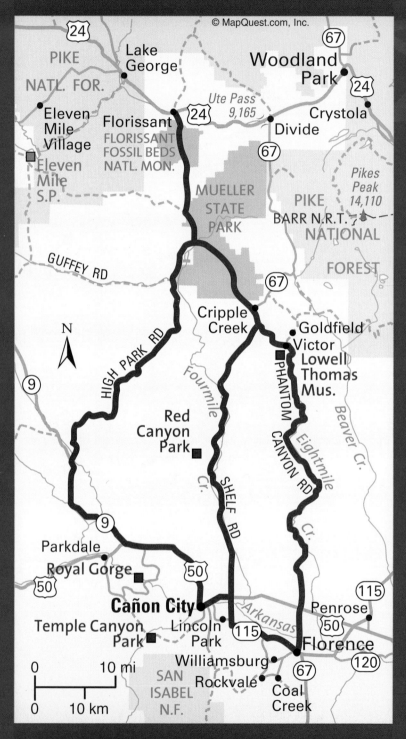

© MapQuest.com, Inc.

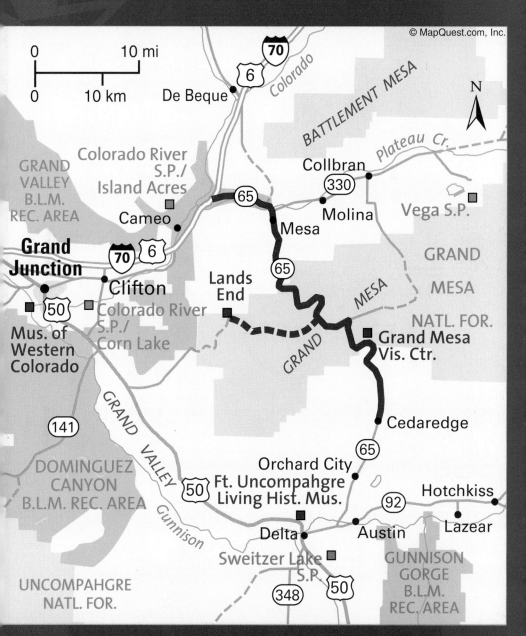

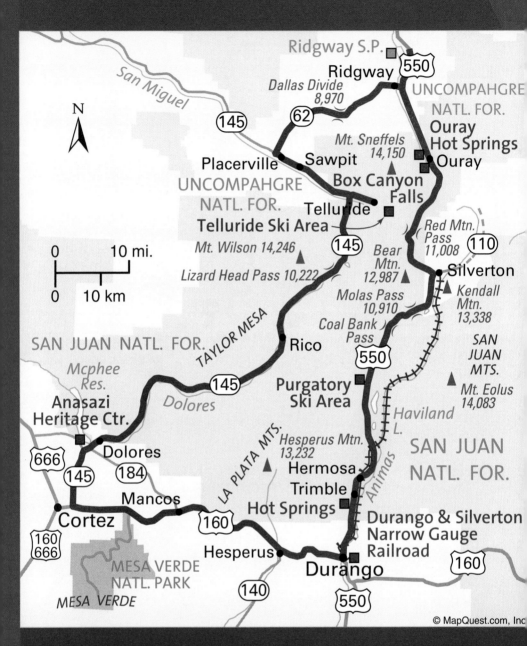

285 Pueblo ○ 287 385 Holly

Westcliffe Bent's Old Fort 50
Kit Carson Mus. N.H.S. Las Lamar
69 165 25 50 Animas
GREAT SAND DUNES N. PARK GREAT SAND DUNES N. PRES. 10 Timpas La Junta 287 385 89

Walsenburg COMANCHE N.G. 160
Alamosa 350 FT. CARSON MIL. RES. 109
160 12
285 SAN SABEL N.F. Trinidad Baca House 160 COMANCHE N.G.
159 Trinidad Lake COLO. S.P. Raton Pass 7,839

N. MEX. Raton 72 Des Moines 410 OK 325 Boise City
CARSON N.F. 64 412
522 Maxwell N.W.R. 64 Grenville 406 64 412
Questa Cimarron Springer 56 412 453 64 87 Clayton 287 RITA BLANCA N.G.
64 64 21 Abbott 56 412 56 412 KIOWA N.G. 87
Taos Rayado Gladstone 102 Dahlhart
285 68 518 120 25 Santa Fe Trail Mus. 120 54
Espanola 161 KIOWA N.G. 402
Buena Vista Wagon Mound N
SANTE FE Ft. Union N.M. 385
Santa Fe 518 N.F. Watrous 419 40
14 Pecos Las Vegas Conchas L. 39 Vega
Pecos N.H.P. 104 Romeroville 385
3 San Jose 104 Tucumcari 40
40 84 129 40 54
41 285 Santa Rosa 209 N. MEX. 0 30 mi
60 54 209 0 30 km
Vaughn 84 © MapQuest.com, Inc.

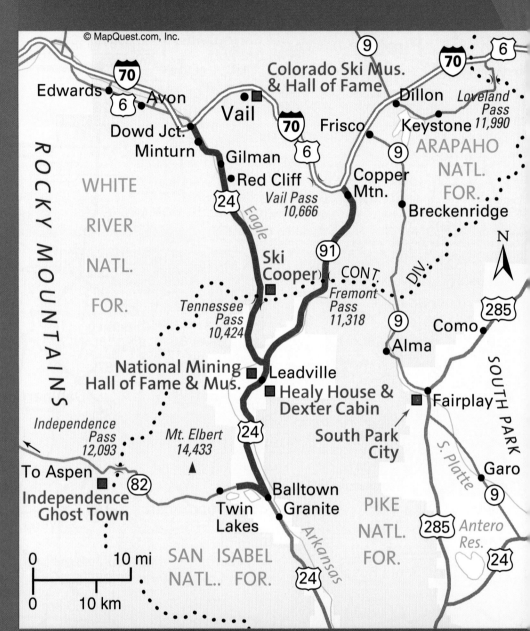

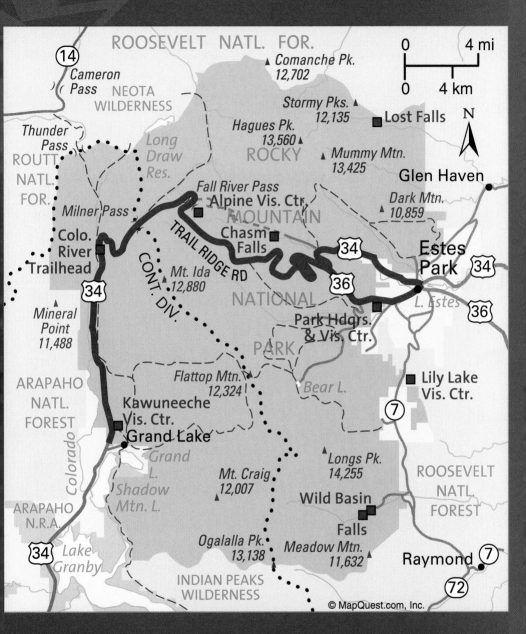

ROOSEVELT NATL. FOR.

(14) Cameron Pass

NEOTA WILDERNESS

▲ Comanche Pk. 12,702

Stormy Pks. ▲ 12,135

■ Lost Falls

Hagues Pk. 13,560 ▲

ROCKY

▲ Mummy Mtn. 13,425

Glen Haven

Thunder Pass

Long Draw Res.

Fall River Pass

Alpine Vis. Ctr.

Dark Mtn. 10,859

ROUTT NATL. FOR.

Milner Pass

MOUNTAIN

Chasm Falls ■

Colo. River Trailhead

(34)

CONT. DIV.

TRAIL RIDGE RD

Mt. Ida 12,880

(34)

Estes Park (34)

(36)

NATIONAL

L. Estes

(36)

Mineral Point 11,488

Park Hdqrs. & Vis. Ctr.

PARK

ARAPAHO NATL. FOREST

Flattop Mtn. 12,324

Bear L.

■ Lily Lake Vis. Ctr.

(7)

Kawuneeche Vis. Ctr.

Grand Lake

Colorado

Grand L.

Shadow Mtn. L.

Longs Pk. 14,255

ROOSEVELT NATL. FOREST

ARAPAHO N.R.A.

Mt. Craig 12,007 ▲

Wild Basin ■■

Falls

(34) Lake Granby

Ogalalla Pk. 13,138

Meadow Mtn. 11,632 ▲

Raymond (7)

INDIAN PEAKS WILDERNESS

(72)

© MapQuest.com, Inc.

0 — 4 mi
0 — 4 km

N

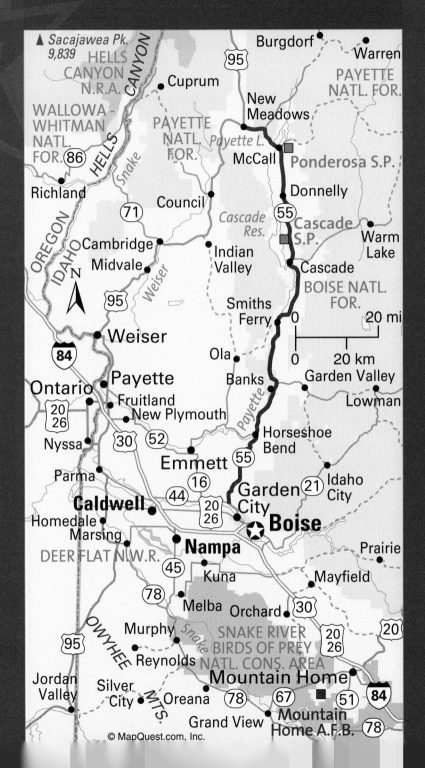

© MapQuest.com, Inc.

ID ✳ Pend Oreille Scenic Byway

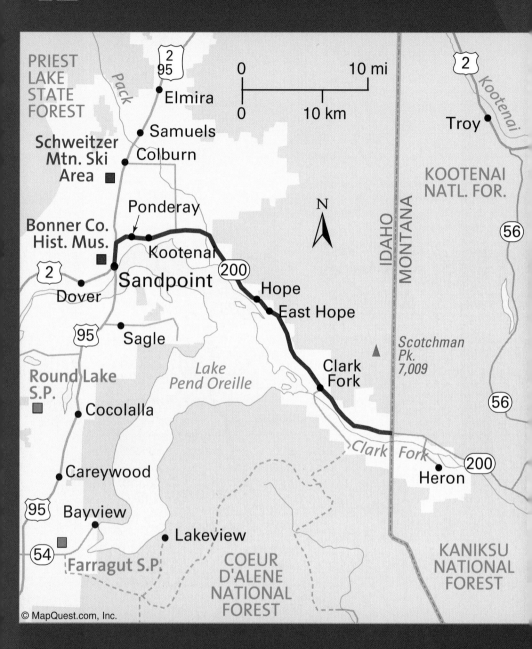

PRIEST LAKE STATE FOREST

Pack

[2] [95]

Elmira

Samuels

Schweitzer Mtn. Ski Area

Colburn

Ponderay

Bonner Co. Hist. Mus.

Kootenai

[2]

Sandpoint

Dover

[95]

Sagle

Round Lake S.P.

Lake Pend Oreille

N

[200]

Hope

East Hope

Clark Fork

IDAHO

MONTANA

KOOTENAI NATL. FOR.

Troy

Kootenai

[2]

[56]

Scotchman Pk. 7,009

[56]

Cocolalla

Careywood

[95]

Bayview

[54]

Lakeview

Farragut S.P.

COEUR D'ALENE NATIONAL FOREST

Clark Fork

[200]

Heron

KANIKSU NATIONAL FOREST

0   10 mi
0   10 km

© MapQuest.com, Inc.

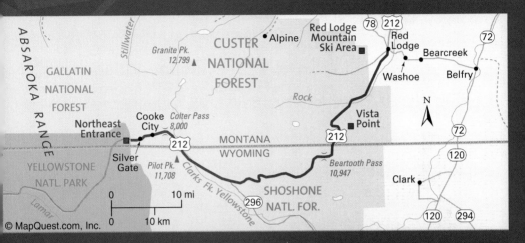

NV Lake Tahoe–Eastshore Drive

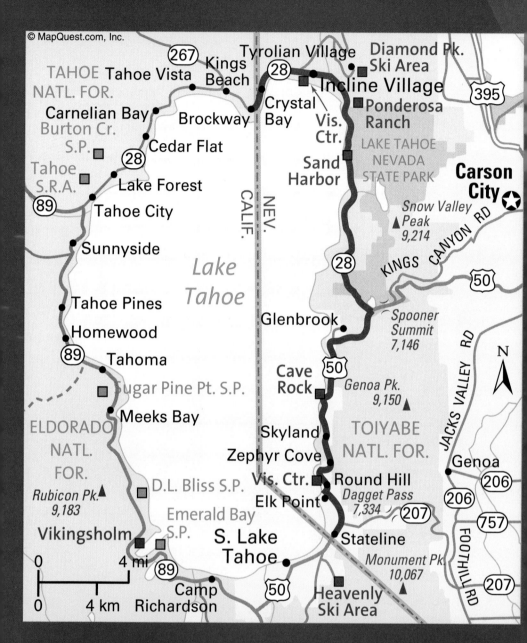

© MapQuest.com, Inc.

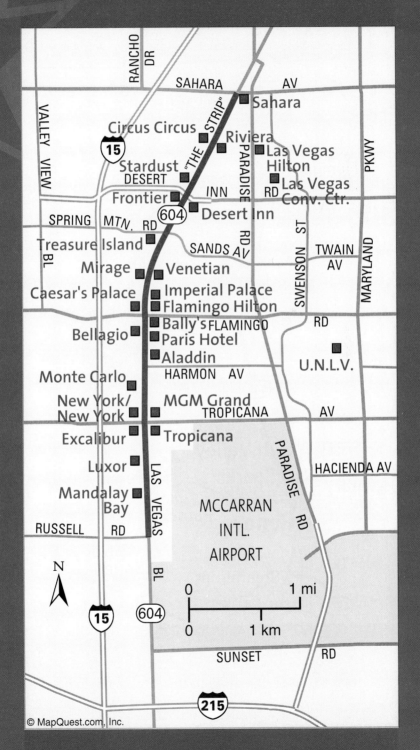

Las Vegas Strip NV

RANCHO DR

SAHARA AV

VALLEY VIEW

"THE STRIP"

15

Circus Circus

Riviera

Sahara

Las Vegas Hilton

PARADISE RD

PKWY

Stardust

DESERT

INN

Las Vegas Conv. Ctr.

Frontier

604

Desert Inn

SPRING MTN. RD

Treasure Island

SANDS AV

BL

ST

SWENSON

TWAIN AV

MARYLAND

Mirage

Venetian

Caesar's Palace

Imperial Palace

Flamingo Hilton

Bally's FLAMINGO

RD

Bellagio

Paris Hotel

Aladdin

HARMON AV

U.N.L.V.

Monte Carlo

New York/ New York

MGM Grand

TROPICANA AV

Excalibur

Tropicana

PARADISE RD

HACIENDA AV

Luxor

Mandalay Bay

LAS VEGAS BL

RUSSELL RD

MCCARRAN INTL. AIRPORT

N

15

604

0   1 mi

0   1 km

SUNSET RD

215

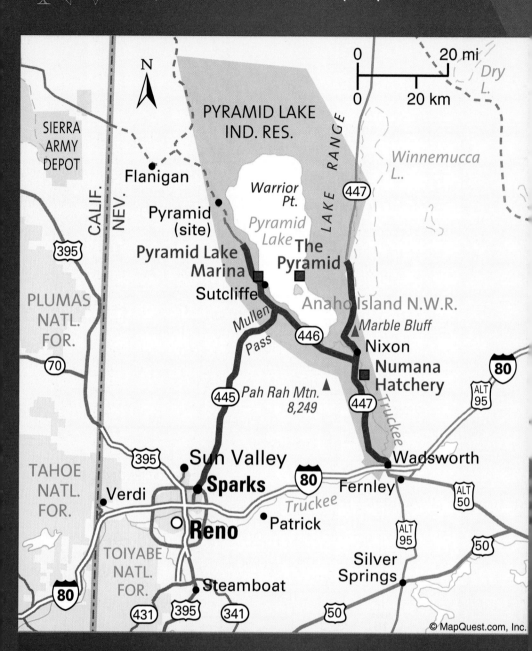

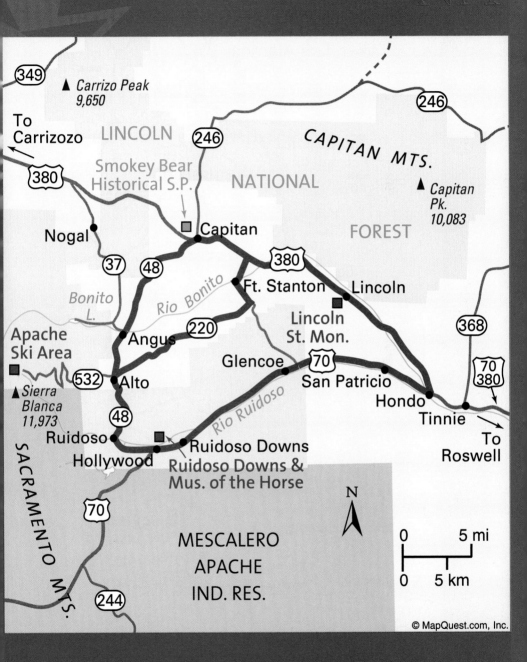

0 ——— 30 mi
0 ——— 30 km

Los Alamos
Bandelier N.M.
84 / 285
SANTA FE N. F.
25
COCHITI PUEBLO
550
16
★ Santa Fe
Pecos Natl. Hist. Park
SANTA FE N. F.
Rio Rancho
Bernalillo
285
Grants
Petroglyph N.M.
○ Albuquerque
84
40
ACOMA PUEBLO
ISLETA PUEBLO
40
EL MALPAIS NATL. MON.
Isleta
41
Belen
60
25
47
54
285
Bernardo
SEVILLETA N.W.R.
Salinas Pueblo Missions Natl. Mon.
N
60
Socorro
380
CIBOLA
LINCOLN N.F.
1
Bosque del Apache N.W.R.
Carrizozo
NATL.
1
54
FOREST
Elephant Butte Lake S.P.
380
Truth or Consequences
WHITE SANDS MISSILE RANGE
Ruidoso
70
MESCALERO APACHE I.R.
Caballo Res.
Tularosa
152
WHITE SANDS N.M.
82
187
Hatch
Alamogordo
26
25
54
LINCOLN
180
185
70
NATL. FOR.
10
FORT BLISS MIL. RES.
Deming
Las Cruces
11
Mesilla
N.MEX
28
TEX.
U.S.
Anthony
62 / 180
MEX.
273
El Paso
Sunland Park
10
Ciudad Juárez
Rio Grande
© MapQuest.com, Inc.

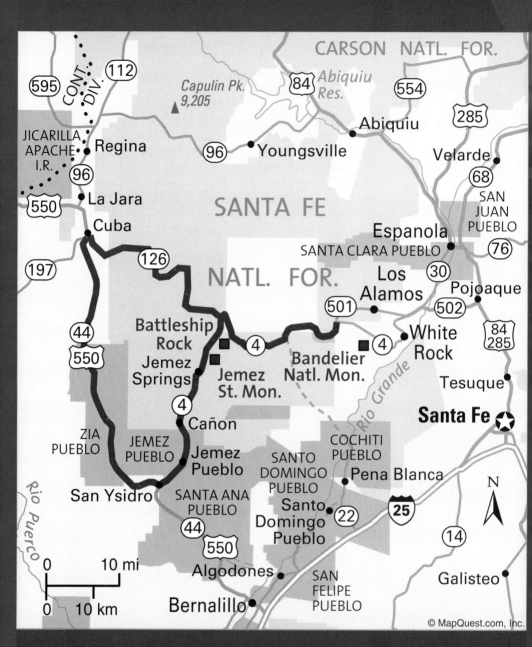

CARSON NATL. FOR.

595
112
CONT. DIV.

Capulin Pk.
9,205

84
Abiquiu
Res.

554

285

JICARILLA
APACHE
I.R.
Regina
96
Youngsville
Abiquiu

Velarde
68

96
La Jara

SAN
FE

Espanola
SANTA CLARA PUEBLO

SAN
JUAN
PUEBLO

76

550
Cuba

197
126

44
550

Battleship
Rock
Jemez
Springs

NATL. FOR.

Los
Alamos
501

30

Pojoaque
502

84
285

4

4
White
Rock

Tesuque

Bandelier
Natl. Mon.

Jemez
St. Mon.

4
Cañon

ZIA
PUEBLO
JEMEZ
PUEBLO
Jemez
Pueblo

San Ysidro

Rio Grande

Santa Fe ✪

SANTA ANA
PUEBLO

44

550

Rio Puerco

0   10 mi

0   10 km

Algodones

Bernalillo

COCHITI
PUEBLO
Pena Blanca

SANTO
DOMINGO
PUEBLO
Santo
Domingo
Pueblo

22

25

N

14

Galisteo

SAN
FELIPE
PUEBLO

© MapQuest.com, Inc.

SANTA FE N. F.

Cochiti Lake

COCHITI PUEBLO

SANTA FE N. F.

Santa Fe ⭐

JEMEZ PUEBLO

Pena Blanca

La Cienega

⑭

I-25

SANTO DOMINGO PUEBLO

⑯

㉒

Domingo

N

SANTA ANA PUEBLO

SAN FELIPE PUEBLO

I-25

Casa Grande Mining Mus.

Madrid

Los Cerrillos

Galisteo

㊽
U.S. 550

Algodones

⑭

Old Coal Mine Mus.

㊶

Bernalillo

⑤②⑧

SANDIA PUEBLO

㉕⑤

Placitas

0   10 mi

0   10 km

③①③

Sandia Cr. 10,678

SANDIA MTN. WILDERNESS

Golden

㉞④

Sandia Crest

⑤③⑥

Cedar Grove

Stanley

Tramway

Tinkertown Mus.

San Antonito

④⑦②

I-25

⑤⑤⑥

⑭

CIBOLA

Cedar Crest

I-40

㊶

Albuquerque

NATL.

Tijeras

③③③

Albuquerque Intl. Sunport

FOR.

Ranger St.

I-40

Edgewood

© MapQuest.com, Inc.

UT

The Energy Loop: Huntington and Eccles Canyons Scenic Byways

0   10 mi

0   10 km

● Indianola

89

Scofield S.P.

Scofield Res.

96

Colton

6

191

Price

Price Canyon B.L.M. Rec. Area

● Milburn

Scofield

264

Kenilworth

Helper ●

Western Mining & Railroad Mus.

6 Spring Glen

31

Fairview

Clear Creek

Prehistoric Mus.

Price

San Pitch

31

116

Mt. Pleasant

Seeley Mtn. 10,362 ▲

Wattis

10

89

● Spring City

MANTI-LA SAL

Hiawatha

122

N ▲

NATIONAL

Elmo

FOREST

Huntington S.P.

31

155

Cleveland

Joes Valley Res.

Huntington

57

10

29

Castle Dale

© MapQuest.com, Inc.

© MapQuest.com, Inc.

0   40 mi
0   40 km

530

FLAMING GORGE NATL. REC. AREA

Flaming Gorge Res.

191

N

414

WYO.

43

Manila

Sheep Creek Canyon

44

Dutch John

Flaming Gorge Dam Vis. Ctr.

Green

318

HIGH UINTAS WILDERNESS AREA

Red Canyon Overlook and Vis. Ctr.

UINTA MTS.

UTAH | COLO.

Marsh Pk.▲ 12,240

191

ASHLEY NATL. FOR.

Red Fleet S.P.

DINOSAUR NATL. MON.

Steinaker S.P.

UINTAH AND OURAY IND. RES.

Utah Field House of Nat. Hist. S.P.

Dinosaur Quarry Vis. Ctr.

Vernal

• **Neola**

121

Naples

149

State Welcome Ctr.

121

40 191

Jensen

45

Green

• **Roosevelt**

• **Fort Duchesne**

40

A Journey Through Time Scenic Byway–
Highway 12

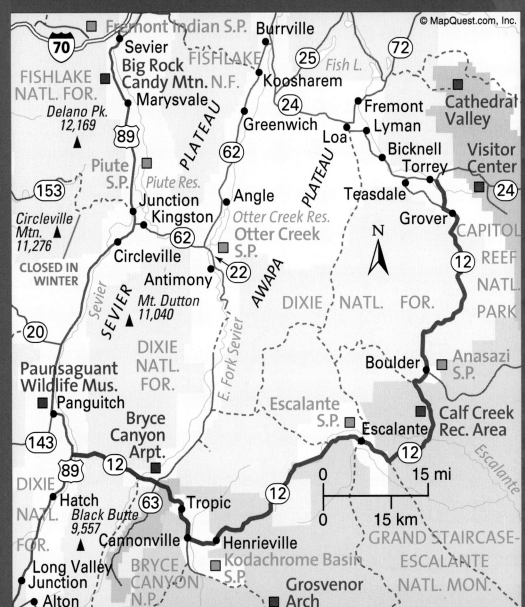

© MapQuest.com, Inc.

CARIBOU
N.F.

Woodruff
36

Weston

Preston

Minnetonka
Cave

St.
Charles

89

Bear
Lake

Fish Haven
IDAHO

Portage

Cornish

Lewiston

Beaver
Mtn.

UTAH

Bear Lake
S.P.

15

Clarkston

61

142

Richmond

Garden City

Plymouth

Newton

Trenton

Bear Lake
(Rendezvous
Beach) S.P.

13

Fielding

218

Smithfield
Utah
State
Univ.

89

Laketown

30

30

23

91

91

WASATCH-
CACHE
N.F.

Logan

Providence

Garland

Tremonton

Wellsville

Hyrum

101

Bear
River
City

Honeyville

38

89
91

Hyrum S.P.

Paradise

Corinne

Brigham City

BEAR RIVER
MIGRATORY
BIRD REFUGE

Mantua

Perry

39

Willard
Bay S.P.

Willard

Powder
Mtn.

CLOSED IN
WINTER

0   15 mi

89

Pleasant
View

Nordic
Valley

0   15 km

15 84

Plain City

North Ogden

39

© MapQuest.com, Inc.

N

BEAR RIVER RANGE

Bear

Logan

84

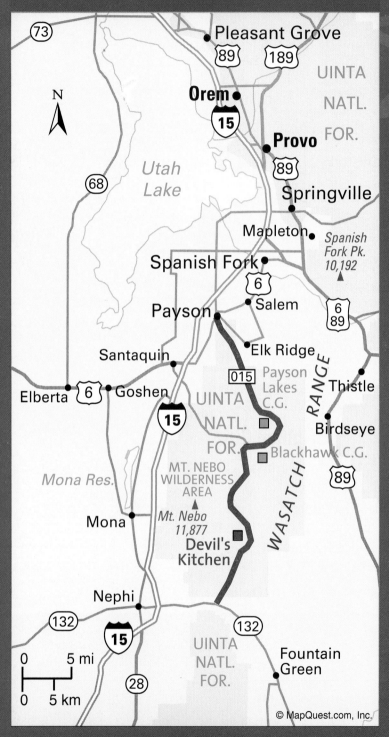

come CLOSER to *the heart and soul of* *your* AMERICA

America's Byways are a distinctive collection of American roads, their stories and treasured places. They are roads to the heart and soul of America. Each and every Byway has unique qualities that make it special, whether it is a coastal highway known for its striking scenery or a historic route that takes travelers on a path through the country's past. The images on these pages give you only a taste of what the Byways in this region have to offer. For more photos, see the individual Byways.

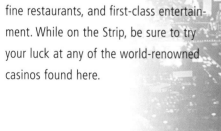

Las Vegas Strip

Dusk falls over the Las Vegas Strip

The Las Vegas Strip dazzles Byway visitors with four and a half miles of luxury hotels, fine restaurants, and first-class entertainment. While on the Strip, be sure to try your luck at any of the world-renowned casinos found here.

Nevada

A Journey Through Time
Scenic Byway – Highway 12

Fossilized rock formations

Along Highway 12, the stone towers, pinnacles, and arches—formed by water and wind over millions of years—present an artistic masterpiece to travelers. Vivid colors and irregular shapes beckon you to look closer.

Utah

Beartooth Scenic Byway

Fisherman in Clarks Fork of Yellowstone River

The area surrounding the Beartooth Scenic Byway offers a wealth of recreational opportunities, including trout fishing. Visitors also enjoy hiking, cross-country skiing, and riding horseback on the area's many trails; watching and photographing wildlife; and camping in any of the 12 national forests along the way.

Wyoming

A Word to Our Readers

Travelers are on the roads in great numbers these days. They're exploring the country on day trips, weekend getaways, business trips, and extended family vacations, visiting major cities and small towns along the way. Because time is precious and the travel industry is ever-changing, having accurate, reliable travel information at your fingertips is critical. Mobil Travel Guide has been providing invaluable insight to travelers for more than 45 years, and we are committed to continuing this service well into the future.

The Mobil Corporation (known as Exxon Mobil Corporation since a 1999 merger) began producing the Mobil Travel Guide books in 1958, following the introduction of the US highway system in 1956. The first edition covered only five southwestern states. Since then, our books have become the premier travel guides in North America, covering the 48 contiguous states and Canada. Now, Mobil Travel Guide presents a brand-new series in partnership with the National Scenic Byways Program. We also recently introduced road atlases and specialty publications; a robust new Web site; as well as the first fully integrated, road-centric travel support program called MobilCompanion, the driving force in travel.

Since its founding, Mobil Travel Guide has served as an advocate for travelers seeking knowledge about hotels, restaurants, and places to visit. Based on an objective process, we make recommendations to our customers that we believe will enhance the quality and value of their travel experiences. Our trusted Mobil One- to Five-Star rating system is the oldest and most respected lodging and restaurant inspection and rating program in North America. Most hoteliers, restaurateurs, and industry observers favorably regard the rigor

of our inspection program and understand the prestige and benefits that come with receiving a Mobil star rating.

The Mobil Travel Guide process of rating each establishment includes:

- Unannounced facility inspections

- Incognito service evaluations for Mobil Four- and Five-Star properties

- A review of unsolicited comments from the general public

- Senior management oversight

For each property, more than 450 attributes, including cleanliness, physical facilities, employee attitude, and courtesy, are measured and evaluated to produce a mathematically derived score, which is then blended with the other elements to form an overall score. These quantifiable scores allow comparative analysis among properties and form the basis that Mobil Travel Guide uses to assign its Mobil One- to Five-Star ratings.

This process focuses largely on guest expectations, guest experience, and consistency of service, not just physical facilities and amenities. It is fundamentally a relative rating system that rewards those properties that continually strive for and achieve excellence each year. Indeed, the very best properties are consistently raising the bar for those that wish to compete with them. These properties proactively respond to consumers' needs even in today's uncertain times.

Only facilities that meet Mobil Travel Guide's standards earn the privilege of being listed in our books. Deteriorating, poorly managed establishments are deleted. A Mobil Travel Guide listing constitutes a positive quality recommendation; every listing is an accolade, a recognition of achievement. Our Mobil One- to Five-Star rating system highlights its level of service. Extensive in-house research is constantly underway to determine new additions to our lists.

• The **Mobil Five-Star Award** indicates that a property is one of the very best in the country and consistently provides gracious and courteous service, superlative quality in its facility, and a unique ambience. The lodgings and restaurants at the Mobil Five-Star level consistently and proactively respond to consumers' needs and continue their commitment to excellence, doing so with grace and perseverance.

• Also highly regarded is the **Mobil Four-Star Award,** which honors properties for outstanding achievement in overall facility and for providing very strong service levels in all areas. These award-winners provide a distinctive experience for the ever-demanding and sophisticated consumer.

• The **Mobil Three-Star Award** recognizes an excellent property that provides full services and amenities. This category ranges from exceptional hotels with limited services to elegant restaurants with a less-formal atmosphere.

• A **Mobil Two-Star property** is a clean and comfortable establishment that has expanded amenities or a distinctive environment. A Mobil Two-Star property is an excellent place to stay or dine.

• A **Mobil One-Star property** is limited in its amenities and services but focuses on providing a value experience while meeting travelers' expectations. The property can be expected to be clean, comfortable, and convenient.

Allow us to emphasize that we do not charge establishments for inclusion in our guides. We have no relationship with any of the businesses and attractions we list and act only as a consumer advocate. In essence, we do the investigative legwork so that you won't have to.

Keep in mind, too, that the hospitality business is ever-changing. Restaurants and lodgings— particularly small chains and standalone establishments—change management or even go out of business with surprising quickness. Although we make every effort to double-check information during our annual updates, we nevertheless recommend that you call ahead to make sure the place you've selected is still open and offers all the amenities you're looking for. We've provided phone numbers; when available, we also list Web site addresses.

We hope that your travels are enjoyable and relaxing and that our books help you get the most out of every trip you take. If any aspect of your accommodation, dining, or sightseeing experience motivates you to comment, please drop us a line. We depend a great deal on our readers' remarks, so you can be assured that we will read your comments and assimilate them into our research. General comments about our books are also welcome. You can write to us at Mobil Travel Guide, 1460 Renaissance Drive, Suite 401, Park Ridge, IL 60068, or send an e-mail to info@mobiltravelguide.com.

Take your Mobil Travel Guide books along on every trip you take. We're confident that you'll be pleased with their convenience, ease of use, and breadth of dependable coverage.

Happy travels!

Overview of the National Scenic Byways Program

WHAT ARE AMERICA'S BYWAYS™?

Under the National Scenic Byways Program, the US Secretary of Transportation recognizes certain roads as National Scenic Byways or All-American Roads based on their archaeological, cultural, historic, natural, recreational, and scenic qualities. There are 96 such designated Byways in 39 states. The Federal Highway Administration promotes the collection as America's Byways™.

America's Byways™ are a distinctive collection of American roads, their stories and treasured places. They are roads to the heart and soul of America. Byways are exclusive because of their outstanding qualities, not because Byways are confined to a select group of people.

Managing the intrinsic qualities that shape the Byway's story and interpreting the story are equally important in improving the quality of the visitors' experience. The National Scenic Byways Program is founded upon the strength of the leaders for individual Byways. It is a voluntary, grassroots program. It recognizes and supports outstanding roads. It provides resources to help manage the intrinsic qualities within the broader Byway corridor to be treasured and shared. Perhaps one of the underlying principles for the program has been articulated best by the Byway leader who said, "The program is about recognition, not regulation."

WHAT DEFINES A NATIONAL SCENIC BYWAY AND AN ALL-AMERICAN ROAD?

To be designated as a National Scenic Byway, a road must possess at least one of the six intrinsic qualities described below. To receive an All-American Road designation, a road must possess multiple intrinsic qualities that are nationally significant and contain one-of-a-kind features that do not exist elsewhere. The road or highway must also be considered a destination unto itself. That is, the road must provide an exceptional traveling experience so recognized by travelers that they would make a drive along the highway a primary reason for their trip.

Anyone may nominate a road for possible designation by the US Secretary of Transportation, but the nomination must be submitted through a state's official scenic byway agency and include a corridor management plan designed to preserve and enhance the unique qualities of the Byway.

The Byways themselves typically are supported through a network of individuals who volunteer their time and effort. It is a bottom-up, grassroots-oriented program. Local citizens and communities create the vision for their Byway, identify the resources comprising the intrinsic qualities, and form the theme or story that stirs the interest and imagination of visitors about the Byway and its resources. Local citizens and communities decide how best to balance goals, strategies, and actions for promoting the Byway and preserving its intrinsic qualities. The vision, goals, strategies, and actions for the Byway are laid out in the required corridor management plan.

Nomination is not about filling out an application. It's all about telling the Byway's story. That's the premise that is driving the FHWA's work on requesting nominations for possible national designation. Nominees might want to think of their Byway's nomination as a combination of the community's guide and a visitor's guide for the Byway.

WHAT ARE INTRINSIC QUALITIES?

An intrinsic quality is a scenic, historic, recreational, cultural, archaeological, or natural feature that is considered representative, unique, irreplaceable, or distinctly characteristic of an area. The National Scenic Byways Program provides resources to the Byway community and enhances local quality of life through efforts to preserve, protect, interpret, and promote the intrinsic qualities of designated Byways.

- **Archaeological quality** involves those characteristics of the Byway corridor that are physical evidence of historic or prehistoric life that is visible and capable of being inventoried and interpreted.

- **Cultural quality** is evidence and expressions of the customs or traditions of a distinct group of people. Cultural features include, but are not limited to, crafts, music, dance, rituals, festivals, speech, food, special events, and vernacular architecture that are currently practiced.

- **Historic quality** encompasses legacies of the past that are distinctly associated with physical elements of the landscape, whether natural or man-made, that are of such historic significance that they educate the viewer and stir an appreciation of the past.

- **Natural quality** applies to those features in the visual environment that are in a relatively undisturbed state. These features predate the arrival of human populations and may include geological formations, fossils, landforms, water bodies, vegetation, and wildlife.

- **Recreational quality** involves outdoor recreational activities directly associated with, and dependent upon, the natural and cultural elements of the corridor's landscape.

- **Scenic quality** is the heightened visual experience derived from the view of natural and man-made elements of the visual environment.

For more information about the National Scenic Byways Program, call 800/4BYWAYS or visit the Web site www.byways.org.

Introduction

America's Byways™ are a distinctive collection of American roads, their stories, and treasured places. They are the roads to the heart and soul of America. This book showcases a select group of nationally designated Byways and organizes them by state, and within each state, alphabetically by Byway. Information in this book is collected from two sources:

- The National Scenic Byways Program (NSBP) provides content about the Byways themselves—quick facts, the Byway story, and highlights. NSBP's information contributors include federal, regional, and state organizations, as well as private groups and individuals. These parties have been recognized as experts in Byways and are an authoritative source for the Byways information that appears in this book.

- Information in this book about lodgings, restaurants, and most sights and attractions along the Byways comes from Mobil Travel Guide, which has served as a trusted aid to auto travelers in search of value in lodging, dining, and destinations since its inception in 1958. The Mobil One- to Five-Star rating system is the oldest and most respected lodging and restaurant inspection and rating program in North America. This trusted, well-established tool directs you to satisfying places to eat and stay, as well as to interesting events and attractions in thousands of locations.

The following sections explain the wealth of information you'll find about the Byways that appear in this book: information about the Byway, things to see and do along the way, and places to stay and eat.

Quick Facts

This section gives you an overview of each Byway, including the following quick facts:

LENGTH: The number of miles from one end of the Byway to the other.

TIME TO ALLOW: How much time to allow to drive the entire length. For some Byways, the suggested time is several days because of the length or the number of attractions on or near the Byway; for others, the time is listed in hours.

BEST TIME TO DRIVE: The season(s) in which the Byway is most appealing. For some Byways, you also discover the peak season, which you may want to avoid if you're looking for a peaceful, uncrowded drive.

BYWAY TRAVEL INFORMATION: Telephone numbers and Web sites for the Byway organization and any local travel and tourism centers.

SPECIAL CONSIDERATIONS: Words of advice that range from the type of clothing you'll want to bring to winter-weather advisories.

RESTRICTIONS: Closings or other cautionary tips.

BICYCLE/PEDESTRIAN FACILITIES: Explains whether the Byway is safe and pleasant for bicycling and/or walking.

THE BYWAY STORY

As explained in the preceding section titled "Overview of the National Scenic Byways Program," a road must possess intrinsic qualities and one-of-a-kind features to receive a National Scenic Byway or All-American Road designation. An All-American Road must also be considered a destination unto itself. This section describes the unique qualities of each Byway, with a separate section for each of its intrinsic qualities. Here you'll find information about the history and culture of the roadway, the wildlife and other natural features found along the Byway, and the recreational opportunities that are available to visitors to the area.

HIGHLIGHTS

Some local Byway organizations suggest tours or itineraries that cover all or part of the Byway. Where these itineraries are available, they're included in this book under the heading "Highlights."

THINGS TO SEE AND DO

Mobil Travel Guide offers information about nearly 20,000 museums, art galleries, amusement parks, historic sites, national and state parks, ski areas, and many other types of attractions. A white star on a black background ⭐ signals that the attraction is a must-see—one of the best in the area. Because municipal parks, public tennis courts, swimming pools, and small educational institutions are common to most towns, they generally are not mentioned.

When a Byway goes through or comes quite close to a particular town, city, or national park, attractions in those towns or parks are included. Otherwise, attractions are limited to those along the Byway.

Attractions for the entire Byway are listed alphabetically by name. Following an attraction's description, you'll find the months, days, and, in some cases, hours of operation; the address/directions, telephone number, and Web site (if there is one); and the admission price category. The following are the ranges we use for admission fees:

- **FREE**
- **DONATION**
- **$** = Up to $5
- **$$** = $5.01-$10
- **$$$** = $10.01-$15
- **$$$$** = $15.01 and up

PLACES TO STAY

For each Byway, recommended lodgings are listed in alphabetical order, based on the cities in which they're located. In general, only lodgings that are close to or located right on the Byway are listed.

Each lodging listing gives the name, address/location (when no street address is available), neighborhood and/or directions from downtown (in major cities), phone number(s), Web site (if available), total number of guest rooms, and seasons open (if not year-round). Also included are details on business, luxury, recreational, and dining facilities on the property or nearby. A key to the symbols at the end of each listing can be found in the "Terms, Abbreviations, and Symbols in Listings" section of this Introduction.

Because most lodgings offer the following features and services, information about them does not appear in the listings unless exceptions exist:

- Year-round operation with a single rate structure
- Major credit cards accepted (note that Exxon or Mobil Corporation credit cards cannot be used to pay for room or other charges)
- Air-conditioning and heat, often with individual room controls
- Bathroom with tub and/or shower in each room
- Cots and cribs available

• Daily maid service

• Elevators

• In-room telephones

For every property, we also provide pricing information. Because lodging rates change frequently, we list a pricing category rather than specific prices. The pricing categories break down as follows:

• ¢ = Up to $90

• $ = $91-$150

• $$ = $151-$250

• $$$ = $251-$350

• $$$$ = $351 and up

All prices quoted are in effect at the time of publication; however, prices cannot be guaranteed. Note that in some locations, short-term price variations may exist because of special events or holidays. Certain resorts have complicated rate structures that vary with the time of year; always confirm rates when making your plans.

All listed establishments have been inspected by experienced field representatives and/or evaluated by a senior staff member. Our ratings are based on detailed inspection reports of the individual properties, on written evaluations of staff members who stay and dine anonymously, and on an extensive review of reader comments. Rating categories reflect both the features a property offers and its quality in relation to similar establishments.

Here are the definitions for the star ratings for lodgings:

• ★★★★★: A Mobil Five-Star lodging provides consistently superlative service in an exceptionally distinctive luxury environment, with expanded services. Attention to detail is evident throughout the hotel, resort, or inn, from bed linens to staff uniforms.

• ★★★★: A Mobil Four-Star lodging provides a luxury experience with expanded amenities in a distinctive environment. Services may include, but are not limited to, automatic turndown service, 24-hour room service, and valet parking.

• ★★★: A Mobil Three-Star lodging is well appointed, with a full-service restaurant and expanded amenities, such as a fitness center, golf course, tennis courts, 24-hour room service, and optional turndown service.

• ★★: A Mobil Two-Star lodging is considered a clean, comfortable, and reliable establishment that has expanded amenities, such as a full-service restaurant on the premises.

• ★: A Mobil One-Star lodging is a limited-service hotel, motel, or inn that is considered a clean, comfortable, and reliable establishment.

PLACES TO EAT

For each Byway, dining establishments are listed in alphabetical order, based on the cities in which they're located. These restaurants and other eateries are either right on or close to the Byway chapter in which they're listed. All establishments listed have a full kitchen and offer table service and a complete menu. Parking on or near the premises, in a lot or garage, is assumed.

Each listing also gives the cuisine type, address (or directions if no street address is available), neighborhood and/or directions from downtown (in major cities), phone number, Web site (if available), meals served, days of operation (if not open daily year-round), reservation policy, and pricing category. We also indicate whether a children's menu is offered. The pricing categories are defined as follows per diner and assume that you order an appetizer, entrée, and one drink:

• $ = Up to $15

• $$ = $16-$35

• $$$ = $36-$85

• $$$$ = $86 and up

All listed establishments have been inspected by experienced field representatives and/or evaluated by a senior staff member. Our ratings are based on detailed inspection reports of the individual properties, on written evaluations of staff members who stay and dine anonymously, and on an extensive review of reader comments. Rating categories reflect both the features a property offers and its quality in relation to similar establishments.

The Mobil star ratings for restaurants are defined as follows:

- ★★★★★: A Mobil Five-Star restaurant offers one of few flawless dining experiences in the country. These establishments consistently provide their guests with exceptional food, superlative service, elegant décor, and exquisite presentations of each detail surrounding a meal.

- ★★★★: A Mobil Four-Star restaurant provides professional service, distinctive presentations, and wonderful food.

- ★★★: A Mobil Three-Star restaurant has good food, warm and skillful service, and enjoyable décor.

- ★★: A Mobil Two-Star restaurant serves fresh food in a clean setting with efficient service. Value is considered in this category, as is family friendliness.

- ★: A Mobil One-Star restaurant provides a distinctive experience through culinary specialty, local flair, or individual atmosphere.

TERMS, ABBREVIATIONS, AND SYMBOLS IN LISTINGS

The following terms, abbreviations, and symbols are used throughout the Mobil Travel Guide lodging and restaurant listings to indicate which amenities and services are available at each establishment. We've done our best to provide accurate and up-to-date information, but things do change, so if a particular feature is essential to you, please contact the establishment directly to make sure that it is available.

Continental breakfast: Usually coffee and a roll or doughnut.

In-room modem link: Every guest room has a connection for a modem that's separate from the main phone line.

Laundry service: Either coin-operated laundry facilities or overnight valet service is available.

Luxury level: A special section of a lodging, spanning at least an entire floor, that offers

Byway experts from around the country recommend special restaurants and/or lodgings along their particular Byways that can make your trip even more pleasant. You'll see these special recommendations throughout this book. Look for this symbol next to the hotel or restaurant name: 😊

increased luxury accommodations. Management must provide no less than three of these four services: separate check-in and check-out, concierge, private lounge, and private elevator service (with key access). Complimentary breakfast and snacks are commonly offered.

MAP: Modified American plan (lodging plus two meals).

Movies: Prerecorded videos are available for rental or check-out.

Prix fixe: A full, multicourse meal for a stated price; usually available at finer restaurants.

Valet parking: An attendant is available to park and retrieve your car.

VCR: VCRs are present in all guest rooms.

VCR available: VCRs are available for hookup in guest rooms.

🐕 Pet allowed

🎣 Fishing

🏇 Horseback riding

⛷ Snow skiing nearby

🏌 Golf, nine-hole minimum, on premises

🎾 Tennis court(s) on premises

🏊 Swimming

🏋 In-house fitness room

🏃 Jogging

✈ Major commercial airport within 10 miles

🚭 Nonsmoking guest rooms

SC Senior citizen rates

🏃 Business center

SPECIAL INFORMATION FOR TRAVELERS WITH DISABILITIES

The Mobil Travel Guide D symbol indicates establishments that are at least partially accessible to people with mobility problems. Our criteria for accessibility are unique to our publications. Please do not confuse them with the universal symbol for wheelchair accessibility.

When the D symbol follows a listing, the establishment is equipped with facilities to accommodate people using wheelchairs or crutches or otherwise needing easy access to doorways and rest rooms. Travelers with severe mobility problems or with hearing or visual impairments may or may not find the facilities they need. Always phone ahead to make sure that an establishment can meet your needs.

All lodgings bearing our D symbol have the following facilities:

- ISA-designated parking near access ramps
- Level or ramped entryways to buildings
- Swinging building entryway doors a minimum of 39 inches wide
- Public rest rooms on the main level with space to operate a wheelchair and handrails at commode areas
- Elevator(s) equipped with grab bars and lowered control buttons
- Restaurant(s) with accessible doorway(s), rest rooms with space to operate a wheelchair, and handrails at commode areas
- Guest room entryways that are at least 39 inches wide

- Low-pile carpet in rooms
- Telephones at bedside and in the bathroom
- Beds placed at wheelchair height
- Bathrooms with a minimum doorway width of 3 feet
- Bath with an open sink (no cabinet) and room to operate a wheelchair
- Handrails at commode areas and in the tub
- Wheelchair-accessible peepholes in room entry door
- Wheelchair-accessible closet rods and shelves

All restaurants bearing our D symbol offer the following facilities:

- ISA-designated parking beside access ramps
- Level or ramped front entryways to the building
- Tables that accommodate wheelchairs
- Main-floor rest rooms with an entryway that's at least 3 feet wide
- Rest rooms with space to operate a wheelchair and handrails at commode areas

Kaibab Plateau–
North Rim Parkway
❄ ARIZONA

Quick Facts

LENGTH: 42 miles.

TIME TO ALLOW: 1 hour or more.

BEST TIME TO DRIVE: Fall; high season is May through October.

SPECIAL CONSIDERATIONS: To avoid long lines at the entrance gate, enter the park before 10 am or after 2 pm. Make arrangements for accommodations and special activities in advance. All roads are winding and steep. You may come upon cows, deer, logging trucks, road construction, or visitors stopping to take photographs, so please drive carefully. Arizona's climate is dry and hot, so be sure to carry plenty of water. Wear proper footwear to minimize the risk of serious injury. There is also the danger of fires, lightning, and flash floods. Ridgetops seem to receive the most lightning strikes.

RESTRICTIONS: Most roads are not maintained during the winter. The Grand Canyon National Park North Rim section is closed from November 15 to May 1; SR 67 is closed from mid-December to mid-May. However, Highway 89A is plowed and maintained year-round. Pets are allowed in Grand Canyon National Park, but they must be restrained at all times and are not allowed below the rim, in park lodgings, or on park buses. The only exception is for certified service dogs.

BICYCLE/PEDESTRIAN FACILITIES: Bicycles are not available for rent in the Grand Canyon. Bicyclists are permitted on all paved and unpaved park roads open to automobile traffic and must obey all traffic regulations. Shoulders are narrow, and vehicle traffic is heavy. Bicycles are prohibited on park trails.

This route crosses over the gorgeous Kaibab Plateau and travels through two forests: the Kaibab National Forest and Grand Canyon National Park. Along the route, you'll find plenty of places to hike and camp. Groves of golden aspen, flowery meadows, ponds, outcrops of limestone, and steep slopes on all sides break up the dominance of the regal coniferous forest. Also, the Colorado and Kanab rivers flow right around the Byway, so opportunities for water sports abound.

THE BYWAY STORY

The Kaibab Plateau–North Rim Parkway tells archaeological, cultural, historical, natural, recreational, and scenic stories that make it a unique and treasured Byway.

Archaeological

People have occupied the Kaibab Plateau for at least 8,000 years. The earliest people inhabiting this region were hunter-gatherers who utilized the plateau extensively for its big game opportunities and for plant and mineral resources. These people, referred to as the Archaic people, were highly nomadic. Between 500 BC and 300 BC, the life and methods of the people using the Grand Canyon area began to change. The first evidence of plant domestication is linked to this period. Archaeologists refer to the people of this era as the Basketmaker people. Although they still depended heavily on hunting and gathering, they were slowly incorporating horticulture into their lifestyle. The Basketmaker period lasted until around AD 800.

Arizona

* Kaibab Plateau–North Rim Parkway

Toward the end of the Basketmaker period, pottery was made and people became less mobile. Over time, it is believed that the Basketmaker culture transitioned into what is now known as the Pueblo culture. The Pueblo people relied more heavily on farming than the Basketmaker people; they also built more permanent village sites that included upright masonry structures and cliff dwellings known as pueblos. They also developed beautiful painted pottery styles. The Pueblo people abandoned the area by the late 1200s. Archaeologists are unsure as to why they left; they suspect that prolonged drought and increased population levels forced the Pueblos to leave.

The Paiute people moved into the area shortly after the Pueblo people left. These people continue to live in the area today. The Paiute people were a hunting and gathering culture that utilized the Kaibab Plateau for its wild plant and animal resources. While some of the Paiute farmed in historic times, they were not originally a farming people. As with the earlier archaic cultures, the Paiute were highly nomadic. Unlike the Pueblo people, who built masonry pueblo structures, the Paiute lived in temporary brush structures called wikiups. This form of housing allowed them to move their camps on a regular basis to where resources were seasonably available. The Paiutes gave the region the name we still use today; Kaibab is the Paiute term meaning "mountain lying down." Today, the Paiute live on the Kaibab Paiute Indian Reservation located near Fredonia, Arizona. They continue to use the Kaibab Plateau for traditional cultural practices.

Cultural

The rich cultural diversity of Arizona is proudly displayed on the Kaibab Plateau–North Rim Parkway. Here, you find a diverse cross-section of Native Americans and pioneer stock. Visit the local towns of Kanab, Glendale, and Fredonia to see the rich heritage that is still maintained today. From good ol' country fairs to the vibrant Western Legends Round Up,

everyone is sure to have a good time. Don't forget Glendale's Apple Festival in October, where you can experience archery contests, booths, crafts, and an apple Dutch-oven cooking contest that is sure to please even the most discerning tastes.

Historical

The Kaibab is rich with the history of preservation and conservation. In 1893, the Grand Canyon Forest Reserve was created, and in the first decade of the 20th century, national forests were designated. Then, in 1906, President Theodore Roosevelt created the Grand Canyon National Game Preserve to protect the Kaibab mule deer, and in 1908, the Grand Canyon Forest Reserve became the Kaibab National Forest.

The historic Jacob Lake Ranger Station was built in 1910 to help administer lands that included what is now Grand Canyon National Park. The ranger station is located along the road that originally led to the North Rim of the Grand Canyon. Eventually, the road to Grand Canyon National Park was moved to its present location, but the Jacob Lake Ranger Station continued to be utilized to administer Kaibab National Forest lands. It is one of the oldest remaining ranger stations in the country and is now an interpretive site presenting the life of a forest ranger. It can be accessed from Highway 67.

After a devastating wildfire in 1910 burned through much of the Idaho panhandle and parts of western Montana, the United States ushered in an era of fire suppression. Prior to that time, little was done to suppress fires. However, after 1910, fire lookouts and trail systems began to be developed in earnest throughout the national forest system. The earliest fire lookouts on the Kaibab consisted of platforms built at the tops of tall trees that were accessed by ladders. Eventually, lookout buildings and towers were built, including the Jacob Lake Tower in 1934. The tower is located on the east side of Highway 67 and can be viewed from the Kaibab Plateau–North Rim Parkway.

Today, the Jacob Lake Ranger Station and Fire Lookout Tower are on the National Register of Historic Places, and the Jacob Lake Fire Lookout Tower is on the National Register of Fire Lookouts.

Natural

The Kaibab Plateau could be called an island of forest; sage and grass cover the lower elevations that surround it. The plateau is bordered on the south by the Grand Canyon and on the east and west by the Colorado River, sometimes reaching elevations of 9,000 feet. Some of the trees found at its higher elevations include Ponderosa pine, Englemann spruce, aspen, blue spruce, oak, piñon, pine, and juniper. At lower elevations, you'll find bitter brush, Gambel oak, sagebrush, and cliffrose.

Within the forest are irregular areas entirely free of tree growth. These parks are found in canyon bottoms, dry southern exposures, and ridge tops near the forest's exterior limits. Naturally occurring water is scarce in the North Kaibab Ranger District; Big Springs and North Canyon are the only two places in the district where the surface water flows year-round. Melting snow seeps through the gravelly soil to emerge as springs several hundred feet below the plateau rim.

The Vermilion Cliffs are spectacular because of their brilliant colors. It is also thrilling to watch the Grand Canyon walls change color as the sun sets; watching the morning sun hit the canyon is just as unforgettable.

The Grand Canyon stands alone as the world's most awesome natural wonder, and the surrounding Kaibab National Forest offers plenty of native forest wildlife. Keep an eye open for large, soaring birds; the endangered California condor was recently introduced to this area.

see page A5 for color map

Recreational

Nonmotorized and motorized trails are maintained for hikers, walkers, bikers, equestrians, cross-country skiers, four-wheel drivers, and snowmobilers. Fifty miles of the cross-state nonmotorized Arizona Trail traverse the district, providing opportunities for day hiking or multi-night trips. Many miles of closed roads provide outstanding mountain biking opportunities for all rider levels. (Remember that wilderness areas do not allow mountain bikes.) Spring and fall are the best seasons for enjoying both the wilderness and the Grand Canyon National Park trails due to extreme summer temperatures and winter inaccessibility. If you plan to stay overnight below the rim of the Grand Canyon, purchase a permit from the Grand Canyon National Park Backcountry Office.

For hunters, the Kaibab Plateau is famous for producing record-class mule deer, with established seasons for bow, black powder, and rifle hunting. Game birds, such as the chukar partridge and Merriam's turkey, also have established seasons. The Arizona Game and Fish Department sets the hunt dates and numbers, and hunters are selected by drawings.

The winter season on the Kaibab Plateau is a unique experience. Lodging is available on the plateau at Jacob Lake and Kaibab Lodge. Nordic skiing and snowmobiling are the most popular activities on the plateau in the winter. The area east of Highway 67 is open only to nonmotorized activities. The North Rim is also open only to nonmotorized activities, with no facilities or services during the winter season. All areas west of Highway 67 are open to motorized and nonmotorized activities. Winter conditions are surprisingly severe on the Kaibab Plateau. Be prepared for 4 to 8 feet of snow, along with cold and windy weather.

On national forest lands, camping is not limited to campgrounds; instead, camping is permissible off of any dirt road or out of the sight of a paved highway at no charge. Backcountry camping is prohibited within 1/4 mile of water to allow wildlife undisturbed access. Backcountry campers also must stay at least 1/2 mile from a developed campground or other facility. Campers are also asked to stay out of meadows, due to the fragile environment.

Jacob Lake area campgrounds open May 15 and close about October 20. Forest Service and National Park Service campgrounds have water and toilets, but no RV hook-ups. Private campgrounds at Jacob Lake or off the plateau do have full RV hook-ups, however. Tents and RVs are welcome at all campgrounds. DeMott Campground is not suitable for large RVs; all other campgrounds can handle any size. Group campsites are available by reservation at Jacob Lake and the North Rim. The Forest Service campgrounds operate on a first-come, first-served basis, and reservations can be made at the North Rim and private campgrounds. The free Jacob Lake picnic area is open May 1 to November 1 during daytime hours. No fee is charged for camping at Indian Hollow Campground, but camping is primitive, and no water is available.

Scenic

In many areas along the Kaibab Plateau–North Rim Parkway, you can get out, stretch your legs, and take one of the trails to scenic overlooks in the Grand Canyon. The golden glow of the red rocks and the lonely sound of the wind in the early morning are enough to inspire the most inexperienced of poets. Be sure to bring a journal and a camera.

HIGHLIGHTS

While visiting the Kaibab Plateau–North Rim Parkway, you can take the following self-guided tour of the Byway.

- **Jacob Lake Junction:** Highway marker 579 or the junction of Highway 67 and State Highway 89A. The **Kaibab Plateau Visitor Center** offers information and interpretive displays about the natural and cultural resources of the plateau. The visitor center also offers books, videos, postcards, and other interpretive sales items through the Public Lands Interpretive Association. **Jacob Lake Inn** is a historic lodge offering accommodations, a restaurant/café, and a gift shop. At **Jacob Lake Campground,** you'll find family sites and group sites available.

- **Jacob Lake Fire Lookout Tower:** Highway marker 580.3 or 1 mile south of the Jacob Lake Junction/Highway 67 and 89A. Visit this historic tower and find out how fires are detected. Views of the **Grand Staircase** are visible from the tower. The tower is usually staffed between 9 am-6 pm and may be closed for two days during the week; check in at the visitor center for current opening.

- **Demotte Park Overlook:** Highway marker 604 or 22 miles south of the Jacob Lake Junction on the Byway. Vehicle pull-off overlooking Demotte Park. Demotte Park is one of the largest meadows on the Kaibab Plateau, and it's filled with deer, coyotes, and numerous species of birds. Wildflower enthusiasts

will also enjoy the diversity and abundance in this meadow. One mile south of this stop is the historic **Kaibab Lodge.** Rustic cabins and restaurant, gift shop, gas station, and convenience store are available.

• **Grand Canyon National Park–North Rim:** 44 miles south on Highway 67. The end of this scenic parkway leads to a spectacular view of the North Rim of the Grand Canyon. Several hiking trails are located at or near the rim. The **North Rim Visitor Center** is open seven days a week 8 am-8 pm. Visitor information, interpretation, and interpretive sale items are available. The **North Rim's Historic Lodge** offers hotel accommodations, restaurant, mule rides, and a gift shop.

THINGS TO SEE AND DO

Driving along the Kaibab Plateau–North Rim Parkway will certainly keep your senses engaged, but if you yearn to get out of the car and stretch your legs, or if you'd like to make a mini-vacation out of your trip, check out these attractions along the route.

GRAND CANYON IMAX THEATER.  *Hwy 64 and US 180, Grand Canyon (86023). Phone 928/638-2203. www.grandcanyonimaxtheater.com.* Large-screen film (35 minutes) highlights features of the Grand Canyon. Open daily. $$

⭐ **GRAND CANYON NATIONAL PARK.** *US 93 and Hwy 169, PO Box 129, Williams (86023). Phone 928/638-7888. www.nps.gov/grca/.* This majestic park encompasses more than 1 million acres. Of the Grand Canyon's 277-mile length, the first 50 or so miles along the Colorado River comprise what is known as Marble

Canyon, where 3,000-foot, near-vertical walls of sandstone and limestone may be seen. US 89A crosses the Navajo Bridge 467 feet above the Colorado River. Camping (fee). Pets must be on a leash and are not allowed on trails below the rim. $$$$ per vehicle; $$ for pedestrians and cyclists. The following activities are available in the park:

• **Hiking down into the canyon.** Not recommended unless you're in good physical condition, because the heat and the 4,500-foot climb back are exhausting. Consult the Backcountry Office staff before attempting a canyon hike and always carry sufficient water and food; neither is available along trails. Reservations and fees are required to camp below the rim; obtain by mail from Backcountry Office, PO Box 129, Grand Canyon (86023) or in person at Backcountry, located adjacent to Maswik Lodge.

• **Mule trip into the canyon.** Easier than walking and quite safe, a number of mule trips are scheduled, all with guides. There are some limitations. Trips take one, two, or three days. Reservations should be made several months in advance (preferably one year prior).

• **Scenic flights over the canyon.** Many operators offer air tours of the canyon. Flights leave from many different airports. For a partial list

Arizona

Kaibab Plateau–North Rim Parkway

of companies, contact the Grand Canyon Chamber of Commerce, PO Box 3007, Grand Canyon (86023); phone 303/297-2757.

- **Evening programs.** Every night, year-round, Park Service ranger-naturalists offer programs in an outdoor amphitheater (during summer) or inside the Shrine of the Ages Building (during the colder months). Daytime talks given all year at Yavapai Observation Station and at the Visitor Center. **FREE**
- **Tusayan Museum.** *1 Main St, South Rim, Grand Canyon National Park (86023).* Exhibits on prehistoric man in the Southwest. Excavated pueblo ruin (circa AD 1185) is nearby. Open daily, weather permitting. **FREE**
- **Yavapai Observation Station.** *1 Main St, South Rim, Grand Canyon National Park (86023).* Scenic views, exhibits, information. Open daily. **FREE**

KAIBAB NATIONAL FOREST. *800 S 6th St, Williams (86046). Phone 928/638-2443. www.fs.fed.us/r3/kai/.* Adjacent to both North and South rims are units of this 1.5-million-acre forest. The Ranger District office for the Tusayan District is located in Tusayan, 4 miles south of the park.

PLACES TO STAY

If you choose to include an overnight stay in your trip along this Byway, Mobil Travel Guide recommends the following lodgings.

★★ JACOB LAKE INN. (icon) *Hwy 89A and Hwy 67, Jacob Lake (86022). Phone 928/643-7232. www.jacoblake.com.* American menu. Lunch, dinner. Featuring distinctive regional cuisine in a country setting. **$**

★★GRAND CANYON LODGE. *Hwy 67, North Rim, Grand Canyon (86052). Phone 928/638-2611. www.grandcanyonnorthrim.com.* 201 rooms. Closed Nov-Apr. Check-out 11 am. Restaurant, bar. Game room. View of the canyon. **¢**
(icons)

★★BEST WESTERN GRAND CANYON SQUIRE INN. *Hwy 64, South Rim, Grand Canyon (86023). Phone 928/638-2681; toll-free 800/780-7234. www.bestwestern.com.* 250 rooms, 3 story. Check-out noon. TV; cable (premium). Laundry services. Restaurant, bar. In-house fitness room, sauna. Game room. Heated pool, whirlpool. Concierge. Cowboy museum; mural of the Grand Canyon. **$$**
(icons)

★★★EL TOVAR. *1 Main St, South Rim, Grand Canyon (86023). Phone 928/638-2631. www.grandcanyonlodges.com.* The premier lodging facility at the Grand Canyon, the El Tovar Hotel (named in honor of the Spanish explorer Don Pedro de Tovar, who reported the existence of the Grand Canyon to fellow explorers) opened its doors in 1905 and was dubbed "the most expensively constructed and appointed log house in America." Just 20 feet from the edge of the Canyon's South Rim, the building is a little Swiss, vaguely Scandinavian, and charmingly rustic. Upon entering, guests are greeted by a roaring fire, striking paintings of the Canyon, copper statues depicting the American West, and a bustling peacefulness that ensures a remarkable stay. The hotel features a fine dining room, lounge, and a gift shop highlighting Native American artisans. With so much to do right at your doorstep—hiking, mule rides, train excursions, interpretive walks, and cultural activities—El Tovar offers the best of the Grand Canyon, combining turn-of-the-century lodge ambience with the highest standard of service on the canyon's edge. Advance reservations are recommended, especially for the summer season, which is usually booked up a year in advance. 78 rooms, 4 story. Check-out 11 am. TV. Restaurant, bar. Concierge. **$**
(icons)

★KACHINA LODGE. *1 Main St, South Rim, Grand Canyon (86023). Phone 928/638-2631. www.xanterra.com.* 49 rooms, 2 story. Check-out 11 am. TV. Canyon tour service. **$**
(icons)

★★**QUALITY INN.** *Hwy 64, South Rim, Grand Canyon (86023). Phone 928/638-2673; toll-free 800/221-2222. www.qualityinn.com.* 232 rooms, 3 story. Check-out 11 am. TV. In-room modem link. Restaurant. Pool, whirlpool. ¢

★**RODEWAY INN RED FEATHER LODGE.** *Hwy 64, South Rim, Grand Canyon (86023). Phone 928/638-2414; toll-free 800/228-2000. www.rodeway.com.* 234 rooms, 2-3 story. Pet accepted; fee. Check-out 11 am. TV. In-house fitness room. $

★**THUNDERBIRD LODGE.** *1 Main St, South Rim, Grand Canyon (86023). Phone 928/638-2631. www.xanterra.com.* 55 rooms, 2 story. Check-out 11 am. TV. Some canyon-side rooms. Canyon tour service. $

PLACES TO EAT

A long day of driving is sure to make you hungry. At the end of your journey, take a table at one of the following restaurants.

★★ **ARIZONA ROOM.** *West Rim Dr, Grand Canyon Village (86023). Phone 303/297-2757.* American menu. Lunch, dinner. An upscale dining room known for its prime steaks and magnificent canyon views. $$

★★ **GRAND CANYON LODGE.** *Hwy 67, North Rim, Grand Canyon (86052). Phone 928/638-2611. www.grandcanyonnorthrim.com.* American menu. Breakfast, lunch, dinner. Featuring spectacular views of the North Rim as a backdrop to the dining experience. ¢

★**STEAKHOUSE AT THE GRAND CANYON.** *Hwy 64 and US 180, Grand Canyon (86023). Phone 928/638-2780. www.kaibab.org/gc/serv/ gc_or_ts.htm.* Steak menu. Dinner. Bar. Children's menu. Hayrides, stagecoach rides Mar-Oct. Covered wagon in front yard. $$

★★★**EL TOVAR DINING ROOM.** *1 Main St, South Rim, Grand Canyon (86023). Phone 928/638-2631. www.kaibob.org/serv/ gc_pr_et.htm.* Perched 20 feet from the South Rim of the Grand Canyon, El Tovar Dining Room (located in the spectacularly rustic and historic El Tovar Hotel) is considered the premier dining establishment at the Grand Canyon. It provides a memorable experience, thanks to spicy regional cuisine and spectacular Canyon views. The atmosphere is casually elegant with native stone fireplaces, Oregon pine vaulted ceilings, Native American artwork, and Mission-style accents. Diners can select from a well-rounded menu of unique dishes created with regional flavors and utilizing contemporary techniques. The restaurant offers multiple vegetarian options and an extensive wine list. Southwestern menu. Breakfast, lunch, dinner. Children's menu. Reservations required for dinner. Totally nonsmoking. $$

Dinosaur Diamond Prehistoric Highway

✳ COLORADO

Part of a multistate Byway; see also UT.

Quick Facts

LENGTH: 112 miles.

TIME TO ALLOW: 2.5 hours to several days.

BEST TIME TO DRIVE: Year-round; high season is summer.

BYWAY TRAVEL INFORMATION: Dinosaurland Travel Board: 800/477-5558; Byway local Web site: www.dinosaurdiamond.org.

SPECIAL CONSIDERATIONS: The mountain passes at Douglas Pass on CO 139 can be treacherous during winter storms. This road is rarely, if ever, officially closed, but sometimes a few hours' delay would be prudent. All points along the Byway are subject to snowfall, with snow cover lasting longer in the northern and higher elevation areas than in the lower elevation and southern portions. Dinosaur trackways are difficult if not impossible to see under snow cover.

BICYCLE/PEDESTRIAN FACILITIES: The Dinosaur Diamond Byway includes portions of the interstate (I-70) and various US Highways. Because of this, bicycle and foot travel along the actual route may be prohibited and/or dangerous. However, numerous trails off the Byway delight visitors who come to the area. The Kokopelli Trail is designed and built for mountain bike travel between Moab and Fruita. Hiking for recreation, solitude, or sightseeing in the area of the Dinosaur Diamond is very popular, and you'll find many trails to follow.

Echoes of the past resonate along the Colorado stretch of the Dinosaur Diamond, with artifacts, such as dinosaur bones and rock art, from an earlier time. The most prominent example of rock art along the Byway may be found at Canyon Pintado, which features visible marks of the Fremont Indians. At the Colorado National Monument, visitors get a chance to view the striking landscape of western Colorado; the openness around Grand Junction fades into the majestic cliffs and canyons that are characteristic in the area. Around Fruita are examples of excavation sites, such as at Dinosaur Hill; Fruita is also home of the Museum of Western Colorado, where dinosaurs come alive. The Byway is a travel back in time, with recreational opportunities; such as biking, hiking, and camping awaiting you along the route.

THE BYWAY STORY

The Dinosaur Diamond Prehistoric Highway tells archaeological, cultural, historical, natural, recreational, and scenic stories that make it a unique and treasured Byway.

Archaeological

The Dinosaur Diamond Prehistoric Highway showcases the archaeological qualities of a time about 1,000 years ago, when Native American cultures lived and hunted in the area. These cultures maintained their way of life in the desert and today, remnants of this culture are located along the Byway. The best evidence of these ancient people is the abundance of petroglyphs and pictographs in the area. (Petroglyphs are pictures that are pecked into rock surfaces using harder rocks, often made into tools; pictographs are pictures painted onto the rocks.)

9

Ancient petroglyph panels show up on cliff sides and rock surfaces along the Byway, because the sheer rock cliffs and walls served as an ideal place to create this rock art. There are panels in both Utah and Colorado, and they are spread out along the Byway. The most prominent petroglyphs are in the Colorado National Monument near Grand Junction. In addition to these, Canyon Pintado, between Douglas Pass and Rangely, has significant examples of rock art, along with roadside interpretive displays.

Cultural

Because of the rural nature of living in the desert, many cultural events have sprung up to give people a reason to congregate and enjoy the splendid outdoors. Festivals and events honoring the heritage and natural features of the area give the Byway a cultural flair.

Stroll by Colorado's largest and most diverse outdoor sculpture exhibit, on display along Grand Junction's downtown shopping park. The exhibit, entitled Art Around the Corner, highlights a unique variety of work by local artists. The nearly 20-year-old ongoing event introduces visitors to many distinct artistic approaches. Informative brochures are available at the Downtown Development Authority Visitor's Center at 350 Main Street, Suite 204; phone 970/245-2926.

Historical

The high mountain desert of western Colorado has drawn people to the area of the present-day Dinosaur Diamond Prehistoric Highway. Evidences of Native American cultures, such as the Fremont and Ute, can be seen in the rock art along the Byway. The Escalante-Dominguez Expedition, followed by scientific and paleontologic expeditions, undertook early exploration of the area, while Mormon settlers, miners, and immigrants from Europe all settled in the area and created a unique and colorful history.

The first recorded venture of Europeans into the area was the Escalante-Dominguez Expedition in 1776. This expedition came from Santa Fe, New Mexico, attempting to blaze a trail to California in order to access the missions located there; however, their journey was unsuccessful due to the barriers formed by the western Utah deserts. The expedition was led by Father Silvestre Velez de Escalante and Father Francisco Dominguez, accompanied by Captain Bernardo de Miera y Pacheco, a retired military engineer. They explored Canyon Pintado from Douglas Pass toward what is now Rangely, Colorado, crossed the Green river near Jensen, Utah, and traveled as far west as Spanish Fork, Utah, before turning back south to return to Santa Fe, New Mexico.

While Escalante and Dominguez came to the area in search of another route west, others have been drawn to western Colorado for more than 150 years because of scientific exploration. Beginning with John C. Fremont in the early 1840s, reports about the majesty of the mountains, the roaring rivers, the expanse and austerity of the deserts, the abundance of game, and the clues to vast mineral resources have enticed adventurers to the intermountain west of the United States. John Wesley Powell, Clarence King, and Ferdinand V. Hayden led extensive geological surveys that helped quantify these resources. In addition, their reports tempted paleontologists with a vast array of undescribed fossils, particularly dinosaurs and prehistoric mammals.

Settlement in the area inevitably brought about great changes on the landscape, such as mining. In the Uintah Basin, gilsonite was the first hydrocarbon to be mined, bringing a small narrow-gage railroad (the Uintah Railroad) into the southeastern edge of the basin near Dragon. Although several attempts were made to build more railroads into the basin, none was successful. As a result, the Uintah Basin remains one of the largest areas of the US to be undeveloped by railroads. After World War II, petroleum development and phosphate mining became integral

see page A6 for color map

to the rural economy. The railroad from Grand Junction, Colorado, to Price, Utah, brought development of the coal resources in both Carbon and Emery counties. As a result of this mining industry, an influx of some 18 different ethnic groups from across southern and eastern Europe and Asia came to work in the mines. This economic development was a great boost to the area.

Natural

The area encompassed by this diamond-shaped Byway is the best place in the world to see dinosaurs in a variety of ways: dinosaurs on display in museums, dinosaur bones still in the ground at the sites where they were discovered, dinosaur bones currently being excavated by paleontologists, and dinosaur trackways preserved in rocks.

Dinosaurs ruled the Earth long ago, and today, the bones and tracks of these extinct animals can be seen at various sites along the Byway. Many of these sites are located in their natural settings, which makes this Byway one of a kind. Actual dinosaur quarries, which are areas where dinosaur bones are excavated, are along the Byway. The Mygatt-Moore Quarry near Fruita preserves the history of dinosaurs in their natural state.

Recreational

River rafting is one popular sport to participate in along the Byway. Both calm water and white water river trips are available through companies out of Grand Junction. The whitewater sections can be frightening even to experienced river runners during the high water levels of spring melt, yet some stretches of both the Green and Colorado rivers have flatwater that may be enjoyable in canoes. Grand scenery awaits the visitor around every bend in the river. In fact,

the Green River in Desolation Canyon has cliffs higher than the Grand Canyon in Arizona.

Hiking opportunities are everywhere along the Byway. The terrain is varied, giving visitors a feel for the many aspects of the Byway. In the mountains, numerous spectacular peaks and lakes are accessible to the hiker; the Uinta Mountain Range is the largest east-west mountain range in the 48 contiguous United States. The desert is another popular place to go hiking, and it is an entirely different experience from alpine hiking. All of the national parks and monuments along the Byway are outstanding places for hiking and camping. Outfitters are available all along the Byway for visitors who want guides, horses, or even llamas to help with the load. Hunting and fishing are also popular recreational activities in the area. Fruita also has excellent mountain biking trails to challenge the expert rider and lure the beginner.

Winter sports are also popular for visitors. Snowshoeing, cross-country skiing, snowmobiling, and ice fishing can be enjoyed in the high country, while hiking without the summer heat is a popular activity in the southern desert areas.

✳ *Dinosaur Diamond Prehistoric Highway*

Scenic

The Dinosaur Diamond Prehistoric Highway has many scenic views that capture the expansive area of land surrounding the Byway. Wide vistas are normal in this desert country, with the horizon stretching on for miles. During hot summer days, it seems like the blue sky is an endless expanse, and sunsets—going on forever—are magnified because of the open sky.

Vistas can include features that are over 100 miles away. Canyons with walls of red, green, beige, purple, gray, and white greet you. These scenes are intermingled with forested mountain passes and snowcapped mountains. As you travel winding roads out of canyons, sweeping views of the valleys below open up before you. Along the northern facet of the Dinosaur Diamond, the Uinta Mountains cut the skyline. Ancient faults and tectonics controlled the development of this maverick mountain range, creating the largest east-west trending mountain range in the lower 48 states. It is unlike the rest of the Rock Mountains that are aligned north to south.

The Green River joins the Yampa River in Dinosaur National Monument at Steamboat Rock. The canyon it forms is spectacular whether viewed from the canyon rim or from the river edge. Farther downstream, the river cuts through Split Mountain and then the Gray Tertiary badlands of the Uinta and Green River formations of Desolation Canyon, the main

drainage for the Book Cliffs. The Colorado River provides further scenic aspects to the Byway, meandering through canyons of red rock. The green vegetation near the river is a nice contrast to the sheer red rock cliffs of the canyons, while snowcapped mountain ranges in the distance offer a break in the desert landscape.

THINGS TO SEE AND DO

Driving along the Dinosaur Diamond Prehistoric Highway will certainly keep your senses engaged, but if you yearn to get out of the car and stretch your legs, or if you'd like to make a mini-vacation out of your trip, check out these attractions along the route.

COLORADO NATIONAL MONUMENT. *CO 340, Grand Junction (81610). www.nps.gov/colm/.* Wind, water, a 10-mile fault, and untold eons have combined to produce spectacular erosional forms. In the 32-square-mile monument, deep canyons with sheer walls form amphitheaters for towering monoliths, rounded domes, and other geological features. Wildlife includes deer, foxes, coyotes, porcupines, and a growing herd of desert bighorn sheep. Rim Rock Drive, accessible from either Fruita or Grand Junction, is a spectacular 23-mile road along the canyon rims. Picnicking and camping facilities within the monument are available all year (fee for camping). The Saddlehorn Visitor Center has geology and natural history exhibits (open daily). Interpretive programs are offered in summer. Hiking and cross-country skiing trails are open in season. **$$**

CROSS ORCHARDS HISTORIC FARM. *3079 Patterson Rd, Grand Junction (81506). Phone 970/434-9814. www.wcmuseum.org/crssorchards .htm.* Operated from 1896 to 1923 by owners of Red Cross shoe company. Living-history farm with historically costumed guides interprets the social and agricultural heritage of western Colorado. Restored buildings and equipment on display; narrow gauge railroad exhibit and country store. Demonstrations, special events. Open Tues-Sun. **$$**

DINOSAUR HILL. *CO 340, Grand Junction (81610).* Self-guided walking trail interprets quarry of paleontological excavations. Daily. **FREE**

⭐ **DINOSAUR NATIONAL MONUMENT/ COLORADO ENTRANCE.** *Box 4545 E Hwy 40, Dinosaur (81610). Phone 970/374-2216. www.nps.gov/dino/.* This 325-square-mile monument in the northwest corner of the state holds one of the largest concentrations of fossilized Jurassic-era dinosaur bones in the world. You can get a close-up view of a quarry wall containing at least 1,500 fossil bones dating back 150 million years. The wall, enclosed in the information-packed Dinosaur Quarry Visitors Center, was once part of an ancient riverbed. The monument itself, spanning more than 300 square miles on the Colorado/Utah border, is distinguished by its ruggedly beautiful landscape of high plateaus and river-carved canyons. Access to the Colorado backcountry section, a land of fantastic, deeply eroded canyons of the Green and Yampa rivers, is via the Harpers Corner Rd, starting at monument headquarters on US 40, 2 miles east of Dinosaur. At Harpers Corner, the end of this 32-mile surfaced road, a 1-mile foot trail leads to a promontory overlooking the Green and Yampa rivers. Camping, picnicking, Dinosaur Quarry, Fishing, River rafting. The visitor centers and one quarry-section campground are open all year; the remainder are often closed by snow approximately mid-November to mid-April. **$$**

MUSEUM OF WESTERN COLORADO. *462 Ute Ave, Grand Junction (81501). Phone 970/242-0971. www.wcmuseum.org.* Features exhibits on regional, social, and natural history of the Western Slope; collection of small weapons; wildlife exhibits. Open Mon-Sat 9 am-5 pm, Sun noon-4 pm; winter Tues-Sat 10 am-3 pm. Tours by appointment. **$**

RABBIT VALLEY TRAIL THROUGH TIME. *30 miles W on I-70, 2 miles from UT border, Grand Junction (81610).* A 1 1/2-mile self-guided walking trail through a paleontologically significant area. Fossilized flora and fauna from the Jurassic Age. No pets allowed. Open daily. **FREE**

RIGGS HILL. *S Broadway and Meadows Way, Grand Junction (81610). Phone 970/241-9210.* A 3/4-mile, self-guided walking trail in an area where bones of the Brachiosaurus dinosaur were discovered in 1900. Open daily. **FREE**

PLACES TO STAY

If you choose to include an overnight stay in your trip along this Byway, Mobil Travel Guide recommends the following lodgings.

★★**ADAM'S MARK.** *743 Horizon Dr, Grand Junction (81506). Phone 970/241-8888; toll-free 888/444-2326. www.adamsmark.com.* 273 rooms, 8 story. Check-out noon, check-in 3 pm. TV; cable (premium). Restaurant, bar. In-house fitness room. Game room. Outdoor pool, whirlpool, poolside service. Outdoor tennis, lighted courts. Lawn games. Free airport transportation. Luxury level. **$**
[icons]

★**BEST WESTERN SANDMAN MOTEL.** *708 Horizon Dr, Grand Junction (81506). Phone 970/243-4150; toll-free 800/780-7234. www.bestwestern.com.* 80 rooms, 2 story. Check-out 11 am, check-in 3 pm. TV. In-room modem link. Coin laundry. Pool, whirlpool. Free airport transportation. **¢**
[icons]

★**BUDGET HOST INN.** *721 Horizon Dr, Grand Junction (81506). Phone 970/243-6050; toll-free 800/283-4678. www.budgethost.com.* 54 rooms, 2 story. Pet accepted; fee. Complimentary continental breakfast. Check-out 11 am, check-in 3 pm. TV; cable (premium). Laundry services. Pool. **¢**
[icons]

★★**GRAND VISTA HOTEL.** *2790 Crossroads Blvd, Grand Junction (81506). Phone 970/241-8411; toll-free 800/800-7796. www.grandvistahotel.com.* 158 rooms, 6 story. Pet accepted, some restrictions; fee. Check-out noon, check-in 3 pm. TV; cable (premium). In-room modem link. Restaurant, bar. Room service. Health club privileges. Indoor pool, whirlpool. Free airport transportation. $
⊠ D ❄ ➲ SC ⊷

★★**HOLIDAY INN.** *755 Horizon Dr, Grand Junction (81506). Phone 970/243-6790; toll-free 800/HOLIDAY. www.holiday-inn.com.* 292 rooms. Pet accepted. Check-out 11 am, check-in 4 pm. TV; cable (premium), VCR available. In-room modem link. Restaurant, bar; entertainment. Room service. In-house fitness room, sauna. Game room. Indoor, outdoor pool, children's pool, whirlpool. Airport transportation. ¢
⊠ D ❄ ➲ SC ⊷

★★**RAMADA INN.** *752 Horizon Dr, Grand Junction (81506). Phone 970/243-5150; toll-free 800/272-6232. www.ramada.com.* 100 rooms, 2 story. Pet accepted, some restrictions; fee. Check-out noon, check-in 3 pm. TV; cable (premium), VCR available. In-room modem link. Laundry services. Restaurant. Outdoor pool, whirlpool. Free airport transportation. ¢
⚹ D ❄ SC ⊷ ➲

PLACES TO EAT

A long day of driving is sure to make you hungry. At the end of your journey, take a table at one of the following restaurants.

★★**FAR EAST RESTAURANT.** *1530 North Ave, Grand Junction (81501). Phone 970/242-8131.* Chinese, American menu. Closed major holidays. Lunch, dinner. Bar. Children's menu. $$
D

★**STARVIN' ARVIN'S.** *752 Horizon Dr, Grand Junction (81506). Phone 970/241-0430.* American menu. Closed Thanksgiving, Dec 25. Breakfast, lunch, dinner. Bar. Children's menu. Casual atmosphere; antique photographs. $
D SC

★★**WINERY RESTAURANT.** *642 Main St, Grand Junction (81501). Phone 970/242-4100.* American menu. Closed Dec 25. Dinner. Bar. Restored 1890s building. Totally nonsmoking. $$
D

Frontier Pathways Scenic and Historic Byway

❋ COLORADO

Quick Facts

LENGTH: 103 miles.

TIME TO ALLOW: 4 hours.

BEST TIME TO DRIVE: Winter and summer; high season is summer.

BYWAY TRAVEL INFORMATION: Greenhorn Valley Chamber of Commerce: 719/676-3000; Byway local Web site: www.coloradobyways.org.

SPECIAL CONSIDERATIONS: Wildfires are an ever-present danger in the dry summer months; follow all posted signs regarding campfires and do not throw cigarettes out the car window. Abandoned mines are extremely dangerous—look and take pictures but do not explore. This Byway traverses high mountain passes; be prepared for all types of weather. High altitudes bring increased sun exposure and reduced oxygen, so wear sunscreen and sunglasses and don't overexert yourself.

RESTRICTIONS: There are rare winter closures due to snowfall.

BICYCLE/PEDESTRIAN FACILITIES: This area is a mountain biker's paradise, with many roads and trails to choose from. Tour biking is also a popular activity, and the highway's paved shoulders, typically 4 feet in width, accommodate these bikers. Virtually every type of pedestrian-based recreational activity is accommodated. Whether you take a walking tour of Pueblo's Union Avenue Historic District, hike a meadow or mountain, take a backpacking trip, or opt for the historic walking tour of Westcliffe and Silver Cliff, you'll experience many wonderful natural attractions. The nationally renowned Rainbow Trail attracts many visitors each year as well.

During the winter of 1806, Lt. Zebulon Pike nearly froze to death in the Wet Mountain Valley within sight of the peak bearing his name. Nevertheless, this valley and its mountain became a beacon to 19th-century settlers, who came to take advantage of the good soil and climate. Today, the valley boasts one of the state's finest collections of historic ranches and farmsteads (some dating to the 1840s), trading posts, and stage stops. Also, this pastoral paradise contrasts with the more severe-looking Hardscrabble Canyon, the white-capped Sangre de Cristos, and the sharp mesas and hogbacks that flank the Arkansas River.

THE BYWAY STORY

The Frontier Pathways Scenic and Historic Byway tells cultural, historical, natural, recreational, and scenic stories that make it a unique and treasured Byway.

Cultural

This Byway chronicles the joys and sorrows that its early residents experienced while breaking in the land. It is a living showcase of the evolution of architecture, transportation, and agriculture that you can experience by visiting the Frontier Pathway's old homesteads, cabins, barns, stage-stops, and settlements. This landscape hasn't changed much in the last 100 years, so you can still see how different groups of people used their ingenuity to harness the land. Evidence of their resourcefulness is found in the area's nationally important high-country homesteading.

Colorado

Frontier Pathways Scenic and Historic Byway

Historical

The Frontier Pathways Scenic and Historic Byway is seeping with nationally significant history. For example, some of the first high-country homesteads, ranches, and farms were developed here. In 1779, the Spanish Governor De Anza, with the help of the Utes, defeated Comanche Chief Cuerno Verde (Greenhorn) right in this very valley. Also, German and English colonists settled here in the mid-1800s, and their heritage still pervades this area.

Natural

The Wet Mountains and Greenhorn Valleys are not well known, even to long-time Coloradoans, making this Byway an excellent getaway. Home for a remarkable number of diverse species of plants and animals, this area attracts naturalists, nature lovers, and botanists. (Note that the Wet Mountains are neither an extension of Colorado's Front Range—the mountains immediately west of Denver—nor are they part of the Continental Divide.)

As the only trout native to Colorado, the greenback cutthroat trout was believed to be extinct until it was rediscovered in a stream near the Frontier Pathways and successfully reintroduced statewide.

Recreational

Year-round opportunities at this recreational mecca include climbing 14,295-foot-high Crestone Peak, shopping and dining in Pueblo's Historic Union Avenue District, and playing in the Wet Mountain Wilderness. You can also trout fish on the banks of Lake Isabel, backpack on the nationally renowned Rainbow Trail, and hike in the Sangre de Cristos or Greenhorn Wilderness.

While the summer sun is out, you may enjoy fishing for trout in streams, mountain biking, and horseback riding. You can also get in some sailing, power boating, or water-skiing at the Lake Pueblo State Recreation Area. Consider

taking time to discover Pueblo Mountain Park, which is on the National Register of Historic Places. During the winter, be sure to cross-country ski, downhill ski, or ice fish on the Pueblo Reservoir.

Scenic

Photographers will need to long-focus their cameras in order to capture a sliver of the 100-mile-long Sangre de Cristo Range. As the backbone of the Rocky Mountains, the Sangre de Cristos' many grand peaks jut into the clear blue sky; seven peaks reach over 14,000 feet, while 39 peaks rise over 13,000 feet.

You can also discover other intriguing photographic subjects among the shops and streets of Pueblo's Union Avenue Historic District or during your descent into dramatic Hardscrabble Canyon.

HIGHLIGHTS

To take in the highlights of the Frontier Pathways Scenic and Historic Byway, consider this must-see tour.

- **Pueblo Museum:** This museum, located in the town of Pueblo, gives you an opportunity to learn about the interaction of several different cultures: American Indian, Mexican, and American. Fascinating artifacts, colorful murals, and interesting stories bring the history of the Pueblo area to life.

- **Wetmore and Early Settlements (on Highway 96 at mile marker 26.4):** More than 150 years ago, buckskin-clad French traders, scrappy American farmers, and fur traders lived in nearby settlements. In the 1830s, three French trappers built a fort on Adobe Creek to facilitate trade with the Ute Indians. It was called Buzzard's Roost, or Maurice's Fort, after Maurice LeDuc. Later settlements in the area included Hardscrabble in 1844 and Wetmore in the late 1870s.

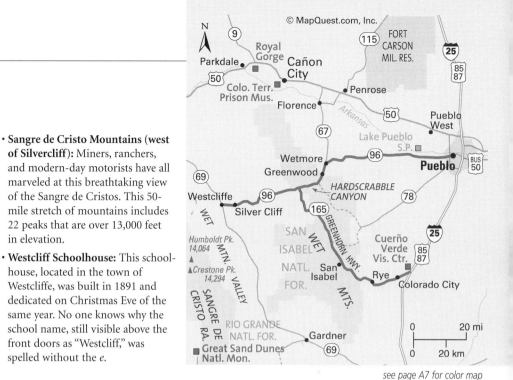

see page A7 for color map

- **Sangre de Cristo Mountains (west of Silvercliff):** Miners, ranchers, and modern-day motorists have all marveled at this breathtaking view of the Sangre de Cristos. This 50-mile stretch of mountains includes 22 peaks that are over 13,000 feet in elevation.
- **Westcliff Schoolhouse:** This schoolhouse, located in the town of Westcliffe, was built in 1891 and dedicated on Christmas Eve of the same year. No one knows why the school name, still visible above the front doors as "Westcliff," was spelled without the *e*.

THINGS TO SEE AND DO

Driving along the Frontier Pathways Scenic and Historic Byway will certainly keep your senses engaged, but if you yearn to get out of the car and stretch your legs, or if you'd like to make a mini-vacation out of your trip, check out these attractions along the route.

EL PUEBLO MUSEUM. *324 W First St, Pueblo (81003). Phone 719/583-0453.* Full-size replica of Old Fort Pueblo, which served as a base for fur traders and other settlers from 1842 to 1855. Exhibits on the Anasazi, steel and ore production, and narrow-gauge railroads. Open daily; closed Thanksgiving, Dec 25. **$$**

THE GREENWAY AND NATURE CENTER OF PUEBLO. *5200 Nature Center Rd, 5 miles W via US 50, Pueblo (81003). Phone 719/549-2414.* Small reptile exhibit, Raptor Center; special nature programs (by appointment). Also 36 miles of hiking and biking trails (rentals). Café. Open Tues-Sun; closed Jan 1, Thanksgiving, Dec 25.

LAKE PUEBLO STATE PARK. *640 Pueblo Reservoir Rd, Pueblo (81005). Phone 719/561-9320.* Swimming, water-skiing, boating; hiking, camping. Open daily. **$$**

MINERAL PALACE PARK. *1500 N Santa Fe, Pueblo (81003). Phone 719/566-1745.* Swimming pool (fee), children's fishing; picnicking. Rose garden, greenhouse. Pueblo Art Guild Gallery with local artists exhibits. Open Sat-Sun; closed Dec-Feb. **FREE**

★ **PIKE NATIONAL FOREST.** *1920 Valley Dr, Pueblo (81008). Phone 719/545-8737. www.fs.fed.us/r2/psicc/.* This forest of more than 1.1 million acres includes the world-famous Pikes Peak; picnic grounds, campgrounds (fee). Other areas of interest include Wilkerson Pass (9,507 feet), 45 miles W on US 24, with visitor information center (Memorial Day-Labor Day); Lost Creek Wilderness, NW of Lake George; Mt Evans Wilderness, NW of Bailey. **FREE**

PUEBLO WEISBROD AIRCRAFT MUSEUM. *31001 Magnuson Ave, Pueblo (81001). Phone 719/948-3355. www.pwam.org/default.htm.* Outdoor museum features a static aircraft display. Adjacent is the B-24 Aircraft Memorial Museum, with indoor displays of the history of the B-24 bomber. Guided tours. Open Mon-Fri 10 am-4 pm, Sat 10 am-2 pm, Sun 2-4 pm; closed holidays. **$$**

❉ *Frontier Pathways Scenic and Historic Byway*

ROSEMOUNT VICTORIAN HOUSE MUSEUM. *419 W 14th St, Pueblo (81003). Phone 719/545-5290. www.rosemount.org.* This 37-room mansion contains original Victorian furnishings and the McClelland Collection of world curiosities. Open Tues-Sat 10 am-4 pm; closed holidays; also closed Jan. **$$**

SAN ISABEL NATIONAL FOREST. *2840 Kachina Dr, Pueblo (81008). Phone 719/545-8737. www.fs.fed.us/r2/psicc/.* On over 1.1 million acres. Three sections of the forest lie adjacent to this highway with picnicking, camping, and two winter sports areas (Monarch and Ski Cooper). In the southern part of the forest is the Spanish Peaks National Natural Landmark. Collegiate Peaks, Mount Massive, and Holy Cross Wilderness areas are also within the forest, as are four wilderness study areas. Colorado's highest peak, Mount Elbert (14,433 feet), is within the forest south of Leadville.

SANGRE DE CRISTO ARTS AND CONFERENCE CENTER. *210 N Santa Fe Ave, Pueblo (81003). Phone 719/295-7200. www.sdc-arts.org.* Four art galleries include the Francis King Collection of Western Art on permanent display; changing art exhibits; children's museum, workshops, dance studios, theater. Open Mon-Sat; closed holidays. **$**

PLACES TO STAY

If you choose to include an overnight stay in your trip along this Byway, Mobil Travel Guide recommends the following lodgings.

★★★**ABRIENDO INN.** 🛁 *300 W Abriendo Ave, Pueblo (81004). Phone 719/544-2703. www.abriendoinn.com.* 10 rooms, 3 story. Children over 6 years only. Complimentary full breakfast. Check-out 11 am, check-in 3:30-9 pm. TV; VCR. In-room modem link. Built in 1906. Totally nonsmoking. **$**
▧

★**COMFORT INN.** *4645 N Freeway Rd (I-25), Pueblo (81008). Phone 719/542-6868; toll-free 800/228-5150. www.comfortinn.com.* 60 rooms, 2 story. Complimentary continental breakfast. Check-out 11 am. TV; cable (premium). In-room modem link. Indoor pool. **¢**
D ▧ ⌇

★**HAMPTON INN.** *4703 N Freeway, Pueblo (81008). Phone 719/544-4700; toll-free 800/426-7866. www.hamptoninn.com.* 111 rooms, 2 story. Complimentary breakfast buffet. Check-out noon. TV; cable (premium), VCR available. In-house fitness room. Pool. **¢**
🕴 D ▧ ⌇

★★**HOLIDAY INN.** *4001 N Elizabeth St, Pueblo (81008). Phone 719/543-8050; toll-free 800/465-4329. www.holiday-inn.com.* 193 rooms, 2 story. Check-out 11 am. TV. In-room modem link. Restaurant, bar. Room service. In-house fitness room. Game room. Indoor pool, whirlpool. Free airport transportation. Business center. **¢**
🕴 🕴 🐾 D ⌇

★★★**MARRIOTT PUEBLO CONVENTION CENTER.** *110 W First St, Pueblo (81003). Phone 719/542-3200; toll-free 888/236-2427. www.marriott.com.* 164 rooms, 7 story. Check-out noon, check-in 3 pm. TV; cable (premium). In-room modem link. Restaurant, bar. In-house fitness room. Indoor pool, whirlpool. Business center. Concierge. **$$**

★**WINGATE INN.** *4711 N Elizabeth St, Pueblo (81008). Phone 719/586-9000; toll-free 800/228-1000. www.wingateinns.com.* 84 rooms, 3 story. Complimentary continental breakfast. Check-out 11 am. TV; cable (premium). In-room modem link. In-house fitness room. Indoor pool, whirlpool. Business center. **¢**

PLACES TO EAT

A long day of driving is sure to make you hungry. At the end of your journey, take a table at one of the following restaurants.

★★**CAFÉ DEL RIO.** *5200 Nature Center Rd, Pueblo (81003). Phone 719/549-2029.* American menu. Closed Mon. Lunch, dinner, Sun brunch. Children's menu. Outdoor seating. Scenic view of the Arkansas River; adobe building built by volunteers. **$$**

★★**GAETANO'S.** *910 Hwy 50 W, Pueblo (81008). Phone 719/546-0949.* Italian, American menu. Closed Sun; Jan 1, Dec 25. Lunch, dinner. Bar. Children's menu. Casual attire. Outdoor seating. **$$**

★★ **LA MELA DI ANGELO.** *123 N Main St, Pueblo (81003). Phone 719-253-7700.* Italian. Lunch, dinner. Serving family style regional Italian cuisine. **$**

★★★**LA RENAISSANCE.** *217 E Routt Ave, Pueblo (81004). Phone 719/543-6367.* Continental menu. Closed Sun, major holidays. Dinner. Bar. Church built in 1886; garden room. Totally nonsmoking. **$$**

★ **PATTI'S RESTAURANT.** *241 S Santa Fe, Pueblo (81003). Phone 719/543-2371. www.pattisonline.com.* American menu. Closed Mon, Tues. Breakfast, lunch, dinner. The oldest continually running restaurant in Pueblo, Patti's has been a local's favorite for over 65 years. **$**

Gold Belt Tour Scenic and Historic Byway

❋ COLORADO

LENGTH: 135 miles.

TIME TO ALLOW: 8 hours.

BEST TIME TO DRIVE: Year-round.

BYWAY TRAVEL INFORMATION: Gold Belt Tour Information/Cañon City Chamber of Commerce: 719/275-2331; Byway local Web site: www.goldbeltbyway.com

SPECIAL CONSIDERATIONS: The Phantom Canyon and Upper Shelf roads have rough, gravel surfaces, so it is better to avoid them in wet weather. A 4-mile segment of the Shelf Road becomes soft and slippery during wet periods and is not recommended for two-wheel-drive vehicles. A four-wheel-drive vehicle is recommended on the Upper Shelf Road.

RESTRICTIONS: Vehicles over 25 feet long are not permitted to travel the Phantom Canyon Road. RVs are not suitable for Shelf Road or Phantom Canyon Road.

On the Gold Belt Tour, the roads themselves are part of the personality of the Byway. The Byway follows historic railroad and stagecoach routes, leading you to North America's greatest gold camp, three world-class fossil sites, and numerous historical sites. The Shelf and Phantom Canyon roads offer adventurous driving experiences along unpaved routes through winding canyons. Paved roads wind through the gently rolling mountain parklands of the High Park route, where Colorado's highest mountain ranges rise in the distance. Teller 1 (a county road) travels through the pastoral Florissant Valley, with Pikes Peak in the background.

The five Byway communities invite you to share in their rich history. In Cripple Creek, the historical hub of the mining district and a National Historic Landmark, visitors enjoy the variety and beauty of the early 1900s architectural styles in the downtown district. The area's mining heritage continues in Victor, the City of Mines. Surrounded by hundreds of historic mines, Victor is the headquarters for a modern gold mine. Victor's downtown district, a National Historic District, includes beautifully restored buildings. To the south, you can enjoy the Royal Gorge as well as restaurants, museums, and historic sites in Cañon City and Florence. Florissant, the Byway's northern gateway, offers the Florissant Heritage Museum to interpret the area's numerous historic sites and Ute cultural sites.

Also located along the Byway are the Garden Park Fossil Area, the Florissant Fossil Beds National Monument, and the Indian Springs Trace Fossil Site. These sites form an internationally important area for paleontological discovery and research. The Florissant Fossil Beds Visitor Center, Dinosaur Depot Museum, wayside exhibits, and trails offer visitors the opportunity to experience these natural wonders.

THE BYWAY STORY

The Gold Belt Tour Scenic and Historic Byway tells archaeological, cultural, historical, natural, recreational, and scenic stories that make it a unique and treasured Byway.

Archaeological

Archaeological sites can be found throughout the Byway and provide a comprehensive look at the past and the creatures that lived in this area millions of years ago. With three fossil beds along the Byway, gold was clearly not the only treasure to be found within the mountains and hills of this section of Colorado. When settlers were done digging for gold, many excavations of the fossil beds in the area began, and the discovery and search for fossils on the Byway continues today. What has been found is one of the most diverse and complete collections of fossils on the continent.

For millions of years, creatures have been preserved in the rock and stone along the Gold Belt Tour; in fact, 460-million-year-old tracks of arthropods have been found at Indian Springs Trace. This discovery led scientists and even visitors to conjecture about the way the world was so many ages ago, and scientists use these fossils to explore new ideas in evolution. The Florissant Fossil Beds include imprints and fossils of creatures and their environment from 35 million years ago. Garden Park Fossil Beds hold bones of many of the favorite dinosaurs, including brachiosaurus and stegosaurus. Exploration of the fossil beds along the Gold Belt Tour gives you a glimpse of the Earth's age and fascinating history. Although visitor fossil hunting is prohibited at these places, in areas outside these parks, you may find a fossil of a prehistoric plant or insect.

Cultural

The Gold Belt Tour once sported a classic culture of the Wild West. Gold miners, saloons, and the untamed land of the Rocky Mountains are all part of the cultural past of this Byway. Although you probably won't experience a gun fight in the streets of a Byway town, the towns along the Gold Belt Tour are fiercely proud of their heritage and bring pieces of the past to the surface for visitors throughout the year.

The mining culture was not the first culture to inhabit the mountains of the Gold Belt Tour. Many native cultures, including the Ute, lived here and developed their own unique way of life. The area was a prime hunting spot and a good place to spend the winter because of its relatively mild climate. The history of these cultures has faded to only a few stories and archaeological artifacts.

In the 1800s, a new culture came to the Gold Belt Tour. Settlers from the east brought with them a new organization of towns, roads, and mines, coupled with all the lawlessness of gunfights and hangings. Respect for the land by the area's predecessors was replaced by a way of life that used up the resources around the people. When the gold boom subsided, however, the communities of the area decreased to smaller sizes, allowing the surrounding regions to continue in their natural beauty.

Now, the culture of the Byway is one that appreciates the natural wonders of the Byway while still remembering the days of miners and cowboys. Many of the towns that exist today along the Byway hold festivals and events throughout the year that both visitors and residents attend.

Historical

The three roads that constitute the Gold Belt Tour are the historic routes that connected the Cripple Creek Mining District to the communities to the north and south. The historic communities of Cripple Creek, Victor, Cañon City, Florence, and Florissant along with the

Byway played important roles in what was the most productive gold mining district in North America.

Cripple Creek was the center of the Gold Boom. Bob Womack discovered gold in 1890, setting off a gold rush that brought people from all over the country and put Cripple Creek on the map. By the year 1900, three railroads, two electric tram lines, modern water and sewer systems, and many other conveniences separated Cripple Creek from the average western mining camp. Cripple Creek became the financial and commercial center of what is known as the Cripple Creek Mining District. Today, many of the historic buildings that played such a prominent role in the days of gold have been restored, and the entire downtown area of Cripple Creek is a National Historic Landmark.

Victor, which lies just southeast of Cripple Creek, was historically the home of the miners and their families. The downtown area of the city boasts several buildings that are on the National Register of Historic Places, and Victor's downtown itself is a National Historic District.

Florissant is north of the Cripple Creek mining district. It stands at the crossroads of two important Ute Indian trails. It was a stopover for Indians, trappers, traders, and mountain men long before silver and gold were discovered in the mountains to the west. In 1886, the railroad came through Florissant and was the closest rail connection to the mining district in the early years of the gold boom.

South of the Cripple Creek Mining District lies the Arkansas River Valley and two more communities that have historical significance. Cañon City and Florence both sought the overflow of wealth coming out of Cripple Creek during the golden years. Both cities were established in the second half of the 1800s and have a rich historical past. Cañon City's downtown area is a National Historic District; visitors can enjoy a tour of some early railroad depots that have been restored.

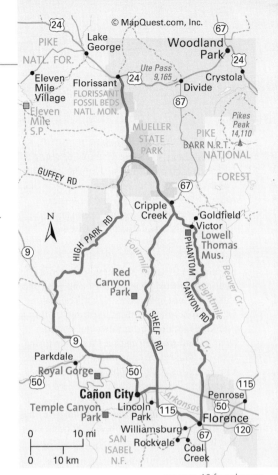

see page A8 for color map

Along with the communities found on the Gold Belt Tour, the routes themselves have historical significance. The Phantom Canyon Road follows the abandoned railroad grade of the Florence and Cripple Creek Railroad, the first railroad to reach the gold mines. Today, travelers on the Phantom Canyon Road go through tunnels, drive over bridges, and see past remnants of train stations used by the railroad back in the 1890s. Shelf Road was constructed in 1892 and was the first direct route from Cripple Creek to the Arkansas River Valley. Today, travelers experience the shelf—a narrow, winding section of road perched high above Fourmile Creek—much the same way that people experienced it in the 1890s.

After you reach the outskirts of Cripple Creek, you pass several historic mines and mills. High Park Road travels through a high-elevation park that is home to modern cattle ranchers.

❋ *Gold Belt Tour Scenic and Historic Byway*

This land and the ranches along High Park Road represent 150 years of ranching history. Historic ranch buildings, such as the Fourmile Community building, lie along the Byway route. Other roads like Skyline Drive near Cañon City provide beautiful views and interesting historical background as well.

Natural

Located in the Rocky Mountains, the Gold Belt Tour is a worthwhile visit for anyone who enjoys outdoor splendor. The landscape along the Byway resulted from multiple alternating periods of mountain-building and flooding by an inland sea; you can see sandstone formations and limestone cliffs that were formed as a result of this geological history. The remains of ancient plants and animals deposited during the flooding produced the rich coal and oil fields in the Arkansas Valley near Florence. It also produced the fossil beds at Garden Park and Indian Springs.

In addition to its unique collection of fossil beds, the Gold Belt Tour is a land with a volcanic history. In the areas of Cripple Creek and Victor, volcanic activity that occurred 6 million years ago formed the terrain. One volcanic cone was nearly 15 miles wide and rose 6,000 feet above surrounding hills. This volcanic activity is the reason the Byway is called the Gold Belt Tour today; it influenced the formation of the gold that was discovered in the early 1800s.

Visitors here can see a wide variety of fossils, from those of insects to petrified trees. The fossils provide insights into the environment of 34 million years ago. Garden Park Fossil Area, located along Shelf Road, has provided the world with many unique and complete dinosaur skeletons. The first major discoveries of large, plant-eating dinosaurs were made here in the 1870s, while the best example of a complete stegosaurus skeleton was found in 1992. You can take a guided tour and view the fossil quarries where these miraculous discoveries were made. Adjacent to Phantom Canyon Road lies the Indian Springs Trace Fossil Area,

which contains portions of an ancient sea floor and was designated a National Natural Landmark in 1979.

The Cripple Creek Caldera, a 24-square-mile basin, is the site of the most productive gold mining area in North America. The caldera formed when a volcanic center collapsed. The collapse shattered the rocks around its edges, and volcanic activity later filled the cracks in the rocks with rich mineral deposits. As you travel the Gold Belt Tour, you can learn about and view the Cripple Creek Caldera at the Cripple Creek overlook.

Recreational

Although it is no more the gold mining district it once was, the Gold Belt Tour is still the road to riches as far as recreation is concerned. Camping is available in several places throughout the area, allowing you to camp your way through the Gold Belt Tour. In addition to outdoor recreation areas, you'll likely be pleased with the historic museums and fossil parks that are just waiting to be explored.

The Royal Gorge Park, owned by Cañon City, is one of Colorado's top tourist destinations. The impressive chasm of the Royal Gorge is spanned by the world's highest suspension bridge. At the bridge, a concessionaire operates an incline railway, aerial tram, and other attractions for visitors. Hiking trails and picnic areas are located throughout the park. Beginning at Cañon City, the Royal Gorge Route leaves on a scenic train ride through the bottom of the gorge. Not only are you treated to a view of the natural wonders in the gorge, but you also catch glimpses of history in ruins from the Royal Gorge War. Cañon City also provides you with opportunities to explore prehistoric creatures at the Garden Park fossil area or the Dinosaur Depot.

A portion of the Arkansas Headwaters Recreation Area is located along the Byway. Colorado's Arkansas River between Leadville and Cañon City is among the nation's most popular whitewater boating destinations, hosting over 300,000 boaters annually. The river also offers some of Colorado's best fly fishing.

Shelf Road Recreation Area attracts rock climbers from around the world. The limestone cliffs offer short but extremely difficult climbs in some places. In other places, they are over 100 feet high and are enticing even to expert climbers. An extensive trail network along the cliffs provides hiking opportunities for climbers and non-climbers alike. On Lower Shelf Road, climbers can picnic at Red Canyon Park. Camping, hiking, and photographing are also excellent pastimes at Red Canyon Park. Many travelers also enjoy picnicking along Phantom Canyon Road after a drive through the forested areas. Here, you may glimpse wildlife or vegetation that are an indication of the area's pristine natural condition.

Scenic

The Gold Belt Tour offers you a wide variety of scenic experiences. From majestic Pikes Peak to the depths of the Royal Gorge, the Gold Belt Tour is a scenery lover's delight. The dramatic changes in terrain and the majestic Rocky Mountains are the elements that give this Byway its unique flavor. The territory echoes with the Old West and the days when gold miners filled the countryside. Historic buildings, scenic roads, and natural splendor give the Gold Belt Tour even more scenic qualities.

Red Canyon Park, along Shelf Road, is filled with spires, windows, and other amazing rock formations eroded from red sandstone monoliths. The park roads provide easy access to a variety of scenic viewpoints. Skyline Drive, located on the western edge of Cañon City, climbs a 600 foot-high tilted sandstone ridge called a hogback. It offers a panoramic view of Cañon City and the lower Arkansas River Valley. The Royal Gorge, located along the High Park segment of the Byway, is one of

Colorado's most famous tourist destinations: you can cross the bridge in a car or on foot or take the incline railway to the bottom of the gorge.

Historic buildings and museums are part of the picturesque towns you drive through along the Gold Belt Tour. Old West main streets and store fronts create a feeling from another time, although they offer modern amenities and attractions. You may drive past an old homestead framed against a Colorado grassland and imagine yourself in the days when gold glittered in the hills and the railroad brought new and interesting people everyday.

Plains and grasslands characterize the southern portion of the Byway near Cañon City. Phantom Canyon and Shelf roads climb out of the valley to the high country, following creeks or clinging to canyon walls hundreds of feet above the canyon floor. As you make your way up the canyons, the plains give way to the forest. As the road nears Cripple Creek and Victor, the scenery opens up to a view of high mountain ranges and majestic Pikes Peak. The area is covered with subalpine forests of Engelmann spruce, subalpine fir, and quaking aspen. Travelers driving through this area are very likely to catch a glimpse of some of the best wildlife the Gold Belt Tour has to offer. In addition, High Park Road and Teller 1 travel through rolling mountain parkland, offering awe-inspiring views of two of Colorado's highest mountain ranges—the Sawatch and Sangre de Cristo ranges.

HIGHLIGHTS

As you travel the Gold Belt Tour, consider following this itinerary.

- **Royal Gorge Bridge:** The first place you'll want to stop is the Royal Gorge Bridge. Travel south out of Cañon City on High Park Road for about 8 miles, turn right, and you'll come to the bridge (and Royal Gorge State Park) in about half a mile. The Royal Gorge Bridge is the world's tallest suspension bridge, spanning the Royal Gorge some 1,053 feet above the waters of the Arkansas River. You can walk or drive the bridge, have a picnic in the surrounding park, or take the world's steepest incline railway to the bottom of the Royal Gorge.

- **Dinosaur Depot and Garden Park Fossil Area:** As you drive back through Cañon City, take time to stop at Dinosaur Depot on Royal Gorge Boulevard. The Depot is a museum that shows some the fossils found at the Garden Park Fossil Area. You can take a guided tour of the museum that includes an informative video showing the removal of famous dinosaur fossils. This is also the place to set up a tour of Garden Park Fossil area, located just north of Cañon City. Garden Park Fossil Area has been the location of the some of the most important discoveries about dinosaurs in North America. Tours should be made in advance; self-guided trails and exhibits are also available at the Garden Park Fossil Area.

- **View of Pikes Peak:** As you travel Shelf Road north to Cripple Creek, you will be treated to a beautiful vista of the west slope of Pikes Peak, named for explorer Zebulon Pike. Pikes Peak towers 14,110 feet and is one of the most breathtaking sights in Colorado.

- **Cripple Creek:** Take the Shelf Road north out of Cañon City, and you'll drive through a scenic canyon and across what's called the shelf, a narrow section of road perched high above Fourmile Creek. When you're 26 miles out of Cañon City, you'll reach historic Cripple Creek, the center of the Cripple Creek Mining District. Cripple Creek is a National Historic Landmark, and many of the buildings that were built during the early 1900s have been restored to their original likeness. Cripple Creek is a great place to stop, have lunch, and see a true piece of American history.

- **Florissant Fossil Beds National Monument:** From Cripple Creek, travel west on Bennett Ave to Teller 1. Seventeen miles from the junction on Teller 1, stop at Florissant Fossil Beds National Monument, which offers walking and guided tours. The fossils found here are renowned for their variety of species: over 80,000 fossilized specimens of tree stumps, insects, seeds, and leaves have been catalogued. The historic **Hornbek Homestead** is also located here. Picnic areas, a visitor's center, and hiking trails are available.

THINGS TO SEE AND DO

Driving along the Gold Belt Tour Scenic and Historic Byway will certainly keep your senses engaged, but if you yearn to get out of the car and stretch your legs, or if you'd like to make a mini-vacation out of your trip, check out these attractions along the route.

BUCKSKIN JOE FRONTIER TOWN & RAILWAY.

1193 County Rd 3A, Cañon City (81212). Phone 719/275-5149. www.buckskinjoes.com. Old West theme park includes an old Western town with 30 authentic buildings, plus a restaurant and saloon. Other activities include daily gunfights, horse-drawn trolley rides, and magic shows. Also a 3-mile, 30-minute train ride to the rim of Royal Gorge. Railway open Mar-Dec, daily. Park open May-Sept, daily. Railway or park only, **$$**; combination ticket **$$$$**.

CAÑON CITY MUNICIPAL MUSEUM. *612 Royal Gorge Blvd, Cañon City (81212). Phone 719/276-5279.* The complex includes Rudd Cabin, a pioneer log cabin constructed in 1860, and Stone House, built in 1881. Second-floor Municipal Building galleries display minerals and rocks, artifacts from settlement of the Fremont County region, and guns. Open early May-Labor Day, Tues-Sun; rest of year, Tues-Sat; closed holidays. **$**

CRIPPLE CREEK CASINOS. *Hwy 67 S, Cripple Creek (80813). Phone toll-free 800/235-2922. www.cripple-creek.co.us.* Historic Cripple Creek has managed to preserve some of its Old West charm despite the frenzied arrival of legalized gambling in the 1990s. More family friendly than the big casino center of Black Hawk, Cripple Creek nevertheless has nearly 20 limited-stakes ($5 bet limit) casinos along its Victorian storefront main street area. The massive Imperial Palace Casino Hotel, built in 1896, offers a multi-tiered gambling parlor with antique décor. For a more Vegas-style experience, check out the glitzy, noisy Double Eagle Hotel & Casino, with more than 600 slot machines, poker, and blackjack tables under a vaulted stained-glass ceiling and a modern, 158-room hotel attached. Both establishments include restaurants or buffets and offer live entertainment. Open daily. **FREE**

CRIPPLE CREEK DISTRICT MUSEUM. *CO 67, Cripple Creek (81212). Phone 719/689-2634. www.cripple-creek.org.* Artifacts of Cripple Creek's glory; pioneer relics, mining and railroad displays; Victorian furnishings. Heritage Art Gallery and Assay Office. Extensive activities for research. Open Memorial Day-mid-Oct, daily; winter and early spring, weekends only. **$$**

CRIPPLE CREEK-VICTOR NARROW GAUGE RAIL-ROAD. *520 Carr St, Cripple Creek (81212). Phone 719/689-2640. www.cripplecreekrailroad.com.* An authentic locomotive and coaches depart from Cripple Creek District Museum. Four-mile round-trip past many historic mines. Open late May-early Oct, daily, departs every 45 minutes. **$$$**

DINOSAUR DEPOT MUSEUM. *330 Royal Gorge Blvd, Cañon City (81212). Phone 719/269-7150; toll-free 800/987-6379. www.dinosaurdepot.com.* Working paleontologists prepare fossils for study and exhibit as you tour the museum's exhibits, including an entire Stegosaurus skeleton that was discovered less than ten miles away. Open daily 9 am-6 pm summer; Wed-Sun 10 am-5 pm winter. **$**

FLORISSANT FOSSIL BEDS NATIONAL MONUMENT. *PO Box 185, 2 miles south on Teller 1, Florissant (80816). Phone 719/748-3253.* Florissant Fossil Beds National Monument consists of 6,000 acres once partially covered by a prehistoric lake. Thirty-five million years ago, ash and mud flows from volcanoes in the area buried a forest of redwoods, filling the lake and fossilizing its living organisms. Insects, seeds, and leaves of the Eocene Epoch are preserved in perfect detail, along with remarkable samples of standing petrified sequoia stumps. On the grounds are nature trails, picnic areas, and a restored 19th-century homestead. Guided tours are available. Visitor center open daily; closed January 1, Thanksgiving, December 25. **$$**

GARDEN PARK FOSSIL AREA. *3170 East Main St, Cañon City (81212). Phone 719/269-8500.* Fossils of well-known species of large dinosaurs have been discovered at this site over the last 120 years; many are on exhibit at museums around the country, including the Smithsonian. Fossils of dinosaurs, dinosaur eggs, and dinosaur tracks have also been discovered in the Garden Park Fossil Area, along with fossils of rare plants. Open daily.

MOLLIE KATHLEEN GOLD MINE. *Hwy 67, Cripple Creek (81212). Phone 719/689-2466. www.goldminetours.com.* Descend 1,000 feet on a 40-minute guided tour through a gold mine. Open May-Oct, daily. **$$$**

★ **ROYAL GORGE.** *4218 County Rd 3A, Cañon City (81212). Phone 719/275-7507.* Magnificent canyon with cliffs rising more than 1,000 feet above the Arkansas River. Royal Gorge

❋ Gold Belt Tour Scenic and Historic Byway

Suspension Bridge, 1,053 feet above the river, is highest in the world (recreational vehicles larger than small van or small camper are not permitted on the bridge). Royal Gorge Incline Railway, the world's steepest, takes passengers 1,550 feet to the bottom of the canyon. A 2,200-foot aerial tramway glides across the spectacular canyon. Theater; entertainment gazebo; petting zoo; restaurants. Open daily.

ROYAL GORGE ROUTE. *401 Water St, Cañon City (81212). Phone toll-free 888/RAILS-4U. www. royalgorgeroute.com.* Travel by train through the Royal Gorge on a two-hour round-trip departing from Cañon City. Open summer; daily.

VICTOR. *5 miles S on CO 67, Cripple Creek (81212). www.tellercountydc.com/victorchamber .htm.* Victor, the City of Mines, actually does have streets paved with gold: low-grade ore was used to surface streets in the early days.

PLACES TO STAY

If you choose to include an overnight stay in your trip along this Byway, Mobil Travel Guide recommends the following lodgings.

★★BEST WESTERN ROYAL GORGE. *1925 Fremont Dr, Cañon City (81212). Phone 719/275-3377; toll-free 800/780-7234. www.bestwestern .com.* 67 rooms, 2 story. Pet accepted, some restrictions; fee. Check-out 11 am. TV; cable (premium). In-room modem link. Laundry services. Restaurant, bar. Pool, whirlpool, poolside service. ¢

D ⬛🔧🈁

★★★CAÑON INN. 🛁 *3075 E US 50, Cañon City (81212). Phone 719/275-8676; toll-free 800/525-7727. www.canoninn.com.* Located at the mouth of Royal Gorge, this simple hotel offers spectacular vistas. 152 rooms, 2 story. Pet accepted, some restrictions; fee. Check-out 11 am. TV; cable (premium). Laundry services. Restaurant, bar. Room service. Pool, whirlpool. Free airport transportation. ¢

D ⬛🔧🈁

★HOLIDAY INN EXPRESS CRIPPLER. *601 E Galena Ave, Cripple Creek (80813). Phone 719/689-2600; toll-free 800/465-4329. www. holidayinncc.com.* 67 rooms, 3 story. Complimentary continental breakfast. Check-out 11 am. TV; cable (premium). Concierge. ¢

⬛ D 🔧🈁

★★VICTOR HOTEL. *4th St and Victor Ave, Victor (80860). Phone 719/689-3553.* 20 rooms, 4 story. Complimentary continental breakfast. Check-out 11 am, check-in noon. TV; cable (premium). Restaurant. Room service. $

⬛ D 🔧🈁

PLACES TO EAT

A long day of driving is sure to make you hungry. At the end of your journey, take a table at one of the following restaurants.

★★ LE PETIT CHABLIS. *512 Royal Gorge Blvd, Cañon City (81212). Phone 719/269-3333.* French. Closed Sun, Mon. Lunch, dinner. A local favorite serving authentic Country French cuisine. $

★★MERLINO'S BELVEDERE. 🛁 *1330 Elm Ave, Cañon City (81212). Phone 719/275-5558.* American, Italian menu. Closed Thanksgiving, Dec 25. Dinner. Bar. Children's menu. $$

D

★★STRATTON DINING ROOM. *123 N 3rd St, Cripple Creek (80813). Phone 719/689-7777.* Breakfast, lunch, dinner. Bar. Authentic Old West décor. Valet parking available. $$

D

Grand Mesa Scenic and Historic Byway

COLORADO

Quick Facts

LENGTH: 63 miles.

TIME TO ALLOW: 2 hours.

BEST TIME TO DRIVE: Late spring through September; high season is summer.

BYWAY TRAVEL INFORMATION: Grand Mesa Scenic Byway Welcome Center: 970/856-3100; Grand Mesa Byway Association: 800/436-3041; Byway local Web site: www.coloradobyways.org.

SPECIAL CONSIDERATIONS: There are no services between Cedaredge and Mesa. Wildfires are an ever-present danger in the dry summer months; follow all posted signs regarding campfires and do not throw cigarettes out the car window. Abandoned mines are extremely dangerous—look and take pictures but do not explore. This Byway traverses high mountain passes; be prepared for all types of weather. High altitudes bring increased sun exposure and reduced oxygen, so wear sunscreen and sunglasses and don't overexert yourself.

RESTRICTIONS: The main road is open year-round. However, Spur Road to Lands End is closed October through May.

The Utes called the Grand Mesa "Thunder Mountain." This name is fitting because, when standing at the Lands End Overlook, the Grand Valley unfolds more than a mile below, and you can imagine yourself as Zeus, ready to hurl thunderbolts from the top. Indeed, this playground in the sky seems too heavenly for mere mortals. The 63-mile route is transcendent as it climbs through the dusty canyon of Plateau Creek to the cool evergreen forests of the mesa top more than 11,000 feet above sea level.

Many scenic overlooks along the Byway allow you to glimpse the extraordinary landscape below. The Lands End Road follows the rim of the mesa for much of the way. From here, you may be able to see the peaks of the LaSal Mountains 60 miles to the west in Utah and may even see the San Juan Mountains in Colorado 90 miles to the south. You won't forget the grand views of the unfolding beauty below.

Every season has its highlights along the Grand Mesa Scenic and Historic Byway. Fall brings a splash of red and yellow to the valleys and mountains, while the mild climate encourages a variety of wildlife to wander in the area of the Byway. Summertime is the season for enjoying the many activities along the Byway. Hiking one of the many trails, fishing in the mesa's 300 lakes, hunting big game, or enjoying a roadside picnic with family or friends makes the Grand Mesa Scenic and Historic Byway one to remember.

�֎ Grand Mesa Scenic and Historic Byway

THE BYWAY STORY

The Grand Mesa Scenic and Historic Byway tells historical, natural, recreational, and scenic stories that make it a unique and treasured Byway.

Historical

The first Europeans known to have come to the Grand Mesa were members of the famous Dominguez-Escalante expedition. In 1776, Ute guides led them over the Mesa because the expedition couldn't find a good land route to California on their own; more Europeans came as fur traders in the mid-1800s.

Early treaties "gave" this land to the Utes, but as white settlers moved to Colorado, the US government made a series of treaties with the Utes that reduced the territory by degrees. In the early 1880s, the Utes were moved to reservations in Utah and southwestern Colorado, and cattle and sheep ranchers soon dominated the area.

Since 1881, the valley floor has been home to farmers, who rely on water from the Grand Mesa for their crops and orchards. Beginning in the late 1800s, numerous water storage and irrigation projects were initiated to bring the water from the mesa. These water conservation systems continue to operate today with enhancements for hydroelectric production and municipal watersheds.

Fishing has been promoted since 1893, when the Mesa Resort Company was established. The company, still in existence today, built several lodges and over 300 summer homes. Skiing on the mesa dates back to 1939, with the construction of the Mesa Creek Ski Area. Relocated in 1964, it is now The Powderhorn of the Grand Mesa Ski Area.

Touring the scenic Grand Mesa began with horse and buggy trips that lasted several days. Access was improved in 1895 with the completion of the first road through Plateau Canyon. A stage line and freight wagons regularly traveled the route. The road was improved with convict labor in 1911 and later became part of the Pikes Peak Ocean-to-Ocean Highway.

A second access route to the top of the mesa was constructed in 1933 by ex-servicemen on a Civilian Conservation Corps (CCC) crew. The twisting, rocky road was then known as the Veteran Road in their honor. It is now called Lands End Road. With the advent of better roads and automobiles, the popularity of Grand Mesa touring has continued to expand.

Natural

Geologically, the Grand Mesa is a lava-capped plateau. Lava flows occurred in ancient river valleys about 10 million years ago. However, unlike many lava flows, no volcanic cone or crater was associated with the Grand Mesa flows. Instead, these flows rose through fissures in the Earth's surface on the eastern part of the mesa. Geologists have identified 25 individual flows, ranging in thickness from less than 10 feet to more than 70 feet. The total thickness of the lava cap of the Grand Mesa ranges from 200 to 600 feet.

Erosion over the last 10 million years has removed the hills that were composed of softer rocks that surrounded the harder lava-filled valleys, leaving the lava-capped terrain as a high plateau. During the Wisconsin Ice Age that occurred 100,000 to 50,000 years ago, glaciers formed on Grand Mesa. Some of these glaciers flowed down the north side of the mesa, over the area where The Powderhorn of the Grand Mesa Ski Area is now located and into the valley of Plateau Creek. The town of Mesa is built upon glacial gravels, and many of the lava boulders in Plateau Canyon were deposited by a glacial river that was much larger than the present-day Plateau Creek.

The drive along the Grand Mesa Scenic and Historic Byway takes you up through numerous ecological transitions that you would normally have to travel a much longer route to see. The ecology includes 5,000-foot elevation

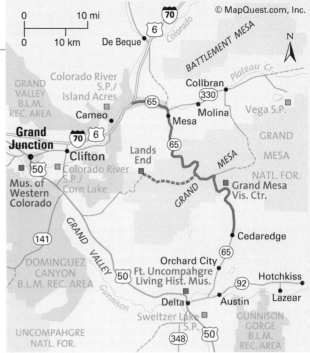

see page A9 for color map

piñon-juniper desert canyons, aspen foothills, lily ponds, and alpine forest at 11,000 feet. The animal life found in each zone changes with the seasons. During the summer, elk and deer roam the cool alpine forests, while winter snow depths of 5 feet or more drive them to the lower elevations. There is a significant change in temperature as the elevation changes, as well. Although it can be hot and dry on the valley floor, the mesa's top may have enough snow for a snowball fight.

Recreational

The Grand Mesa offers excellent outdoor recreational opportunities. Over 300 stream-fed lakes are scattered across the mesa, teaming with rainbow, cutthroat, and brook trout. Numerous roads and trails offer sightseeing and hiking adventures. In the winter, the Grand Mesa provides premier cross-country skiing, downhill skiing at The Powderhorn of the Grand Mesa Ski Area, and snowmobiling. Big game hunting, horseback riding, mountain biking, and boating are also popular activities.

Scenic

The Grand Mesa Scenic and Historic Byway offers a unique experience to travelers seeking an alternative to the typical fast-paced travel routes. Colorado Highway 65 provides for safe, comfortable year-round passage along this nationally designated Byway, which incorporates the world's largest flat-top mountain. Lands End Road provides a unique and safe travel experience seasonally, offering magnificent vistas from a 10,000-foot elevation. The Byway passes through shimmering aspen and aromatic pine forests, by meadows of wildflowers, and among endless sparkling lakes. You have the opportunity to observe major changes and diversity in the landscape, from desert-like approaches to dense

forests atop the Grand Mesa. Scenic overlooks, rest areas, trails, and picnic areas are clearly marked along the Byway, offering easy access to a variety of opportunities to take in the scenery. Interpretive and other information is available at two visitor centers on the Byway and at the Byway Welcome Center in Cedaredge.

HIGHLIGHTS

You can begin this Grand Mesa must-see tour in either of two locations: starting from the Lands End Observatory and proceeding south or starting from the town of Cedaredge and proceeding north. If you are beginning this tour from Cedaredge, start at the bottom of the list and work your way up.

• **Lands End Observatory:** This spur of the Byway ends at the spectacular views around the Lands End Observatory. This structure, which is listed on the Register of Historic Sites, was built in the late 1930s as a public-works project. It is perched on the edge of Grand Mesa and offers views of the valley 6,000 feet below and the LaSal mountains in Utah to the west.

- **Land-O-Lakes Overlook:** When you return back to Highway 65, proceed south to the sign for the Land-O-Lakes Overlook. Due to the area's unique geology, the Grand Mesa is dotted with over 300 streams and reservoirs. A 100-yard trail to this overlook provides a great view that displays many of these lakes and the West Elk Mountains in the east.

- **Grand Mesa Visitor Center:** This beautiful log structure is located at the intersection of Highway 65 and Forest Development Road 121. It is open from 9 am to 5 pm, seven days a week from June to September, with the same hours on weekends for most of the rest of the year. This facility provides visitor information, sales of interpretive materials, and an interpretive hiking trail.

- **Cedaredge Welcome Center and Pioneer town:** These facilities are located together in the town of Cedaredge. Exhibits are open to the public daily from 9 am to 5 pm, Memorial Day to Labor Day. The facilities provide visitor information, exhibits and a tour of a reconstructed town that depicts the life of early pioneers in the area.

THINGS TO SEE AND DO

Driving along the Grand Mesa Scenic and Historic Byway will certainly keep your senses engaged, but if you yearn to get out of the car and stretch your legs, or if you'd like to make a mini-vacation out of your trip, check out these attractions along the route.

✪ **GRAND MESA NATIONAL FOREST.** *US 50, Grand Junction (81416). Phone 970/874-6600. www.fs.fed.us/r2/gmug/.* This 346,221-acre alpine forest includes a flat-top, basalt-capped tableland at 10,500 feet. The forest encompasses more than 300 alpine lakes and reservoirs, many with trout; boat rentals are available. The mesa is also a big-game hunting area, with horses available for rent. Excellent areas for cross-country skiing, snowmobiling, picnicking, and camping (fee at some campgrounds), also a lodge and housekeeping cabins. The rim of Lands End, the westernmost spot on Grand Mesa, offers a spectacular view of much of western Colorado. Also located within the forest is **The Powderhorn Ski Resort** and the **Crag Crest National Recreational Trail.**

POWDERHORN SKI RESORT. *4828 Powderhorn Rd, Mesa (81643). Phone 970/268-5700; toll-free 800/241-6997. www.powderhorn.com.* Quad, two double chairlifts; surface lift; patrol, school, rentals, snowmaking; snack bar, restaurants, bar, day-lodge. Twenty-nine runs; longest run 2 miles; vertical drop 1,650 feet. Cross-country trails (7 miles), snowboarding, snowmobiling, sleigh rides. Half-day rates. Summer activities include fishing, rafting trips, biking, horseback riding, and cookouts. Open mid-Dec-mid-Apr, daily. $$$$

PLACES TO STAY

If you choose to include an overnight stay in your trip along this Byway, Mobil Travel Guide recommends the following lodgings. Grand Junction is less than 20 miles from the northwestern end of the Byway.

★★**BEST WESTERN SUNDANCE.** *903 Main St, Delta (81416). Phone 970/874-9781; toll-free 800/780-7234. www.bestwesternsundance.com.* 41 rooms, 2 story. Pet accepted, some restrictions; fee. Complimentary full breakfast. Check-out 11 am. TV; cable (premium). In-room modem link. Restaurant, bar. Room service. In-house fitness room. Pool, whirlpool. ¢

★**COMFORT INN.** *180 Gunnison River Dr, Delta (81416). Phone 970/874-1000; toll-free 800/228-5150. www.comfortinn.com.* 47 rooms, 2 story. Pet accepted; fee. Complimentary continental breakfast. Check-out 11 am, check-in 2 pm. TV; cable (premium), VCR available (movies). Health club privileges. Sauna. Game room. Pool privileges, whirlpool. ¢

★★ **ADAMS MARK.** *743 Horizon Dr, Grand Junction (81506). Phone 970/241-8888; toll-free 888/444-2326. www.adamsmark.com.* 273 rooms, 8 story. Check-out noon, check-in 3 pm. TV; cable (premium). Restaurant, bar. In-house fitness room. Game room. Outdoor pool, whirlpool, poolside service. Outdoor tennis, lighted courts. Lawn games. Free airport transportation. Luxury level. $

★★ **GRAND VISTA HOTEL.** *2790 Crossroads Blvd, Grand Junction (81506). Phone 970/241-8411; toll-free 800/800-7796. www.grandvistahotel .com.* 158 rooms, 6 story. Pet accepted, some restrictions; fee. Check-out noon, check-in 3 pm. TV; cable (premium). In-room modem link. Restaurant, bar. Room service. Health club privileges. Indoor pool, whirlpool. Free airport transportation. $

PLACES TO EAT

A long day of driving is sure to make you hungry. At the end of your journey, take a table at one of the following restaurants.

★★ **FAR EAST RESTAURANT.** *1530 North Ave, Grand Junction (81501). Phone 970/242-8131.* Chinese menu. Closed major holidays. Lunch, dinner. Bar. Children's menu. $$

★ **STARVIN' ARVIN'S.** *752 Horizon Dr, Grand Junction (81506). Phone 970/241-0430.* American menu. Closed Thanksgiving, Dec 25. Breakfast, lunch, dinner. Bar. Children's menu. Casual atmosphere; antique photographs. $

★★ **WINERY RESTAURANT.** *642 Main St, Grand Junction (81501). Phone 970/242-4100.* American menu. Closed Dec 25. Dinner. Bar. Restored 1890s building. Totally nonsmoking. $$

San Juan Skyway

✳ COLORADO

AN ALL-AMERICAN ROAD

Quick Facts

LENGTH: 233 miles.

TIME TO ALLOW: 1 to 2 days.

BEST TIME TO DRIVE: June through October. The Byway can be enjoyed year-round, and each season has its own attractions. Fall is one of the most spectacular seasons along the Byway because of the many fall colors. High season is in July and August.

BYWAY TRAVEL INFORMATION: San Juan National Forest Visitors Center: 970/247-4874; Byway local Web site: www.coloradobyways.org.

SPECIAL CONSIDERATIONS: The country along the San Juan Skyway is exciting to explore, but safety should always be a major concern. Old, unstable mills, mines, and timber structures may be decaying and hazardous. Be prepared for changing weather both while driving and while hiking. If you are not accustomed to high altitudes, get plenty of rest and resist overdoing activities during your first two days at high altitude.

RESTRICTIONS: This Byway is maintained year-round. Mountain passes are sometimes closed for an hour or two (sometimes even a day or two) in the case of heavy snowstorms or slides during the winter. The two-lane road between Ouray and Silverton has incredibly beautiful views; it is also narrow and steep, has many hairpin switchbacks and a tunnel, includes tremendous drop-offs with no railings or shoulders, and offers few places to pass. Some curves are signed at 10 mph.

BICYCLE/PEDESTRIAN FACILITIES: The San Juan Skyway is a popular and extremely challenging bicycle route. Shoulders are always adequate, but in some places they are tight. Be particularly alert on the Ouray to Silverton segment, where the road is narrow, high, steep, and curvy, and views ahead are limited.

Travel to the top of the world and back in time on the San Juan Skyway. This loop trip through the San Juan Mountains of southwest Colorado follows more than 200 miles of state-maintained highways on a journey from towering mountains and alpine forests to the rolling vistas and ancient ruins of Native American country.

On this Byway, you drive through the heart of 5 million acres of the San Juan and Uncompahgre national forests. The skyway takes you over high mountain passes and through quaint historic towns. Crashing waterfalls can be seen in the spring as the snow melts in the higher mountains; wildflowers are in full bloom during the pleasant summer months; the golden colors of aspens delight visitors in the fall; and winter brings a quieting blanket of snow to the Byway.

You also find plenty of action along the route: four-wheeling, hiking, backpacking, bicycling, hunting, fishing, kayaking, dirt biking, and motorcycle touring.

You find rest and relaxation, too, by browsing town shops, soaking in historic hot springs, staying in a Victorian lodge, or sleeping under the stars in a forest campground. During the winter, skiing is one of the premier activities you can enjoy at quality resort areas like Telluride and Purgatory. The beauty of the surrounding mountains and the historic towns will remind you of the varied and complex history of the area. Ancestral Pueblos lived and worked the land long ago, and the cliff dwellings at Mesa Verde National Park exemplify the complexity of this culture. Spanish exploring parties made their way through the area, and the discovery of gold in the Rocky Mountains forever changed the nature of the surrounding country. Mining towns sprung up in the mountains, and the railroad helped maintain this growth.

THE BYWAY STORY

The San Juan Skyway tells archeological, historical, natural, recreational, and scenic stories that make it a unique and treasured Byway.

Archaeological

Among this Byway's many archaeological sites, Mesa Verde (located in Mesa Verde National Park) is arguably the most outstanding site. Mesa Verde (Spanish for green table) offers an unparalleled opportunity to see and experience a unique cultural and physical landscape. The culture represented at Mesa Verde reflects more than 700 years of history. From approximately AD 600 through AD 1300, people lived and flourished in communities throughout the area. They eventually built elaborate stone villages, now called cliff dwellings, in the sheltered alcoves of the canyon walls. In the late 1200s and within only one or two generations, they left their homes and moved away.

The archaeological sites found in Mesa Verde National Park are some of the most notable and best preserved in the United States. Mesa Verde National Park offers visitors a spectacular look into the lives of the ancestral Pueblo. Scientists study the ancient dwellings of Mesa Verde in part by making comparisons between the ancestral Pueblo and their descendants who live in the Southwest today—24 Native American tribes in the Southwest have an ancestral affiliation with the sites at Mesa Verde.

Historical

The discovery of precious metals led to the exploration and settlement of areas along the San Juan Skyway during the late 19th century. Narrow-gauge railroads played an important role during the mining era and in the history of Southwest Colorado as a whole.

With their rails set 3 feet apart as opposed to the standard gauge of nearly 5 feet, the narrow-gauge lines made it possible for trains to operate in mountainous country with tight turns and steep grades. Evidence of these defunct, narrow-gauge lines is manifested by the water tanks, bridges, trestles, and sections of railroad bed found along the Byway. One narrow-gauge railroad, the Durango & Silverton, continues to operate as a tourist line. It was constructed in 1881-1882 by the Denver & Rio Grande Railroad to haul ore and provisions, and in 1968 the line was designated a National Historic Civil Engineering Landmark. As it travels along the Animas River amidst majestic mountains, the Durango & Silverton Railroad offers you spectacular scenic vistas and the experience of riding an authentic coal-fired, steam-powered railroad. It is one of southwest Colorado's major attractions and carries more than 200,000 passengers a year.

Natural

The already spectacular San Juan Skyway takes on especially vibrant beauty in the fall. The lush green of deciduous vegetation on the mountainsides is transformed into shades of gold, red, bronze, and purple, with evergreens adding their contrasting blues and greens.

The aspen trees are the first to turn shades of gold and rosy red. With their shimmering leaves, the aspen groves glow when the sun shines through them. The cottonwood trees, located along rivers and creeks, are next to turn gold, and a variety of shrubs complement the scene with their fall hues of red, purple, bronze, and orange.

Autumn is a favorite time for locals and tourists alike to enjoy the warm days, cool and crisp nights, and breathtakingly beautiful scenery of the San Juan Skyway.

Recreational

Summer activities include hiking, mountain biking, kayaking, four-wheeling, hunting, and fishing. Winter activities include snowshoeing, ice climbing, snowmobiling, and downhill and cross-country skiing.

Durango Mountain Resort at Purgatory offers downhill skiing and a Nordic center with a groomed track. In summer, the lift takes visitors up the mountain for sightseeing and wildflower viewing. The lift is also a way to get to the top of the mountain biking trail system and to the top of the toboggan-like Alpine Slide.

see page A10 for color map

Scenic

The brawny and pine-furrowed Rockies lounge around this Byway, and their uneven ridges yield to tree-packed forests, flashing streams, and slate-blue lakes. The scene extends into stretches of breezy grasslands divided occasionally by hand-hewn weathered fences. This Byway is known as the Million Dollar Highway not only for its connection to gold and silver mining, but also for its first-class scenery.

HIGHLIGHTS

The following tour begins in Mesa Verde National Park and ends in the town of Ouray. If you are beginning the tour from Ouray, simply begin at the bottom of the list and work your way up.

- **Mesa Verde:** At this national park, explore cliff dwellings made by the Anasazi Indians. These dwellings were mysteriously abandoned by the Anasazi approximately 200 years before Columbus discovered America.

- **Durango:** This authentic Old West town, founded in 1880, still retains its Victorian charm. Restored historic landmarks line downtown streets, while nearby ski resorts beckon to adventurous winter travelers.

- **Silverton:** This remote mining community can be reached either by taking the historic Durango & Silverton narrow-gauge railroad or by driving over the 10,910-foot Molas Divide pass. Many of the beautiful Victorian buildings in Silverton are registered as National Historical Sites.

- **Ghost towns:** The ghost towns of Howardsville, Eureka, and Animas Forks are all located within 14 miles of Silverton. At Animas Forks, you can walk through the remnants of a 19th-century mining town or wander through beautiful meadows of wildflowers.

- **Million Dollar Highway:** The section of highway from Silverton to Ouray has been named the Million Dollar Highway because of the immense amounts of silver and gold that were carted through these passes. This road is quite possibly the most beautiful section of byway anywhere in the country and is not to be missed.

Colorado

THINGS TO SEE AND DO

Driving along the San Juan Skyway will certainly keep your senses engaged, but if you yearn to get out of the car and stretch your legs, or if you'd like to make a mini-vacation out of your trip, check out these attractions along the route.

BACHELOR SYRACUSE MINE TOUR. *1222 County Rd 14, Ouray (81427). Phone 970/325-0220.* This mine has been in continuous operation since 1884. You can take a guided tour aboard a mine train, advancing 3,350 feet horizontally into Gold Hill. Within the mine, you'll see mining equipment, visit work areas, and find out how explosives are used. Gold panning is available, as is an outdoor café. Open late May-Sept, daily; closed July 4. $$$$

BEAR CREEK FALLS AND TRAIL. *1230 Main, Ouray (81427). Phone 970/325-4746.* This area offers a 2-mile canyon walk with views of a tiered waterfall. Open May-Oct.

BOX CAÑON FALLS PARK. *1/2 mile S on US 550, Ouray (81427). Phone 970/325-4464.* Canyon Creek has cut a natural canyon 20 feet wide, 400 feet deep—a view of thundering falls from the floor of the canyon is reached by stairs and suspended bridge. Picnic tables are available in beautiful settings. Children must be accompanied by an adult. Open daily.

BRIDAL VEIL FALLS. *2 1/2 miles E on CO 145, Telluride (81435).* Bridal Veil Falls is the highest waterfall in Colorado. The structure at top of the falls was once a hydroelectric power plant that served the Smuggler-Union Mine operations. It has been renovated and now provides auxiliary electric power to Telluride.

DIAMOND CIRCLE THEATRE. *7th and Main, Durango (81302). Phone 907/247-3400; toll-free 877/325-3400. www.diamondcirclemelodrama.com.* Professional turn-of-the-century melodrama and vaudeville performances, located in the Strater Hotel. Advance reservations are advised. Performances June-Sept, nightly (except Sun). $$$$

DURANGO & SILVERTON NARROW GAUGE RAILROAD. *479 Main Ave, Durango (81301). Phone 970/247-2733; toll-free 888/TRAIN-07. www.durangotrain.com.* This historic narrow gauge railroad, in operation since 1881, links Durango in southwest Colorado with the Victorian-era mining town of Silverton, 45 miles away. A journey on this coal-fired, steam-powered locomotive up the Animas River and through the mountainous wilderness of the San Juan National Forest gives you the chance to relive history while taking in some of the most breathtaking scenery Colorado has to offer. Round-trip travel takes approximately nine hours. Same-day travelers may opt to return by bus; others can stay overnight in historic Silverton with a return train ride the next day. During the winter season, the train makes a shorter, round-trip journey to and from Cascade Canyon. Wheelchair-accessible cars are available; reservations for all riders are highly recommended. Open May-Oct, with shorter routes during the winter months. $$$$

DURANGO & SILVERTON NARROW GAUGE RAILROAD MUSEUM. *www.durangorailway.com/museum.htm.* This museum, operated in conjunction with Durango & Silverton Narrow Gauge Railroad, contains exhibits on steam trains, historic photos, railroad art, and restored railroad cars. You can even enter a locomotive. $$

HOT SPRINGS POOL. *1200 Main, Box 468, Ouray (81427). Phone 970/325-4638.* This outdoor, million-gallon pool is fed by natural mineral hot springs and is sulfur-free. Bathhouse; spa. Open daily. $$

✪ MESA VERDE NATIONAL PARK. *Cortez (81321). Phone 970/529-4465. www.nps.gov/meve/.* In the far southwest corner of Colorado exists the largest—and arguably the most fascinating—archaeological preserve in the nation. Mesa Verde National Park, with 52,000 acres encompassing

4,000 known archaeo-
logical sites, is a treasure
trove of ancestral
Pueblo cultural artifacts,
including the magnifi-
cent, mysterious Anasazi
cliff dwellings.
Constructed in the 13th
century, these huge,
elaborate stone villages
built into the canyon
walls are spellbinding.
To fully appreciate their
significance, first take a
walk through the park's
Chapin Mesa Museum
for a historical overview. A visit to the actual sites
can be physically challenging but is well worth the
effort. Several of the sites can be explored year-
round, free of charge; others require tickets for
ranger-guided tours in summer months only.
Tour tickets can be purchased at the park's Far
View Visitors Center. Open daily. $$

OLD HUNDRED GOLD MINE TOUR. *721 County
Rd 4A, Silverton (81433). Phone 970/387-5444;
toll-free 800/872-3009. www.minetour.com.* This
guided one-hour tour of an underground mine
offers a view of mining equipment, crystal
pockets, and veins. Find out more about meth-
ods of hard-rock mining. Open Memorial
Day-Sept, daily. $$$

OURAY COUNTY HISTORICAL MUSEUM. *420
6th Ave, Ouray (81427). Phone 970/325-4576.
www.ouraycountyhistoricalsociety.org.* This
former hospital constructed in 1887 now
houses artifacts from mining and ranching
and exhibits Ute relics. Open daily. $$

RED MOUNTAIN PASS. *1315 Snowden, Silverton
(81433). Phone 970/387-5838.* Traveling
through the towering San Juan Mountains, the
23-mile stretch of US 550 between Ouray and
Silverton passes through some of Colorado's
wildest country. Traversing numerous gorges,

past cascading falls and tunnels, the road rises
to 11,075 feet to cross the Red Mountain Pass,
a favorite spot for hikers, rock climbers, moun-
tain bikers, and backcountry ski enthusiasts.
Abandoned log cabins and mining equipment,
still visible from the roadside, are evidence of
the region's history. Open as weather permits.

**SAN JUAN COUNTY HISTORICAL SOCIETY
MUSEUM.** *1315 Snowden, Silverton (81433).
Phone 970/387-5838. www.silvertonhistorical
society.org.* Located in an old three-story jail,
this museum exhibits mining and railroad
artifacts from Silverton's early days. Open
Memorial Day-mid-Oct, daily. $$

SAN JUAN NATIONAL FOREST. *15 Burnette Ct,
Durango (81301). Phone 970/247-4874.
www.fs.fed.us/r2/sanjuan/.* This forest of nearly
2 million acres includes the Weminuche
Wilderness, Colorado's largest designated wilderness, with several peaks topping 14,000 feet. The
forest also includes the South San Juan and
Lizard Head wildernesses. The Colorado Trail
begins in Durango and traverses the backcountry all the way to Denver. Recreation includes
fishing in high mountain lakes and streams,
boating, whitewater rafting, hiking, biking,
camping, and four-wheel driving. Open daily.

TELLURIDE GONDOLA. *Phone toll-free 888/376-9770. www.telluride.com/about_telluride/Gondola.asp.* Passengers are transported from downtown Telluride, over a ski mountain, and to Mount Village. You can find four gondola terminals: Station Telluride, Oak St; Station St. Sophia, on the ski mountain; and stations Mount Village and Village Parking in Mount Village. Open early June-early Oct and late Nov-mid-Apr, daily. **FREE**

TELLURIDE HISTORICAL MUSEUM. *317 N Fir St, Telluride (81435). Phone 970/728-3344. www.telluridemuseum.com.* Built in 1893 as a community hospital, this historic building houses artifacts, historic photos, and exhibits that show what Telluride was like in its Wild West days. Open Tues-Sun. **$**

TELLURIDE SKI RESORT. *565 Mt Village Blvd, Telluride (81435). Phone toll-free 800/801-4832. www.telski.com.* The ski resort offers a three-stage gondola; four quad, two triple, and two double chairlifts; one surface lift; patrol, school, rentals; restaurants; nursery. Sixty-six runs; longest run 3 miles; vertical drop 3,522 feet. Cross-country skiing, heliskiing, ice skating, snowmobiling, sleigh rides. Shuttle bus service and two in-town chairlifts. Open Thanksgiving-early Apr, daily. **$$$$**

PLACES TO STAY

If you choose to include an overnight stay in your trip along this All-American Road, Mobil Travel Guide recommends the following lodgings.

Bayfield

★★★**WIT'S END GUEST RANCH AND RESORT.** *254 County Rd 500, Bayfield (81122). Phone 970/884-4113; toll-free 800/236-9483. www.witsendranch.com.* 35 kitchen cabins, 1-2 story. No A/C. Check-out 10 am, check-in 4 pm. TV; VCR (free movies). In-room modem link. Stone fireplaces, knotty pine interiors. Laundry services. Dining room, bar; entertainment. Room service. Free supervised children's activities (June-Labor Day), from 5 years. Heated pool; whirlpool. Tennis. Cross-country ski on site. Horse stables. Hay rides. Snowmobiles, sleighing. Mountain bikes. Social director. Fishing, hunting guides. Picnic tables, grills. Airport transportation. In a valley on 550 acres; all cabins are adjacent to a river or pond. Totally nonsmoking. **$$$$**

Dolores

★★ **RIO GRANDE SOUTHERN HOTEL AND BED & BREAKFAST.** *101 S 5th St, Dolores (81323). Phone toll-free 800/258-0434. www.riograndesouthernhotel.com.* 7 rooms, 2 story. Historic building constructed in 1892 with wood floors and an on-site restaurant. **$**

Durango

★★**LELAND HOUSE BED & BREAKFAST SUITES.** *721 E 2nd Ave, Durango (81301). Phone 970/385-1920; toll-free 800/664-1920. www.leland-house.com.* 10 rooms, 2 story. Pet accepted. Complimentary full breakfast. Check-out 11 am, check-in 3 pm. TV; cable (premium), VCR available. In-room modem link. Fireplaces. Restored apartment building (1927); many antiques. Totally nonsmoking. **$$**

★★★**LIGHTNER CREEK INN.** *999 County Rd 207, Durango (81301). Phone 970/259-1226; toll-free 800/268-9804. www.lighnercreekinn.com.* This mountain getaway is located only five minutes from downtown and fine dining. This inn, built in 1903, resembles a country French manor and offers finely decorated rooms filled with antiques. 10 rooms, 2 story. No A/C. Children over 6 years only. Check-out 11 am, check-in 4 pm. Totally nonsmoking. **$$**

★★★**NEW ROCHESTER HOTEL.** *726 E 2nd Ave, Durango (81301). Phone 970/385-1920; toll-free 800/664-1920. www.rochesterhotel.com.* Built in 1892, this hotel offers guest rooms named after historic figures from the Old West. 15 rooms, 2 story. Pet accepted, some restrictions. Complimentary continental breakfast. Check-out 11 am, check-in 3 pm. TV; cable (premium), VCR available. Totally nonsmoking. $$

Mesa Verde

★★**FAR VIEW LODGE.** *1 Navajo Hill, Mile 15, Mesa Verde National Park (81328). Phone 970/529-4421; toll-free 800/449-2288.* 150 rooms, 1-2 story. No A/C. No room phones. Pet accepted, some restrictions. Check-out 11 am. Restaurant, dining room, bar. Room service 24 hours. Hiking trails. Mesa Verde tours available. General store, take-out service, coin showers. Educational programs. Camping sites, trailer facilities. View of canyon. Totally nonsmoking. ¢

Mountain Village

★★★**WYNDHAM PEAKS RESORT.** *136 Country Club Dr, Telluride (81435). Phone 970/728-6800; toll-free 800/789-2220. www.thepeaksresort.com.* 174 rooms, 6 story. Closed mid-Apr-mid-May, mid-Oct-mid-Nov. Pet accepted; fee. Check-out noon, check-in 4 pm. TV; cable (premium), VCR. In-room modem link. Dining room, bar. Room service. Supervised children's activities. Babysitting services available. In-house fitness room, spa, massage, sauna. Indoor, outdoor pools; children's pool; whirlpool; poolside service. Golf; greens fee $160 (includes cart). Outdoor tennis, lighted courts. Downhill, cross-country ski on site; rentals. Hiking, sleighing, snowmobiles. Valet parking available. Free airport transportation. Business center. Concierge. $$$

Ouray

★**BOX CANYON LODGE & HOT SPRING.** *45 Third Ave, Ouray (81427). Phone 970/325-4981; toll-free 800/327-5080. www.boxcanyonouray.com.* 38 rooms, 2 story. No A/C. Check-out 11 am. TV; cable (premium). Fireplace in suites. At the mouth of the canyon; scenic view. Near the river. $

★**CASCADE FALLS LODGE.** *120 6th Ave, Ouray (81427). Phone 970/325-4394; toll-free 888/466-8729. www.ouraycascadefallslodge.com.* 19 rooms, 1-2 story. No A/C. Closed mid-Oct-mid-Apr. Complimentary continental breakfast. Check-out 10:30 am. TV; cable (premium). Balconies. Refrigerators, microwaves. Restaurant nearby. Playground. Whirlpool. Picnic tables. ¢

★★★**DAMN YANKEE COUNTRY INN.** *100 6th Ave, Ouray (81427). Phone 970/325-4219; toll-free 800/845-7512. www.damnyankeeinn.com.* This inn, complete with a natural hot springs pool, is located in the San Juan Mountains. Rooms are furnished with ceiling fans, two-person whirlpools, and remote-controlled gas fireplaces. 10 rooms, 3 suites, 3 story. Children over 16 years only. Complimentary full breakfast. Check-out 11 am, check-in 3 pm. TV; cable (premium), VCR available. Balconies. Restaurant nearby. Whirlpool in gazebo. Totally nonsmoking. ¢

★★**OURAY VICTORIAN INN.** *50 3rd Ave, Ouray (81427). Phone 970/325-7222; toll-free 800/846-8729. www.ouraylodging.com.* 38 rooms, 4 suites, 2 story. No A/C. Pet accepted. Complimentary continental breakfast (Oct-May). Check-out 11 am. TV; cable (premium). In-room modem link. Restaurant nearby. Playground. Two whirlpools. Picnic tables. Business services. On the river. ¢

★★★**ST. ELMO HOTEL.** *426 Main St, Ouray (81427). Phone 970/325-4951; toll-free 866/243-1502. www.stelmohotel.com.* The guest rooms

41

at this inn are all individually decorated in Victorian style and feature period antiques. Guests can enjoy a wine and cheese social hour every afternoon in the parlor. 9 rooms, 2 story. No room phones. Complimentary full breakfast. Check-out 11 am, check-in 1 pm. TV in sitting room; cable (premium). Restaurant, bar. Whirlpool. Sauna. Business services. Restored 1898 hotel. Totally nonsmoking. ¢

Silverton

★★**ALMA HOUSE BED AND BREAKFAST.** *220 E 10th St, Silverton (81433). Phone 970/387-5336; toll-free 800/267-5336.* 10 rooms, 6 with bath, 4 share bath, 2 1/2 story. No room phones. Pet accepted, some restrictions; $10. TV; cable (premium). Complimentary full breakfast. Check-out 11 am, check-in 2 pm. Luggage handling available. Built in 1898. Victorian furnishings. Some fireplaces. Totally nonsmoking. ¢

★★★**WYMAN HOTEL.** *1371 Greene St, Silverton (81433). Phone 970/387-5372; toll-free 800/609-7845. www.silverton.org/wymanhotel.* 18 rooms, 2 story. Pet accepted; $15. Complimentary full breakfast. Check-out 10:30 am, check-in after 3-8 pm. TV; cable (premium), VCR, free videos. In-room modem link. Some refrigerators. Restaurant nearby. Built in 1902. Victorian furnishings. Totally nonsmoking. $

Telluride

★★★**COLUMBIA HOTEL.** *300 W San Juan Ave, Telluride (81435). Phone 970/728-0660; toll-free 800/201-9505. www.columbiatelluride.com.* 21 rooms, 4 story. No A/C. Pet accepted, some restrictions; $25. Check-out 11 am. TV; cable (premium), VCR (movies). In-room modem link. Fireplaces. Laundry. Restaurant, bar. Room service. In-house fitness room. Downhill, cross-country ski; snowboard on site. $$

★**MANITOU LODGE.** *333 S Fir St, Telluride (80751). Phone 970/728-4011; toll-free 800/538-7754.* 12 rooms, 2 story. No A/C. Complimentary continental breakfast. Check-out 10 am, check-in 4 pm. TV; cable (premium). Restaurant nearby. Downhill ski 1 block, cross-country ski on site. $$

★★★**NEW SHERIDAN HOTEL.** *231 W Colorado Ave, Telluride (81435). Phone 970/728-4351; toll-free 800/200-1891. www.newsheridan.com.* Built in 1891, this hotel is located in the heart of Telluride. Many of the elegant guest rooms feature mountain views and separate sitting rooms. Warm up with a hearty gourmet breakfast and relax in the afternoon with a complimentary glass of Pine Ridge wine at the New Sheridan Bar. 26 rooms, 3 story. Closed mid-Apr-mid-May. Complimentary continental breakfast. Check-out 11 am, check-in 2 pm. TV; cable (premium). In-room modem link. Restaurant, bar. Babysitting services available. In-house fitness room. Game room. Whirlpool. Downhill, cross-country ski 2 blocks. Valet parking available. Concierge. Totally nonsmoking. $$

★**THE VICTORIAN INN.** *401 W Pacific St, Telluride (81435). Phone 970/728-6601; toll-free 800/611-9893. www.tellurideinn.com.* 32 rooms, 2 story. No A/C. Complimentary continental breakfast. Check-out 10 am, check-in 4 pm. TV. Restaurant nearby. Sauna. Downhill, cross-country skiing. Totally nonsmoking. ¢

PLACES TO EAT

A long day of driving is sure to make you hungry. At the end of your journey, take a table at one of the following restaurants.

Durango

★★**ARIANO'S ITALIAN RESTAURANT.** *150 E College Dr, Durango (81301). Phone 970/247-8146.* The turn-of-the-century building in which this restaurant is housed was originally a saloon and brothel. Northern Italian menu. Closed Thanksgiving, Dec 25. Dinner. Bar. Children's menu. Casual attire. Totally nonsmoking. **$$**

★**CARVER BREWING CO.** *1022 Main Ave, Durango (81301). Phone 970/259-2545.* American, Southwestern menu. Closed Jan 1, Thanksgiving, Dec 25. Breakfast, lunch, dinner. Bar, brewery. Children's menu. Casual attire. **$**
D

★★★**CHEZ GRAND-MERE.** *3 Depot Pl, Durango (81301). Phone 970/247-7979. www. chezgrand-mere.com.* French menu. Lunch, dinner. Six-course prix fixe menu changes nightly. Largest wine list in the region. **$$$**

★★**FRANCISO'S.** *619 Main Ave, Durango (81301). Phone 970/247-4098.* Mexican, American menu. Mexican décor. Lunch, dinner. Bar. Children's menu. Casual attire. **$**
D SC

★**LADY FALCONBURGH.** *640 Main St, Durango (81301). Phone 970/382-9664.* American menu. Lunch, dinner, late night. Bar. Children's menu. Casual attire. **$**

★**PALACE.** *505 Main Ave, Durango (81301). Phone 970/247-2018. www.palacerestaurants.com.* American menu. Closed Sun Nov-May; Dec 25. Lunch, dinner. Bar. Casual attire. Reservations accepted. Outdoor seating. **$$**
D

★★**RED SNAPPER.** *144 E 9th St, Durango (81301). Phone 970/259-3417.* Seafood, steak menu. Closed Thanksgiving, Dec 25. Dinner. Bar. Children's menu. Turn-of-the-century building (1904). Casual attire. Totally nonsmoking. **$$**
D

Ouray

★★**BON TON.** *426 Main St, Ouray (81427). Phone 970/325-4951; toll-free 866/243-1502. www.stelmohotel.com/bonton.htm.* Italian menu. Closed Dec 25. Dinner, Sun brunch. Bar.

Children's menu. Outdoor seating. Built in 1898. Totally nonsmoking. **$$**
D

★**BUEN TIEMPO.** *515 Main St, Ouray (81427). Phone 970/325-4544; toll-free 866-243-1502. www.stelmohotel.com/buentiempo.htm.* Mexican, Southwestern menu. Closed Dec 25. No A/C. Dinner. Bar. Outdoor seating. Casual dining. In an 1891 building, originally a hotel. Totally nonsmoking. **$$**
D

★**CECILIA'S.** *630 Main St, Ouray (81427). Phone 970/325-4223.* American menu. Closed mid-Oct-mid-May. Breakfast, lunch, dinner. Children's menu. Specializes in homemade soup, pastries. Entertainment. In a vintage movie theater. **$$**
D

Telluride

★★★**ALLRED'S.** *2 Coonskin Ridge, Telluride (81435). Phone 970/728-7474. www. allredsrestaurant.com.* American menu. Closed mid-Apr-mid-June, late Sept-mid-Dec. Dinner. Bar. Children's menu. Casual attire. Reservations required. **$$$**
D

★★★**COSMOPOLITAN.** *300 W San Juan, Telluride (81435). Phone 970/728-1292.* Located just across from the gondola in the Hotel Columbia, this fine-dining restaurant features a weekly changing menu comprised of dishes from around the globe. French, American menu. Closed mid-Apr-mid-May, also the last week of Oct. Dinner. Bar. Entertainment. Children's menu. Casual attire. Reservations required. Totally nonsmoking. **$$**
D

★**FLORADORA.** *103 W Colorado Ave, Telluride (81435). Phone 970/728-3888.* Southwestern, American menu. Lunch, dinner. Bar. Children's menu. Stained-glass windows, Tiffany-style lamps. Totally nonsmoking. **$$**
D

Santa Fe Trail Scenic and Historic Byway

✳ COLORADO

Part of a multistate Byway; see also NM.

Quick Facts

LENGTH: 188 miles.

TIME TO ALLOW: 4 hours.

BEST TIME TO DRIVE: Early spring through late fall.

BYWAY TRAVEL INFORMATION: Colorado Welcome Center in Lamar: 719/336-3483; Byway local Web site: www.coloradobyways.org.

BICYCLE/PEDESTRIAN FACILITIES: This Byway is well equipped for passenger vehicles and bicyclists, offering flat or slightly rolling terrain. Highways 160 and 350 from Trinidad to La Junta have two undivided lanes. From La Junta east to the Kansas border on State Highway 50, the highway varies between two and four lanes. These road segments can easily accommodate passenger vehicle traffic because they have light traffic volume, 12-foot-wide lanes, and good sight lines. However, the road shoulders are fairly narrow at 2 feet wide. Even though specifically designated bicycle routes are not available, long-distance bicyclists can be found riding the route on a typical day. The communities along the Byway are small, with populations under 10,000 people, so local traffic has minimal impact on visiting pedestrians, bicyclists, and vehicle traffic. Bicyclists are permitted on I-25 because there are no alternative routes. Pedestrian usage is concentrated in commercial areas where sidewalks are available.

The Santa Fe Trail Scenic and Historic Byway is a rich legacy of the many people who made their way across southeastern Colorado. This transportation route served as a corridor to the West and resulted in the meshing of many cultures and traditions. Today along the Byway, festivals and museums honor the many men and women who left a distinctive mark on the area, including early Native Americans, military personnel, ranchers, miners, and railroad passengers.

On a clear spring day, a sharp observer can still discern the wagon-wheel ruts of the Santa Fe Trail wending their way across the prairie. The cultural legacies of this historic trade route, which saw its heaviest use between the 1820s and 1870s, remain just as distinct today. The Byway, which comprises a 188-mile portion of the trail, traverses one of the last strongholds of the nomadic Plains Indians and one of the first toeholds of Anglo-American pioneers who began homesteading along the Arkansas River in the 1860s. The Mountain Branch of the Santa Fe Trail traveled through the present-day city of Trinidad. It then crossed Raton Pass, a mountain gap used by Native Americans for centuries. The Byway's midpoint is Bent's Old Fort, once a trading post and cultural melting pot and now a National Historic Site.

Travelers on the Santa Fe Trail today enjoy the area for the variety of attractions and activities that it offers. The rich history of the area is reflected in many historic sites and museums along the Byway, and recreational sites offer enjoyment for the entire family. Fishing, camping, hunting, and hiking are all popular activities. John Martin Reservoir is the largest body of water in southeastern Colorado and provides a great deal of recreational opportunity for modern-day travelers of the Santa Fe Trail.

THE BYWAY STORY

The Santa Fe Trail Scenic and Historic Byway tells archaeological, cultural, historical, natural, recreational, and scenic stories that make it a unique and treasured Byway.

Archaeological

Early man has left signs of habitation along the Santa Fe Trail Scenic and Historic Byway in many forms, including rock art, Native American teepee rings and fire circles, and other evidence of prehistoric and settlement-era activities. Numerous rock art sites document continuous habitation of this region for over 5,000 years, covering Paleo-Indian, Archaid, Ceramic, and Protohistoric/Historic stages.

Southeastern Colorado has many sites that have both petroglyphs and pictographs. (Petroglyphs are images that are pecked into the rock, while pictographs are painted on to the rock.) These images speak of days long past, and part of the enjoyment of viewing rock art is hypothesizing about what the images may mean. Perhaps these symbols were religious in meaning, were used as calendars, or conveyed information about natural resources.

Visitors to the Santa Fe Scenic and Historic Byway will find sites where this rock art is located. Archaeological sites exist at Picket Wire Canyonlands, Picture Canyon, Comanche National Grassland, and Piñon Canyon. A 1997 archaeological survey documented more than 70 sites in the Timpas Creek (Comanche Grassland) area alone. Louden-Henritzie Archaeological Museum in Trinidad features exhibits on the area's geology, fossils, and archaeology.

Cultural

The culture of the Santa Fe Scenic and Historic Byway has been shaped by the many people who have traveled along the Santa Fe Trail. The Byway has signs of Mexican influence, as well as the impact of a variety of other people. The tradition of county fairs and local rodeos can be found all along this route, and community celebrations highlight some of the unique features of the area.

Southeastern Colorado is embedded with Mexican culture; the area was a Mexican territory longer than it has been a part of the United States. Even after the US acquired Mexico's northern provinces in 1848, the Santa Fe Trail served as a conduit for exchange between Spanish, Native American, and American cultures. Communities along the Byway continue to celebrate the diverse inhabitants through traditional celebrations, culturally representative architecture (such as adobe structures), religious folk art, and Hispanic culture at Trinidad's Baca House Museum (located in the Trinidad History Museum) and A. R. Mitchell Museum. Large murals depicting the Santa Fe Trail and Western history are painted on the exterior of commercial buildings as reminders of past and present cultural contributions.

Local community events highlight the area's rich traditions. The Santa Fe Trail saw many people moving from place to place, and this movement brought a variety of people and many new celebrations to the area located along the Byway. Local fairs and rodeos are held in Kiowa County, Bent County, and Crowley County, and they host parades and good old-fashioned fun. The Sand and Sage Roundup in Prowers County has a variety of events, including a rodeo, carnival, exhibits, and a host of other activities. Oktoberfest in Lamar celebrates in the Germanic tradition, with a parade, food, arts, crafts, and a street dance.

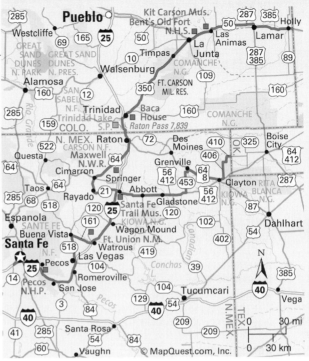

see page A11 for color map

Historical

The Santa Fe Scenic and Historic Byway parallels the Santa Fe Trail, which served as a trade route between Missouri and the Mexican frontiers from 1821 to 1880. Traders, miners, military, and settlers all used this route in the settlement and exploration of the West. Even during the Civil War, the area saw action as Colorado volunteers fought against Confederate troops. With the coming of the railroad, the Santa Fe Trail entered a new phase of its history.

The Santa Fe Trail extended for 900 miles from Missouri to Santa Fe and was instrumental in carrying people and goods across the land. The Mountain Route of the Santa Fe Trail was traveled by caravans of traders, often journeying four horses abreast. Although the Mountain Route was 100 miles longer than the Cimarron Route and included the difficult climb over Raton Pass, the Mountain Route was preferred because water was more accessible and the area was less vulnerable to attacks from Native Americans.

Travel on the trail was beneficial but dangerous for those making the journey. In 1834, Charles and William Bent and Ceran St. Vrain, built a fort to protect trading activities between the Americans, Mexicans, and Native Americans. Visitors can visit Bent's fort today and see what fort life was like. Miners heading to California in search of gold often chose the shorter, although more dangerous, route of the Santa Fe Trail rather than the Oregon Trail.

After the railroad came through the area, the nature of the Santa Fe Trail changed, and in 1861, the Barlow-Sanderson stage line was established. This line provided a weekly schedule, and Trinidad was a major stop on this line. With America embroiled in the Civil War, the Colorado Territory also saw an increase in military traffic.

Visitors traveling the route today can discover the magic of the trail and retrace authentic steps taken by pioneers. Travelers of the trail today are able to recreate life along the Trail by viewing existing historic sites, including trading posts (Bent's Old Fort), stage stops, visible wagon ruts, graves, ruins of Trail-era ranches, and statues commemorating pioneers. Exhibits, interpretive displays, and living-history presentations that convey the history of the Trail are accessible to the public and can be explored at will.

Natural

The Santa Fe Trail corridor provides an opportunity to discover an undisturbed, pristine landscape while observing the wide diversity of wildlife habitats. Southeastern Colorado varies from prime agricultural land to expanses of native grassland; four state wildlife areas in the corridor cover over 10,000 acres. Rivers have carved canyons and valleys, where striking geology and unusual rock formations can be found.

Wildlife consists of free-ranging antelope, mule deer, bighorn sheep, bobcats, foxes, coyotes, and mountain lions, as well as small mammals, amphibians, reptiles, fish, and birds. Comanche National Grassland alone provides habitat for

47

approximately 275 species of birds, 60 species of mammals, 40 species of reptiles, 11 species of fish, and 9 species of amphibians.

The Comanche National Grassland offers an area of rich natural qualities. The features of this landscape vary from short and midgrass prairies to deep canyons and arroyos. Although it may be hard to imagine, this area was once the site of an ancient sea and today, fossils of pre-historic creatures of this sea have been found in the Comanche National Grassland. In addition to these fossils, there is a set of dinosaur tracks south of La Junta that is the longest set of tracks in North America.

Recreational

The Santa Fe Scenic and Historic Byway offers over 30,000 acres of public land that supports a variety of recreational activities. Fishing, hunting, boating, golfing, four-wheeling, hiking, horseback riding, biking, wildlife viewing, and camping are all activities that you can enjoy along the Byway. Several warm-water lakes, state parks, and wildlife areas serve as multiple-use recreation areas. Picnic areas, trailheads, municipal parks, and golf courses are also found in communities and parks on the route.

The Arkansas and Timpas rivers follow the Byway for a good portion of the route, providing many opportunities to enjoy the riverbanks. In addition, the John Martin Reservoir is the largest body of water in Southeastern Colorado. The blue waters of the lake give you a chance to enjoy a fun day of swimming, picnicking, camping, boating, water-skiing, sailing, or windsurfing. Fishing is another popular activity both on the lake and in nearby rivers. A number of lakes and reservoirs located just off of the Byway provide additional opportunities to enjoy the recreational qualities of the area.

In addition to the many types of fish in the lakes and rivers, an abundance of additional wildlife are located along the Byway. Numerous state wildlife areas are situated on the Byway and give you a chance to view the wildlife of the area. Desert bighorn sheep, eagles, cranes,

pelicans, lesser prairie chickens, and humming-birds can often be spotted in the area. Hunters come to southeastern Colorado for prime hunting opportunities; in fact, Prowers County is known as the goose hunting capital of the nation and in December, hunters come from all over to participate in the annual Two Shot Celebrity Goose Hunt.

Scenic

Scenic qualities along the Byway range from panoramic vistas of the Spanish Peaks, Fisher Peak, and Raton Pass to the verdant, irrigated croplands of Colorado's high plains. A sense of isolation is found on the expansive grasslands, one of the nation's disappearing resources. Because much of the Byway is virtually undeveloped, you can experience what traveling the Santa Fe Trail must have been like in the 1800s. Picturesque windmills and evidence of homesteads provide travelers with a glimpse of life as a settler. In addition, the Byway passes through communities that are scenic in their own right, from the Corazon de Trinidad National Historic District, with its period architecture and brick streets, to quaint rural farm towns with roadside stands selling locally grown produce.

HIGHLIGHTS

The Santa Fe Trail historical tour begins at Bent's Old Fort and follows the trail westward toward Trinidad. If you're beginning the tour from Trinidad, simply start at the bottom of the list and work your way up.

• **Bent's Old Fort:** This National Historical Site is a reconstruction of Bent's Fort, which was built in the 1830s. The fort played an important role as a trading post for trappers and the Plains Indians and also as a supply depot during the Mexican-American War.

• **Sierra Vista Overlook:** For Santa Fe Trail travelers heading south, the changing horizon from plains to mountains was a major milestone on their journey. One of their guiding landmarks was the distant Spanish Peaks, which came into view along this section of the trail. A short walk up the side of a bluff gives you an excellent view of the Rocky Mountains and surrounding prairie, much like what early travelers saw. To reach this overlook, drive southwest from La Junta on Highway 350 for 13 miles. Turn right (north) at Highway 71 for 1/2 mile, and then turn left (west) to the parking lot.

- **Trinidad History Museum:** This museum complex, operated by the Colorado Historical Society, houses five attractions in one location. Visitors to the site can visit the Santa Fe Trail Museum, the Baca House, the Bloom Mansion, the Historic Gardens, or the bookstore.

THINGS TO SEE AND DO

Driving along the Santa Fe Trail Scenic and Historic Byway will certainly keep your senses engaged, but if you yearn to get out of the car and stretch your legs, or if you'd like to make a mini-vacation out of your trip, check out these attractions along the route.

A. R. MITCHELL MEMORIAL MUSEUM OF WESTERN ART. *150 E Main St, Trinidad (81082). Phone 719/846-4224.* Features Western paintings by Arthur Roy Mitchell, Harvey Dunn, Harold von Schmidt, and other famous artists; Western and Native American artifacts; Hispanic religious folk art. Housed in a 1906 former department store with original tin ceiling, wood floors, and a horseshoe-shaped mezzanine. Open Apr-Sept, Mon-Sat; also by appointment; closed holidays. **FREE**

BENT'S OLD FORT NATIONAL HISTORIC SITE. *35110 CO 194 E, La Junta (81050). Phone 719/838-5010. www.nps.gov/beol/.* The fort has been reconstructed as accurately as possible to its appearance in 1845-1846; the furnishings are antique and reproductions. The original structure, located on the Santa Fe Trail, was built as a privately-owned frontier trading post (circa 1833). The old fort played a central role in the opening of the west. For 16 years, until its abandonment in 1849, the fort was an

important frontier hub of American trade and served as a rendezvous for trappers, Native Americans, and Hispanic traders on the Santa Fe Trail. It also served as the center of Army operations to protect the traders using the Santa Fe Trail. Self-guided tour. Summer living history programs. Open daily; closed Jan 1, Thanksgiving, Dec 25. **$**

BIG TIMBERS MUSEUM. *7517 US 50, Lamar (81052). Phone 719/336-2472.* Named for the giant cottonwoods on the banks of the Arkansas River. Newspapers, art, drawings, and artifacts of area history. Open daily, afternoons; closed holidays. **FREE**

⚀ **KOSHARE INDIAN KIVA MUSEUM.** *115 W 18th St, La Junta (81050). Phone 719/384-4411; toll-free 800/693-5482. www.koshare.org.* Housed in a domed building, a copy of ceremonial kivas in the Southwest, the museum features Native American baskets, arrowheads, paintings, and carvings, as well as paintings by Southwestern artists. Open daily; closed holidays. **$** Held here are

- **Koshare Indian Dances.** Dances by a nationally famous Boy Scout troop. Sat evenings in late June-early Aug.

- **Koshare Winter Night Ceremonial.** Nightly performances. Week of Dec 25 and first weekend in Jan.

OTERO MUSEUM. *218 Anderson, La Junta (81050). Phone 719/384-7500.* History of Otero County and surrounding areas. Santa Fe Railroad history; artifacts. Open June-Sept, Mon-Sat. **FREE**

TRINIDAD HISTORY MUSEUM. *300 E Main St, Trinidad (81082). Phone 719/846-7217.* Colorado Historical Society administers this museum complex. The Baca House (1870) is a restored nine-room, two-story adobe house purchased by a wealthy Hispanic sheep rancher. The Bloom House (1882) is a restored Victorian mansion and garden built by cattleman and banker Frank C. Bloom. The Santa Fe Museum is also here. Guided tours (Memorial Day-Sept, daily; rest of year, by appointment). **$**

TRINIDAD LAKE STATE PARK. *32610 State Hwy 12, Trinidad (81082). Phone 719/846-6951.* A 2,300-acre park with a 900-acre lake. Water-skiing, fishing, boating (ramps); nature trails, mountain biking, picnicking, playground, camping (electrical hookups, showers). Interpretive programs (Memorial Day-Labor Day, Fri, Sat, holidays). Open daily. **$**

PLACES TO STAY

If you choose to include an overnight stay in your trip along this Byway, Mobil Travel Guide recommends the following lodgings.

La Junta

★★**QUALITY INN.** *1325 E Third St, La Junta (81050). Phone 719/384-2571; toll-free 800/228-5151. www.qualityinn.com.* 76 rooms, 2 story. Pet accepted, some restrictions; fee. Complimentary breakfast. TV; cable (premium), VCR available (movies). Restaurant, bar. Room service. In-house fitness room. Indoor/outdoor pool, whirlpool, poolside service. Free airport transportation. **¢**

Lamar

★★**BEST WESTERN COW PALACE INN.** *1301 N Main St, Lamar (81052). Phone 719/336-7753; toll-free 800/678-0344. www.bestwestern.com.* 95 rooms, 2 story. Pet accepted. Complimentary breakfast buffet. Check-out 11 am. TV; cable (premium), VCR available. Restaurant, bar. Room service. Health club privileges. Indoor pool, whirlpool, poolside service. Free airport transportation. **¢**

★**BLUE SPRUCE.** *1801 S Main St, Lamar (81052). Phone 719/336-7454.* 30 rooms. Pet accepted; fee. Complimentary continental breakfast. Check-out 11 am. TV; cable (premium). Pool. Free airport transportation. **¢**

Las Animas

★★**BEST WESTERN BENT FORT'S INN.** *10950 US 50, Las Animas (81054). Phone 719/456-0011; toll-free 800/780-7234. www.bestwestern.com.* 38 rooms, 2 story. Pet accepted. Complimentary breakfast. Check-out 11 am. TV. In-room modem link. Restaurant, bar. Room service. Pool. Free airport transportation. **¢**

Trinidad

★**BUDGET HOST DERRICK MOTEL.** *10301 Santa Fe Trl, Trinidad (81082). Phone 719/846-3307; toll-free 800/BUDHOST. www.trinidadco.com/budgethost.* 26 rooms. Pet accepted, some restrictions; fee. Complimentary continental breakfast. Check-out 11 am. TV. Whirlpool. Lawn games. Free airport transportation. Features a 107-foot oil derrick. **¢**

★**BUDGET SUMMIT INN.** *9800 Santa Fe Trl, Trinidad (81082). Phone 719/846-2251.* 44 rooms, 2 story. Pet accepted; fee. Complimentary continental breakfast.

Check-out 11 am. TV. In-room modem link.
Laundry services. Whirlpool. Lawn games. ¢

★**HOLIDAY INN.** 3125 Toupal Dr, Trinidad
(81082). Phone 719/846-4491; toll-free 800/465-
4329. www.holiday-inn.com. 113 rooms, 2 story.
Pet accepted. Check-out noon. TV; cable
(premium). In-room modem link. Restaurant,
bar. Room service. In-house fitness room.
Game room. Indoor pool, whirlpool, poolside
service. Lawn games. $

PLACES TO EAT

A long day of driving is sure to make you
hungry. At the end of your journey, take
a table at one of the following restaurants.

★**CHIARAMONTE'S.** 27696 Harris Rd, La Junta
(81050). Phone 719/384-8909. Continental menu.
Closed major holidays. Lunch, dinner. Bar. $$

★ **BLACKWELL STATION.** 1301 S Main St,
Lamar (81052). Phone 719/3367575. American
menu. Lunch, dinner. Featuring authentic local
cuisine and prime aged steaks. $

★★**CHEF LIU'S CHINESE RESTAURANT.**
1423 Santa Fe Trl, Trinidad (81082). Phone
719/846-3333. Chinese menu. Closed
Thanksgiving; also Mon Thanksgiving-Mar.
Dinner. Bar. $$

★ **MAIN STREET BAKERY CAFÉ.** 121 W Main
St, Trinidad (81082). Phone 719/846-8779.
www.mainstreetbakery.net. American menu.
Breakfast, lunch. Serving modern American
cuisine in a family setting. $

★ **NANA & NANO MONTELEONE'S DELI
& PASTA HOUSE.** 418 E Main St, Trinidad
(81082). Phone 719/846-2696. Italian. Closed
Sun, Mon. Lunch, dinner. A local favorite
known for its homemade sausages and
authentic Italian cuisine. $

Top of the Rockies Scenic Byway

❊ COLORADO

Quick Facts

LENGTH: 75 miles.

TIME TO ALLOW: 2.5 hours to 1 day.

BEST TIME TO DRIVE: Year-round; summer is the high season.

BYWAY TRAVEL INFORMATION: Greater Leadville Area Chamber of Commerce: 719/486-3900; Byway local Web site: www.coloradobyways.org.

SPECIAL CONSIDERATIONS: The only part of this Byway that ever closes is the Vail Pass segment of I-70; bypass it by taking Highways 24 and 91, which take a little more time to travel. Due to the amount of snowfall along the Byway, use normal winter precautions when traveling this route. Wildfires are an ever-present danger in the dry summer months; follow posted signs regarding campfires and do not throw cigarettes out the car window. Abandoned mines are extremely dangerous—look and take pictures but do not explore. High altitudes bring increased sun exposure and reduced oxygen, so wear sunscreen and sunglasses and don't overexert yourself. Be prepared for cold mornings, even in August.

RESTRICTIONS: Highway 82, the Independence Pass Road between Twin Lakes and Aspen, is closed during the winter months at a point about 5 miles beyond the southwestern terminus of the Byway.

BICYCLE/PEDESTRIAN FACILITIES: Bicyclists and pedestrians share the road with cars. You'll find wide shoulders along some stretches of the road, especially around Leadville and the Twin Lakes area.

The cool mountain air and fresh scent of pine trees beckons you to the Top of the Rockies Scenic Byway. Traveling through two different national forests, thick stands of pine trees cover the mountainside. Towering peaks flank the highways, and open lowlands give you a rest from steep mountain passes. However, don't be fooled by these "lowlands," because Leadville, the hub of the Byway, is the highest incorporated community in the US, located 10,200 feet above sea level. Mount Elbert (14,433 feet) and Mount Massive (14,421 feet)—the highest and second highest mountains in Colorado—stand just outside of Leadville.

The colossal peaks of this area yielded huge fortunes in the 19th century as miners pulled millions of dollars of precious mineral from the ground. The most fortunate of them, Horace Tabor, became one of the titans of Colorado's silver industry. Leadville was the hub of activity during those silver mining days, with outlying areas acting as small mining towns and stopovers for travelers and miners alike.

While mining is still an integral part of the industry of the area, the town of Leadville is known more for its Victorian charm, colorful history, and historic buildings and churches. In addition, you'll find many activities and recreational opportunities along this 82-mile route that crosses the Continental Divide twice and traces the Arkansas River nearly to its source in the vicinity of Fremont Pass. Hiking, biking, skiing, and fishing are some of the most popular activities along the Byway.

THE BYWAY STORY

The Top of the Rockies tells historical, natural, recreational, and scenic stories that make it a unique and treasured Byway.

Historical

Mining shaped a way of life along the Top of the Rockies many years ago. The rich mines of the area led to the growth of communities such as Twin Lakes, Minturn, Leadville, and Redcliff. The military presence of the 10th Mountain Division at Camp Hale added another distinct chapter in the history of the Byway.

In 1860, the mountains and hills came alive as gold was discovered in California Gulch. Soon, silver was also discovered in the area, bringing individuals such as Horace Tabor, David May, J. J. and Margaret Brown, the Guggenheims, and the Boettchers. Fortunes were made, and communities soon developed to meet the needs of the growing mining populations. Many of these towns, such as Kokomo, Recen, and Robinson, are now nonexistent, having been destroyed by fires or other natural disasters. Other towns, such as Leadville and Twin Lakes, still retain a strong mining influence.

While mining brought many people to the area, when fortunes were harder to come by, many residents turned to farming, and thus the boomtowns remained lively communities. Leadville today maintains the Victorian charm and influence that kept people in town after the mining boom was over. Harrison Avenue boasts many historic structures, and the National Mining Museum relates the story of the importance of mining in the area and around the world. The wealth made in the nearby mines created well-to-do individuals, and the colorful stories of these individuals are still told today in the town. The Healy House and Dexter Cabin show what wealth did for individuals and allow you to see how they lived.

Mining was—and continues to be—one of the most important aspects of the area, but other factors contributed to its historical development.

The 10th Mountain Division, which trained at Camp Hale near Ski Cooper, fought in the military campaign in Italy during World War II. Camp Hale was the training site of the Invisible Men on Skis. The troops used the high elevation, steep slopes, and winter conditions to train for mountain and winter warfare in the Apennine Mountains of Italy. The 10th Mountain Division did see action during the war, and a memorial to those who lost their lives in this campaign stands at the entrance to Ski Cooper.

Natural

The many impressive peaks along the Top of the Rockies Scenic Byway combined with the national forests in the area give the Byway a wealth of natural features. The Byway threads through three national forests—the Pike National Forest, the San Isabel National Forest, and White River National Forest—and one of the largest concentrations of congressionally designated Rare II Wildernesses. The area is so noteworthy that the Rocky Mountain Region of the US Forest Service has designated it a Center of Excellence. In all, six wilderness areas cover about 900 square miles. These primitive lands are being protected to ensure that future generations will be able to explore and experience this rugged and pristine wilderness.

The Mount Massive Wilderness Area covers 18,000 acres. Located in the San Isabel National Forest, this area is characterized by Mount Massive (14,421 feet), the second highest peak in Colorado. The processes of uplift, warping, buckling, and, to a lesser extent, glaciation, have given shape to the peaks in the Sawatch Mountain range and created many hidden mountain lakes. The Rocky Mountains and Continental Divide reach a higher point here than anywhere else between the Arctic Ocean and the Isthmus of Panama.

Recreational

Recreation along the Top of the Rockies is both diverse and abundant. During the winter and summer, you can enjoy a wide variety of

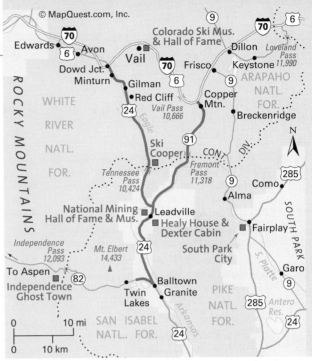

© MapQuest.com, Inc.

see page A12 for color map

recreational opportunities. The many lakes and streams provide rafting and fishing adventures, while the high Rocky Mountains lend themselves to camping, hiking, skiing, or mountain biking. Popular four-wheel drive vehicle trails take you off the beaten track to various destinations. Mount Massive Golf Course outside of Leadville claims the distinction of being the highest golf course on the continent.

The Arkansas and Colorado rivers give you a chance to enjoy rafting—from high water rapids to float trips, the area has something for everyone. These same rivers boast outstanding fishing. Twin Lakes and Turquoise Lake afford opportunities to fish, camp, and boat along the tranquil shores of the mountain lakes.

These lakes and rivers are set among and near some of the highest mountains in the Rocky Mountains. The Sawatch Mountain Range near Leadville has two peaks over 14,000 feet, and the Colorado and Continental Divide trails provide many opportunities for hiking. Numerous mountain biking trails are also in the area. Wilderness areas are the perfect place for extensive rugged outdoor adventure, such as backpacking, camping, picnicking, hunting, horseback riding, four-wheeling, and climbing. You can visit over 300 miles of hut-to-hut trails associated with the 10th Mountain Hut and Trail System, one of the most extensive backcountry hut-to-hut systems in North America.

World-class skiing facilities along the Byway also make this one of the major recreational draws for the area. Both Copper Mountain Resort and Ski Cooper provide opportunities to ski. Other wintertime activities include backcountry skiing, cross-country skiing, and snowmobiling.

Scenic

Driving the Top of the Rockies Byway is an adventure set among some of the highest country in Colorado. With Leadville located at just over 10,000 feet and Mount Elbert and Mount Massive both over 14,000, you are literally at the top of the Rocky Mountains. Both Tennessee Pass (10,424 feet) and Fremont Pass (11,318 feet) take you over the tops of these grand mountains, offering never-ending views of mountaintops and deep canyons. Cool air, even in the summer months, provides a perfect environment for exploring the many attractions along the Byway.

Every turn on State Route 91 and US 24 going to Leadville yields another view of a peak jutting into the sky. The forested mountainsides offer you a chance to witness the many shades of green that can be seen within the forests. Within each of the three national forests (Pike, San Isabel, and White River), woodland creatures, such as deer, may be spotted alongside the road. Clear mountain lakes and tumbling streams are easily accessible and seen from the road.

The open valley around Leadville is flanked on the west side by the Sawatch Mountain Range, with Mount Elbert (14,433 feet) and Mount Massive (14,421 feet) standing guard over the valley. Colorado's largest glacial lake, Twin Lakes, is set at the base of Twin Peaks and offers a peaceful and tranquil setting for the Byway traveler.

HIGHLIGHTS

The Top of the Rockies historical tour begins in the town of Dowd, which is about 5 miles west of Vail along Interstate 70. If you're beginning the tour from Leadville, simply start at the bottom of the list and work your way up.

- **Dowd and Minturn:** The Byway passes briefly through these small mountain communities, and then quickly gains elevation as it winds its way up and over rugged mountain passes. Be sure to bring a camera, because views from the road to the valleys below are incredible, especially in the fall.

- **Camp Hale Memorial and Historic Interpretive Site:** This site is located on the Byway near milepost 160 and features several plaques detailing the history of the 10th Mountain Division that trained here before serving in Europe in World War II.

- **National Mining Museum and Hall of Fame:** Located in Leadville, visitors can see displays of hundreds of fine specimens of gold, silver, ore, and minerals, including spectacular examples loaned from the Smithsonian Institute and the Harvard Mineralogical Museum.

- **Tabor Opera House:** When it opened in 1879, the Tabor Opera House was said to be the finest theater between St. Louis and San Francisco. This building is one of only a few Tabor-associated buildings still standing in Colorado.

- **Annunciation Church:** Started in 1879, this historic church in Leadville was dedicated on New Year's Day, 1880. This church's steeple has become a prominent landmark of this area. It houses an enormous bell that weighs more than 3,000 pounds.

THINGS TO SEE AND DO

Driving along the Top of the Rockies Scenic Byway will certainly keep your senses engaged, but if you yearn to get out of the car and stretch your legs, or if you'd like to make a mini-vacation out of your trip, check out these attractions along the route.

EARTH RUNS SILVER. *809 Harrison Ave, Leadville (80461). Phone 719/486-3900; toll-free 800/933-9301.* A multimedia presentation features Leadville's legendary mining camp with music and narration. Open daily; closed Jan 1, Thanksgiving, Dec 25. **$$**

HEALY HOUSE AND DEXTER CABIN. *912 Harrison Ave, Leadville (80461). Phone 719/486-0487.* The restored Healy House, built in 1878, contains many fine Victorian-era furnishings. Dexter Cabin, built by early mining millionaire James V. Dexter, appears on the outside to be an ordinary two-room miner's cabin; built as a place to entertain wealthy gentlemen, the cabin's interior is surprisingly luxurious. Open Memorial Day-Labor Day, daily. **$$**

HERITAGE MUSEUM AND GALLERY. *9th St and Harrison Ave, Leadville (80461). Phone 719/486-1878.* Diorama and displays depict local history; scale-model replica of Ice Palace, Victorian costumes, memorabilia of mining days. Changing exhibits of American art. Open mid-May-Oct, daily. **$$**

LEADVILLE NATIONAL FISH HATCHERY. *2844 Hwy 300, Leadville (80461). Phone 719/486-0189. leadville.fws.gov.* The original hatchery building constructed in 1889 is still in use. Approximately 45 tons of brook, lake, brown, and cutthroat trout are produced here each year. Hiking and ski-touring trails are nearby. Open daily. **FREE**

LEADVILLE, COLORADO & SOUTHERN RAILROAD TRAIN TOUR. *326 E 7th St, Leadville (80461). Phone 719/486-3936. www.maintour.com/colorado/railroad.htm.* Departs from the old depot for a 23-mile round-trip scenic ride following the headwaters of the Arkansas River through the Rocky Mountains. Open Memorial Day-Sept 30, daily. **$$$$**

THE MATCHLESS MINE. *E 7th St, Leadville (80461). Phone 719/486-1899. www. matchlessmine.com.* When H. A. W. Tabor died in 1899, his last words to his wife, Baby Doe, were "Hold on to the Matchless," which had produced as much as $100,000 a month in its bonanza days. Faithful to his wish and ever hopeful, the once fabulously rich Baby Doe lived on in poverty in the little cabin next to the mine for 36 years; in it, she was found frozen to death in 1935. The cabin is now a museum. Open June-Labor Day, daily. **$$**

NATIONAL MINING MUSEUM AND HALL OF FAME. *120 W 9th St, Leadville (80461). Phone 719/486-1229. www.leadville.com/ miningmuseum/.* This museum features history and technology exhibits of the mining industry, with a Hall of Fame dedicated to those who have made significant contributions to the industry. Open May-Oct, daily; rest of year, Mon-Fri; closed winter holidays. **$$**

SKI COOPER. *Summit of Tennessee Pass, 10 miles N on US 24, Leadville (80461). Phone 719/486-3684. www.skicooper.com.* Triple, double chairlift; Pomalift, T-bar; patrol, school, rentals; snowcat tours; cafeteria, nursery. Twenty-six runs; longest run 1 1/2 miles; vertical drop 1,200 feet. Groomed cross-country skiing 15 miles. Open late Nov-early Apr, daily. **$$$$**

⭐ TABOR OPERA HOUSE. *308 Harrison Ave, Leadville (80461). Phone 719/486-8409. www.taboroperahouse.net.* Now a museum, this theater was elegantly furnished when it was constructed in 1879. At the time, Leadville had a population of 30,000 (it is now closer to 2,000). The theater was host to the Metropolitan Opera, the Chicago Symphony, and most of the famous actors and actresses of the period. Their pictures still line the corridors. Many of the original furnishings, much of the scenery, and the dressing areas are still in use and on display. The

Tabor box, where many dignitaries were Tabor's guests, is part of the theater tour. Summer shows (inquire locally). Self-guided tours. Open Memorial Day-Sept, daily. **$$**

PLACES TO STAY

If you choose to include an overnight stay in your trip along this Byway, Mobil Travel Guide recommends the following lodgings.

★★DELAWARE HOTEL. *700 Harrison Ave, Leadville (80461). Phone 719/486-1418; toll-free 800/748-2004. www.delawarehotel.com.* 36 rooms, 3 story. No A/C. No elevator. Complimentary continental breakfast. Check-out 11 am, check-in 2 pm. TV; cable (premium). Restaurant. Whirlpool. Historic hotel (1886); Victorian lobby. **$**

★★ICE PALACE INN BED & BREAKFAST. *813 Spruce St, Leadville (80461). Phone 719/486-8272; toll-free 800/754-2840. www.icepalaceinn.com.* 5 rooms, 2 story. No room phones. Complimentary full breakfast. Check-out 11 am, check-in 4 pm. TV; VCR (movies). Fireplaces. Whirlpool. Built in 1879. Totally nonsmoking. **$**

Colorado

★★ **THE LEADVILLE COUNTRY INN.** ⊙ *127 E 8th St, Leadville (80461). Phone 719/486-2354; toll-free 800/748-2354. www.leadvillebednbreakfast .com.* 9 rooms, 3 story. This stately 15-room Victorian mansion was built in the 1800s and has been an inn since 1999. **$$**

★★ **PERI & ED'S MOUNTAIN HIDEAWAY.** *201 W 8th St, Leadville (80461). Phone 719/486-0716; toll-free 800/933-3715. www.mountainhideaway .com.* 10 rooms, 2 story. This large Victorian boarding house features private baths, a large breakfast, and great views. **$$**

★**SUPER 8.** *1128 S Hwy 24, Leadville (80461). Phone 719/486-3637; toll-free 800/800-8000. www.super8.com.* 58 rooms, 3 story. No A/C. No elevator. Complimentary continental breakfast. Check-out 10 am, check-in 2 pm. TV; cable (premium). In-room modem link. Sauna. Game room. **¢**
〰️ D

PLACES TO EAT

A long day of driving is sure to make you hungry. At the end of your journey, take a table at one of the following restaurants.

★★ **THE BLUE SPRUCE.** *20 W Main Ave, Frisco (80443). Phone 970/668-5900. www.thebluespruce .com.* American menu. Dinner. Situated in the pine forests of Frisco, serving regional American cuisine. **$$**

★ **MATTEO'S.** *106 3rd Ave, Frisco (80433). Phone 970/668-3773.* Italian. Lunch, dinner. Notable for its New York-style pizza and great sandwiches. A local favorite. **$**

★**HIGH COUNTRY.** *115 Harrison Ave, Leadville (80461). Phone 719/486-3992.* American menu. Closed some major holidays. Lunch, dinner. Bar. Children's menu. Casual attire. Outdoor seating. Three dining areas. Mounted wildlife. **$**
D

★★★ **TENNESSEE PASS COOKHOUSE.** *1892 Hwy 25, Leadville (80461). Phone 719/486-8114. www.tennesseepass.com.* American menu. Lunch, dinner. This skiing-oriented dining room serves one prix fixe meal nightly, with entrees ordered 24 hours in advance. Reservations only for lunch and dinner. **$$$**

★**CHILI WILLY'S.** *101 Main St, Minturn (81645). Phone 970/827-5887.* Tex-Mex menu. Closed Thanksgiving, Dec 25. Lunch, dinner. Bar. Children's menu. Rustic décor; casual atmosphere. Outdoor seating. **$$**
D

★**MINTURN COUNTRY CLUB.** *131 Main St, Minturn (81645). Phone 970/827-4114.* American menu. Closed Dec 25. Dinner. Entertainment. Children's menu. **$$$**
D

Trail Ridge Road/ Beaver Meadow Road

✳ COLORADO

AN ALL-AMERICAN ROAD

Quick Facts

LENGTH: 53 miles.

TIME TO ALLOW: 2 hours or more.

BEST TIME TO DRIVE: Open to through traffic Memorial Day to mid- or late October; closed by snow the rest of the year. High season includes June, July, and August, and the heaviest traffic is between 10 am and 4 pm.

BYWAY TRAVEL INFORMATION: Rocky Mountain National Park Information Center: 970/586-1206; Byway local Web site: www.coloradobyways.org.

SPECIAL CONSIDERATIONS: You can't get fuel inside Rocky Mountain National Park, so you'll have to fill up in Estes Park or Grand Lake. Beware of vapor lock, a common occurrence for vehicles from low altitudes. Speed limits are generally 35 mph.

RESTRICTIONS: Rocky Mountain National Park is closed during the winter from mid- to late October until the Friday of Memorial Day weekend. Park entrance fees are required: $10 per carload for seven days, $5 per pedestrian, bicyclist, or motorcyclist for seven days; commercial bus fees vary.

BICYCLE/PEDESTRIAN FACILITIES: The road is narrow and has no shoulder or guardrail. At different points along the route, the drop-off is up to 2,000 vertical feet. Take extreme caution if biking this scenic road.

Sitting in a national park encompassed by national forests, the Trail Ridge Road/Beaver Meadow Road is arguably one of the most beautiful Byways in Colorado. The overarching characteristic of the Byway is its many overlooks, all of which bestow stirring vistas of 415 square miles of the towering (14,000+ feet) southern Rockies.

The clear atmosphere of this alpine tundra makes seeing the night sky from one of the overlooks incomparable. Constellations, planets, meteor showers, and phases of the moon seem brighter than ever and just beyond arm's reach.

Because this is such a protected area, elk, deer, mountain sheep, coyotes, moose, beavers, ptarmigans, marmots, pikas, eagles, and peregrine falcons can be seen more often than in other (unprotected) areas of Colorado and the nation. Also, the tender tundra wildflowers, which generally peak in July, are an exceptional treat.

THE BYWAY STORY

The Trail Ridge Road/Beaver Meadow Road tells historical, natural, recreational, and scenic stories that make it a unique and treasured Byway.

Historical

The first white men to see this area were French fur traders. In 1859, Joel Estes and his son, Milton, rode into the valley that now bears their name. A few others had settled in this rugged county by 1909 when Enos Mills, a naturalist, writer, and conservationist, began to campaign for preservation of the pristine area, part of which became the Rocky Mountain National Park in 1915.

Colorado

❋ *Trail Ridge Road/Beaver Meadow Road*

Natural

One-third of the park is above the tree line, and the harsh, fragile alpine tundra predominates. The uniqueness of this area is a major reason why it has been set aside as a national park. Just below that, at the upper edges of the tree line, the trees are twisted, grotesque, and hug the ground. Here, more than one-quarter of the plants are also found in the Arctic.

Just below that, forests of Englemann spruce and subalpine fir take over in a subalpine ecosystem. Openings in these cool, dark forests expose wildflower gardens of rare beauty and luxuriance in which the blue Colorado columbine reigns. And in the foothills, open stands of ponderosa pine and juniper grow on the slopes facing the sun; on cooler north slopes grow Douglas fir.

Recreational

The recreational opportunities on this route are varied and excellent. For example, you can enjoy horseback riding, camping, fishing, rock climbing, and various winter activities.

Several campgrounds beckon, some of which are open year-round. The Rocky Mountain National Park maintains more than 260 miles of trails for private and commercial horse users. Hire horses and guides at two locations on the east side of the park or from a number of liveries outside the park boundaries during the summer season.

Four species of trout live in the mountain streams and lakes of Rocky Mountain National Park: German brown, rainbow, brook, and cutthroat trout. These cold waters may not produce large fish, but you do get to enjoy the superb mountain scenery as you fish. Rocky Mountain National Park also offers a variety of challenging ascents throughout the year for climbers. The Colorado Mountain School is the park's concessionaire, operating a climbing school and guide service.

Winter brings cross-country skiing in the lower valleys and winter mountaineering in the high country. Access roads from the east are kept open and provide you with a panorama of the high mountains.

Scenic

The highest continuous road in the United States, this route affords an almost-too-rapid sequence of scenic overlooks as it skips along the roofs of some of the tallest Rockies (over 12,000 feet). From these wind-scoured peaks, you can gaze out to the dark masses of other Rockies, posed like hands of cards in the distance. The land adjacent to the Byway is otherworldly; the tundra's twisted, ground-creeping trees, crusted snow, and hard-faced boulders seem like they belong to a colder, more distant world.

HIGHLIGHTS

While visiting the Trail Ridge Road/Beaver Meadow Road, you can take a self-guided tour of the Byway. If you enter the park from the east (either the Fall River or Beaver Meadows entrance), start at the beginning and move down the list. If you are entering from the west (Grand Lake Entrance), begin at the bottom of the list and work your way up.

• **Rainbow Curve Overlook:** At 10,829 feet, this overlook is more than 2 vertical miles above sea level. At this elevation, every exposed tree is blasted by wind, ice, and grit into distinctive flag shapes. Tree branches here survive only on the downwind side of tree trunks. Higher still, trees survive only where the severely pruned shrubs are covered and protected by winter snowdrifts.

• **Forest Canyon Overlook:** Here, the erosive force of glacial ice is unmistakable. Although the ice did not reach as high as the overlook, it still lay more than 1,500 feet thick in a V-shaped stream valley. With the grinding of a giant rasp, the ice scoured the valley into the distinctive U shape of today.

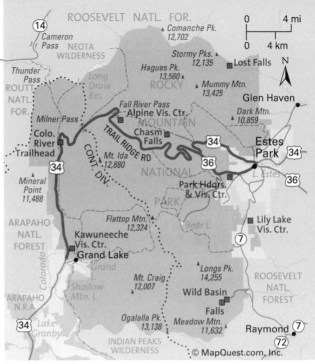

see page A13 for color map

- **Rock Cut Overlook:** Here on the roof of the Rockies, the climate is rigorous. Severe weather can come at any time. Periods of drought may occur in both summer and winter, and winter blizzards are frequent. Temperatures remain below freezing all winter, and they frequently drop below freezing in summer. Wind speeds here can exceed 150 miles per hour in either summer or winter, and ultraviolet radiation is twice what it is at sea level. Sunlight is 50 percent more intense.

- **Fall River Pass and Alpine Visitor Center:** Besides the Visitor Center, there is a gift shop and a short trail to an overlook at 12,003 feet.

- **Milner Pass:** Here, Trail Ridge Road crosses the Continental Divide. At this point, waters enter either the Atlantic or Pacific drainages. The Rockies divide these two great watersheds, but the Continental Divide may be a mountaintop, a ridge, or a pass.

- From this point, a short trail leads past Poudre Lake, headwaters of the Cache La Poudre River, and up to Old Fall River Road. This road was the original road over the Continental Divide. The trail then connects with another trail leading to Mount Ida, at 1,288 feet. This is a 4 1/2-mile hike.

THINGS TO SEE AND DO

Driving along the Trail Ridge Road/Beaver Meadow Road will certainly keep your senses engaged, but if you yearn to get out of the car and stretch your legs, or if you'd like to make a mini-vacation out of your trip, check out these attractions along the route.

ENOS MILLS ORIGINAL CABIN. *6760 Hwy 7, Estes Park (80517). Phone 970/586-4706.* On this family-owned 200-acre nature preserve stands the cabin of Enos Mills, regarded as the Father of Rocky Mountain National Park.

In the shadow of Longs Peak, the cabin contains photos, notes, and documents of the famed naturalist. Nature guide (fee) and self-guided nature trails. Open May-Oct, daily; rest of year, by appointment. **FREE**

ESTES PARK AREA HISTORICAL MUSEUM. *200 Fourth St, Estes Park (80517). Phone 970/586-6256. www.estesnet.com/museum.* The museum includes three facilities, including a building that served as headquarters of Rocky Mountain National Park from 1915 to 1923. Exhibits on the history of the park, the town, and the surrounding area. Open Apr-Sept, daily; Oct-Mar, weekends only. **$$**

★ ROCKY MOUNTAIN NATIONAL PARK. *Estes Park (80517). Phone 970/586-1206. www.nps.gov/romo/.* More than 100 years ago, Joel Estes built a cabin on Fish Creek, one of the higher sections of north-central Colorado. Although the Estes family moved away, more settlers soon followed, and the area became known as Estes Park. Described by Albert Bierstadt (one of the great 19th-century landscape artists of the West) as America's finest composition for the painter, the land west of where Estes settled was set aside as Rocky Mountain National Park in 1915. Straddling the Continental Divide, with valleys 8,000 feet in elevation and 114 named peaks more than 10,000 feet high, the 415-square-mile park contains a staggering profusion of peaks, upland meadows, sheer canyons, glacial streams, and lakes. Longs Peak dominates the scene with its east face towering 14,255 feet above sea level. The park's forests and meadows provide sanctuary for more than 750 varieties of wildflowers, more than 260 species of birds, and such indigenous mammals as deer, wapiti (American elk), bighorn sheep, beaver, and other animals. **$$**

ROOSEVELT NATIONAL FOREST. *240 W Prospect Rd, Estes Park (80517). Phone 970/498-1100. www.fs.fed.us/arnt/.* Forest lands include more than 780,000 acres of icy streams, mountains, and beautiful scenery. Trout fishing, hiking trails, winter sports area, picnicking, and camping. Of special interest are the Cache la Poudre River and five wilderness areas. **FREE**

PLACES TO STAY

If you choose to include an overnight stay in your trip along this All-American Road, Mobil Travel Guide recommends the following lodgings.

Estes Park

★**ALPINE TRAIL RIDGE INN.** *927 Moraine Ave, Estes Park (80517). Phone 970/586-4585; toll-free 800/233-5023. www.alpinetrailridgeinn.com.* 48 rooms. No A/C. Closed mid-Oct-Apr. Check-out 10:30 am. TV. Restaurant, bar. Heated pool. Airport transportation. Refrigerators; microwaves available. Some balconies. Mountain views. ¢

★★**ASPEN LODGE RANCH.** *6120 Hwy 7, Estes Park (80517). Phone 970/586-8133; toll-free 800/332-6867. www.aspenlodge.net.* 59 units, 36 rooms in lodge, 23 cottages. No A/C. Check-out 11 am, check-in 4 pm. TV in lobby. Dining room (public by reservation). Box lunches, barbecue, breakfast rides. Bar. Free supervised

children's activities (June-Sept), ages 3-12. Playground. Exercise room, sauna. Sports director. Game room, recreation room. Pool, whirlpool. Tennis. Cross-country ski on site. Picnic tables, grills. Lawn games, handball. Paddle boats. Entertainment. Hayrides, overnight cookouts. Ice skating, snowshoeing. Mountain bike rentals. Airport transportation. Business center. Concierge. Gift shop. Petting zoo (summer months). **$$**

★★★**BOULDER BROOK ON FALL RIVER.** *1900 Fall River Rd, Estes Park (80517). Phone 970/586-0910; toll-free 800/238-0910. www.estes-park.com/boulderbrook.* Fall asleep listening to the Fall River gurgle outside your back door or watch it from the Spa Room. Fishing is available in the lake, river, stream, or creek. 16 rooms, 1-2 story. Check-out 10 am, check-in 2:30 pm. TV; cable (premium), VCR. In-room modem link. Some fireplaces. Cross-country ski 7 miles. Airport transportation. On the banks of the Fall River. Totally nonsmoking. **$**

★**PONDEROSA LODGE.** *820 Fall River Rd, Estes Park (80517). Phone 970/586-4233; toll-free 800/628-0512. www.estes-park.com/ponderosa.* 23 rooms, 2 story. No A/C. No room phones. Summer 2-, 3-, 5-day minimum. Check-out 10 am, check-in 2 pm. TV; cable (premium). Fireplaces. Cross-country ski 2 miles. Fishing, hiking. **$**

★★★**ROMANTIC RIVERSONG INN.** *1765 Lower Broadview Rd, Estes Park (80517). Phone 970/586-4666. www.romanticriversong.com.* A gurgling trout stream, gazebo, and pond all add to the charm of this bed-and-breakfast. Rooms are named after wildflowers. Located on 27 acres adjacent to Rocky Mountain National Park, the inn offers some breathtaking views. 16 rooms, 1-2 story. No A/C. No room phones. Children over 12 years only. Complimentary full breakfast. Check-out noon, check-in 4-7 pm.

Fireplaces. Airport transportation. Built in 1928; decorated with a blend of antique and modern country furnishings. Dinner with advance reservation. Many ponds, trails. Totally nonsmoking. $$

★**WIND RIVER RANCH.** *5770 S St. Vrain, Estes Park (80517). Phone 970/586-4212; toll-free 800/523-4212. www.windriverranch.com.* 15 units, 4 rooms in lodge, 13 (1-3 bedroom) cottages. June-Aug, AP, 3-day minimum. Closed rest of year. No room phones. Check-out 10 am, check-in 3 pm. Many private porches. Many fireplaces. Grocery, coin laundry, package store 7 miles. Dining room. Box lunches. Free supervised children's activities (June-Aug). Playground. Heated pool, whirlpool. Hiking, rafting. Airport transportation. Business center. $$

Grand Lake

★**BIGHORN LODGE.** *613 Grand Ave, Grand Lake (80447). Phone 970/627-8101; toll-free 888/315-2378.www.rkymtnhi.com/bighorn.* 20 rooms, 2 story. TV. Whirlpool. Restaurant nearby. Check-out 10 am. Business services available. Some refrigerators, microwaves. ¢

★**GRAND LAKE LODGE.** *15500 US 34, Grand Lake (80447). Phone 970/627-3967. www. grandlakelodge.com.* 56 kitchen units, 1-2 story. No room phones. Closed Oct-May. Check-out 10 am. Check-in 4 pm. Laundry services. Dining room, bar; entertainment Wed-Sun. Game room. Heated pool, whirlpool. Lawn games. ¢

★★**SPIRIT MOUNTAIN RANCH.** *3863 County Rd 41, Grand Lake (80447). Phone 970/887-3551. www.spiritmtnranch.com.* 4 rooms, 2 story. No room phones. Children over 10 years only. Complimentary full breakfast, afternoon refreshments. Check-out 11 am, check-in 4 pm. Whirlpool. Game room. Downhill ski 15 miles, cross-country ski on site. Picnic tables, grills. Lawn games. Bicycles. Business services. Totally nonsmoking. $

★**WESTERN RIVIERA.** *419 Garfield St, Grand Lake (80447). Phone 970/627-3580. www. westernriv.com.* 25 rooms, 2 story, 6 kitchen cabins. Check-out 10 am. TV. Fireplace in lobby. Cross-country ski 1 mile. On lakefront; scenic view. ¢

PLACES TO EAT

A long day of driving is sure to make you hungry. At the end of your journey, take a table at one of the following restaurants.

Estes Park

★★★**BLACK CANYON INN.** *800 MacGregor Ave, Estes Park (80517). Phone 970/586-9344. www.blackcanyoninn.com.* Continental menu. Closed Mon. Reservations accepted. Lunch, dinner. Bar. Children's menu. Specializes in seafood, wild game. Built in 1927 out of rough-cut logs. Two-story moss and rock fireplace. **$$**
[D]

★**MAMA ROSE'S.** *338 E Elkhorn Ave, Estes Park (80517). Phone 970/586-3330.* Italian menu. Closed major holidays; Jan, Feb; also Mon-Wed (winter). Breakfast, dinner. Bar. Children's menu. Outdoor seating. Victorian décor; large fireplace. Totally nonsmoking. **$$**
[D]

★★**NICKY'S.** *1350 Fall River Rd, Estes Park (80517). Phone 970/586-5376.* Continental menu. Breakfast, lunch, dinner. Bar. Children's menu. Outdoor seating available. Beautiful mountain views. **$$$**
[D]

Grand Lake

★★★**CAROLINE'S CUISINE.** *9921 US 34 #27, Grand Lake (80447). Phone 970/627-9404. www.sodaspringsranch.com/cc.htm.* French, American menu. Closed two weeks in Apr, two weeks in Nov. Dinner. Children's menu. Entertainment: pianist (Sat). Outdoor seating. Three dining rooms; European décor. Art gallery upstairs. Large windows offer views of either the mountain or the hills. **$$**
[D]

★**E. G.'S GARDEN GRILL.** *1000 Grand Ave, Grand Lake (80447). Phone 970/627-8404.* Specialties: catfish, baby back ribs, enchiladas. Closed Dec 25. Reservations accepted. No A/C. Lunch, dinner. Bar. Children's menu. Outdoor seating. Totally nonsmoking.
[D]

★★**GRAND LAKE LODGE RESTAURANT.** *15500 US 34, Grand Lake (80447). Phone 970/627-3967.* Steak menu. Closed mid-Sept-May. Breakfast, lunch, dinner. Bar. Children's menu. Casual attire. Outdoor seating. **$$**
[D]

Northwest Passage Scenic Byway

※ IDAHO

Quick Facts

LENGTH: 90 miles.

TIME TO ALLOW: 3 hours to 3 days.

BEST TIME TO DRIVE: Year-round. Summer is the high season.

BYWAY TRAVEL INFORMATION: North Central Idaho Travel Association: 800/473-3543; Byway local Web site: www.northcentralidaho.info.

SPECIAL CONSIDERATIONS: US 12 above Kooskia is a winding, two-lane road with occasional passing lanes and slow vehicle turnouts.

RESTRICTIONS: During winter months, drivers may experience some snow-covered roads near Lolo Pass at the Montana border.

BICYCLE/PEDESTRIAN FACILITIES: Pedestrians, equestrians, and bicyclists all use the Byway. In many cases, however, there may not be a sufficient amount of shoulder room along all portions of the Byway, so nonmotorized travelers use a portion of traffic lanes, making this mode of travel challenging. Beautiful nature and cycling trails can be found all along the Northwest Passage Scenic Byway.

Follow the footsteps of Meriwether Lewis and William Clark as they searched, at the request of President Thomas Jefferson, for the Northwest Passage—a link between the Missouri River and the Columbia River through the unexplored Rocky Mountains. Lewis and Clark's arduous journey proved that no easy route existed; however, they were led by Sacagawea to the trail through the mountains that had been used by generations of Nez Perce Indians.

Traverse the Northwest Passage Scenic Byway through the winding Clearwater River canyon, and then climb south to the Camas Prairie. Along the way, you will see numerous Nez Perce cultural sites and Lewis and Clark Expedition campsites. View displays, cultural demonstrations, and a historical movie featuring the traditions of the Nez Perce tribe when you visit the Nez Perce National Historical Park Museum at Spalding.

Enjoy the patchwork of wheat, barley, peas, alfalfa, and wildflowers that wave in the gentle breeze of the Camas Prairie. Have your camera ready when you drive this panoramic route between Lewiston and Grangeville; this is scenery you'll definitely want to take with you.

THE BYWAY STORY

The Northwest Passage Scenic Byway tells archaeological, cultural, historical, natural, recreational, and scenic stories that make it a unique and treasured Byway.

❋ *Northwest Passage Scenic Byway*

Archaeological

As archaeologists have looked for traces of the past in the land of the Northwest Passage, they have not come up empty-handed. Two significant archaeological sites have been found along the corridor. At Big Eddy, evidence of early native occupation has been discovered. In Eimers Park's Tolo Lake, the remains of mammoths and an extinct species of bison were discovered at the bottom of the lake in 1994. During the excavation, archaeologists determined that the bones excavated were only a fraction of what is actually at the bottom of Tolo Lake. A display of the mammoth is now located at the Idaho Museum of Natural History in Pocatello. When you come upon an archaeological site along the Byway, informational signs point you in the right direction.

Cultural

Although a conglomeration of cultures and people make up the Northwest Passage, none of the cultures has preserved its heritage like the Nez Perce. Agriculture and industry fostered by the coming of homesteaders and gold miners exist side by side with the customs of the Nez Perce. As the Nez Perce work to restore and preserve their culture, they invite visitors to experience one of their powwows or to visit the Nez Perce National Historic Park, where local arts and crafts are displayed. The Nez Perce commemorate historic events and battles with gatherings and perhaps a pipe ceremony. You can also experience this Northwest Passage culture through events, historical displays, and information centers. Within their reservation, the Nez Perce also offer a language program and have begun to breed Appaloosa horses as they once did in the past.

One of the most significant sites to the Nez Perce is also located along the Byway. A rock formation in the Clearwater River is known to the Nez Perce as the Heart of the Monster in one of their oldest legends. Visitors today can follow a path to the rock formation and listen to its history on an audio program featured here. Keep your eyes open as you drive the rest of the Byway to get the most out of culture on the Northwest Passage.

Historical

Before the Northwest Passage became a nationally recognized corridor, the route was a home to the Nez Perce, and it remains their home even today. For thousands of years, this native culture built villages and camps along the Clearwater River. The Northwest Passage was a main route for the Nez Perce as they traveled through the mountains and forests of what is now northern Idaho. The society of the Nez Perce met the society of European culture when Lewis and Clark traveled through the area in 1805 and 1806. Known as the Corps of Discovery, the company of Lewis and Clark had a difficult crossing of the Bitteroot Mountains after which they were close to starvation. When three Nez Perce children discovered them, the explorers received help from the Nez Perce and continued their journey.

After the coming of the Lewis and Clark Expedition, new visitors wanted to do more than explore. Trappers, missionaries, and miners soon followed and tried to influence the land and its native people. For a time, people gathered in the area in hopes of discovering gold. The mining districts from this period in history eventually became the towns that are now present on the Byway.

In the 1870s, conflict mounted between the Nez Perce and the US government. Battles occurred as the Nez Perce tried to regain their lands. The conflict ended with many of the Nez Perce dead; the rest were moved to reservations. Today, the Byway travels along the Nez Perce Indian Reservation and passes Nez Perce National Historic Parks in Spalding and Kamiah. As you journey the Byway, you begin to understand why so many people through history have appreciated this beautiful land.

see page A14 for color map

Natural

Few evergreen forests and wilderness areas can compete with the Northwest Passage for the grandest of undisturbed nature. Although many of the valleys are now green agricultural fields, the mountainsides are covered in trees, and the sights and smells of the forest still have an overwhelming presence on the Byway. Canyons and valleys appear along the Byway to display the varied topography of the area. Rocks exposed along the Byway are part of basalt lava flows from the Columbia Plateau that formed millions of years ago. Volcanoes in Washington and Oregon made cracks in the Earth's crust that caused an outpouring of molten rock. Some of this rock reached northern Idaho to harden there and remain for geologists and travelers to observe today.

In addition to the scenery, wildlife also thrives here. The rivers are filled with fish, such as steelhead trout and Chinook salmon, and the forests are home to deer, elk, and other species. The variety of tree and plant life that grows along the Byway creates a habitat for all these creatures.

With only small communities along the way, this Byway is far from being urbanized, and the rural, rugged landscape is one of the primary attractions.

Recreational

If you can canoe down a river, have fresh trout for lunch, and hike to a campsite under a stand of pine trees for a beautiful night under the stars, you might be vacationing along the Northwest Passage Scenic Byway. Sublime outdoor recreation awaits you as you explore this enchanted land that was once known only to native tribes who also loved its forested wilderness. From the rivers to the forests, an outdoor adventure beckons to travelers on the Byway.

The road is surrounded by rivers. Along the Byway, travelers can hardly escape the allure of the Clearwater River and its forks. Nearby, you will also find the Snake, Salmon, Selway, and Lochsa Rivers. And whether you choose to enjoy what's in the water or the water itself, you won't be disappointed. Chinook salmon swim in the waters and fly fishing for steelhead trout is one of the reasons people return again and again to the Northwest Passage.

Whitewater rafting on one of the Byway rivers is also irresistible. From beginning rafters to expert kayakers, the rivers can accommodate everyone, depending on location and the time of year. The Lochsa River is named the Native American word for "rough water," and with good reason; the river boasts 40 rapids that rate 4 or above on the whitewater rafting European rating system. Whether you want to try the extreme river or the swiftly rushing stream, outfitters and guides are available to newcomers and experienced adventurers.

If you ever get enough of the water, a walk in the woods may entice you. Travelers take trails through mountains for the sweeping vistas they enjoy along the way. National forests, wilder-

Idaho

✻ *Northwest Passage Scenic Byway*

ness areas, and even state parks give you the opportunity to find trails and go exploring. You can hike your way to the top of a mountain or into one of the Byway communities, where the small town atmosphere is sure to make you feel at home. Plenty of campsites, lodges, and bed-and-breakfasts are also available along the Byway.

Scenic

From canyon to valley to a riverside drive, the Northwest Passage provides a breathtaking variety of scenery. Communities and homesteads provide a pastoral alpine scene against the mountains and deep green forests of the Byway.

Four different landscapes can be found on the Northwest Passage: open canyon, closed canyon, valleys, and panoramic views. From Spalding to Orofino, enjoy the sights of an open canyon, where the water moves along the flat bottom of the canyon between sloping hills. From the hillsides, you will enjoy panoramic views of the river and surrounding land. Near Orofino and Harpster, closed canyon dominates the landscape with steep canyon walls and dense forests of ponderosa pine and Douglas fir. The closed canyon is where the river moves faster around corners and down hills through the trees. Sometimes, a glimpse of the water is enough to make visitors want to stop and explore this beautiful area. In the closed canyon area, rocky outcroppings add to the rugged mountain atmosphere.

The valley landscape from Kamiah to Stites is characterized by a much calmer river and agricultural fields of green. From Harpster to Eimers, the view from the road is broad and sweeping. National forest lands are perennially beautiful, and the nearby pastoral fields change with the seasons, just as the river does. From colors of crystal turquoise to a demure blue, the Clearwater River changes moods all along the way. On this Byway, views from above and below allow you to truly appreciate the land that makes up the Northwest Passage.

THINGS TO SEE AND DO

Driving along the Northwest Passage Scenic Byway will certainly keep your senses engaged, but if you yearn to get out of the car and stretch your legs, or if you'd like to make a mini-vacation out of your trip, check out these attractions along the route.

BORDER DAYS. *Rte 95, Grangeville (83530). Phone 208/983-0460.* Three-day rodeo and parades, dances. Art in the park; food. Held July 4 weekend.

HELL'S CANYON NATIONAL RECREATION AREA. *Grangeville (83520). Phone 541/426-4978.* Created by the Snake River, at the Idaho/Oregon border, Hell's Canyon is the deepest gorge in North America: 1 1/2 miles from He Devil Mountain (elevation 9,393 feet) to the Snake River at Granite Creek (elevation 1,408 feet). Overlooks at Heaven's Gate, west of Riggins. The recreation area includes parts of the Nez Perce and Payette national forests. Activities include float trips, jet boat tours; auto tours, backpacking, and horseback riding; and boat trips into the canyon from Lewiston, Grangeville, and Riggins, also via Pittsburg Landing or the Hell's Canyon Dam. Developed campgrounds; much of the area is undeveloped, and some is designated wilderness. Be sure to inquire about road conditions before planning a trip; some roads are rough and open for a limited season.

HELL'S GATE STATE PARK. *Lewiston (83501). Phone 208/799-5015.* 960 acres on the Snake River, 40 miles north of Hell's Canyon National Recreation Area. Swimming, fishing, boating (marina, concession, ramp); hiking and paved bicycle trails, horseback riding area, picnicking, playground, tent and trailer campsites (hookups, dump station; 15-day maximum). Info center, interpretive programs, exhibits; excursion boats. Open Mar-Nov.

LUNA HOUSE MUSEUM. *306 3rd St, Lewiston (83501). Phone 208/743-2535.* On the site of the first hotel in town (1861). Exhibits on Nez

Perce and pioneers; displays on the town and county history. Open Tues-Sat; closed holidays. **FREE**

⭐ **NEZ PERCE NATIONAL FOREST.** *Main St and E Hwy 13, Grangeville (83530). Phone 208/983-1950.* More than 2.2 million acres with excellent fishing; camping, cabins (fee at some campgrounds), picnicking, cross-country skiing, and snowmobiling. The Salmon (the River of No Return), Selway, South Fork Clearwater, and Snake rivers, all classified as Wild & Scenic, flow through or are adjacent to the forest. Pack and float trips are available; contact the Idaho Outfitters and Guides Association, PO Box 95, Boise 83701; phone 208/342-1438. High elevations are open only in summer and fall; low elevations are open Mar-Nov.

NEZ PERCE NATIONAL HISTORICAL PARK. *US 95 S, Spalding (83541). Phone 208/843-2261.* The park is composed of 38 separate sites scattered throughout Washington, Oregon, Montana, and Idaho. All of the sites relate to the culture and history of the Nez Perce; some relate to the westward expansion of the nation into homelands. **FREE**

SNOWHAVEN. *Grangeville (83530). Phone 208/983-3866.* Nonprofit, city-owned facility. Two chairlifts: one T-bar, one rope tow. Elevation 5,600 feet, vertical drop 440 feet. Lodge. Lessons, rentals. Bar. Open Sat-Sun 10 am-4 pm. **$$$**

WHITE BIRD HILL. *Rte 95, Grangeville (83530). Phone 208/983-0460.* Site of the famous Whitebird Battle of the Nez Perce Indian Wars. View of Camas Prairie, canyons, mountains, and Seven Devils Peaks. Self-guided tour brochures available from the Chamber of Commerce.

PLACES TO STAY

If you choose to include an overnight stay in your trip along this Byway, the Mobil Travel Guide recommends the following lodgings.

★★ **RED LION HOTEL.** *621 21st St, Lewiston (83501). Phone 208/799-1000; toll-free 800-RED-LION. www.westcoasthotels.com.* 183 rooms, 4 story. Pet accepted, some restrictions. Check-out noon, check-in 3 pm. TV; cable (premium). Laundry services. Restaurant, bar. Room service. Pool, whirlpool, poolside service. Airport transportation. Concierge. **$**
D⬛🐾SC🌊

★ **RIVERVIEW INN.** *1325 Main St, Lewiston (83501). Phone 208/746-3311.* 75 rooms, 4 story. Pet accepted. Check-out noon, check-in 3 pm. TV; cable (premium). In-room modem link. In-house fitness room. Pool. **$**
D⬛🐾🌊🏃

★ **SACAJAWEA SELECT INN.** *1824 Main St, Lewiston (83501). Phone 208/746-1393.* 90 rooms, 2 story. Pet accepted, some restrictions; fee. Complimentary continental breakfast. Check-out noon, check-in 1 pm. TV; cable (premium). In-room modem link. Laundry services. Restaurant, bar. In-house fitness room. Outdoor pool, whirlpool. Airport transportation. **$**
D⬛🐾🌊🏃

Payette River Scenic Byway

✳ IDAHO

Quick Facts

LENGTH: 112 miles.

TIME TO ALLOW: 2 days.

BEST TIME TO DRIVE: Year-round. High season is summer.

BYWAY TRAVEL INFORMATION: Idaho Division of Tourism Development: 208/334-2470.

SPECIAL CONSIDERATIONS: The roadway is a narrow, winding, two-lane road with occasional passing lanes and slow vehicle turnouts.

BICYCLE/PEDESTRIAN FACILITIES: Numerous hiking trails are available along the Byway.

A drive along the Payette River Scenic Byway can be distracting for motorists. Rather than watching the road, you may be more inclined to watch the river as it crashes and tumbles its way over rocks and through the narrow river valley. Be sure to take advantage of the occasional pull-offs that allow you to view wilder parts of the river and treat your senses to the sights, sounds, smells, and rhythms of Idaho's famous white water.

Enjoy the scenic drive along the river through the Boise and Payette national forests before arriving in the high, picturesque mountain valley dotted with the resort towns of Cascade, McCall, and New Meadows. Between the thunderous roll of the whitewater and the quiet serenity of the valley landscapes, you will find a thrilling adventure as you travel this mountain Byway.

THE BYWAY STORY

The Payette River Scenic Byway tells historical, natural, recreational, and scenic stories that make it a unique and treasured Byway.

Historical

The people and events associated with this river stretch thousands of years back in time, creating generational ties between the past and present and between old-timers and new arrivals in Idaho. But most of the recorded history of this area started only a couple hundred years ago. Fur trappers of the early 1800s, working for Hudson's Bay Company, named the Payette River in honor of their comrade, Francois Payette, a French-Canadian who explored much of southwestern Idaho. After explorers mapped the territory, pioneers began to settle the area.

Idaho

* Payette River Scenic Byway

The city of McCall, built by these early settlers, is well worth a visit. Much of the city's history is on display at the Central Idaho Cultural Center, one of the interpretive centers of the Payette River Scenic Byway. This center occupies the original Southern Idaho Timber Protective Association (SITPA) buildings. The SITPA was a cooperative fire organization established in 1919 to oversee private, state, and federal lands. These buildings were constructed by troops stationed in McCall during the 1930s. Hollywood then discovered McCall in 1936. The famous movie *Northwest Passage,* starring Robert Young and Spencer Tracy, was filmed on the shores of Payette Lake and on the North Fork of the Payette River.

Around that same time, people began the construction of a bridge now called the North Fork Bridge, although locals refer to it as the Rainbow Bridge because of its arch. It crosses the North Fork of the Payette River above Smith's Ferry. Built in 1933, it displays an open-spandrel design introduced to Idaho in the 1920s. Unlike other bridges of this type, the North Fork Bridge has not been altered over the years and is listed on the National Register of Historic Places.

Natural

Along the Payette River Scenic Byway rests the Idaho Batholith, which offers a wealth of knowledge for geologists as well as precious samples for gemologists. This unique geological feature covers much of the area and is made up of primarily granite. A lot of this batholith formation began millions of years ago, when magma pushed up on the Earth's crust and created many of the Idaho mountains. The magma eventually hardened below the surface and is now known as the batholith; through erosion, you can see the cooled rock today. Yet much has happened to the land in the last 12,000 years, making Idaho a geologically active place. Quite recently (relatively speaking),

magma oozed out of the Earth's crust in many places and has also shot out of volcanoes, warping the land and changing the environment.

Due to differences in the magma's cooling times and conditions, the Idaho Batholith contains many rare and valuable minerals, including the star garnet, jasper, and opal, making Idaho an ideal place for gemologists to collect gems. (Idaho is, after all, known as the Gem State.) The area also boasts many gold, silver, copper, and zinc veins.

This batholith created a unique landscape that interests sightseers as well as geologists. There are mountains made out of solid granite and valleys carved out of this hard mineral. And because many areas near this Byway are still quite new (geologically speaking), several rugged peaks still have not bowed down to the effects of gravity. Furthermore, people can see the traces of glaciers, as these, too, have not yet disappeared with the passing of time.

Recreational

If you are looking for fun, particularly the life-long, memorable kind that nature offers, come to Payette River Scenic Byway. Activities are never far away, and the majestic mountains in the background (which offer some of these activities) enhance the recreation. No matter what time of the year, there's always something fun available.

Of all the activities available here, whitewater rafting ranks perhaps as the most popular. People find braving the rapids on the Payette River enjoyable, too: there is a quantity of white water along the Byway, and rafters rarely experience a boring moment. The rapids range in different sizes, so rafters with less adventuresome spirits can usually avoid the more commanding waves. As you raft in the Payette River, you'll witness sparkling, clean water and gorgeous, jagged peaks looming high above the canyon. This privileged view alone is reason enough for many rafters to experience this river.

Other than rafting, you can find numerous places to settle down for a relaxing picnic, enjoy world-class trout fishing, and hike or bike the plentiful mountain trails. Many enjoy viewing wildlife in the wetlands around this area, which attract bald eagles, ospreys, and Canadian geese. During the cold winter months, snowmobiling replaces rafting as the most popular activity, although skiing and snowshoeing follow close behind. Whatever your preference for fun, the Payette River Scenic Byway is sure to offer memorable and exhilarating experiences.

Scenic

The scenic beauty found along the Payette River Scenic Byway is one of the road's strongest features, an aspect most people remember years after traveling here. For approximately 20 miles, travelers are lulled by the flow of the main Payette River and exhilarated by the turbulent North Fork of the river. Nearly every mile along this stretch makes an ideal setting for pictures.

Driving a little farther along the Byway, Lake Cascade, with its calm serenity and abundant wildlife, can be glimpsed around the corners of the mountains and through the Long Valley surrounding it. Visitors can pull off into access areas, watch the trout anglers, and gaze at bald eagles and ospreys flying overhead. Several picnic grounds also offer you clean mountain air and an opportunity to soak up the natural scenery. The spectacular view of Payette Lake, nestled among mountains and trees, is a thrill not only for first-time travelers to the city of McCall but also for those who have witnessed it many times before.

Not all scenic features along the Byway are natural, however; manmade features like the Old Tate Barn are reminiscent of old-time America. The agricultural and Finnish culture of the area is preserved on Farm-to-Market Road and Elo Road. An old Finnish church, with a cemetery next to it, still stands today and gives a glimpse of what the area was once like. By seeing manmade attractions such as these, you can experience another aspect of the Byway.

see page A15 for color map

THINGS TO SEE AND DO

Driving along the Payette River Scenic Byway will certainly keep your senses engaged, but if you yearn to get out of the car and stretch your legs, or if you'd like to make a mini-vacation out of your trip, check out these attractions along the route.

BOGUS BASIN SKI RESORT. *2405 Bogus Basin Rd, Boise (83702). Phone toll-free 800/367-4397 (except ID).* Four double chairlifts, two high-speed quad, paddle tow; patrol, school, rentals; two lodges, restaurants, bar; day care. Longest run 1 1/2 miles; vertical drop 1,800 feet. Night skiing (Nov-Apr, daily). Cross-country trails. $$$$

BOISE RIVER FESTIVAL. *7032 S Eisenman Rd, Boise (83702). Phone 208/338-8887.* Night parade, contests, entertainment, fireworks. Held the last full weekend in June.

✳ *Payette River Scenic Byway*

BOISE NATIONAL FOREST. *1387 S Vinnell, Boise (83702). Phone 208/373-4007.* This 2,646,341-acre forest includes the headwaters of the Boise and Payette rivers, abandoned mines and ghost towns, and access to the Sawtooth Wilderness and the River of No Return Wilderness. Trout fishing, swimming, rafting; hunting, skiing, snowmobiling, mountain biking, motorized trail biking, hiking, picnicking, and camping. Visitor center.

BRUNDAGE MOUNTAIN SKI AREA. *McCall (83638). Phone 208/634-4151; toll-free 888/ALL-SNOW (snow conditions).* Two triple chairlifts, Quadlift, Pomalift, platter tow; patrol, school, rentals; bar, cafeteria; nursery. Open mid-Nov-mid-Apr, daily. $$$$

CASCADE DAM RESERVOIR. *25 miles S on ID 55, Cascade (83702).* Fishing, boating.

DISCOVERY CENTER OF IDAHO. *131 Myrtle St, Boise (83702). Phone 208/343-9895.* Hands-on exhibits explore various principles of science; large bubblemaker, catenary arch, magnetic sand. Open Tues-Sun; closed holidays. $$

IDAHO BOTANICAL GARDENS. *2355 N Penitentiary Rd, Boise (83702). Phone 208/343-8649.* Twelve theme and display gardens include meditation, cactus, rose, water, and butterfly/hummingbird gardens; 3/4-mile nature trail; plaza. Open daily. $$

IDAHO STATE HISTORICAL MUSEUM. *610 N Julia Davis Dr, Boise (83702). Phone 208/334-2120.* History of Idaho and the Pacific Northwest. Ten historical interiors; Native American exhibits; fur trade, mining, ranching, and forestry displays. Open daily. $

★ **JULIA DAVIS PARK.** *1104 Royal Blvd, Boise (83702). Phone 208/384-4240.* Rose garden, tennis courts, picnicking (shelters), playground. Boat rentals, Gene Harris Bandshell.

MCCALL FOLK MUSIC FESTIVAL. *University of Idaho Field Campus, Ponderosa State Park, McCall (83638). Phone 208/634-7631.* Fiddle music; Western, swing, Irish, folk, blues, and jazz; square dancing. Held the third weekend in July.

M-K NATURE CENTER. *600 S Walnut St, Boise (83702). Phone 208/334-2225.* The river observatory allows visitors to view activities of fish life; aquatic and riparian ecology displays; also a visitor center with hands-on computerized exhibits; nature trails. Open Tues-Sun. $$

PAYETTE NATIONAL FOREST. *800 W Lakeside, McCall (83638). Phone 208/634-0700.* More than 2.3 million acres surrounded by the Snake and Salmon rivers, the River of No Return Wilderness, Hell's Canyon National Recreation Area, and the Boise National Forest. Trout and salmon fishing in 300 lakes and 3,000 miles of streams, boating; 2,100 miles of hiking trails, hunting, camping, and picnic areas; winter sports. Open daily.

PONDEROSA STATE PARK. *Miles Standish Rd, McCall (83638). Phone 208/634-2164.* Approximately 1,280 acres. A large stand of ponderosa pines. Swimming, water-skiing, fishing, boating (ramps); hiking; cross-country skiing, picnicking, camping (except winter; reservations accepted Memorial Day-Labor Day); tent and trailer sites (hookups; 15-day maximum; dump station). Open daily.

SALMON RIVER OUTFITTERS. *1734 W Roseberry Rd, Donnelly (83615). Phone toll-free 800/346-6204.* Offers five- and six-day guided raft trips along the Salmon River. **$$$$**

TABLE ROCK. *4 miles E at end of Shaw Mt Rd, Boise (83702).* Provides a panoramic view of the entire valley, 1,100 feet below. The road may be closed in winter.

WINTER CARNIVAL. *McCall (83638). Phone 208/634-7631.* Parades, fireworks; ice sculptures, snowmobile and ski races, snowman-building contest, carriage and sleigh rides, ball. Held over ten days in early Feb.

WORLD CENTER FOR BIRDS OF PREY. *5668 W Flying Hawk Ln, Boise (83702). Phone 208/362-TOUR.* Originally created to prevent extinction of the peregrine falcon; the scope has been expanded to include national and international conservation of birds of prey and their environments. Visitors can see a breeding chamber of California condors and other raptors at an interpretive center. Open daily; closed Jan 1, Thanksgiving, Dec 25. **$$**

ZOO BOISE. *355 N Julia Davis Dr, Boise (83702). Phone 208/384-4260.* Home to 285 animals; large birds of prey area; otter exhibit, primates, variety of cats, petting zoo. Education center; gift shop. Open daily; closed Jan 1, Thanksgiving, Dec 25. **$$**

PLACES TO STAY

If you choose to include an overnight stay in your trip along this Byway, the Mobil Travel Guide recommends the following lodgings.

Boise

★ **BOISE CENTER GUESTLODGE.** *1314 Grove St, Boise (83702). Phone 208/342-9351.* 50 rooms, 2 story. Pet accepted, some restrictions. Complimentary continental breakfast. Check-out noon, check-in 1 pm. TV; cable (premium). Pool. Airport transportation. **$**

★★ **DOUBLETREE HOTEL BOISE-RIVERSIDE.** *2900 Chinden Blvd, Boise (83714). Phone 208/343-1871; toll-free 800/222-TREE. www.doubletree.com.* Right on the banks of the Boise River, this hotel is only 1 mile from the city center, near golf, white water rafting and the Bogus Basin Ski Area. 304 rooms, 2 story. Pet accepted, some restrictions; fee. Check-out noon, check-in 3 pm. TV. In-room modem link. Restaurant, bar. Room service. In-house fitness room. Outdoor pool, children's pool, whirlpool, poolside service. Airport transportation. **$**

★★ **IDAHO HERITAGE INN.** *109 W Idaho St, Boise (83702). Phone 208/342-8066; toll-free 800/342-8445. www.idheritageinn.com.* 6 rooms, 3 story. Complimentary full breakfast. Check-out 11 am, check-in 3 pm. TV; cable in 3 rooms. In-room modem link. Free parking. Built in 1904. **$**

★★★ **OWYHEE PLAZA HOTEL.** *1109 Main St, Boise (83702). Phone 208/343-4611; toll-free 800/233-4611. www.owyheeplaza.com.* This historic property (built in 1910) in the Owyhee Mountains offers an outdoor pool, two restaurants, and a complimentary airport shuttle, making the beauty of Idaho accessible. 100 rooms, 3 story. Pet accepted, some restrictions; fee. Check-out noon, check-in 3 pm. TV; cable (premium), VCR available. In-room modem link. Laundry services. Restaurant, bar; entertainment. Room service. Pool, poolside service. Free airport transportation. **$**

★★ **STATEHOUSE INN.** *981 Grove St, Boise (83702). Phone 208/342-4622; toll-free 800/243-4622. www.statehouse-inn.com.* 112 rooms, 6 story. Complimentary full breakfast. Check-out 1 pm, check-in 1 pm. TV; cable (premium), VCR. In-room modem link. Laundry services. Restaurant, bar. Room service. In-house fitness room, sauna. Whirlpool. Free garage parking. Free airport transportation. **$**

★ **UNIVERSITY INN.** *2360 University Dr, Boise (83706). Phone 208/345-7170.* 84 rooms, 2 story. Complimentary continental breakfast. Check-out noon, check-in 3 pm. TV; cable (premium). In-room modem link. Laundry services. Outdoor pool, whirlpool, poolside service. Free parking. Free airport transportation. **$**

[D][⇥][SC][≈][✕]

McCall

★ **BEST WESTERN.** *415 N 3rd St, McCall (83638). Phone 208/634-6300; toll-free 800/780-7234. www.bestwestern.com.* 79 rooms, 2 story. Pet accepted, some restrictions. Check-out 11 am, check-in 2 pm. TV; cable (premium), VCR available. In-room modem link. Laundry services. In-house fitness room. Indoor pool, whirlpool. Downhill, cross-country ski 10 miles. **¢**

[D][⇥][🏊][SC][➤][≈][🏃]

★★ **HOTEL MCCALL.** *1101 N 3rd St, McCall (83638). Phone 208/634-8105.* 32 rooms, 3 story. Complimentary continental breakfast. Check-out 11 am, check-in 2 pm. TV; cable (premium), VCR available. In-room modem link. Totally nonsmoking. **¢**

[D][⇥]

★ **WOODSMAN MOTEL AND CAFÉ.** *402 N 3rd St, McCall (83638). Phone 208/634-7671.* 88 rooms, 1-2 story. No A/C. Check-out 11 am, check-in 4 pm. TV. Restaurant. Cross-country skiing. Airport transportation. **¢**

[⇥][➤][✕]

PLACES TO EAT

A long day of driving is sure to make you hungry. At the end of your journey, take a table at one of the following restaurants.

Boise

★★ **MILFORD'S FISH HOUSE.** *405 S 8th St #100, Boise (83702). Phone 208/342-8382.* Seafood menu. Closed major holidays. Dinner. Bar. Children's menu. Former railroad freight warehouse. Casual attire. Outdoor seating. **$$$**

[D]

★ **RICK'S CAFE AMERICAN AT THE FLICKS.** *646 Fulton St, Boise (83702). Phone 208/342-4288.* International menu. Closed July 4. Dinner. Bar. Casual attire. Outdoor seating. Totally nonsmoking. **$$**

[D]

McCall

★★ **MILL STEAKS & SPIRITS.** *24 N 3rd St, McCall (83638). Phone 208/634-7683.* Steak menu. Closed Thanksgiving, Dec 25. Dinner. Bar; entertainment weekends. Children's menu. Photo collection of the history of the Northwest. **$$$**

Pend Oreille Scenic Byway

✴ IDAHO

Quick Facts

LENGTH: 33 miles.

TIME TO ALLOW: 2 hours.

BEST TIME TO DRIVE: The Byway can be traveled year-round. High season is summer.

BYWAY TRAVEL INFORMATION: Hope-Clark Fork-Trestle Creek Chamber of Commerce: 208-266-1552; Byway local Web site: www.pendoreillescenicbyway.org.

SPECIAL CONSIDERATIONS: Idaho 200 is a two-lane road with no passing lanes. It can be icy during winter months, so drive with caution. Also remember that the Pend Oreille Scenic Byway and most of northern Idaho is in the Pacific time zone.

BICYCLE/PEDESTRIAN FACILITIES: This Byway is one segment of a national cross-country bicycle tour promoted by Adventure Cycling of Missoula, Montana. Paved shoulders along the highway are narrow, but the Byway does see frequent bicycle users, both local and visiting bikers. The narrow shoulders do not promote a great deal of pedestrian traffic, except along the Byway in Hope and East Hope, where shoulders are noticeably wider.

Visit the Pend Oreille Scenic Byway and discover a water-lover's paradise! The Byway follows the shore of Lake Pend Oreille (pronounced PEND oh RAY) for the majority of the length of the Byway, and then winds alongside the Clark Fork River to the Montana state line. You'll find yourself beneath towering mountains that are reflected in the many miles of water along the Byway.

The area is largely undeveloped, ensuring that you are treated to the serene outdoors of Idaho by viewing waterfowl, other species of wildlife, and a variety of plants. Be sure to take advantage of the many pull-outs along the road and experience an uninhibited view of this majestic area.

The area around the Byway has been full of activity for thousands of years. See landscapes formed over 10,000 years ago by the many glacial cycles that created flooding, which reached across Oregon and Washington before hitting the Pacific Ocean. Watch for evidence of the Kalispel people, Native Americans who inhabited the area after the waters receded. Imagine the traders, trappers, and miners who passed through the area, helping to make it what it is today.

These days, there's never a dull moment with Lake Pend Oreille and the Clark Fork River nearby. You can go boating, fishing, sailing, canoeing, kayaking, and swimming in the lake, rivers, and streams that line the Byway. If water sports aren't your thing, spend some time viewing the abundant wildlife, especially waterfowl, or go camping, hiking, biking, horseback riding, or golfing. In the wintertime, hit the slopes at Schweitzer Mountain Ski Resort. Whatever your recreational interests, be assured that you can find plenty to do on the Pend Oreille Scenic Byway.

THE BYWAY STORY

The Pend Oreille Scenic Byway tells historical, recreational, and scenic stories that make it a unique and treasured Byway.

Historical

Throughout time, people have been drawn to water. Towns, roads, and groups of people have been concentrated along rivers and lakes, making water one of the most important factors in the shaping of the land. Lake Pend Oreille and the Clark Fork River have been important in the development of the area that is now the Pend Oreille Scenic Byway. Before humans had an impact on the environment, however, glacial Lake Missoula had a significant impact on the land. Subsequent glacial cycles caused cataclysmic flooding, which began in the area of Cabinet Gorge, near the Idaho/Montana border, and then spread across Oregon and Washington before reaching the Pacific Ocean. This tremendous phenomenon created many of the geological formations seen in the area today.

After the glacial ice abated, the land became habitable, and the native Kalispel people lived in the area. The Clark Fork River was an important aspect of their existence, and the Kalispels hosted an annual regional tribal gathering at the mouth of the river. There, they hunted, fished, picked berries, and traded. The importance of this event and the key location at the mouth of the river continued as traders and trappers moved through the area, exploring the west. One British explorer, David Thompson, established a trading post on the banks of Lake Pend Oreille while he was searching for the headwaters of the Columbia River, and he was instrumental in the settlement of the Pend Oreille region.

As traffic through the West and Northwest continued to grow, new routes of transportation were needed. With the creation of the steamboat in 1866, the waterways in the area of the Pend Oreille Scenic Byway became connected, enabling people to travel efficiently from one place to another. When the Northern Pacific Railroad was being built in the Pend Oreille section, many structures, such as bridges, were built to span the many areas of water. The wooden bridge built to cross the Pack River was the longest structure in the entire transcontinental system.

With each passing era, the water and waterways of the Pend Oreille Scenic Byway continue to shape the history and people of the area.

Recreational

With unspoiled landscapes and clean country air, it is no wonder that Idaho is known for its many outdoor activities. Pend Oreille Scenic Byway is no exception, and with 100 miles of shoreline along Lake Pend Oreille, water recreational opportunities are never far away and are in great abundance. Boating, fishing, sailing, and other water sports are all available along the Byway. The water is clean and pure, and it draws visitors from around the country and world. In addition to the scenic and recreational Lake Pend Oreille, two rivers are accessible along the Byway. The Clark Fork River stretches across 2 miles of delta and wetland; the river itself is a popular place to go fishing. The Pack River does not create such a vast delta, but it provides wonderful opportunities for canoeing and kayaking. The Byway is located in Bonner County, which accounts for 20 percent of the total surface water in Idaho's 44 counties, so the Byway follows either a lake or river for its entire length.

Water sports may dominate the recreational scene along the Byway, but a look toward the forests to the sides of the lake reveal an area rich in other recreational opportunities. A number of trails are accessible through the Kaniksu National Forest, affording you the chance to go hiking, biking, or horseback riding. Hunting, berry picking, and snowmobiling are additional activities that you can enjoy along the Byway. Every season has its charm along the Byway. Fall colors dazzle visitors in the autumn, winter encourages visits to

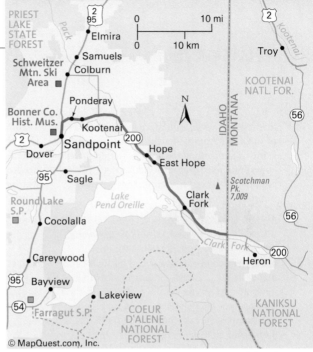

© MapQuest.com, Inc.

see page A16 for color map

Schweitzer Mountain Ski Resort, and spring and summer provide the perfect weather for a game of golf on the two courses adjacent to the Byway.

A drive along the Pend Oreille Scenic Byway opens your eyes to the beauty of the outdoors, including many different types of wildlife. The abundance of water along the Byway makes this an ideal route to travel for bird-watching. The delta area at the confluence of the Clark River provides prime opportunity to see different waterfowl up close in the marshes and wetlands. A variety of fish can also be found on the lake and rivers of the Byway, and 20-plus-pound rainbow or mackinaw trout can be caught during week-long fishing derbies that begin in May and end in November. You may also spot deer and moose all along the Byway and near the water.

Scenic

With over 100 miles of shoreline, Lake Pend Oreille dominates the area. Glassy water reflects the Cabinet Mountains, sunsets, and farming scenes, and the water draws wildlife to its shores. A drive along the Pend Oreille Scenic Byway is a journey into an area that remains largely undeveloped, providing you with the chance to enjoy nature as it was intended to be experienced. You do not have to go far, either, to enjoy breathtaking vistas. Numerous turnouts along the road allow you to experience the outdoors right off of the Byway. Crashing waterfalls and tranquil lake and river scenes await you along the Byway.

Picturesque farms and farmlands are plentiful along the Byway, providing a look at a lifestyle that America was founded on and one that continues to be an important factor in the country's economy. From fields that are almost ready to be harvested to soaring eagles and curious deer, the Pend Oreille Scenic Byway provides a glimpse into a life filled with beauty and serenity.

Every season has its own type of beauty along the Byway, from the explosion of color in the fall to the quiet white world of a northern Idaho winter. Summer may be spent enjoying the water on Lake Pend Oreille or marveling at the brilliance of a sunset. Through every season, you will continually be reminded of the beauty of the area.

THINGS TO SEE AND DO

Driving along the Pend Oreille Scenic Byway will certainly keep your senses engaged, but if you yearn to get out of the car and stretch your legs, or if you'd like to make a mini-vacation out of your trip, check out these attractions along the route.

COLDWATER CREEK ON THE CEDAR STREET BRIDGE. *334 N 1st Ave, Sandpoint (83864). Phone 208/263-2265.* This shopping mall was built on a bridge over Sand Creek. Inspired by the Ponte Vecchio in Florence, Italy, the Coldwater Creek shops provide panoramic views of Lake Pend Oreille and nearby mountains. Open daily.

LAKE PEND OREILLE. *Sandpoint (83864).* The largest lake in Idaho, one of the largest natural lakes wholly within the US; more than 43 miles long, 6 miles wide, with more than 111 miles of shoreline. Approximately 14 varieties of game fish, including the famous Kamloops, the largest rainbow trout in world (average 16-26 pounds). Boating, swimming, water-skiing; camping, picnicking.

ROUND LAKE STATE PARK. *10 miles S on US 95, then 2 miles W, near Sagle (83860). Phone 208/ 263-3489.* Approximately 140 acres of coniferous woods. Swimming, skin diving, fishing, ice fishing, ice skating, boating (ramp, no motors); hiking, cross-country skiing, sledding, tobogganing, snowshoeing in winter, picnicking. Camping (15-day maximum; no hookups), dump station. Campfire programs. Open daily.

SANDPOINT PUBLIC BEACH. *Foot of Bridge St, E edge of town, Sandpoint (83864).* Nearly 20 acres. Bathhouse, swimming, water-skiing, boat docks, ramps; picnic tables, fireplaces, volleyball and tennis courts; concession (seasonal). Open daily. **FREE**

SCHWEITZER MOUNTAIN RESORT. *10000 Schweitzer Mountain Rd, Sandpoint (83864). Phone toll-free 800/831-8810.* In the Selkirk Mountains of the Idaho Panhandle National Forests. Five chairlifts, high-speed quad; school, rentals; lodging, restaurants, bars, cafeteria; nursery. Longest run 2.7 miles; vertical drop 2,400 feet. Open Nov-Apr, daily. Summer chairlift rides (fee). **$$$$**

WINTER CARNIVAL. *Sandpoint (83864). Phone 208/263-2161.* Two weekends of festivities include snow sculpture, snowshoe softball, other games, races, and a torchlight parade. Held in mid-Jan.

PLACES TO STAY

If you choose to include an overnight stay in your trip along this Byway, the Mobil Travel Guide recommends the following lodgings.

★★ **BEST WESTERN EDGEWATER RESORT.** *56 Bridge St, Sandpoint (83864). Phone 208/263-3194; toll-free 800/780-7234. www.bestwestern.com.*

55 rooms, 3 story. No elevator. Pet accepted; fee. Complimentary breakfast. Check-out noon. Check-in 3 pm. TV; VCR available. Restaurant, bar. Room service. Sauna. Indoor pool, whirlpool. **$**

★ **LA QUINTA INN.** *415 Cedar St, Sandpoint (83864). Phone 208/263-9581; toll-free 800/742-6081. www.laquinta.com.* 70 rooms, 3 story. Check-out 1 pm. TV; cable (premium), VCR available. In-room modem link. Laundry services. Restaurant, bar. Health club privileges. Pool, whirlpool. Downhill, cross-country skiing 9 miles. **$**

★ **LAKESIDE INN.** *106 Bridge St, Sandpoint (83864). Phone 208/263-3717.* 50 rooms, 3 story. No elevator. Pet accepted, some restrictions; fee. Complimentary continental breakfast. Check-out 11 am, check-in 2 pm. TV. Laundry services. Sauna. Whirlpool. Lawn games. Free airport transportation. **¢**

★★ **QUALITY INN SANDPOINT.** *807 N 5th Ave, Sandpoint (83864). Phone 208/263-2111; toll-free 877-424-6423. www.qualityinn.com.* 53 rooms, 2 story. Pet accepted; fee. Check-out noon, check-in 3 pm. TV; VCR available. Laundry services. Restaurant, bar. Indoor pool, whirlpool. Downhill, cross-country ski 11 miles. **¢**

★ **SUPER 8 MOTEL.** *476841 Hwy 95 N, Sandpoint (83864). Phone 208/263-2210. www.super8.com.* 61 rooms, 2 story. Check-out 11 am, check-in 3 pm. TV; cable (premium). In-room modem link. Whirlpool. ¢
D▸SC

PLACES TO EAT

A long day of driving is sure to make you hungry. At the end of your journey, take a table at one of the following restaurants.

Hope

★★ **FLOATING RESTAURANT.** *Hwy 200 E, Hope (83836). Phone 208/264-5311.* Seafood menu. Closed Nov-Mar. Lunch, dinner, Sun brunch. Bar. Children's menu. Outdoor seating. Totally nonsmoking. On lake. $$
D

Sandpoint

★★ **BANGKOK CUISINE.** *202 N 2nd Ave, Sandpoint (83864). Phone 208/265-4149.* Thai menu. Closed Sun, Labor Day, Thanksgiving, Dec 25. Lunch, dinner. $$
D

★ **HYDRA.** *115 Lake St, Sandpoint (83864). Phone 208/263-7123.* Closed Thanksgiving, Dec 25. Lunch, dinner, Sun brunch. Bar. $$
D

★★ **IVANO'S RISTORANTE.** *102 S First Ave, Sandpoint (83864). Phone 208/263-0211.* Italian menu. Closed Easter, Thanksgiving, Dec 25. Dinner. Bar. Children's menu. Outdoor seating. Cathedral ceiling in the main dining room. $$
D

★ **JALAPENO'S.** *314 N 2nd Ave, Sandpoint (83864). Phone 208/263-2995.* Mexican menu. Closed some major holidays. Lunch, dinner. Children's menu. Outdoor seating. Totally nonsmoking. Wall murals. $$
D

Beartooth Highway

✺ MONTANA   AN ALL-AMERICAN ROAD

Part of a multistate Byway; see also WY.

Quick Facts

LENGTH: 54 miles.

TIME TO ALLOW: 3 hours.

BEST TIME TO DRIVE: Driving from Red Lodge to Cooke City (east to west) in the morning and west to east in the afternoon reduces glare. High season extends throughout the summer.

BYWAY TRAVEL INFORMATION: Red Lodge Area Chamber of Commerce: 406/446-1718.

SPECIAL CONSIDERATIONS: The alpine climate is rigorous, and severe weather conditions can occur any month of the year. Summer temperatures range from the 70s on sunny days to below freezing during sudden snowstorms.

RESTRICTIONS: The entire length of the Byway is open from Memorial Day weekend through about mid-October. Snow conditions close sections. Check with the local ranger district office before planning a trip in May or September.

The Beartooth Highway is one of the most spectacular national forest routes on this continent. To many, it's known as "the most beautiful highway in America." From its beginning at the border of the Custer National Forest to its terminus near the northeast entrance to Yellowstone National Park, the Beartooth Highway (US 212) offers travelers the ultimate high country experience as it travels through the Custer, Shoshone, and Gallatin national forests.

Since its completion in 1936, the highway has provided millions of visitors a rare opportunity to see the transition from a lush forest ecosystem to alpine tundra in the space of a few miles. The Beartooths are one of the highest and most rugged areas in the lower 48 states, with 20 peaks over 12,000 feet in elevation. Glaciers are found on the north flank of nearly every mountain peak over 11,500 feet in these mountains.

Recreational opportunities are abundant in the area traversed by the Byway. You can cross-country ski in June and July, hike across the broad plateaus, view and photograph wildlife (Rocky Mountain goats, moose, black bears, grizzly bears, marmots, and mule deer), take a guided horseback trip, fish for trout in the streams and lakes adjacent to the Byway, and camp in the 12 national forest campgrounds in the area. Even when the highway is formally closed to automobiles, snowmobilers may travel the route and enjoy a spectacular winter wonderland.

THE BYWAY STORY

The Beartooth Highway tells archaeological, cultural, historical, natural, recreational, and scenic stories that make it a unique and treasured Byway.

Archaeological

Many of the ancient remains found here show a people who treasured their spirituality. We can best understand this by seeing the challenges they went through, from both severe climate and extreme environment, to come to this area to practice religion. Archaeologists have found numerous small, limited-use camps that offer isolated finds and resource extraction sites. Because of the specimens found in the camps, the location of the camps, and even the frequency of the camps, archaeologists believe the area was used for spiritual purposes rather than primarily for food (which was previously thought).

Even though Native Americans dwelt in various places throughout present-day Montana, archaeological evidence from the Beartooth Mountains is somewhat limited. The high elevation most likely restricted living there on a permanent basis, largely because there is only a short time during the summer to hunt and gather plants specially adapted to high elevations before the cold returns. The rest of the year, deadly weather conditions contribute to making it a hostile environment. Coming here, rather than staying in the fertile plains in the low country, can mean only that the steep mountains held deep significance for them.

Despite the harsh climate, many people have found ancient obsidian arrowheads and spearheads from the people who lived hundreds of years ago, giving more evidence of archaeological activity. Some of these finds can be viewed in museums and visitor centers along the Byway. Whether these Native Americans came to hunt, worship, or a combination of the two, it is clear that they went through great physical strains to travel to the lofty Beartooth Mountains.

Cultural

The Beartooth Highway's most important cultural value is the chance to appreciate some of the activities that flourish in natural environments. By better understanding the people's occupations and interests in this part of Montana, you can more fully experience this Byway. Visitors often leave with a longing to return to the simple yet strenuous life found here. Furthermore, gaining this understanding gives a glimpse at the past, rugged life of Montana's homesteaders.

Some of the locals' occupations and hobbies include ranchers raising livestock that graze on the vast, open range; lumberjacks who spend their days in the dark timber lands managing wood in national forests; sportsmen hunting in steep, barren habitats; and anglers fishing in cold, wild streams. These and other similar activities thrive today along this Byway, continuing a long tradition of utilizing the natural resources of these public lands.

Historical

The first recorded travel across the Beartooth Pass area occurred in 1882, when General Sheridan with a force of 129 soldiers and scouts, with 104 horses and 157 mules, pioneered and marked a route across the mountains from Cooke City to Billings. A year later, Van Dyke, a packer, modified the trail and located a route off the Beartooth Plateau into Rock Creek and Red Lodge. Van Dyke's trail was the only direct route between Red Lodge and Cooke City until the Beartooth Highway was constructed in 1934 and 1935. Remnants of Van Dyke's trail are visible from the Rock Creek Overlook parking lot, appearing as a Z on the mountain between the highway switchbacks about 1/2 mile south of the parking lot.

Doctor Siegfriet and other visionaries from the Bearcreek and Red Lodge communities foresaw, in the early 1900s, the value of a scenic route over the mountains to connect to Yellowstone Park. These men spent many years promoting

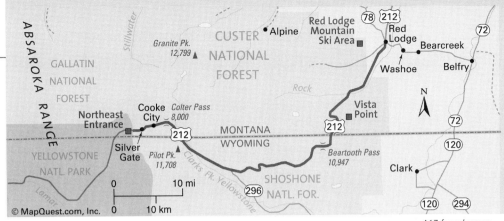

see page A17 for color map

the construction of a road over the mountains and even began the construction of a road with hand tools and horse-drawn implements.

Other routes were surveyed from 1920 to 1925, and, in 1931, President Herbert Hoover signed the Park Approach Act, which was the forerunner to the funding of the road now known as the Beartooth Highway.

Natural

A variety of theories exist on the formation of the Beartooth Mountains, but geologists generally agree that the mountains resulted from an uplifting of an Archean block of metamorphic rocks that were eroded, flooded with volcanic lava on the southwest corner, and covered with glaciers. Seventy million years of formation went into making this section of the Rocky Mountains.

The Palisades that stretch along the Beartooth Front were first sedimentary rocks originally deposited as flat-lying beds in an ancient sea. Thrust skyward, they have become conspicuous spires. Pilot and Index peaks are the remainders of an extensive volcanic field that came into existence 50 million years ago.

Changes are continuing into the present. Yellowstone National Park has been an active volcanic center for more than 15 million years. Erosional forces are still at work. Glaciers have shaped the mountains into the range they comprise today. The glaciers edged their way down just 10,000 years ago. Younger rocks are the sources of coal exploited by the early settlers of Red Lodge.

The Stillwater Complex, a body of igneous magma formed along the northern edge of

the mountain range 2.7 million years ago, is one of the rarest and least understood geologic occurrences in the world. It is the site of the only source of the platinum group of metals in the western hemisphere, mined by Stillwater Mining Company of Nye, Montana.

Recreational

Recreational opportunities are abundant in the area traversed by the Beartooth Highway. You can cross-country ski on the snowfields in June and July; hike across the broad plateaus and on Forest Service trails (some of which are National Recreation Trails); camp; picnic; fish for trout in the streams and lakes adjacent to the highway; view and photograph nature at its finest, including wildflowers and wildlife (moose, Rocky Mountain goats, mule deer, black bears, grizzly bears, marmots, and pikas); visit a guest ranch; take a guided horseback trip from Cooke City; bicycle; and downhill ski on the headwalls. Even when the highway is formally closed to automobiles, snowmobilers may travel the route in a spectacular winter wonderland.

If you enjoy skiing, each summer in June and July, the Red Lodge International Ski Race Camp is conducted on the north side of the East Summit on the Twin Lakes Headwall. This camp is for aspiring Olympic-caliber skiers and provides a viewing opportunity for highway travelers. The ski area is not open to the public for skiing at this time.

Each summer, the Red Lodge Chamber of Commerce sponsors a one-day, unannounced "Top of the World Bar" in a snowbank at or near the West Summit and provides complimentary nonalcoholic beverages, horse rides, complimentary photos at the Bar, and, on occasion, even a live pink elephant.

Scenic

The spire known as the Bears Tooth was carved in the shape of a large tooth by glacial ice gnawing inward and downward against a single high part of a rocky crest. Beartooth Butte is a remnant of sedimentary deposits that once covered the entire Beartooth Plateau. The red-stained rock outcrop near the top of Beartooth Butte was a stream channel some 375 million years ago, so fossils are found in abundance in the rocks of Beartooth Butte.

In these treeless areas, near or above timberline, vegetation is often small, low-growing, and compact—characteristics that are vital to the survival of the plants at this elevation. Wildflowers, often as tiny as a quarter-inch across, create a literal carpet of color during the 45-day or shorter growing season.

In contrast, the common flowers found below the timberline in wet meadows are Indian paintbrush, monkeyflower, senecio, and buttercups; and in drier areas are lupine, beards-tongue, arrowleaf balsamroot, and forget-me-nots. The colors and the flowers change weekly as the growing season progresses, but mid-July is generally the optimum for wildflower displays.

Wildlife in Beartooth Country varies from the largest American land mammal, the moose, to the smallest land mammal, the shrew. Other animals commonly seen along the highway are mule deer, whitetail deer, elk, marmots (rock chucks), and pine squirrels. Bighorn sheep, Rocky Mountain goats, black bears, and grizzly bears are residents of the area, but are seldom visable. Birds include the golden eagle, raven, Clarks nutcracker, Stellars jay, robin, mountain bluebird, finch, hawk, and falcon. Watch for the water ouzel darting in and out of—and walking along the bottoms of—streams.

The snowbanks often remain until August near Beartooth Pass, and remnants of some drifts may remain all summer. A pink color often appears on the snow later in the summer, which is caused by the decay of a microscopic plant that grows on the surface of the snowbank. When the plant dies, it turns red and colors the snow pink.

THINGS TO SEE AND DO

Driving along the Beartooth Highway will certainly keep your senses engaged, but if you yearn to get out of the car and stretch your legs, or if you'd like to make a mini-vacation out of your trip, check out these attractions along the route.

GALLATIN NATIONAL FOREST. *10 E Babcock St, Bozeman (59715). Phone 406/587-6701. www.fs.fed.us.* Over 1.7 million acres, including mountain peaks, pine and fir forest, winter sports, pack trips, picnicking, camping, fishing, and hunting; 574,788-acre Absaroke-Beartooth Wilderness south of Livingston, 253,000-acre

Lee Metcalf Wilderness, and Gallatin Gateway to Yellowstone. Forest rangers provide interpretive programs in the summer at the Madison River Canyon Earthquake Area.

GRASSHOPPER GLACIER. *14 miles NE on a mountain trail in the Absaroka-Beartooth Wilderness, Custer National Forest, Cooke City (59081).* One of the largest icefields in the United States; so named because of the millions of grasshoppers frozen in its 80-foot ice cliff. Accessible only by trail, the last 2 miles are reached only by foot; be prepared for adverse weather. The grasshoppers are visible only during brief periods; glacial ice must be exposed by snow melt, which generally does not occur until mid-August, while new snow begins to accumulate in late August.

PLACES TO STAY

If you choose to include an overnight stay in your trip along this All-American Road, Mobil Travel Guide recommends the following lodgings.

★ **HOOSIER'S MOTEL & BAR.** *Corner Hwy 212 and Huston N, Cooke City (59020). Phone 406/838-2241.* 12 rooms, 1 story. No A/C. Check-out 10 am, check-in 12 pm. TV; cable (premium). Bar. Totally nonsmoking. ¢

★ **BEST WESTERN LUPINE INN.** *702 S Hauser Ave, Red Lodge (59068). Phone 406/446-1321; toll-free 888/567-1321. www.bestwestern.com.* 47 rooms, 2 story. Pet accepted, some restrictions. Complimentary continental breakfast. Check-out noon, check-in 3 pm. TV; cable (premium). In-room modem link. In-house fitness room, sauna. Game room. Indoor pool, whirlpool. Downhill, cross-country ski 6 miles. ¢

★ **COMFORT INN.** *612 N Broadway, Red Lodge (59068). Phone 406/446-4469; toll-free 888/733-4661. www.choicehotels.com.* 53 rooms, 2 story. Pet accepted; fee. Complimentary continental breakfast. Check-out 11 am, check-in 2 pm. TV; VCR available. In-room modem link. In-house fitness room. Indoor pool, whirlpool. Downhill, cross-country ski 6 miles. ¢

★★ **POLLARD HOTEL.** *2 N Broadway, Red Lodge (59068). Phone 406/446-0001; toll-free 800/765-5273. www.pollardhotel.com.* 38 rooms, 5 with shower only, 3 story. Complimentary full breakfast. Check-out noon, check-in 4 pm. TV; DVD available. In-room modem link. Restaurant. Room service. In-house fitness room, sauna. Whirlpool. Downhill, cross-country ski 6 miles. Racquetball courts. Restored hotel built in 1893. Totally nonsmoking. ¢

★★★ **ROCK CREEK RESORT.** *HC 49, Red Lodge (59068). Phone 406/446-1111; toll-free 800/667-1119. www.rockcreekresort.com.* Situated below Beartooth Pass and beside Rock Creek, this resort features such adventurous activities as snowmobiling, skiing, kayaking, and golf. 85 rooms, 2-3 story. No A/C. Complimentary continental breakfast. Check-out 11 am, check-in 3 pm. TV; cable (premium), VCR available. In-room modem link. Restaurant, dining room. Room service. Children's activity center. In-house fitness room, sauna. Indoor pool, whirlpool. Outdoor tennis. Downhill ski 11 miles. Lawn games. Free airport transportation. $

★ **SUPER 8.** *1223 S Broadway Ave, Red Lodge (59068). Phone 406/446-2288; toll-free 800/813-8335. www.super8.com.* 50 rooms, 2 story. Pet accepted, some restrictions; fee. Complimentary continental breakfast. Check-out 11 am, check-in 2 pm. TV; cable (premium). Game room. Indoor pool; whirlpool. Downhill, cross-country ski 5 miles. ¢

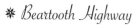

❉ *Beartooth Highway*

PLACES TO EAT

A long day of driving is sure to make you hungry. At the end of your journey, take a table at one of the following restaurants.

★★★ **ARTHUR'S GRILL.** *2 N Broadway, Red Lodge (59068). Phone 406/446-0001.* American menu. Dinner, Sun brunch. Bar. Children's menu. Totally nonsmoking. **$$**
D SC

★★ **OLD PINEY DELL.** *US 212, Red Lodge (59068). Phone 406/446-1196.* Dinner. Bar. Casual attire. Totally nonsmoking. **$$**
D

★ **LOG CABIN CAFÉ.** *US 212, Silver Gate (59081). Phone 406/838-2367.* Continental menu. Closed mid-Sept-mid-May. Dinner. Children's menu. Casual attire. Outdoor seating. Totally nonsmoking. **$$**

Lake Tahoe–Eastshore Drive

❋ NEVADA

Quick Facts

LENGTH: 28 miles.

TIME TO ALLOW: 1 hour.

BEST TIME TO DRIVE: Year-round; high season is July through September and the last week of December.

BYWAY TRAVEL INFORMATION: Tahoe Douglas Chamber of Commerce & Visitors Center: 775/588-4591; Byway travel and tourism Web site: www.tahoechamber.org.

RESTRICTIONS: There are occasional brief road closures during snowstorms.

Called the most beautiful drive in America, the 72-mile Lake Tahoe–Eastshore Drive affords breathtaking views of spectacularly clear Lake Tahoe. The pristine alpine lake is surrounded by the snow-capped mountains of the Sierras. The Byway is mostly undeveloped, except for the fabulous recreational opportunities afforded by the lake, including the Zephyr Cove Resort, stables, campgrounds, the Tahoe Rim Trail, ski resorts, hotels and casinos, and fabulous golf courses. As part of the Pony Express trail and home to the historic sacred grounds of the Washo Indians, Lake Tahoe's eastern shore offers a wide variety of activities during every season. The Lake Tahoe–Eastshore Drive Byway is one of the most beautiful winter Byways in the country, with the draw of an alpine climate and the ever-crystalline lake. Throughout the year, visitors come from miles around to enjoy Lake Tahoe.

THE BYWAY STORY

The Lake Tahoe–Eastshore Drive tells cultural, historical, natural, recreational, and scenic stories that make it a unique and treasured Byway.

Cultural

Lake Tahoe is well known for its diverse and interesting culture of both recreation and arts. Events take place through the year that attract visitors for reasons ranging from high drama to downhill ski relays. During the summer months, artists gather at Lake Tahoe for exhibitions and workshops, making the area one of the best places to find cutting-edge and classic artwork. While Tahoe's art is a sight to behold, don't miss out on any of the many festivals that take place throughout the year. The festivals themselves are works of art.

Perhaps Lake Tahoe's best known summer festival is the Lake Tahoe Shakespeare Festival at Sand Harbor, which takes place every August. Imagine relaxing on a beautiful sand beach while enjoying your favorite Shakespearean drama. Enjoy the first-class performance near crystal blue waters, set against the stately backdrop of the Sierra Nevada, under a thousand glittering stars. The Lake Tahoe Shakespeare Festival has been voted the Best Summer Event and the Best Cultural Event at the lake. The theater was recently rebuilt and is magnificent. Bring a jacket, a blanket, and some edibles, and then sit back, relax, and enjoy high drama in one of the most stunning locations imaginable.

Lake Tahoe offers a variety of winter festivals as well. Winter begins early here with the Native American Festival and Snow Dance. During the Snow Dance, a two-day event held the first weekend in October, Native Americans dance in full regalia and pray for snow to ensure an abundantly snowy winter. Lake Tahoe also heralds the arrival of winter with other festivals such as the Northern Lights Winter Festival and Snow Fest. During Snow Fest, a ten-day festival with a huge variety of events, you can take part in ice-carving competitions, snow-sculpture contests, parades, and a polar bear swim in the still-frigid Lake Tahoe. Snow Fest's opening-night ceremonies feature activities such as a torchlight parade of skiers, fireworks, a bonfire, and music. Activities throughout the festival also include downhill finals, the largest cross-country ski races in the western US, and celebrity races. The closing weekend has included the nationally televised Incredible Snow Dog Challenge, which featured snow competitions of the canine variety, such as freestyle Frisbee, agility, search and rescue, and dog sledding.

Historical

Lake Tahoe was originally a peaceful, earthy place, connected to the rest of the world by narrow trails over high mountain passes. Native tribes would gather in the summer to fish,

hunt, and harvest nuts and berries for the long winter spent in Nevada's high desert. The native tribes called their special place Da ow aga, meaning "the edge of the lake." It is believed that Tahoe got its name from the white settlers' mispronunciation of the first two syllables. Tahoe remains a gathering place for people hunting for the ultimate vacation.

While on an expedition in search of the mythical Buenaventura River in 1844, explorers Kit Carson and John C. Fremont instead stumbled on Lake Tahoe, letting out the secret that had long been kept from the outside world. Fremont's accurate accounts of his High Sierra travels led other curious explorers to the mountain lake. Soon after, gold and silver prospectors flocked to Lake Tahoe, but their explorations failed. However, in 1859, rich silver deposits in nearby Virginia City began a logging boom. While the Comstock Lode opened the area to big business, it nearly stripped the Lake Basin of its first growth of trees because its lumber was used for timber supports in the underground mines.

As more white men laid eyes on the natural treasure, word of the wondrous lake spread through the land. Among these proclaimers was humorist Mark Twain, who described the area as so wholesome and pure that "three months of camp life on Lake Tahoe would restore an Egyptian mummy to his pristine vigor and give him an appetite like an alligator." Stage stops over the Sierra exposed visitors to Tahoe's scenic beauty and tranquility. Many were lured to stay because they felt that they had found paradise.

Westerners began to develop Lake Tahoe's shore in the early 1900s as a summer retreat for San Francisco's elite. Plush hotels sprang up, and guests amused themselves at Lucky Baldwin's Tallac House and Casino, known today as the Tallac Historic Site at South Shore. Gambling was illegal on the California side of the lake, but enforcement was sporadic, and arrangements with cooperative authorities were routine. Raiding lawmen often found patrons playing nothing more objectionable than

see page A18 for color map

pinochle and canasta. By 1941, the Tahoe Tattle was reporting that Tahoe's number two industry was nightlife, a close second to the resorts. Each weekend, an estimated 3,000 people would flock to the bars, casinos, and dance halls and spend anywhere from 25 cents for a glass of beer to $50,000 for an expensive game.

A boom of another kind was soon occurring at Lake Tahoe. Using Nevada's advantageous tax laws as bait, an enterprising businessman name Norman Blitz convinced more than 80 of the nation's most rich and famous to make Lake Tahoe their home. This effort sparked the development of a thriving real estate and construction industry at the lake.

Natural

Lake Tahoe is a masterpiece of nature. Surrounded by mountains, Lake Tahoe is the highest lake in the United States, the third deepest lake in North America, and the tenth deepest lake in the world. The lake holds more than 39 trillion gallons of water: if it were to be drained, it would take 700 years to refill. Lake Tahoe is incredibly blue because the thin, clear mountain air allows the lake's pure, crystal-clear water to reflect the blue sky above. For this reason, the lake also appears a dramatic red during sunsets and reflects a somber, churning gray during storms. The spectacular shoreline is 71 miles long, 29 miles of which is on the Nevada side. Beautiful vegetation and numerous kinds of wildlife inhabit the area.

Lake Tahoe was created millions of years ago through the shifting of geological faults. Immense forces began the process with the tilting of the Sierra Nevada block. As a result, two parallel faults were developed. One margin created the Carson Range, and the other created the Sierra Nevada. About 2 million years ago, volcanic activity reshaped the entire landscape of the region. Lava formed a barrier across the basin's northeastern outlet, creating a natural dam and, eventually, Lake Tahoe. Next, vast glaciers formed in the surrounding mountains. These gradually moved down the V-shaped canyons on the western side of the lake. The massive glaciers scoured away any loose rock, and the canyons were reshaped into the wide, U-shaped valleys of Emerald Bay, Fallen Leaf Lake, and Cascade Lake.

Lake Tahoe has a variety of unique plant and animal life that make hikes and walks an exciting experience. One particularly striking plant, a fairly common sight when the snow is melting, is the snowplant. This member of the wintergreen family is an asparagus-like plant that doesn't photosynthesize, but receives nourishment from the roots of neighboring plants and decaying organic matter. Despite its somewhat disturbing means of survival, the plant is extremely lovely, rare, and (fortunately) protected by law. Another beautiful flower is the crimson columbine, a well-known flower appreciated for its delicate features that grows in moist areas. The lupine is also easily recognized by the palmate leaf resembling the fingers of a hand and striking blue flowers.

While the Lake Tahoe area is full of a variety of animal life, from coyotes to bears, you will likely see various kinds of birds most often. The western tanager is a beautiful bird and one of the most colorful in the Lake Tahoe Basin, with a red head and a bright yellow body and black markings on its back, wings, and tail. Another common bird in the area is the mountain chickadee, the most common bird in the Tahoe Basin. This bird is small with a black cap, a black bib, and a white line over each eye. It is acrobatic and swings from branches as it hunts for insects and seeds; it also makes a distinctive three-note whistle.

Recreational

When it comes to winter activities, Lake Tahoe has it covered (literally). Tahoe has more snow (averaging about 400 inches per season), more variety, and more ways to play than just about any other place. Lake Tahoe has the largest concentration of ski resorts in North America, including six world-class resorts you won't want to miss. The terrain ranges from leisurely bowls to steep hills that make your heart thump. However, excellent skiing and snowboarding are not all that Lake Tahoe has to offer. Snowmobiling, snowshoe treks, snow tubing, and cross-country treks open up the millions of acres of national forest land waiting to be explored. Ice skating, sleigh rides, and sledding are fun activities close to the Byway. Lake Tahoe also hosts numerous special events all winter long. Snow Fest is a unique experience taking place in the beauty of the High Sierras, with 50 fun and diverse events. The events are not to be missed and include ice-carving competitions, snow-sculpture contests, parades, a polar bear swim in the frigid Lake Tahoe, and an opening night ceremony with a torchlight parade of skiers, fireworks display, a bonfire, and music.

If you prefer warmer weather, Lake Tahoe's links are second to none. Extra altitude makes even the worst golfer feel like a pro, and the breathtaking backdrops and outstanding course architecture will make bogeys seem a little less burdensome. The Lake Tahoe region boasts 12 courses accessible to all levels of play: Bijou Municipal, Glenbrook Golf Course, Lake Tahoe Golf Course, Incline Village Championship Course, The Mountain Course, Northstar-at-Tahoe Golf Course, Ponderosa Golf Course, Old Brockway Golf Course, Resort at Squaw Creek, Tahoe City Golf Course, Tahoe Donner Golf Course, and Tahoe Paradise Golf Course.

Surrounded by national forest lands, wilderness, and state parks, Lake Tahoe possesses some of the country's most spectacular scenery. With almost 300 miles of trails, hikers have plenty of room to roam. Backcountry buffs can trek up waterfall trails, hike along wildflower-carpeted meadows, or visit serene alpine lakes and stunning overlooks of Lake Tahoe. There are trails to suit every ability—flat, steep, and moderate. Looping its way around the lake, the Tahoe Rim Trail, a hiking and equestrian trail, offers 165 miles of trail, with elevations ranging from 6,300 feet to 9,400 feet. This trail is generally moderate in difficulty, with a 10 percent average grade, and provides views of Lake Tahoe, the high desert, and snow-capped peaks of the Sierra Nevada. Trailheads accessible along the Byway include Tahoe Meadows Trailhead to Tunnel Creek Road (Highway 431), Spooner Summit Trailhead (Highway 50), and Spooner Summit South to Kingsbury

Grade. The Tunnel Creek Station Road Trail starts at Highway 28 across from Hidden Beach about one mile past Ponderosa Ranch (there's no sign, so look for the gate). This is a steep trail road, about 1 1/2 miles each way, located at the ruins of the western portal of the old log flume tunnel. There is limited parking along Highway 28. The Marlette Lake Trail starts near the Spooner Lake Picnic Area at the junction of Highway 28 and 50 at the green metal gate on the east side of Highway 28. This trail is about 5 miles each way to the lake and passes through mostly mild terrain.

A combination of one of the world's top single-track trails, spectacular views, and miles of open backcountry beckons bikers from around the world to the Lake Tahoe basin. The best-known Tahoe bike trail is the spectacular Flume Trail, carved out of the edge of a mountain some 2,000 feet above the lake's stunning east shore. The Flume Trail follows a precarious route dug out of the granite cliffs more than a century ago by laborers developing a water supply and lumber transport for the mines of the Comstock Lode. Today, the 14-mile Flume Trail offers a challenging ride with a 1,000-foot elevation gain and sweeping views, all within Nevada's Lake Tahoe State Park. The common starting point for this trail is Spooner Lake, which features parking and trail information. Located at the junction of Highways 28 and 50, Spooner Lake is a 15-minute drive south from Incline Village. Groves of aspen trees, towering peaks, old-growth pine, and high mountain lakes greet bikers along the Flume Trail. After a quick turn onto a small outlet creek, the trail suddenly clings to a slope overlooking the azure Lake Tahoe. The northern terminus of the trail can take the rider to either Sand Harbor or the Ponderosa Ranch. For the ambitious rider, a loop via Tunnel Creek Road, Red House, and Hobart Lake creates a 25-mile loop back to Marlette Lake, as well as a stunning downhill ride to Spooner.

Scenic

Lake Tahoe has rightly been called the most beautiful drive in America. Many people find they don't have words to describe its exquisite beauty and often rely upon Mark Twain's well-worded acclaim and praise. After his first vision of the lake, Twain wrote, "The Lake burst upon us—a noble sheet of blue water uplifted six thousand three hundred feet above the level of the sea, and walled in by a rim of snow-clad mountain peaks that towered aloft full three thousand feet higher still! . . . As it lay there with the shadows of the mountains brilliantly photographed upon its still surface I thought it must surely be the fairest picture the whole Earth affords." He also wrote that "Down through the transparency of these great depths, the water was not merely transparent, but dazzlingly, brilliantly so. All objects seen through it had a bright, strong vividness, not only of outline, but of every minute detail, which they would not have had when seen simply through the same depth of atmosphere."

While it has been many years since Mark Twain visited Lake Tahoe, the startling beauty of the area has not diminished. Lake Tahoe still looks like a "beautiful relic of fairy-land forgotten and left asleep in the snowy Sierras when the little elves fled from their ancient haunts and quitted the Earth." Painters find their brushes inadequate to capture the deep-pines crowding the craggy cliffs, the crimson sunsets burnishing the skies, and the clear aquamarine waters reflecting the Sierra Nevada Range swathed in icy snow. Weather cooperates while visitors take in the splendor of their surroundings, and the sun shines an average of 307 days a year. The atmosphere "up here in the clouds is very pure and fine, bracing and delicious. And why shouldn't it be? It's the same the angels breathe." And while the pristine silence of the lake that Twain once enjoyed has been replaced by happy tourists, the majesty of Lake Tahoe still affords solitude and a purely heavenly ambience.

Nevada

✽ *Lake Tahoe–Eastshore Drive*

HIGHLIGHTS

To hit the highlights of the Lake Tahoe–Eastshore Drive, consider following this itinerary.

- You may want to begin traveling the Byway at the northern terminus at Crystal Bay along the California/Nevada border. There are several **casinos** in this area to enjoy.

- From here, the highway winds toward **Incline Village,** one of Tahoe's finest communities. A side trip up Mount Rose Highway, approximately 4 miles, leads to a lookout over the entire Tahoe Basin.

- Back on Highway 28, the **Ponderosa Ranch** is the location of TV's legendary *Bonanza* series that made Lake Tahoe famous worldwide. The Ponderosa offers Cartwright Ranch House tours, an Old West town with shops and memorabilia, summer hay-wagon breakfasts, and more.

- The Byway continues south down the east shore. One of Tahoe's most beautiful beaches, **Sand Harbor,** is located here in the Nevada Lake Tahoe State Park. Following the bouldered Nevada shore, the highway continues south through forests of pine and fir. Stop at **Spooner Lake** for wooded picnic areas and a walk along the water. Turn right at the intersection of Highway 50 and head south past historic **Glenbrook,** once a busy logging town and now an exclusive community and golf course.

- Your next landmark is **Cave Rock,** where the highway passes through 25 yards of solid stone. This is a holy spot for the native Washoe Indians who put their deceased to rest in the cold waters below the outcropping. Farther along is **Zephyr Cove** with its beautiful old lodge, beach, and tour boats.

- The tour now returns you to South Lake Tahoe and the high-rise hotel/casinos in the **Stateline** area; a perfect place to stop at a restaurant or lounge, take in a show, or try your luck in the casinos.

THINGS TO SEE AND DO

Driving along the Lake Tahoe–Eastshore Drive will certainly keep your senses engaged, but if you yearn to get out of the car and stretch your legs, or if you'd like to make a mini-vacation out of your trip, check out these attractions along the route.

DIAMOND PEAK SKI RESORT. *1210 Ski Way, Incline Village (89451). Phone 775/775/832-1177. www.diamondpeak.com.* Three quad, three double chairlifts; patrol, school, rentals, snowmaking; cafeteria, bar, lodge. Thirty runs; longest run approximately 2 1/2 miles; vertical drop 1,840 feet. Open mid-Dec-mid-Apr, daily. $$$$

LAKE TAHOE NEVADA STATE PARK. *2005 Hwy 28, Incline Village (89451). Phone 775/831-0494. parks.nv.gov.* Approximately 14,200 acres on the eastern shore of beautiful Lake Tahoe consisting of five management areas. Gently sloping sandy beach, swimming, fishing, boating (ramp); hiking, mountain biking, cross-country skiing. Picnic tables, stoves. No camping. Open daily.

PONDEROSA RANCH WESTERN STUDIO AND THEME PARK. *100 Ponderosa Ranch Rd, Incline Village (89451). Phone 775/831-0691. www.ponderosaranch.com.* Cartwright House seen in the *Bonanza* television series. Frontier town with an 1870 country church; vintage autos; breakfast hayrides (fee); amusements May-Oct. Open mid-Apr-Oct, daily 9:30 am-6 pm. $$$

PLACES TO STAY

If you choose to include an overnight stay in your trip along this Byway, Mobil Travel Guide recommends the following lodgings.

Crystal Bay

★★**CAL NEVA RESORT.** *2 Stateline Rd, Crystal Bay (89402). Phone 775/832-4000; toll-free 800/225-6382. www.calnevaresort.com.* Guests will enjoy the beauty of Lake Tahoe and the Sierra Mountains from this hotel. Every room has a view of the lake. 200 rooms, 9 story. Check-out noon. TV. Restaurant, bar. In-house fitness room, sauna. Heated pool, whirlpool. Outdoor tennis. Concierge. ¢

★★**TAHOE BILTMORE HOTEL AND CASINO.** *5 NV 28, Crystal Bay (89402). Phone 775/831-0660; toll-free 800/245-8667. www.tahoebiltmore.com.* 92 rooms, 4 story. Complimentary full breakfast. Check-out 11 am. TV; cable (premium). Some refrigerators, microwaves. Restaurant open 24 hours. Bar; entertainment. Pool. Downhill, cross-country ski 5 miles. ¢

Incline Village

★★★**HYATT REGENCY LAKE TAHOE RESORT & CASINO.** *1111 Country Club Dr, Incline Village (89450). Phone 775/832-1234; toll-free 800/553-3288. www.hyatt.com.* This hotel is a top pick for rustic luxury accommodations on the north shore of Lake Tahoe. Although it's not located on a ski mountain, the resort makes every effort to help guests get to and enjoy the sights around the lake, and activities including skiing, snowmobiling, hiking, tennis, golf, and water sports. Spa services are offered through the fitness center. The hotel itself boasts a small but charmingly old-style casino, a private hotel beach, and a destination restaurant with arguably one of the best dining views of the lake, as well as three additional restaurants in the main resort building. 449 rooms, 12 story. Check-out 11 am. TV; cable (premium). Restaurant, bar. Room service. Supervised children's activities (open daily in season; Fri, Sat evenings off-season), ages 3-12. Heated pool, whirlpool, poolside service. Downhill ski 1 1/2 mile, cross-country ski 6 miles. Lawn games. Bicycles available. Free valet parking. Business center. Concierge. Luxury level. Casino. Children's arcade. $$

★**INN AT INCLINE AND CONDO.** *1003 Tahoe Blvd (NV 28), Incline Village (89451).*

Phone 775/831-1052; toll-free 800/824-6391. www.innatincline.com. 38 rooms, 2 story. No A/C. Complimentary continental breakfast. Check-out 11 am, check-in 4 pm. TV; cable (premium). Sauna. Indoor pool, whirlpool. Downhill ski 1 mile, cross-country ski 6 miles. $

Stateline

★★★**CAESARS TAHOE.** *55 US 50, Stateline (89449). Phone 775/588-3515; toll-free 888/829-7630. www.caesars.com.* All of the rooms at this casino hotel feature lake or mountain views. You can try your luck in the casino or spend time relaxing by the lagoon-style pool or having treatments administered in the spa. Don't miss a trip on the Odyssey, the hotel's private yacht. 440 rooms, 15 story. Check-out noon. TV; cable (premium). Restaurant open 24 hours. Bar; entertainment. In-house fitness room, massage, sauna, steam room. Game room. Indoor pool, whirlpool. Outdoor tennis, lighted courts. Free valet parking. Business center. Concierge. Casino. ¢

★★★**HARRAH'S LAKE TAHOE.** *Hwy 50, Stateline (89449). Phone 775/588-6611; toll-free 800/648-3773. www.harrahstahoe.com.* This casino hotel offers plenty of recreation options for visitors. Shop at the Galleria, swim in the glass-domed pool, tan on the sun deck in the summer months, or try your hand at the casino. 532 rooms, 18 story. Pet accepted, some restrictions; fee. Check-out noon. TV; VCR available. Restaurant, bar; entertainment. Room service 24 hours. In-house fitness room, massage, sauna, steam room. Game room. Indoor pool, whirlpool, poolside service. Free covered valet parking. Concierge. Casino. ¢

★★★**HARVEY'S LAKE TAHOE.** *US 50, Stateline (89449). Phone 775/588-2411; toll-free 800/427-2789. www.harveys.com.* Most rooms at this hotel have views of Lake Tahoe or the Sierra Nevada mountains. 740 rooms, 19 story.

Check-out noon. TV. Restaurant, bar; entertainment. Room service 24 hours. In-house fitness room. Game room. Pool, whirlpool, poolside service. Covered parking; free valet, self-parking. Airport transportation (fee). Business center. Concierge. Casino. Tahoe's first gaming establishment (1944). $

🏃 🧍 D ⏃ SC ⚓

★HORIZON CASINO RESORT. *50 US 50, Stateline (89449). Phone 775/588-6211; toll-free 800/648-3322. www.horizoncasino.com.* 539 rooms, 15 story. Check-out noon. TV. Restaurant open 24 hours. Bar; entertainment. In-house fitness room, massage. Game room. Heated pool, whirlpool, poolside service. Downhill ski 1 mile, cross-country ski 15 miles. Concierge. Casino. $

🧍 D ⏃ SC ⚓ ⚓

★★LAKESIDE INN & CASINO. *Hwy 50 at Kingsbury Grade, Stateline (89449). Phone 775/588-7777; toll-free 800/624-7980. www.lakesideinn.com.* 124 rooms, 2 story. Check-out noon. TV. Restaurant open 24 hours. Bars. Game room. Pool. Downhill, cross-country ski 2 miles. Casino. ¢

⏃ SC ⚓ ⚓ D

PLACES TO EAT

A long day of driving is sure to make you hungry. At the end of your journey, take a table at one of the following restaurants.

Incline Village

★LAS PANCHITAS. *930 Tahoe Blvd, Incline Center, Incline Village (89451). Phone 775/831-4048.* Mexican menu. Closed Thanksgiving, Dec 25. Lunch, dinner. Bar. Outdoor seating. $

Stateline

★★CHART HOUSE. *392 Kingsbury Grade, Stateline (89449). Phone 775/588-6276. www.chart-house.com.* Seafood menu. Dinner. Bar. Children's menu. Outdoor seating. $$$

D

★★★FRIDAY'S STATION STEAK & SEAFOOD GRILL. *US 50, Stateline (89449). Phone 775/588-6611.* The view of the lake from this restaurant, located on the 18th floor of Harrah's, is breathtaking. Seafood, steak menu. Dinner. Bar. $$$

D

★★★LEWELLYN'S. *US 50, Stateline (89449). Phone 775/588-2411.* High atop Harvey's on the 19th floor, Llewellyn's offers a spectacular view of Lake Tahoe and an innovative menu with beautiful presentations. International menu. Dinner. Bar. Valet parking available. Totally nonsmoking. $$$

D

★★★SAGE ROOM. *US 50, Stateline (89449). Phone 775/588-2411.* Since 1947, the Sage Room Steak House has been world renowned for its Old West ambience and fine cuisine. Dine among the works of Russell and Remington while enjoying traditional steakhouse fare highlighted by tableside flambé service. Top off your meal with the Sage Room's famous Bananas Foster. Continental, American menu. Dinner. Bar. Valet parking available. $$$

D

★★★SUMMIT. *US 50, Stateline (89449). Phone 775/588-6611.* Located on the 16th and 17th floors of Harrah's, this restaurant has stunning views of the lake and mountains. Continental menu. Dinner. Bar. Valet parking available. Totally nonsmoking. $$$$

D

Las Vegas Strip

✳ NEVADA

AN ALL-AMERICAN ROAD

Quick Facts

LENGTH: 4.5 miles.

TIME TO ALLOW: From half an hour to several hours.

BEST TIME TO DRIVE: Las Vegas is warm year-round. The Strip is usually fairly crowded and congested. Nighttime is usually busier than daytime, and holidays are especially busy.

BYWAY TRAVEL INFORMATION: Nevada Commission on Tourism: 775/687-4322.

SPECIAL CONSIDERATIONS: This is a pedestrian-rich environment, so be on the alert when driving. Consider driving the Byway once each direction. This way, you will be able to view all the sites that line both sides of the street and catch some that you may have missed.

BICYCLE/PEDESTRIAN FACILITIES: Sidewalks line the Strip and provide plenty of room for walking. Cyclists are welcome, but they must observe the same traffic laws as automobiles.

Often referred to as the Jewel of the Desert, Las Vegas has long been recognized as the entertainment vacation capital of the country, and the Las Vegas Strip—at the heart of this playland—sparkles like no other place on Earth. More than 31 million visitors from around the world are drawn to the lights of the Strip each year to experience its unique blend of exciting entertainment, scenic beauty, and lavishly land-scaped resorts. An array of theme resorts can transport you to various exotic realms, from a medieval castle to a Parisian sidewalk café, a lake-side Italian village, or a pyramid in ancient Egypt.

The Las Vegas Strip hosts thousands of motorists a week; after you arrive on the Strip, however, you may be surprised to find that it's also a very enjoyable walking environment. The Strip is the only Byway that is more scenic at night than during the day. In fact, 365 days of the year, 24 hours a day, the Neon Trail offers a fascinating foray past spectacular resorts featuring a variety of visual delights. Whether it's pirates plundering, fiery volcanoes spouting, or tropical gardens luring the weary, the Las Vegas Strip offers a variety of fascinating visual experiences that enchant and mesmerize visitors of all ages. The many facets of this corridor make it truly a one-of-a-kind destination.

THE BYWAY STORY

The Las Vegas Strip tells cultural, historical, recreational, and scenic stories that make it a unique and treasured Byway.

Cultural

While Las Vegas is perhaps best known for its gaming culture—the popularity and influence of which have spread to cities all over the

Nevada

❋ *Las Vegas Strip*

world—the Las Vegas Strip possesses many other outstanding cultural amenities. The diversity and virtuosity of the architecture of the hotels and resorts along the Strip are certainly worth noting. Some of the world's most talented architects have created complex fantasylands all along the Strip. Just a few of the more recent projects include reproductions of the streets of New York, a bayside Tuscany village, the canals of Venice, and a replica of the Eiffel Tower and the Arc de Triomphe.

Many of the resorts on the Las Vegas Strip also feature world-class art galleries full of paintings by world-renowned artists, such as Renoir, Monet, and Van Gogh. Other resorts hold galleries of other unique items, like antique automobiles or wax figures. The Guinness World of Records Museum offers an interesting array of the unusual, and the World of Coca-Cola Las Vegas features an interactive storytelling theater.

Various hotels on the Las Vegas Strip feature a variety of top-caliber theatrical and dance shows. Several hotels and casinos host world-class sporting events and concerts featuring top-name entertainers. And no matter where you go on the Strip, you are bound to run into the dazzling light displays that permeate the area. The magical re-creations found along the Byway are the symbols of our society's most fantastic dreams of luxury.

Historical

The Las Vegas Strip, world-renowned for its neon glitter, possesses an equally colorful historical past. The unique history of Las Vegas is undeniably entwined with the culture of gaming. Gambling was legalized in Nevada in 1931, and the first casino opened downtown that same year. Competition was intense, and casino builders soon were looking to land outside the city limits just south of downtown along Highway 91 (the Old Los Angeles Highway), which is now known as the Las Vegas Strip.

Most of the Las Vegas Strip is not really located within the Las Vegas city limits, but along a corridor of South Las Vegas Boulevard located in unincorporated Clark County. The area was sparsely developed until 1938, when the first resort property was built 4 miles south of downtown Las Vegas at the corner of San Francisco Avenue (now Sahara) and Highway 91 (South Las Vegas Boulevard). Reportedly, city officials had denied licenses to certain businessmen with questionable connections who had applied to build a casino downtown. Undaunted, they decided to build outside the city limits, just south of the downtown district.

In 1941, construction began on El Rancho Vegas resort at the corner of San Francisco Avenue and Highway 91. The original El Rancho Vegas introduced a new style of recreation and entertainment to the Nevada desert by combining lodging, gambling, restaurants, entertainment, shops, a travel agency, horseback riding, and swimming in one resort. El Rancho Vegas was followed a year later by the Last Frontier Resort Hotel & Casino. The well-known Little Church of the West was originally constructed in the resort's Frontier Village. Listed on the National Register of Historic Places, the small chapel has survived four moves on the Strip.

One of the Strip's more colorful (and infamous) characters, Ben "Bugsy" Siegel (reputed hit man for New York mobster Lucky Luciano), oversaw the construction of the fabulous Flamingo Hotel, the third major (and most extravagant) resort to be built on the Strip. Although Siegel met his unfortunate demise soon after the resort's 1946 opening, his prophecies for the future of Las Vegas came true. This new popular playground of Hollywood stars prospered, with the Flamingo setting the stage for the many luxurious resorts yet to be imagined.

As the 1950s began, only four major resorts stood along the Strip, but three more major players were about to hit the scene. The Desert Inn, the Sahara, and the Sands all arrived on

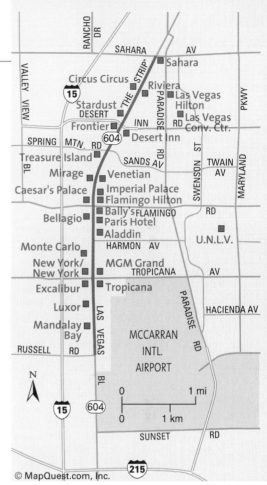

see page A19 for color map

the Strip in the early 1950s, further enhancing the Strip's image as a self-contained playground by featuring elaborate tennis courts, an 18-hole golf course, larger casinos, and fabulous showrooms with Broadway's and Hollywood's brightest stars. Las Vegas has continued to build on this legacy, developing newer and more elaborate resorts every year to make certain that Las Vegas retains the image of the most fabulous playground on Earth.

Recreational

The simplest and easiest recreation on the Strip is strolling and sightseeing along the Boulevard. Intriguing arrays of fantasylands in lush surroundings welcome you to the Strip. But the excitement only begins with sightseeing. From comfortable and plush hotels to exciting displays of lights and fountains, Las Vegas creates a dreamlike lifestyle with color, sound, and light all combined to make the experience on the Las Vegas Strip memorable.

For the more adventuresome, roller coasters featured at several hotels provide a ride that twists, loops, and turns to your delight. Other resorts provide 3-D ride films appealing to the senses of sight, sound, and motion. Many of these rides feature the latest technologies for extra thrills. Most of the resorts along the Strip offer displays of grandeur for every visitor to enjoy. Anyone driving the Byway can stop to see erupting volcanoes, dueling ships, dancing fountains, circus acts, and lush tropical gardens.

In addition to a variety of theatrical and dance shows, the resorts offer varied spectator sports, such as boxing matches. There isn't a resort on the Strip that doesn't offer visitors every amenity imaginable. World-class spas, pools, and exercise rooms are as enticing as the casinos. When you aren't searching for slot machines, you may choose to browse through the many stores and boutiques each resort has to offer. You will find everything from designer fashion to specialty candies to Las Vegas souvenirs. Whatever you choose to do, you can find it in Las Vegas.

Scenic

As one of the most geographically isolated major cities in the continental United States, Las Vegas provides you with an extraordinary visual experience. The matchless Las Vegas Strip serves as the gateway to a host of memorable experiences that are distinctly Las Vegas. The Strip's incredible array of resorts are constructed around themes that transport visitors to different exotic realms, including a medieval castle, the Parisian Eiffel Tower, a lakeside Italian village, and a pyramid in ancient Egypt. Day or night, the Neon Trail provides a fascinating foray past spectacular resorts that offer a variety of visual delights to pedestrians and motorists alike.

HIGHLIGHTS

The Southern Las Vegas Strip Walking Tour begins at South Las Vegas Blvd and Russell

Road, although you can go the opposite way by reading this list from the bottom up.

- The famous "Welcome to Fabulous Las Vegas" sign announces that you're on the right track. On the east side of the Strip, you see **The Little Church of the West,** the site of many celebrity weddings and a favorite place today to have the perfect wedding.

- Park the car at the free parking garage at **Mandalay Bay** (most of the large hotels offer plenty of covered free parking). Explore the tropical themed hotel, including a fun sand and surf beach. Mandalay Bay is one of the newest hotels on the Strip (built in 1999), and that makes it a popular attraction.

- From Mandalay Bay, you can walk north to **Luxor,** the great black glass pyramid. (If you prefer, hop on the free tram that takes you right to the front doors of Luxor—you may want to save your energy for later in the trip.) While at Luxor, don't miss the **King Tut Tomb exhibit**—an exact replica of the ancient Egyptian pharaoh's tomb. A rotating **IMAX** film experience is also a popular attraction here. This unique hotel is amazing and has one of the largest atriums in the world.

- After spending time at Luxor, hop on the tram that takes you over to **Excalibur.** This is the place for an exciting dinner and show. The majestic castle offers adventure at its **Fantasy Faire Midway**—an arena of games appropriate for everyone in the family.

- After spending time at the medieval castle, cross the over street walkway into 1930s- and '40s-inspired **New York-New York.** Billed as "the Greatest City in Las Vegas," New York-New York has attractions that are all themed to the New York life. Park Avenue shopping, a fast-paced Manhattan roller coaster, and Greenwich Village eateries help keep the theme intact.

- It's not time to stop yet. **The Monte Carlo,** just north of New York-New York, is just as classy, but with a purely European twist.

- After a jaunt to Monte Carlo, walk farther north, getting close to the halfway point. The big lake and fantastic fountains are part of **Bellagio,** a hotel that strives for utter perfection. Check out the art gallery here—it houses some fantastic pieces. The gallery has original paintings by Van Gogh, Monet, Renoir, Cezanne, and other masters.

- Now, at Flamingo Boulevard, cross the street to the east—over to **Paris.** This is the midpoint of the tour, and this area is full of areas to sit and rest or to grab a bite to eat. While at Paris, tour the **Eiffel Tower.** This is an exact replica, in half scale, of the original in France. The plans for the original were lent to the developers of the hotel so they could be as accurate as possible. There's also a two-thirds-scale replica of *L'Arc de Triomphe* near the hotel entrance—complete with Napoleon's victories inscribed on it.

- The next stop on this tour is the **MGM Grand.** This very large hotel strives to make visitors feel like stars. Elegance abounds at this hotel. Don't miss the **Lion Habitat** here: a walk-through tour that showcases some beautiful lions, some of which are descendants of Metro, the MGM marquee lion. The only thing separating you and the lions is a glass wall on both sides—an exciting experience.

- Just south of the MGM Grand is the famous **Tropicana,** home to the longest-running show on the Strip.

- After the Tropicana, cross the street again and take the tram from Excalibur to Mandalay Bay. At Mandalay Bay, get back in your car and cross the street to see the **Glass Pool Inn.** This motel was originally called The Mirage but sold the rights to its name to the much larger entity many years ago. The motel features an unusual above-ground pool with portal windows that has been featured in many movies.

- Finish off the tour of the Southern Las Vegas Strip by driving north back past the Tropicana and MGM Grand and beyond. The drive provides amazing views that you may have been missed along the walk.

THINGS TO SEE AND DO

Driving along the Las Vegas Strip will certainly keep your senses engaged, but if you yearn to get out of the car and stretch your legs, or if you'd like to make a mini-vacation out of your trip, check out these attractions along the route.

🔲 **BELLAGIO GALLERY OF FINE ART.** *Bellagio, 3600 Las Vegas Blvd S, Las Vegas (89109). Phone 702/693-7111; toll-free 877/957-9777. www.bgfa.biz.* A refined retreat amid the Sin City madness, the Bellagio Gallery of Fine Art mounts rotating exhibitions organized by a New York gallery on subjects ranging from Faberge eggs to Calder mobiles. The gallery's fine shop stocks arty souvenirs. Open daily 9 am-9 pm. **$$$**

DESERT PASSAGE. *Aladdin, 3663 Las Vegas Blvd S, Las Vegas (89109). Phone 702/866-0710; toll-free 888/800-8284. www.desertpassage.com.* Among the largest shopping centers on the Strip, Aladdin's Desert Passage models a North African bazaar with Moroccan archways, mosaic tiles, fountain courtyards, and stucco walls. The circular center tallies over 130 shops and 14 restaurants, most more affordable than those at Caesars Palace's designer-driven Forum Shops. Key tenants include cookware specialist Sur La Table, beauty supplier Sephora, trendsetter North Beach Leather, and outdoor outfitter Eddie Bauer. Direct from New Orleans, Commander's Palace restores the shop-weary lunch set. Open Sun-Thurs 10 am-11 pm, Fri-Sat 10 am-midnight.

EIFFEL TOWER EXPERIENCE. *Paris Las Vegas, 3655 Las Vegas Blvd S, Las Vegas (89109). Phone 702/946-7000; toll-free 888/266-5687.* The City of Light immigrates to Las Vegas in the form of a 50-story half-scale replica of the Eiffel Tower. A glass elevator whisks you to 460 feet for panoramic views of the mountain-ringed valley by day and the neon canyon by night. The 11th-floor restaurant Eiffel Tower serves the fine French food of native Frenchman (and longtime Chicago chef) Jean Joho. Open daily 10 am-1 am. **$$**

🔲 **THE FORUM SHOPS AT CAESARS.** *Caesars Palace, 3500 Las Vegas Blvd S, Las Vegas (89109). Phone 702/893-4800.* With piazzas, fountains, and an ever-changing (painted) sky overhead, the Forum Shops evoke an ancient Roman street in keeping with landlord Caesars Palace. Time your visit to catch one of the hourly shows at the Festival Fountain, where the statues of Bacchus, Venus, Apollo, and Mars come to life in an animatronic bacchanal (there's also a similar show at the other end of the mall involving Atlas). Stores scale toward luxury retailers like Bulgari, Escada, Gucci, and Fendi, but also include crowd-pleasers like Gap, FAO Schwarz, and Niketown. Several good restaurants, including Spago and Chinois, both from Wolfgang Puck, warrant a visit even for the shopping shy. Open Sun-Thurs 10 am-11 pm, Fri-Sat 10 am-midnight.

🔲 **FOUNTAINS OF BELLAGIO.** *Bellagio, 3600 Las Vegas Blvd S, Las Vegas (89109). Phone 702/693-7111.* A Busby Berkeley chorus line with water cannons subbing for gams, the Fountains of the Bellagio perform daily to a roster of tunes ranging from campy to operatic. The razzle-dazzle really roils after dark, when 4,500 lights dramatize the 1,000-nozzle, 27-million-gallon performances. Crowds tend to stake out spots along the wall ringing the hotel-fronting lake several minutes before every evening show. But if you're a hotel guest, you can catch it on the TV's Bellagio channel. Open Mon-Fri 3 pm-midnight; Sat-Sun noon-midnight.

FREMONT STREET EXPERIENCE. *425 Fremont St, Las Vegas (89101). Phone 702/678-5600.* Old downtown Las Vegas aimed to compete with Strip neon via the Fremont Street Experience, a light and sound show broadcast on a 90-foot-high canopy over a four-block stretch of Fremont Street installed in 1995. And the $70 million gamble paid off. Embedded with 2.1 million lights and 218 speakers, the overhead show synchronizes music and colored-light-derived images in each six-minute show. Only the hottest hands in the ten casinos that border the thoroughfare (also sponsors of the Experience) can resist filing outside for the on-the-hour shows. Each computerized performance per night is different, keying off various musical styles from calypso to disco to country western. Hourly shows dusk-midnight. **FREE**

GAMBLERS GENERAL STORE. *800 Main St, Las Vegas (89101). Phone 702/382-9903; toll-free 800/322-2447. www.gamblersgeneralstore.com.* Take the casino action home with you courtesy of Gamblers General Store, an emporium for the wagering addicted. Wares range from portable poker chip sets and playing cards to roulette wheels, slot machines, and raffle drums—all shippable. Did the tables teach you an expensive lesson? Bone up for a return visit through the store's library of gaming books and videos. Open daily 9 am-5 pm; closed holidays.

GRAND CANAL SHOPPES AT THE VENETIAN. *The Venetian, 3355 Las Vegas Blvd S, Las Vegas (89109). Phone 702/414-1000.* A 1,200-foot-long replica of the Grand Canal bisects the Grand Canal Shoppes, making this one of the Strip's more elegant retail emporiums. Venetian bridges, arches, and arcades dress up the mall. International luxury purveyors like Burberry, Jimmy Choo, and Wolford make a strong showing here. Try Il Prato or Ripa de Monte for Venetian paper goods, carnival masks, and Murano glass. When you're ready to drop, there's a food court and a number of full-service restaurants, many with patio seating. Open Sun-Fri 10 am-11 pm, Sat 10 am-midnight.

⚅ GUGGENHEIM HERMITAGE MUSEUM. *3355 Las Vegas Blvd S, Las Vegas (89109). Phone 702/414-2440. www.guggenheimlasvegas.org.* A venue for rotating exhibitions, the Guggenheim Hermitage is actually managed by a trio of museums, including the New York Guggenheim, Russia's Hermitage, and the Kunsthistorisches Museum in Vienna. Its open-ended, long-running show "Art Through the Ages" features 40 paintings that take a sweeping look at art history, from the 15th century's Jan Van Eyck,

through the popular French Impressionist period, to the Expressionism of Jackson Pollack. Hot Dutch architect Rem Koohaas designed the showcase, breaking ground here by using textured industrial metal walls in place of the velvet used at the Hermitage and providing a modern counterpoint to the baroque trimmings of the Venetian that houses it. Open daily 9:30 am-8:30 pm. **$$$**

LION HABITAT. *The Mirage, 3799 Las Vegas Blvd S, Las Vegas (89109). Phone 702/891-1111; toll-free 800/646-7787.* MGM's mascot lions lounge by day near the casino floor in a skylit habitat surrounded by waterfalls, acacia trees, and a pond. For close encounters, pass through it via a see-through tunnel as the lions pad above and below. Feline expert Keith Evans trucks up to six big cats daily to the Strip from his ranch 12 miles away. Open daily 11 am-11 pm. **FREE**

NEON MUSEUM. *3rd and Fremont sts, Las Vegas (89101). Phone 702/387-6366.* In an effort to preserve the outrageous neon signs for which the city is famed, Las Vegas' Neon Museum currently consists of ten vintage ads, refurbished and remounted in two outdoor "galleries," on 3rd and Fremont streets downtown. Neon touting Dot's Flowers (from 1949), the Nevada Motel (1950), Anderson Dairy's delivery boy (1956), and the Red Barn bar's martini glass (1960) seem almost quaint beside today's more elaborately evolved wattage. Guided tours $. Open 24 hours. **FREE**

RED ROCK CANYON NATIONAL RECREATION AREA. *Red Rock Scenic Dr, Las Vegas (89124). From Las Vegas Blvd, go 17 miles W on Charleston Blvd to Red Rock Scenic Dr. Phone 702/515-5340. www.redrockcanyon.blm.gov.* As the days wear on in Vegas and the trilling of slot machines wears you down, head to the red rocks that form the western view from Strip hotel windows. Although only 10 miles from the city limits, Red Rock Canyon couldn't be more dissimilar from the Neon Gulch. The 13-mile drive through the conservation area on a one-way road takes you to its most entertaining features, including several trailhead stops for day hikes and an almost certain photo op with the assertive wild burros that thrive here. Thirty miles of Mojave Desert trails take hikers deep into the petrified sand dunes, past ancient pictographs and mysterious waterfalls. Difficulty varies, but there's something here for everyone, from the Sunday stroller to the intermediate scrambler and advanced climber. Bureau of Land Management rangers often lead interpretive walks; call for details. Open winter 6 am-5 pm, spring and fall to 7 pm, summer to 8 pm; visitor center, winter 8 am-4:30 pm, summer to 5:30 pm. $$

RUMJUNGLE. *3950 Las Vegas Blvd S, Las Vegas (89119). Phone 702/632-7408.* One of the hottest scenes in Las Vegas, rumjungle pours on the eye candy, from platform-top dancing girls to gushing waterfalls. Until 9 pm weekdays and 11 pm on weekends, the nightspot opens as an eatery, dishing up global island fare with loads of sharable, martini-friendly finger foods. After hours, the place turns full-on nightclub with a blend of house and Latin music. When House of Blues shows nearby let out, rumjungle packs them in. Open Sun-Wed 5 pm-2 am, Thurs-Sat 5 pm-4 am.

SPORTS BOOK AT THE MIRAGE HOTEL AND CASINO. *3400 Las Vegas Blvd S, Las Vegas (89109). Phone 702/791-7111.* Most casinos have one, but sports books are shrinking in newer hotels. The Mirage boasts a 10,000-square-foot sports betting palace. If there's a sport that can be bet on, it's on the busy tote boards and televisions here, easily accounting for the visual confusion of neophytes. If you don't understand the odds, ask the window clerks. Sports bookies have dreamed up myriad ways to bet: not just who wins, who loses, and the point spread, but who wins the coin toss, what the halftime score will be, and who will score more points today, an individual NBA star or the Green Bay Packers. Big events, including the Super Bowl, the Kentucky Derby, and the NBA Finals, are predictably jammed. But niche sports like NCAA basketball and World Cup soccer draw sizable

contingents to the book as well, making seats scarce. Open 24 hours.

WET 'N WILD LAS VEGAS. *2601 Las Vegas Blvd S, Las Vegas (89109). Phone 702/765-9700. www.wetnwildlv.com.* Primed to cool the kiddies in the desert dog days, the conveniently located Wet 'n Wild pumps nearly 2 million gallons of water through chutes, flumes, slides, a lazy river, and a wave pool. Some features, including seven-story plummets, are restricted to teens and adults. For the littlest, there's a pirate ship-cum-playground over the shallowest of pools. Rafts, tubes and lockers are available for rent. May-Sept, open daily at 10 am; closed Oct-mid-Apr. $$$$

PLACES TO STAY

If you choose to include an overnight stay in your trip along this All-American Road, Mobil Travel Guide recommends the following lodgings.

★★★★**BELLAGIO.** *3600 Las Vegas Blvd S, Las Vegas (89109). Phone 702/693-7111; toll-free 888/987-6667. www.bellagiolasvegas.com.* Bellagio is a visual masterpiece. From its bold designs and world-class artwork to its acclaimed entertainment and award-winning cuisine, Bellagio delights the senses. The lobby draws attention with its dazzling bursts of color from the 2,000 hand-blown glass flowers by renowned artist Dale Chihuly. The rooms delightfully combine European élan with American comfort. A fantastic casino is only the beginning at this all-encompassing resort, which hosts an impressive swimming pool and fountain area, an arcade of fine shopping, and a Conservatory and Botanical Gardens under its roof. Discriminating diners will applaud the culinary works of art created in the resort's many fine dining establishments. Figuring largely in the Bellagio experience is its 8-acre lake, where mesmerizing fountains perform to a symphony of sounds and lights every half-hour or so. Bellagio is also home to Cirque du Soleil's *O*, a heart-stopping aquatic

performance that is simply not to be missed. 3,005 rooms, 36 story. Adults only.
TV; cable (premium). Restaurants, bars. In-house fitness room. Spa. Massage. Heated pool; whirlpool, poolside service. Entertainment. $$

[D] [SC] [⌕] [⼊]

★★★**CAESARS PALACE.** *3570 Las Vegas Blvd S, Las Vegas (89109). Phone 702/731-7110; toll-free 800/634-6661. www.caesars.com.* The Roman-themed Caesars was the Strip's first mega-resort when it opened in 1966. And though little lasts long in Vegas, Caesars still reigns, constantly growing and challenging competitors to keep up. To its Italian façade, Caesars recently added a replica of Rome's Coliseum in which singer Celine Dion entertains. The hotel's swimming deck, modeled on Pompeii, trims three pools in marble statues. The confusing layout of the casino floor is an open play to keep you in-house. But there's plenty to recommend it, including 808 and Bradley Ogden restaurants as well as the high-end Forum Shops. Standard guest quarters include a couch as well as a marble bathroom. 2,500 rooms, 14-32 story. Check-out noon, check-in 5 pm. TV; cable (premium), VCR available (movies). In-room modem link. Restaurant, bar; entertainment. In-house fitness room, massage, sauna, steam room. Game room. Three pools, whirlpool. Handball. Racquetball. Free parking. Business center. Concierge. Casino. $$

[⼊] [D] [⼤] [⌕]

★★★★**FOUR SEASONS HOTEL LAS VEGAS.** *3960 Las Vegas Blvd S, Las Vegas (89119). Phone 702/632-5000; toll-free 877/632-5000. www.fourseasons.com.* The Four Seasons Hotel is a palatial refuge in glittering Las Vegas. Located on the southern tip of the famous strip, the Four Seasons remains close to the attractions of this dynamic city while providing a welcome respite from the hustle and bustle. This non-gaming hotel occupies the 35th through 39th floors of the Mandalay Bay Resort tower, yet it is distinctively Four Seasons with its sumptuous décor and inimitable service. Guests surrender

to the plush furnishings in the stylish rooms, and floor-to-ceiling windows showcase exhilarating views of the strip's neon lights or the stark beauty of the Nevada desert. Steak lovers rejoice at Charlie Palmer Steak, while the sun-filled Verandah offers a casual dining alternative. The glorious pool is a lush oasis with its swaying palm trees and attentive poolside service. Lucky visitors retreat to the sublime spa, where JAMU Asian techniques soothe the weary. 424 rooms, 5 story. Pet accepted, some restrictions. Check-out noon, check-in 3 pm. TV; cable (premium). Restaurant, bar. Room service 24 hours. Outdoor pool, children's pool. Spa. Concierge. $$

[D] [➤] [SC] [⌕]

★★★**HARRAH'S HOTEL AND CASINO.** *3475 Las Vegas Blvd S, Las Vegas (89109). Phone 702/369-5000; toll-free 800/427-7247. www.harrahs.com.* The gaming powerhouse Harrah's runs this Strip hotel, where the emphasis, as you might expect, is on the casino. Bolstering the hotel and casino's carnival theme décor, an outdoor plaza showcases entertainers, trinket vendors, and snack booths. Spacious but rather bland rooms are lodged in a 35-story tower behind the gaming floor, although guests spend most of their time at the many tables, in the Olympic-size swimming pool, boutique spa, or eight eateries. Popular entertainer Clint Holmes rules the showroom here with song and dance. 2,673 rooms, 35 story. Check-out noon, check-in 4 pm. TV. Laundry services. Restaurant, bar; entertainment. In-house fitness room, spa, massage, sauna. Game room. Outdoor pool. Valet parking available. Casino. Wedding chapel. ¢

[D] [⼤] [SC] [⌕] [⼊]

★★★**LUXOR HOTEL AND CASINO.** *3900 Las Vegas Blvd S, Las Vegas (89119). Phone 702/262-4000; toll-free 888/288-1000. www.luxor.com.* A 30-story glass pyramid in the desert, the thoroughly thematic Luxor emulates ancient Egypt from its sphinx figurehead outdoors to gold-costumed employees within. Elevators travel the pyramid's incline to deposit guests at room hallways that overlook the world's largest atrium. Five pools, a fitness center, and a spa provide recreation, while an IMAX theater, two-story game room for the kids, and a museum devoted to King Tut entertain. The inventive performance artists Blue Man Group headline Luxor's stage options. 4,400 rooms, 30 story. Check-out 11 am, check-in 3 pm. TV; cable (premium), VCR available. Restaurant, bar; entertainment. In-house fitness room, spa, massage, sauna. Outdoor pool, children's pool. Business center. Concierge. Casino. ¢

★★★MANDALAY BAY RESORT AND CASINO.
3950 Las Vegas Blvd S, Las Vegas (89119). Phone 702/632-7777; toll-free 877/632-7000. www.mandalaybay.com. Even in over-the-top Las Vegas, Mandalay Bay exceeds expectations. This all-encompassing resort captures the spirit of the tropics with its 11-acre sandy beach and three pools with lazy river ride. The stylish accommodations flaunt a tropical flavor, and the casino is a paradise of lush foliage and flowing water, yet this resort is perhaps best known for its mystifying Shark Reef. This facility goes far beyond the ordinary aquarium and takes the entire family on an unforgettable adventure. In true Vegas style, this resort has it all, including a 30,000-square-foot spa and terrific shopping. Thirteen restaurants offer a taste of the world, while an astounding variety of entertainment options include everything from live music to Broadway-style shows. 3,215 rooms, 403 suites, 36 story. Check-out 11 am, check-in 3 pm. TV; cable (premium). In-room modem link. Restaurant, bar; entertainment. Room service 24 hours. In-house fitness room, spa, massage. Beach. Outdoor pool, children's pool, whirlpool. $

★★★MGM GRAND HOTEL AND CASINO.
3799 Las Vegas Blvd S, Las Vegas (89109). Phone 702/891-7777; toll-free 877/880-0880.

www.mgmgrand.com. The largest hotel on the Strip, the MGM Grand virtually pulses with Las Vegas energy. If you've come for nonstop thrills, check in here, where the attractions work well to keep you out of your comfortable room. In the casino, a glassed-in lion habitat with waterfalls showcases a wild pride. The outdoor pool includes a current-fed lazy river, and the spa specializes in cutting-edge treatments. MGM eateries Coyote Café, NobHill, and Craftsteak are thought to be some of the best in the city. The party crowd crows for the dance club Studio 54 and the lounge Tabu. 5,005 rooms, 29 story. Check-out 11 am. Check-in 3 pm. TV; cable (premium). Internet access. Restaurant, bar; entertainment. Supervised children's activities, ages 3-12. Exercise room, spa, steam room. Game room. Pool, whirlpool, poolside service. Free parking. Airport transportation. Business center. Concierge. ¢

★★★THE MIRAGE HOTEL AND CASINO.
3400 Las Vegas Blvd S, Las Vegas (89177). Phone 702/791-7111; toll-free 800/374-9000. www.mgm-mirage.com. The Strip-side volcano—which erupts every 15 minutes at night—marks the Mirage and its exotic theme. Tropical fish tanks back the registration desks, the route to room elevators passes through a cascade of jungle foliage, and a lavish pool deck is ringed by towering palms. Among Mirage's many eateries, Renoir is one of town's tops for fine dining, while the Brazilian-style Samba makes a celebration of meat-eating. One of Vegas' most popular shows—impersonator Danny Gans—plays the Mirage. Rooms, recently and smartly renovated, include spacious, marble-trimmed baths. 3,044 rooms, 30 story. Check-out noon, check-in 2 pm. TV; VCR available. In-room modem link. Restaurants, bars; entertainment. Exercise room, massage. Pool, whirlpool. Valet parking available. Business center. Concierge. Casino. $$

★★★**PARIS LAS VEGAS.** *3645 Las Vegas Blvd, Las Vegas (89109). Phone 702/946-7000; toll-free 877/796-2096. www.parislasvegas.com.* A half-scale model of the Eiffel Tower landmarks Paris Las Vegas, an ode to French savoir faire complete with a copy of the Arc de Triomphe and costumed landscape painters fronting the Strip-side pavilion. Its charms continue inside, where three legs of the Eiffel Tower rest in the casino and a cobblestone street wends its way through the shopping arcade. Rooms underscore the theme with French fabrics and custom furniture. Request a Strip view to see the dancing Bellagio fountains across the street. Most of the restaurants here are French, including the charming Mon Ami Gabi, which offers outdoor seating on a Las Vegas Boulevard terrace that allows for prime people-watching. 2,916 rooms, 30 story. Pet accepted. Check-out 11 am, check-in 3 pm. TV. In-room modem link. Restaurants, bars; entertainment. In-house fitness room, massage, sauna. Outdoor pool, children's pool. Business center. Casino. $

★★**RIVIERA HOTEL AND CASINO.** *2901 Las Vegas Blvd S, Las Vegas (89109). Phone 702/734-5110; toll-free 800/634-6753. www.theriviera.com.* 2,072 rooms, 170 suites, 24 story. Check-out 11 am, check-in 3 pm. TV; cable (premium). In-room modem link. Restaurant, bar; entertainment. In-house fitness room, sauna, steam room. Outdoor pool, children's pool. Outdoor tennis, lighted courts. Business center. Casino. ¢

★★**TROPICANA HOTEL & CASINO.** *3801 Las Vegas Blvd S, Las Vegas (89193). Phone 702/739-2222; toll-free 888/826-8767. www.tropicanalv.com.* More than 1,800 spacious guest rooms, including two towers of suites, overlook 5 acres of gardens and pools at this popular resort. Guests can enjoy the *Folies Bergère,* said to be Las Vegas' longest-running show. 1,878 rooms, 22 story. Check-out 11 am, check-in 3 pm. TV; cable (premium). In-room

modem link. Restaurant, bar; entertainment. Sauna. Outdoor pool. Business center. Casino. $

★★★★**THE VENETIAN RESORT HOTEL & CASINO.** *3355 Las Vegas Blvd S, Las Vegas (89109). Phone 702/414-1000; toll-free 877/283-6423. www.venetian.com.* From the masterfully re-created Venetian landmark buildings to the frescoed ceilings and gilded details, the Venetian Resort Hotel & Casino faithfully re-creates the splendor that is Venice in the heart of the Las Vegas Strip. Guests amble down the winding alleys and glide past ornate architecture in gondolas in this perfect reproduction of the golden island that has inspired countless artists for centuries. Inside, the Venetian is glamorous and refined. This all-suite property ensures the comfort of its guests in its spacious and luxurious accommodations. After winning a hand in the casino, head for the upscale boutiques displaying world-famous brands alongside signature Murano glass and Carnival masks. Some of the biggest names in American cuisine operate award-winning restaurants here, while the Venetian's Guggenheim and Madame Tussaud's Wax Museum always delight. Guests soak away their sins at the Canyon Ranch Spa Club. 3,036 rooms, 35 story. Check-out noon, check-in 3 pm. TV; cable (premium). In-room modem link. Restaurants, bars; entertainment. In-house fitness room, sauna, spa. Outdoor pool, children's pool. Valet parking available. Business center. Casino. $$

PLACES TO EAT

A long day of driving is sure to make you hungry. At the end of your journey, take a table at one of the following restaurants.

★★★★**AQUA.** *Bellagio, 3600 Las Vegas Blvd S, Las Vegas (89109). Phone 702/693-7223. www.bellagiolasvegas.com.* After strolling through the Bellagio Conservatory & Botanical

Gardens on the way to dinner, guests find a luxurious, contemporary dining room bathed in blond wood, creamy neutral tones, and golden light. The menu here is in the care of a talented group of chef-creators trained and transported from the original Aqua in San Francisco. The kitchen is passionate about the sea; delicious dishes tend to concentrate on the creatures of the deep blue ocean jazzed up with California ingredients. Aqua serves the kind of food that begs to be licked off the plate. You won't be able to contain yourself. The menu is extensive and offers à la carte selections in addition to a pair of five-course tasting menus, one vegetarian and one seasonal. The wine list focuses on American producers and contains some gems from small vineyards as well; you'll find lots of fish-friendly options. Contemporary American menu. Jacket required. Reservations required. Valet parking available. **$$$$**
D

★★★★AUREOLE. *Mandalay Bay Resort and Casino, 3950 Las Vegas Blvd, Las Vegas (89119). Phone 702/632-7401. www.aureolelv.com.* A branch of chef Charlie Palmer's New York original, Aureole wows patrons with its centerpiece four-story wine tower. Be sure to order a bottle just to see the catsuit-clad climber, suspended by ropes, locate your vintage. Its 12,000 bottles complement Palmer's seasonal contemporary American cuisine typified by dishes like Peking duck with foie gras ravioli and roast pheasant with sweet potato gnocchi. The modern but romantic room with encircling booths sets the stage for event dining at Mandalay Bay. American menu. Dinner. Jacket required. **$$$$**

★★★CHINOIS. *Caesars Palace, 3500 Las Vegas Blvd S, Las Vegas (89109). Phone 702/737-9700. www.wolfgangpuck.com.* A spin-off of chef Wolfgang Puck's acclaimed Chinois on Main in Santa Monica, California, Las Vegas' Chinois features similar Asian fusion fare in the Forum Shops. The spare, artifact-decorated shop-level café, specializing in pan-Asian fare often

lightened California style to please western palettes, is a well-located lunch spot. The broad-ranging menu includes sushi and sashimi, dim sum, wok-fried meat and vegetable recipes such as kung pao chicken, and Asian noodle dishes like pad Thai. Asian menu. Lunch, dinner. Bar. Children's menu. Reservations required. Valet parking available. **$$$**
D

★★CAMELOT. *Excalibur Hotel and Casino, 3850 Las Vegas Blvd S, Las Vegas (89109). Phone 702/597-7449. www.excalibur.com.* Camelot serves gourmet dishes in a romantic setting. A cigar room, a wine cellar, a fireplace, and an open kitchen are some of the classic elements found here. Steak menu. Closed Mon, Tues. Dinner. Bar. Casual attire. Reservations accepted. Valet parking available. **$$$**
D

★★IL FORNAIO. *3790 Las Vegas Blvd S #13, Las Vegas (89109). Phone 702/650-6500. www.ilfornaio.com.* Italian menu. Dinner. Contemporary Italian cuisine and an on-site bakery. **$$$**
D

★★★LE CIRQUE. *3600 Las Vegas Blvd S, Las Vegas (89109). Phone 702/693-8100. www.lecirque.com.* The hallowed temple of cuisine for New York's financial elite has made it to Las Vegas. Restaurateur and charmer Sirio Maccioni, the face and creative force behind the Gotham power scene, brought a branch to the Bellagio. Like its New York City sibling, this Le Cirque is a shining jewel of a restaurant, awash in bold colors and warm fabrics, with a bright, silk-tented ceiling that brings a festive big-top feel to the intimate dining room. The three-course prix fixe menu features rustic French fare that includes something for everyone: snails, fish, lamb, beef, and game, as well as salads and pasta. In signature Maccioni style, each dish is prepared with precision and

delivered with care. Caviar service is available for those seeking extreme luxury, and the wine list boasts several stellar choices. French menu. Jacket required. Reservations required. Valet parking available. $$$
D

★★★★**PICASSO.** *Bellagio, 3600 Las Vegas Blvd S, Las Vegas (89109). Phone 702/693-7223. www. bellagiolasvegas.com.* The Bellagio is home to some of the finest restaurants in Las Vegas, and Picasso stands out among them. It offers exquisite food in a serene space, and it's one of those two-for-one experiences. If you're trying to decide between visiting a museum and having an elegant and inspired meal, you can do both at Picasso. The master painter's original works don the walls of this beautiful, cozy, country-style room with soaring wood-beamed ceilings, sage-toned upholstery, and a stunning view of the lake. The menu is also artwork. The kitchen uses French technique as a canvas for layering Spanish and Mediterranean flavor. (You can opt for a four-course tasting menu or a chef's degustation menu as well.) To match the museum-worthy food, you'll be offered a rare and magnificent selection of international wines. If the weather is warm, you can also dine al fresco by the lake—nature's art. French cuisine with Spanish flair. Closed Wed. Dinner. Jacket required. Reservations required. Valet parking available. $$$$
D

★★★**PRIME.** *Bellagio, 3600 Las Vegas Blvd S, Las Vegas (89109). Phone 702/693-7223. www.bellagiolasvegas.com.* Famed New York fusion chef Jean-Georges Vongerichten opened his first and only steakhouse with the stylish Prime. Located in the Bellagio with waterside views of the dancing fountains, Prime serves superior cuts of beef, veal, and lamb with a range of sauces, from standard béarnaise to very Vongerichten tamarind. Ample fish and chicken selections and creative appetizers entice lighter appetites. Elegant and romantic surrounds, including Baccarat crystal chandeliers and velvet draperies, distract from the expense-account prices. Steak menu. Dinner. Reservations required 60 days in advance. $$$$
D

★**STAGE DELI.** *3500 Las Vegas Blvd S, Las Vegas (89109). Phone 702/893-4045. www.arkrestaurants.com.* American, deli menu. Breakfast, lunch, dinner. Bar. Children's menu. Casual attire. Valet parking available. $
D

★★**THE STEAK HOUSE.** *2880 Las Vegas Blvd, Las Vegas (89114). Phone 702/734-0410.* Steak menu. Dinner, Sun brunch. Bar. Reservations accepted. Valet parking available. $$$
D

★★★**TOP OF THE WORLD.** *Stratosphere Hotel and Casino, 2000 S Las Vegas Blvd, Las Vegas (89104). Phone 702/380-7711. www.stratlv.com.* In a town of few casino windows and even fewer restaurant views, Top of the World atop the Stratosphere Hotel tower stands out. The circular room revolves once every 90 minutes, offering 360-degree nighttime views of Vegas by neon. Few scenery-centric restaurants push the culinary envelope, and Top of the World is no exception, although it does a nice job with steaks and continental classics like lobster bisque. A mini Stratosphere in chocolate is a must for dessert, serving two. American menu. Lunch, dinner. Bar; entertainment. Reservations required. Valet parking available. $$$
D

★**WOLFGANG PUCK CAFÉ.** *MGM-Grand Hotel and Casino, 3799 Las Vegas Blvd S, Las Vegas (89109). Phone 702/895-9653. www.wolfgangpuck.com.* International menu. Breakfast, lunch, dinner. $$

Pyramid Lake Scenic Byway

❋ NEVADA

Quick Facts

LENGTH: 37 miles.

TIME TO ALLOW: 2 hours to 1 day.

BEST TIME TO DRIVE: Year-round; high season is July and August.

SPECIAL CONSIDERATIONS: Many of the road shoulders are sandy, and vehicles can get stuck easily. The best place to fill up with gasoline is in Wadsworth, near I-80.

Pyramid Lake is a bright jewel in the arid Nevada landscape. Fish, animal, and plant life are sustained by its 300-foot-deep waters and by the fresh water flowing in the Truckee River. In addition to the cui-ui fish, the lake is known for the Lahontan cutthroat trout that the tribe manages through its fisheries program. The mountains surrounding the lake support deer, antelope, and bighorn sheep. The lake is also a resting place for a variety of migrating waterfowl. Anaho Island, a National Wildlife Refuge, is the breeding ground for the largest colony of American white pelicans. It is also home to a variety of other shorebirds. The tufa formations found at this lake are some of the lake's most distinctive natural features. These formations are calcium carbonate deposits formed by precipitation over hot springs. They include the Pyramid (which gives the lake its name) and the Needles.

THE BYWAY STORY

The Pyramid Lake Scenic Byway tells archaeological, cultural, historical, natural, recreational, and scenic stories that make it a unique and treasured Byway.

Archaeological

Since time immemorial, the Northern Paiute people were comprised of many bands that occupied northwestern Nevada and southeastern Oregon. By roaming in small, family-centered groups, these remarkable people developed an ingenious technology that made life possible in a high desert environment. One band centered its territory around Pyramid Lake and were called Kuyuidokado, or cui-ui eaters. Cui-ui is an indigenous fish species found only in Pyramid Lake.

On display at the Pyramid Lake Visitors Center are tools and artifacts that reflect the ancient culture that was essential to these people's survival. Much of the collection has established a timeline for archaeologists in determining when these tools were used.

Cultural

The Pyramid Lake Paiute Tribe is governed by ten tribal council members who are elected biannually in December and on staggered two-year terms. The majority of enrolled tribal members, numbering around 1,700 people, reside on the reservation, and approximately 12 percent of this membership reside in other areas throughout the western United States.

Given the strong cultural ties between the lake and the Paiute Tribe, the cultural attributes of the Byway are best described by the following speech given by a Tribal Chairman during Cui-Day in 1993:

"Welcome to our festival. This gathering was an annual time of celebration for our people, the Kuyuidokado, cui-ui eaters. It was in recognition of the renewal of life in the spring, which included the renewal of our lives as well. There was a time when the cui-ui run meant the continuation of our existence. If there was no cui-ui, a winter of hardship and great difficulty would follow for our people. The absence of a run would mean many of our people would not see the next spring. Our dependence on the land and our traditional way of life changed with the arrival of non-Indians. This change did not always come as a way of choice, but as a necessity. Our ability to live by our traditional way was no longer possible. This was the result of both the cultural and environmental changes brought by this new culture.

"There was a time when heavy snow in the mountains meant the river would flow and we could expect a good harvest of fish. But this pattern changed this century. Dams built on the river kept the snow water from reaching the Lake. And our cui-ui that used to follow the water up the river began to diminish. Feelings of despair replaced that feeling of anticipation in the spring.

"Our Tribe's repeat attempts to return the flow of the river to the Lake met with failure. Our contact with the non-Indian community was fraught with conflict. But today we welcome the non-Indian community to our celebration because we believe we can share the waters of Truckee [River] and [Pyramid] Lake in a way that would benefit all of our communities.

"There is no doubt that our Tribe's culture and society has changed over the years, and our past way of life will not be our future. But we will survive as a people, and the cui-ui will be part of our culture. Much as the eagle is the symbol of freedom for the people of the United States, the cui-ui represents life for our people. It is a sad statement that both of these animals are endangered. We as cultures must work together to see they survive."

Historical

Hundreds of years before white man traveled through Nevada, the Paiute Indians lived near Pyramid Lake, then called Coo-yu-ee Pah. According to a Paiute legend, the lake was also called Wano, meaning a conical basket turned upside down. This name stems from the legend of the Stone Mother, which says a grief-stricken mother cried so much over her sons, her tears filled her basket and overflowed to fill the entire lake.

The Paiute people have always lived near the lake. Their traditional culture was centered around the lake, and they were called Cui-ui Ticutta, or cui-ui eaters. The lake was the center of the Paiute tribe's life. They depended on the cui-ui fish to survive. Unfortunately, in 1859, the Paiute Indian Reservation was formed, giving only a fraction of the land to the Paiute people. They continued to live as they had been and create a culture rich in history and family.

The present name of the lake was given by John C. Fremont on January 10, 1844. The first band of white explorers stumbled upon the lake after a difficult journey through the harsh desert that lasted several weeks. They pitched their camp near a striking 400-foot-high rock island outcropping. Fremont wrote in his journal on January 14, "We encamped on the shore, opposite a very remarkable rock in the lake, which attracted our attention for many miles. It rose, according to our estimate, 600 feet above the water, and, from the point we viewed it, presented a pretty exact outline of the great pyramid of Cheops. This striking feature suggested a name for the lake, and I called it Pyramid Lake." The explorers were also captivated by the stone needles, pinnacles, and steaming sulfur springs, which the Paiute people still hold sacred today.

Natural

The present-day vision of Pyramid Lake took millions of years to form. It is the remnant of an inland sea, Lake Lahontan, that covered over 8,000 square miles about 11 million years ago. Today, Pyramid Lake is 26 miles long, 4 to 11 miles wide, and 350 feet deep at its deepest point. It has been called the world's most beautiful desert lake and presents a range of colors from turquoise to emerald green to deep blue. Because Pyramid Lake used to be part of an inland sea, it is a very alkaline lake, the type found in semiarid or arid environments. Visiting the lake is almost like going to the beach. Unlike the beach, however, Pyramid Lake has a number of interesting formations scattered around and throughout its waters. The lake is also home to a variety of wildlife that visitors usually don't see at the beach.

Tufa needs just the right kind of conditions to form, and Pyramid Lake is the world's largest producer of tufa rock. It forms when the following environment is present: a stable lake,

see page A20 for color map

a source of calcium, high water temperatures, and a stable bedrock or substrate. When all of these conditions are present, all that is necessary is a branch or rock around which the carbonate can form. Pyramid Lake demonstrates its age through the tufa formations. Changes in color and texture of the rock, as well as primary sill level changes, also indicate what kinds of weather Pyramid Lake has survived, including winds, droughts, floods, and glacial activity.

Other tufa formations attract attention, too. The primary area, the Needles, is located at the northwest end of the lake, in the hot springs area. This area of continuing geothermal activity contains more tufa depositions than anywhere else in the world. Other types of formations exist around the lake, such as the Stone Mother and her basket. The basket is actually a rounded, hollowed rock, but a legend exists about the Stone Mother that goes like this: In the ancient days, a mother had four sons. They could not get along and were forced to leave. Their mother, in terrible grief, sat in the middle of the desert and cried so many tears that they filled the lake. She was in such despair she just dropped her basket beside her, and then the mother and her basket turned to stone.

Anaho Island, located in Pyramid Lake, is a National Wildlife Refuge that is one of only eight nesting grounds for white pelicans in North America. As many as 9,500 pelicans nest on the island in the spring, so both the federal government and the Paiute Tribe carefully protect the island from intruding boats or visitors. The best place to view the pelicans is from the southeastern or southwestern shores with binoculars; the best time of year to see them is March through October. Numerous other types of birds, including double-crested cormorants, California gulls, blue herons, golden and bald eagles, rock wrens, owls, falcons, snowy egrets, and California quail, draw bird-watchers.

Because the nature of the lake is so well protected and preserved by the Paiute Tribe, an uncommon amount of wildlife lives undisturbed at Pyramid Lake. Not only do many birds live here, but also burros, big horn sheep, bobcats, wild horses, mountain lions, pronghorn antelope, coyotes, and jack rabbits. There are few spots in the county where visitors can see such a range of wildlife.

Recreational

Pyramid Lake offers all kinds of opportunities to enjoy the surrounding nature. You can hike, rock climb, ride horseback, backpack, and do so much more. And after a full day of activity, hot springs at the north end of the lake among the needle rocks allow you to relax while enjoying Pyramid Lake's famous tufa formations. The lake itself draws the most recreationists; it is a favorite of anglers, who throughout the history of the lake have gone from fishing as a means of survival to fishing as a business venture to fishing for sport.

Fishing at Pyramid Lake is an experience all its own. The water is unlike most lake water and a startling pastel blue. The surroundings are pure desert, with little vegetation. After some practice, many fishermen have discovered that the best way to catch fish in Pyramid Lake is from the top of a five-foot ladder or other tall object. The

fish come into the shallows, and the added altitude gives anglers a better view, as well as a longer casting range. Be careful, though. While you can see the fish, the fish can also see you. Fish often roam the edges of the lake near a series of ledges or drop-offs. If you stand on a tall object and wear polarizing lens, you can actually see the fish take the fly ten feet away. Pyramid Lake has also been known for the size of its fish, especially the cutthroat trout. In 1925, a Paiute named Johnny Skimmerhorn caught the world's record cutthroat—a 41-pounder. In the '20s and '30s, photographs show celebrities like Clark Gable struggling to hold up a pair of massive cutthroat. Another photograph shows a group of Nevadans peeking out from behind a line of shimmering fish that stretches eight feet long from a day's catch. Unfortunately, the fish are no longer as large due to extensive fishing, but 5- to 10-pounders are not uncommon.

Scenic

Travelers driving to Pyramid Lake for the first time may be surprised at the scenic beauty that a cold, blue lake offers in the middle of the desert. The lake is situated in a valley amid distant hills and snowcapped mountains. It is an unexpected oasis in the middle of the dry landscape of Nevada. Upon reaching Pyramid Lake, you can view the tufa rock formations that decorate the lake's shores, including one in

the middle of the lake, a pyramid-shaped rock formation standing 400 feet tall. The lake was named for this feature by John C. Fremont in 1844.

A drive around Pyramid Lake offers an enchanting view of this remnant of an ancient inland sea that changes from green to turquoise to deep blue. The sunset casts a red glow on the lake and surrounding formations that you can behold at scenic turnouts. During the day, just the sight of the deep blue waters of Pyramid Lake is a refreshing experience for hot travelers.

HIGHLIGHTS

On this Pyramid Lake must-see tour, you can start in either Sparks or Wadsworth, because the driving directions given here start and end in the Reno/Sparks area.

- Start your trip by taking I-40 to West Wadsworth. Follow State Route 427 into town, and then drive north along State Route 447, following the course of the Truckee River. You can stop at the **Numana Hatchery Visitor Center** to learn about the area's natural history and the tribe's fisheries program or take a walk along the wetlands nature trail, where you experience the unique habitats of the river valley.

- As you continue to drive north, you will come over a rise and see the lake spread out before you. Just ahead is the **Scenic Byway Visitor Center and Tribal Museum.** From here, you can take a side trip north on Route 447 into the town of **Nixon,** site of the Tribal Headquarters, and beyond to **Marble Bluff** and **Lake Winnemucca.**

- You can also head west on Route 446 toward Sutcliffe. Route 446 follows the west shore of **Pyramid Lake,** with plenty of beaches for swimming, fishing, or enjoying a picnic lunch. In **Sutcliffe,** you'll find the **Pyramid Lake Marina,** with a visitor center and museum, as well as stores and visitor services. North of Sutcliffe are more beaches, especially at **Pelican Point** and **Warrior Point.**

- Returning south from Sutcliffe, take State Route 445 south toward Sparks. As you drive up toward **Mullen Pass,** you can stop at the turnout on the left for a scenic vista of the lake. If you get a chance to visit here as the sun sets, the Pyramid, Anaho Island, and the slopes of the Lake Range may be bathed in a red glow, offering a dramatic counterpoint to the urban glitter awaiting you as you return to Reno.

THINGS TO SEE AND DO

Driving along the Pyramid Lake Scenic Byway will certainly keep your senses engaged, but if you yearn to get out of the car and stretch your legs, or if you'd like to make a mini-vacation out of your trip, check out these attractions along the route.

FLEISCHMANN PLANETARIUM. *1650 N Virginia St, Reno (89557). Phone 775/784-4812.* Northern Nevada's only planetarium, this facility features star shows, movies, astronomy museum, telescope viewing (Fri evenings), and more. Open daily; closed Jan 1, Thanksgiving, Dec 25. $$

MACKAY SCHOOL OF MINES MUSEUM. *9th and Virginia sts, Reno (89557). Phone 775/784-6987.* Minerals, rocks, fossils, and mining memorabilia. Open Mon-Fri; closed holidays. FREE

MOUNT ROSE SKI AREA. *22222 Mt. Rose Hwy, Reno (89511). Phone 775/849-0704; toll-free 800/SKI-ROSE (exc NV).* Two quads, two triple, one six-person chairlift; patrol, rentals, school; bar, cafeteria, deli; sport shop. Longest run 2 1/2 miles; vertical drop 1,440 feet. Open mid-Nov-mid-Apr, daily. $$$$

NATIONAL AUTOMOBILE MUSEUM. *10 Lake St S, Reno (89501). Phone 775/333-9300.* More than 220 cars on display. Theater presentation; period street scenes. Open daily; closed Thanksgiving, Dec 25. $$

NEVADA HISTORICAL SOCIETY MUSEUM. *1650 N Virginia St, Reno (89503). Phone 775/688-1190.* Prehistoric and modern Native American artifacts; ranching, mining, and gambling artifacts. Carson City Mint materials; museum tours; research and genealogy library (open Tues-Sat). Open Mon-Sat; closed holidays, Oct 31.

NEVADA MUSEUM OF ART. *100 S Virginia St, Reno (89501). Phone 775/329-3333.* Changing art exhibits by international, national, regional, and local artists. Open Tues-Sun; closed holidays. **$$**

PYRAMID LAKE. *Pyramid Way and NV 445, Reno (89512). Phone 775/476-1155.* Surrounded by rainbow-tinted, eroded hills, this is a remnant of prehistoric Lake Lahontan, which once covered 8,400 square miles in western Nevada and northeastern California. The largest natural lake in the state, Pyramid is about 30 miles long and from 7 to 9 miles wide, with deep-blue sparkling waters. It is fed by scant water from the diverted Truckee River and by brief floods in other streams. Since the Newlands Irrigation Project deprives it of water, its level is receding. Pyramid Lake abounds with Lahonton cutthroat trout; it is one of the top trophy trout lakes in the United States. All rights belong to the Native Americans. For information about roads, fishing, and boat permits, contact the Sutcliffe Ranger Station or Pyramid Lake Fisheries, Star Rte, Sutcliffe (89510); 775/476-0500. Camping, boating, and fishing at Pyramid Lake are considered by many to be the best in the state. Visitor centers, located in the hatcheries at Sutcliffe and between Nixon and Wadsworth, describe the land, lake, and people through photographs and displays Open daily. **$$$**

RODEO. *1350 N Wells St, Reno Livestock Events Center, Reno (89512).* Downtown contests and celebrations on closed streets. Phone 775/329-3877. Held in late June.

TOIYABE NATIONAL FOREST. *1200 Franklin Way, Sparks (89431). Phone 775/331-6444.* Approximately 3 million acres, partly in California. Trout fishing; big-game hunting, saddle and pack trips, campsites (fees vary), picnicking, winter sports. Berlin-Ichthyosaur State Park, Lake Tahoe, and Mt Charleston Recreation Area are in the forest. Open daily. **FREE**

PLACES TO STAY

If you choose to include an overnight stay in your trip along this Byway, the Mobil Travel Guide recommends the following lodgings.

Reno

★★ **BEST WESTERN AIRPORT PLAZA HOTEL.** *1981 Terminal Way, Reno (89502). Phone 775/348-6370; toll-free 800/780-7234. www.bestwestern.com.* 270 rooms, 3 story. Check-out noon. TV; cable (premium), VCR available. In-room modem link. Restaurant, bar. Room service. In-house fitness room, sauna. Health club privileges. Pool, whirlpool. Airport transportation. Business center. Mini-casino. **$**
🐕 🧍 D ⊠ ⊷

★★★ **ELDORADO HOTEL CASINO.** *345 N Virginia St, Reno (89505). Phone 775/786-5700; toll-free 800/648-5966. www.eldoradoreno.com.* In addition to ten restaurants, extensive gaming facilities, and a sports bar with 80 beers from around the world, guests can enjoy live entertainment and a heated outdoor pool with a sun deck at this casino. 817 rooms, 26 story. Check-out noon. TV. In-room modem link. Restaurant open 24 hours. Bar; entertainment. Room service 24 hours. Health club privileges. Heated pool, whirlpool, poolside service. Garage; free valet parking. Airport transportation. Concierge. Casino. **$**
🧍 D ⊠ ⊷

★★ **FITZGERALD'S CASINO HOTEL.** *255 N Virginia St, Reno (89501). Phone 775/785-3300; toll-free 800/353-LUCK. fitzgeraldsreno.com.* 351 rooms, 16 story. Check-out 11 am. TV. Restaurant open 24 hours. Bar; entertainment. Room service. Free valet parking. Casino. **$**

★★★ **GOLDEN PHOENIX HOTEL AND CASINO.** *255 N Sierra St, Reno (89501). Phone 775/322-1111; toll-free 800/648-1828. www.goldenphoenixreno.com.* Formerly The Flamingo Reno. Located in the heart of downtown Reno, this hotel with views of Reno and the Sierra Mountains holds a 24-hour nonstop casino. There are five restaurants and a fitness center on the property. Golf, a driving range, bowling, horseback riding, and shopping are nearby attractions. 604 rooms, 20 story. Check-out 11 am. TV. In-room modem link. Restaurant open 24 hours. Bar; entertainment. Room service 24 hours. In-house fitness room. Free valet parking. Airport transportation. Business center. Casino. **$**

★★★ **HILTON.** *2500 E Second St, Reno (89595). Phone 775/789-2000; toll-free 800/501-2651. www.renohilton.com.* With a 40,000-square-foot Fun Quest Center and a recreational vehicle park, this casino resort is for the whole family. Other available activities include hang gliding, bungee jumping, sky diving, bowling, a health and fitness center, an aquatic driving range, an indoor golf and sports center, six restaurants, a comedy club, and a swimming pool. 2,000 rooms, 27 story. Check-out 11 am. TV. Restaurant, bar; entertainment. In-house fitness room, massage, sauna, steam room. Pool, whirlpool, poolside service. Free valet parking. Airport transportation. Business center. Casino. **$**

★ **LA QUINTA INN AIRPORT.** *4001 Market St, Reno (89502). Phone 775/348-6100; toll-free 800/742 6081. www.laquinta.com.* 130 rooms, 2 story. Pet accepted, some restrictions. Complimentary continental breakfast. Check-out noon. TV. Pool. Airport transportation. **$**

★★★ **SILVER LEGACY RESORT CASINO.** *407 N Virginia St, Reno (89501). Phone 775/329-4777; toll-free 800/687-8733. www.silverlegacyreno.com.* One of the largest resorts in town, this property has a contemporary décor with Victorian accents. 1,720 rooms, 38 story. Check-out 11 am. TV. Restaurant open 24 hours. Bar. Pool, whirlpool, poolside service. Airport transportation. **$**

★ **VAGABOND INN.** *3131 S Virginia St, Reno (89502). Phone 775/825-7134.* 129 rooms, 2 story. Pet accepted; fee. Complimentary continental breakfast. Check-out 11 am. TV; cable (premium). Health club privileges. Pool. Airport transportation. **$**

Sparks

★★★ **JOHN ASCUAGA'S NUGGET.** *1100 Nugget Ave, Sparks (89431). Phone 775/356-3300; toll-free 800/648-1177. www.janugget.com.* This northern Nevada location has views of the Sierra Nevada mountains. The casino has more than 1,500 slot machines and offers eight restaurants to choose from. The Best in the West Nugget Rib Cook Off is a big draw on Labor Day weekend. 1,407 rooms, 29 story. Check-out 11 am. TV. Restaurant open 24 hours. Bar; entertainment. In-house fitness room, massage. Indoor pool, outdoor pool, whirlpool, poolside service. Free valet parking. Airport transportation. Business center. Concierge. Casino. **$**

★★ JOHN ASCUAGA'S NUGGET COURTYARD.

1100 Nugget Ave, Sparks (89431). Phone 775/356-3300; toll-free 800/648-1177. www.janugget .com/hotel/courtyard.cfm. 157 rooms, 5 story. Check-out 11 am. TV. Health club privileges. Heated pool, poolside service. Free parking. Airport transportation. Wedding chapel. **$**

PLACES TO EAT

A long day of driving is sure to make you hungry. At the end of your journey, take a table at one of the following restaurants.

Reno

★★ BRICKS RESTAURANT AND WINE BAR.

1695 S Virginia St, Reno (89502. Phone 775/786-2277. Continental menu. Closed Sun; major holidays. Lunch, dinner. Bar. **$$**

D

★★ FAMOUS MURPHY'S. *3127 S Virginia St,*
Reno (89502). Phone 775/827-4111. Seafood, steak menu. Closed Sun. Lunch, dinner. Bar. Children's menu. **$$**

D

★★ PALAIS DE JADE. *960 W Moana Ln #107,*
Reno (89509). Phone 775/827-5233. Chinese menu. Closed most major holidays. Lunch, dinner. Bar. **$$**

D

★★ RAPSCALLION. *1555 S Wells Ave, Reno*
(89502). Phone 775/323-1211. Seafood menu. Closed Thanksgiving, Dec 25. Dinner, Sun brunch. Bar. Outdoor seating. **$$**

D

Sparks

★ BLACK BEAR DINER. *235 N McCarren Blvd,*
Sparks (89431). Phone 775/356-1138. American menu. Breakfast, lunch, dinner. Bar. Children's menu. Casual attire. **$**

D

Billy the Kid Trail

✵ NEW MEXICO

Quick Facts

LENGTH: 84 miles.

TIME TO ALLOW: 2 hours.

BEST TIME TO DRIVE: Summer and fall; high season is July and August.

BYWAY TRAVEL INFORMATION: Village of Ruidoso: 505/258-4343; Byway local Web site: www.zianet.com/billythekid.

SPECIAL CONSIDERATIONS: The altitude along this Byway ranges from 6,500 to 7,000 feet above sea level. There are few, if any, seasonal limitations. All of the roadways are paved, and snow is cleared in the wintertime when there is significant accumulation.

BICYCLE/PEDESTRIAN FACILITIES: Sidewalks and bicycle trails are available in some of the communities along the Byway. Some areas of the roadway also have shoulders for pedestrians.

The Lincoln County area surrounding the Billy the Kid Trail is rich in history. It has been home to Billy the Kid, the Lincoln County War, the Mescalero Apache tribe, Kit Carson, "Black Jack" Pershing, the Buffalo Soldiers, the world's richest quarter horse race, and Smokey Bear.

The area is also rich in tradition, as well as in recreational opportunities.

THE BYWAY STORY

The Billy the Kid Trail tells archaeological, cultural, historical, natural, recreational, and scenic stories that make it a unique and treasured Byway.

Archaeological

A fingerprint, carbon-dated to be roughly 28,000 years old, was recently discovered in a cave 70 miles south of Ruidoso in the Tularosa Basin. It is the earliest known evidence of man's presence in North America. Members of the Paleo-Indian cultures converged in the area from 9000 BC to 6000 BC to hunt the woolly mammoth and now-extinct species of bison that roamed the area.

Cultural

While many consider Santa Fe the cultural capital of New Mexico, Lincoln County is more than willing to rival this claim. Spectacular annual events showcase the cultural dynamics along the Billy the Kid Trail throughout the year: you can always find something brewing! From chuck wagon cookouts to arts festivals, from Blues festivals to community concerts, Lincoln County offers year-round cultural enjoyment.

New Mexico

❋ Billy the Kid Trail

Some of the best art in New Mexico can be found in Ruidoso. The Harris Poll has recognized the Ruidoso Art Festival, held each year in late July, as one of the most outstanding juried art shows in the Southwest. The cool pines create a beautiful mountain setting for spectacular art. Over 125 accomplished, professional artists display paintings, drawings, photography, glass, porcelain, woodwork, metalwork, jewelry, batik, pottery, weaving, fabric, leather, and sculpture.

If you have a kick for western cooking and music, be sure to catch the Lincoln County Cowboy Symposium. Held at Ruidoso Downs the second weekend of October, the Symposium gathers the world's finest cowboy poets, musicians, chuck wagon cooks, and artisans.

For a better glimpse at the real West and American Indian cultures, be sure to see the Mescalero Apache Ceremonial Dances. Held during the first week of July, these ceremonial dances celebrate the Apache Spirit.

The cultural qualities of Lincoln County would be unfinished without mentioning the Spencer Theater for the Performing Arts. Opened in 1997, the Spencer Theater creates a year-round venue for world-class performances in theater, music, and dance. An aristocrat among theaters, the $22 million structure is splendid and elegant, yet intimate and welcoming.

Historical

The largely mysterious character of Billy the Kid and many other Old West icons lived in Lincoln County, giving the Byway the flair it has today. Henry McCarty, better known as Bonney or Billy the Kid, is the most well-known person from this area. His involvement in the Lincoln County War ensured that he would be remembered as one of the greatest stories of the Old West.

Billy the Kid is believed to have been born in New York City sometime in 1859 or 1860. His family moved to Indiana, and then to Wichita, Kansas. In 1874, his mother died, and Billy the Kid was placed in foster homes and worked

washing dishes. He soon ran into trouble with the law and was sent to jail, only to escape through the chimney. Billy the Kid wandered from ranch to ranch, and eventually wound up in trouble with the law again when he killed a man at a saloon in Arizona.

When Billy the Kid returned to New Mexico, he and his gang of rustlers became embroiled with the feud going on between James Dolan, John Tunstall, and Alex McSween. The Kid started on Dolan's side, but when he was thrown in jail, he made a deal with Tunstall and became a part of the Regulators, a group that took the law into their own hands after some of their men had been killed.

After the Lincoln County War, Billy the Kid made his living by gambling and rustling cattle. He spent his time eluding the law, usually from Pat Garrett, whose job was to hunt for Billy the Kid. In December 1880, the Kid surrendered to Garrett and was put in jail in Lincoln County. On April 28, 1881, he made his escape to Fort Sumner, only to be followed in July by Garrett. Billy the Kid died in Pete Maxwell's bedroom at the hand of Garrett on July 14, 1881.

One small ferrotype is the only existing authentic photograph of Billy the Kid. Taken by an unknown itinerant photographer outside Beaver Smith's saloon in Old Fort Sumner in 1879, it reveals (as the Las Vegas Gazzette reported in 1880) a young man ". . . about 5 feet 8 or 9 inches tall, slightly built and lithe, weighing about 140; a frank open countenance, looking like a school boy, with the traditional silky fuzz on his upper lip; clear, blue eyes, with a roguish snap about them; light hair and complexion. He is, in all, quite a handsome looking fellow, the only imperfection being two prominent teeth, and he has agreeable and winning ways." The rumpled hat and layers of utilitarian clothing, especially the oversized, open-weave sweater, immediately clash with Hollywood's images of the outlaw. In the photo, he wears a gambler's pinkie ring on his left hand that means he may

118

Map labels

(349) ▲ Carrizo Peak 9,650

To Carrizozo LINCOLN (246) CAPITAN MTS. (246)

(380) Smokey Bear Historical S.P. NATIONAL ▲ Capitan Pk. 10,083

Nogal ◻ Capitan FOREST

(37) (48) (380) ▶ Ft. Stanton Lincoln

Bonito Rio Bonito (220) Lincoln St. Mon. (368)

Apache Ski Area Angus Glencoe (70) (70)(380)

▲ Sierra Blanca 11,973 (532) Alto San Patricio Hondo

(48) Rio Ruidoso Tinnie To Roswell

Ruidoso ◻ Ruidoso Downs

SACRAMENTO MTS. Hollywood Ruidoso Downs & Mus. of the Horse

(70) MESCALERO APACHE IND. RES. N

(244) 0 5 mi 0 5 km

© MapQuest.com, Inc.

see page A21 for color map

---

have cheated at cards. His colt pistol jaunts from his right hip—because the photo was accidentally reversed for many years, people thought the Kid was a lefty. Historians who examined the photo knew that the gun really was on his right hip by looking at the right-loading breech on his Winchester carbine. That's the only way Winchester manufactured them.

The Kid's real name, Henry McCarty, is rather ordinary, but his alias carries a lyrical quality that still gallops across the high plains of our imagination. Of all of America's outlaws, the name of Billy the Kid churns up powerful images and emotions that are forever linked to the Old West.

Natural

A drive along the Billy the Kid Trail not only provides Byway enthusiasts with glimpses into New Mexico's desperado past, but also offers grand views of the natural treasures afforded this region. From towering snowcapped peaks in the Lincoln National Forest to the river bottoms of the Rio Bonito and Rio Ruidoso rivers, the Billy the Kid Trail deals you a royal flush of nature's beauty.

The Lincoln National Forest is host to two prominent mountain ranges, the Sacramento Mountains to the south and the Capitan Mountains to the north. These ranges surround the Billy the Kid Trail and provide natural views guaranteed to beat the house. Each of these mountainous ranges holds towering peaks in an otherwise flat and arid region. Capitan Peak (10,083 feet) and Sierra Blanca (11,973 feet) provide stunning views and are solid bets for viewing wildlife.

Recreational

The Billy the Kid Trail features many recreational opportunities through natural resources as well as man-made recreational features and cultural attractions. The historic district of Lincoln, the Museum of the Horse, Fort Stanton, the Spencer Theater for the Performing Arts, the Ruidoso Downs Race Track, the Smokey Bear Museum and State Park in Capitan, and Ski Apache all lend appeal to the area.

As wild as the West (and kids) can be, the Museum of the Horse is a place the whole family will enjoy. The hands-on displays let kids of all ages get a true feel for history. Visitors can climb in the saddle and sit in the starting gates just like real jockeys, or they can try on period Western clothing and brightly colored jockey silks. Practice your draw (with crayons, that is) at the special children's coloring area.

Scenic

The Billy the Kid Trail travels through a region marked by exceptional natural beauty and diversity. From grassy plains to dense pine forests, the region is known for its stunning views and cool mountain climate. Teeming with fish and wildlife, this area beckons hunters, anglers, skiers, and photographers from around the country. Visually, it is breathtakingly different from the arid desert that surrounds it.

HIGHLIGHTS

Consider taking the following historic tour of Billy the Kid country.

- This tour of Billy the Kid country begins at the **Byway Visitor Center.** The center is located on US Highway 70 in Ruidoso Downs. Spend time here viewing the exhibits and talking with the informative helpers at the center. A gift shop is available here, too.

- Right next door to the Visitors Center is the **Hubbard Museum of the American West.** Here, exhibits, artifacts, and fine art tell of the special history of the area.

- Heading west on US Highway 70, you pass through the village of **Ruidoso,** and then turn north on NM Highway 48. Traveling about 26 miles along NM Highway 48, notice the beautiful Sierra Blanca to the west.

- The next stop of the tour is in **Capitan** at the junction of NM Highway 48 and US Highway 380. Here, the **Smokey Bear Museum and State Park** is a must-see; Smokey is actually buried here. The museum offers exhibits, games, and films about fire safety. Of particular interest is the documentary film about the life of Smokey available at the Park Theater.

- Traveling southeast on US Highway 380, **Fort Stanton** soon appears. The fort itself is not accessible; however, be sure to stop at the Fort Stanton Post Office and speak with Willie Mae Hobbs, an expert about the Fort Stanton area who can direct you to the best places to see. The **Fort Stanton Cemetery and Cave** are definite stops along the tour. If a visit to the cave is in order, plan to spend several hours or camp overnight.

- After Fort Stanton, along US Highway 380, drive southeast until you arrive in the village of **Lincoln.** The Lincoln County War started here, and this is also where Billy the Kid made his last escape. Museums and markers are all over this village that looks almost exactly as it did in the 1850s.

- Wrapping up a visit in Lincoln, finish the Billy the Kid Byway by continuing down US Highway 380 to US Highway 70 in **Hondo.** Then, drive west on US Highway 70 through San Patricio, Glencoe, and back to Ruidoso Downs.

THINGS TO SEE AND DO

Driving along the Billy the Kid Trail will certainly keep your senses engaged, but if you yearn to get out of the car and stretch your legs, or if you'd like to make a mini-vacation out of your trip, check out these attractions along the route.

BILLY THE KID MUSEUM. See *"Things to See and Do" on the Historic Route 66 Byway.*

HUBBARD MUSEUM OF THE AMERICAN WEST. *841 Hwy 70 W, Ruidoso Downs (88346). Phone 505/378-4142. www.hubbardmuseum.org.* Western-themed exhibits relating to cowboys, horses, and pioneer life. Also houses **The Museum of the Horse.** Open daily; closed Thanksgiving, Dec 25. $$$

LINCOLN STATE MONUMENT. *US 380, Ruidoso (88345).* Lincoln was the site of the infamous Lincoln County War and a hangout of Billy the Kid. Several properties have been restored, including the Old Lincoln County Courthouse and the mercantile store of John Tunstall. Guided tours (summer, reservations required). Open daily; closed holidays. $$

OLD DOWLIN MILL. *Sudderth and Paradise Canyon rds, Ruidoso (88345). Phone 505/257-2811; toll-free 800/253-2255. www.historicoldmill .com.* A 20-foot waterwheel still drives a mill that's more than 100 years old.

SKI APACHE RESORT. *NM 532 in Lincoln National Forest, Ruidoso (88345). Phone 505/336-4356; 505/257-9001 (snow report). www.skiapache.com.* The resort has a four-passenger gondola; quad, five triple, two double chairlifts; surface lift; patrol, school, rentals;

snack bars, cafeteria, bar. Fifty-two runs, longest run more than 2 miles; vertical drop 1,900 feet. Open Thanksgiving-Easter, daily. **$$$$**

SMOKEY BEAR HISTORICAL STATE PARK. *118 Smokey Bear Blvd, Capitan (88316). Phone 505/354-2748.* Commemorates the history and development of the national symbol of forest fire prevention. The original Smokey, who was orphaned by a fire raging in the Lincoln National Forest, is buried here within sight of the mountain where he was found. Fire prevention exhibit, film. Open daily; closed Jan 1, Thanksgiving, Dec 25. **$**

SMOKEY BEAR MUSEUM. *102 Smokey Bear Blvd, Capitan (88316). Phone 505/354-2298. www.smokeybear.org/museum/.* Features 1950s memorabilia of this famed fire-fighting bear found in the nearby Capitan Mountains. Open daily; closed holidays. **FREE**

THE SPENCER THEATER FOR THE PERFORMING ARTS. *NM 48, Ruidoso (88345). Phone 505/336-4800; toll-free 888/818-7872. www.spencertheater.com.* Stunning $22 million structure offers 514 seats for professional touring musical and theater productions. Created from 450 tons of Spanish limestone, the building's design calls forth images of pyramids, mountain peaks, and sci-fi star cruisers. Inside are multiple blown-glass installations by Seattle artist Dale Chihuly. Tours (Tues, Thurs). Call for a schedule.

PLACES TO STAY

If you choose to include an overnight stay in your trip along this Byway, Mobil Travel Guide recommends the following lodgings.

Alto

★**HIGH COUNTRY LODGE.** *Hwy 48, Alto (88312). Phone 505/336-4321; toll-free 800/845-7265. www.ruidoso.net.* 32 rooms. No A/C. Pet accepted; fee. Check-out 11 am. TV; cable

(premium). Fireplaces. In-house fitness room, sauna. Game room. Indoor pool, whirlpool. Outdoor tennis. Lawn games. **¢**

Capitan

★ **SMOKEY BEAR MOTEL.** *316 Smokey Bear Blvd, Capitan (88316). Phone 505/354-2253; toll-free 800/766-5392. www.smokeybearmotel.com.* 9 rooms, 1 story. Restaurant. This roadside motel is located in the birthplace of the original Smokey Bear. **$**

★★★**CASA DE PATRON BED AND BREAKFAST INN.** *Hwy 380 E, Lincoln (88338). Phone 505/653-4676; toll-free 800/524-5202. www.casapatron.com.* This inn was the home of Juan Patron, the youngest Speaker of the House in the Territorial Legislature. Legendary figures such as Billy the Kid and Pat Garrett are said to have spent the night here. 5 rooms. No A/C. No room phones. Complimentary full breakfast. Check-out noon, check-in 3-8 pm. Restaurant nearby. Casitas, sauna. Built in 1860; antiques. Totally nonsmoking. **¢**

Mescalero

★★★**INN OF THE MOUNTAIN GODS.** *Caprizo Canyon Rd, Mescalero (88340). Phone 505/464-6173; toll-free 800/545-9011.*

www.innofthemountaingods.com. 253 rooms, 2-5 story. Check-out noon, check-in 4 pm. TV; cable (premium). Dining room, bar; entertainment. Room service. Sauna. Game room. Pool, children's pool, whirlpool, poolside service. 18-hole golf, pro, putting green. Outdoor tennis, lighted courts. Lawn games. Dock; rowboats, paddleboats. Airport transportation. Casino. **$**

Ruidoso

★★**BEST WESTERN SWISS CHALET INN.** *1451 Mechem Dr, Ruidoso (88355). Phone 505/258-3333; toll-free 800/47-SWISS. www.ruidoso.net/swisschalet.* 81 rooms, 2 story. Pet accepted, some restrictions; fee. Check-out noon. TV; cable (premium), VCR available (movies). Restaurant, bar. Room service. Sauna. Indoor pool, whirlpool. On a hilltop. **¢**

★**ENCHANTMENT INN & SUITES.** *307 Hwy 70 W, Ruidoso (88355). Phone 505/378-4051; toll-free 800/435-0280. www.ruidoso.net/enchantment.* 81 rooms, 2 story. Check-out 11 am. TV; cable (premium). Coin laundry. Restaurant, bar. Room service. Indoor pool, whirlpool. **¢**

★**INNSBRUCK LODGE.** *601 Sudderth Dr, Ruidoso (88345). Phone 505/257-4071; toll-free 800/680-4447. www.ruidoso.net/innsbruck.* 48 rooms, 30 with A/C, 18 with shower only, 2 story. Check-out 11 am. TV. **¢**

★**VILLAGE LODGE.** *1000 Mechem Dr, Ruidoso (88345). Phone 505/258-5442; toll-free 800/722-8779. www.villagelodge.com.* 28 rooms, 2 story. Check-out 11 am. TV; cable (premium). **¢**

PLACES TO EAT

A long day of driving is sure to make you hungry. At the end of your journey, try the following restaurant.

★ **SMOKEY BEAR RESTAURANT.** *316 Smokey Bear Blvd, Capitan (88316). Phone 505/354-2253. www.smokeybearmotel.com.* American menu. Breakfast, lunch, dinner. Interesting Western food with a strong local following in a unique setting. **$**

El Camino Real
❋ NEW MEXICO

One of the most important of the historic trails of New Mexico, El Camino Real is not only the first European road in what is now the United States, but for many years it was the longest road in North America. The northern portions of El Camino Real followed the Rio Grande Pueblo Indian Trail, which existed for centuries before the Spanish explorers arrived. The land area along El Camino Real has been a meeting ground of peoples and a haven of cultural diversity through the centuries.

El Camino Real follows the Rio Grande River from the US/Mexico border to Santa Fe. It traverses a land rich in history and culture. The scenic beauty of El Camino Real is as varied and colorful as its culture, history, and people. From the low-lying flatlands of the south to the soaring peaks of the northern mountains, the terrain climbs 10,000 feet in altitude, creating a landscape of dramatic contrasts.

THE BYWAY STORY

El Camino Real tells archaeological, cultural, historical, natural, recreational, and scenic stories that make it a unique and treasured Byway.

Archaeological

Many archaeological attractions are found along El Camino Real in New Mexico. Kuana Pueblo was one of the Rio Grande Valley villages visited by Francisco Vasquez de Coronado in 1540. He called this region the Tiquex Province because its inhabitants spoke a common language, Tiwa. Abandoned before the 1680 Pueblo Revolt against Spanish rule, this large and important site, called the Coronado State Monument, has been excavated and partially restored.

New Mexico

✻ El Camino Real

The San Miguel mission in Santa Fe was established in the early 1600s. Records of its early history were destroyed during the Pueblo Revolt, but the adobe walls were left unharmed. In the early 1700s, the mission walls were reinforced with stone buttresses. An audio presentation is available for visitors.

Over 15,000 petroglyphs (rock drawings) have been carved into the lava rock that covers the mesa west of the Rio Grande. The earliest of these rock drawings were made by prehistoric inhabitants almost 3,000 years ago. Many others were added by Pueblo peoples, and more were added later by Spanish explorers and settlers. This gallery of ancient art is interpreted at Petroglyph National Monument.

Cultural

The cultural landscape along El Camino Real includes a rich variety of people and places. A number of American Indian Pueblos played a significant role in the history of El Camino Real, particularly in establishing trade routes before the arrival of the Spanish. Some Pueblos are open to the public year-round and encourage tourism and recreation. Others are open only by invitation during special events (such as feast day celebrations and dances). In addition, the cultural history of New Mexico and El Camino Real can be enjoyed at a number of museums throughout the Byway, including the Maxwell Museum of Anthropology in Albuquerque and the Geronimo Springs Museum in Truth or Consequences.

Historical

El Camino Real, also called the Royal Highway of the Interior Lands, linked New Mexico with New Spain (Mexico) in the Spanish colonial period (1598-1821), the Mexico national period (1821-1848), and the US Territorial period (1848-1912). El Camino Real ran from Mexico City to Chihuahua City, then crossed the desert to El Paso del Norte on what is now the US-Mexico border. After reaching El Paso del Norte, it more or less paralleled the Rio Grande (called Rio Bravo del Norte) as far as Santa Fe in northern New Mexico.

El Camino Real is one of the most important historic trails in New Mexico. The northern portions of El Camino Real followed the Rio Grande Pueblo Indian Trail, which existed for centuries before the Spanish explorers arrived. This route allowed the Pueblo Indians of New Mexico to have interregional trade with the pre-Columbian Indian civilizations of Mesoamerica. Throughout the Byway, you'll discover many historic places to visit.

Natural

The Lower Sonoran life zone covers much of the southern quarter of El Camino Real. At an altitude below 4,500 feet, these arid flatlands support cholla, prickly pear, creosote, and yucca, along with cottonwood, olive, and cedar trees. The Upper Sonoran life zone, ranging in elevation from 4,500 to 6,500 feet, encompasses the northern two-thirds of New Mexico. As in the Lower Sonoran, cacti and desert grasses thrive, but piñon and oak trees replace the yucca and creosote. In Santa Fe, the Transition zone (6,500 to 8,500 feet) consists of ponderosa pine, oak, juniper, spruce, and Douglas fir.

You'll find many natural features along El Camino Real, including the Sandia Mountains and other mountain ranges, many national forests, and several national wildlife refuges.

Recreational

El Camino Real provides a wealth of recreational sites and facilities for visitors to enjoy. From the Bosque del Apache and Caballo Lake in the south to Cochiti and Isleta lakes in the north, recreational sites lure many outdoor enthusiasts to the Land of Enchantment. Elephant Butte Lake State Park, the largest lake and park in New Mexico, hosts over a million visitors every year.

Scenic

The scenic beauty of the Camino Real is as diverse and colorful as its culture, history, and people. From the low-lying flatlands of the south to the soaring peaks of the northern mountains, the terrain climbs 10,000 feet in altitude, creating a landscape of dramatic contrasts.

HIGHLIGHTS

This El Camino Real must-see tour begins in Santa Fe and continues south to Las Cruces. If you're traveling in the other direction, simply start at the bottom of the list and work your way up.

- The town of **Santa Fe** offers a bevy of sights, sounds, foods, and festivals. Stop for an hour or a week—you'll never tire of the offerings here.

- A visit to **Pecos National Historic Park** just south of Santa Fe is a great stop to learn about 10,000 years of history, including the ancient Pueblo of Pecos, two Spanish colonial missions, and the site of the Civil War battle of Glorieta Pass. Visits to nearby **Bandelier National Monument** and **Fort Union** are also fantastic adventures.

- Venturing south toward Albuquerque, be sure to stop at **Coronado State Park** near **Bernalillo.** Once in **Albuquerque,** stop in at **Petroglyph National Monument** before visiting this rich and diverse city.

- Shortly south of Albuquerque, stop at the **Isleta Pueblo.** Take time to examine the amazing art produced there—a treat best appreciated in person.

- A small side trip will bring a great afternoon at the **Salinas Pueblo Missions National Monument** in Abo. Passing into Soccorro County, the landscape flattens a little, and the Byway is surrounded by National Wildlife refuges, including **Bosque Del Apache** just south of San Antonio and Laborcita.

see page A22 for color map

- Stop in the town of **Truth or Consequences** (T or C, for short), but visit **Fort Carig** first. And don't forget the **Geronimo Springs Museum** in downtown T or C.

- Back on El Camino Real, stop at **Elephant Butte State Park** in Elephant Butte, and then head south toward **Las Cruces.** On Interstate 10, head east toward Alamogordo, where a real treat awaits you at **White Sands National Monument.** Be sure to pick a day when missiles are not being tested, though: the highway is often closed during times of testing. Scheduling information is available by calling the monument. Spending an evening in Las Cruces is a perfect end to the exploration of El Camino Real.

125

THINGS TO SEE AND DO

Driving along El Camino Real will certainly keep your senses engaged, but if you yearn to get out of the car and stretch your legs, or if you'd like to make a mini-vacation out of your trip, check out these attractions along the route.

AGUIRRE SPRING RECREATION SITE. *17 miles E via US 70, 5 miles S on unnumbered road, Las Cruces (88002). Phone 505/525-4300.* Organ Mountain area formed by monzonite intrusions—molten rock beneath the surface. Wearing away of the crust left organ-pipe rock spires. Baylor Pass and Pine Tree hiking trails. Picnicking, camping (centrally located rest rooms; no drinking water). Open daily. **$$**

ALBUQUERQUE BIOLOGICAL PARK. *903 Tenth St SW, Albuquerque (87102). Phone 505/764-6200. www.cabq.gov/biopark/.* The biological park consists of the **Albuquerque Aquarium,** the **Rio Grande Botanic Garden,** and the **Rio Grande Zoo.** The aquarium features a shark tank, eel tunnel, and shrimp boat. The botanic gardens display formal walled gardens and a glass conservatory. The zoo exhibits include koalas, polar bears, sea lions, and shows. Open daily 9 am-5 pm, until 6 pm in summer; closed Jan 1, Thanksgiving, Dec 25. **$$**

ALBUQUERQUE INTERNATIONAL BALLOON FIESTA. *401 Alameda Pl NE, Albuquerque (87103). Phone 505/821-1000.* As many as 100,000 people attend this annual event, the largest of its kind in the world, that fills Albuquerque's blue skies with rainbows of color. You can catch your own balloon rides from **Rainbow Ryders, Inc.** (phone 505/823-1111). Held the first Sat in Oct through the following Sun.

ALBUQUERQUE MUSEUM. *2000 Mountain Rd NW, Albuquerque (87103). Phone 505/243-7255. www.cabq.gov/museum/.* A regional museum of art and history; traveling exhibits; solar-heated building. Across the street from the New Mexico Museum of Natural History and Science. Open Tues-Sun 9 am-5 pm; closed Mon, holidays. **$$**

ATALAYA MOUNTAIN HIKING TRAIL. *Camino Cruz Blanca, Santa Fe (87507).* The Atalaya Mountain Trail, accessible from the parking lot at St. John's College, is one of the most popular and easily accessible hiking trails in Santa Fe. Hikers have the option of taking the longer route (Trail 174), which is approximately 7 miles roundtrip, or parking farther up near the Ponderosa Ridge development and doing a 4.6-mile loop (Trail 170), instead. Both trials eventually join and take you toward the top of Atalaya mountain, a 9,121-foot peak. The first few miles of the trail are relatively easy but become increasingly steep and strenuous as you near the summit of Atalaya Mountain. Hikers who make it to the top are afforded great views of the Rio Grande valley and the city below.

BOSQUE DEL APACHE NATIONAL WILDLIFE REFUGE. *1001 NM 1, San Antonio (87832). Phone 505/835-1828.* A 12-mile self-guided auto tour loop allows visitors to view a variety of wildlife. Also walking trails. Nov-mid-Feb are best viewing months. Visitor center has brochures and exhibits (open daily). Tour loop (open daily; phone for hours and fee).

CABALLO LAKE STATE PARK. *18 miles S on I-25, Truth or Consequences (87901). Phone 505/743-3942.* The Caballo Mountains form a backdrop for this lake. Swimming, windsurfing, water-skiing, fishing (bass, crappie, pike, trout, catfish), boating (ramp); hiking, picnicking, playground, camping (hookups). Open daily. **$$**

CATHEDRAL OF ST. FRANCIS. *Santa Fe (87501). Phone 505/982-5619.* This French Romanesque cathedral was built in 1869 under the direction of Archbishop Lamy, who served as the proto-type for Bishop Latour in Willa Cather's *Death Comes for the Archbishop.* La Conquistadora Chapel, said to be the country's oldest Marian shrine, is here. Tours (summer). Open daily.

CIBOLA NATIONAL FOREST. *2113 Osuna Rd NE, Albuquerque (87113). Phone 505/346-3900.* More than 1.5 million acres located throughout central New Mexico. The park includes Mount

Taylor (11,301 feet), several mountain ranges, and four wilderness areas: **Sandia Mountain, Manzano Mountain, Apache Kid,** and **Withington.** Scenic drives; bighorn sheep in Sandia Mountains. Fishing; hunting, picnicking, and camping (some fees). La Cienega Nature Trail is for the disabled and visually impaired.

CORONADO STATE MONUMENT. *485 Kuaua Rd, Bernalillo (87004). Phone 505/867-5351.* Coronado is said to have camped near this excavated pueblo in 1540 on his famous but unsuccessful quest for the seven golden cities of Cibola. Reconstructed, painted kiva; visitor center devoted to Southwestern culture and the Spanish influence on the area. Picnicking. Open Wed-Mon 8:30 am-5 pm; closed Tues, holidays. **$**

CROSS OF THE MARTYRS. *Paseo de la Loma, Santa Fe (87504). Phone 505/983-2567.* An ideal destination for history buffs and anyone looking for a sensational city view, this large, hilltop cross weighing 76 tons and standing 25 feet tall honors the memory of more than 20 Franciscan priests and numerous Spanish colonists who were killed during the 1680 Pueblo Revolt against Spanish dominion. Dedicated in 1920, this cross shouldn't be confused with the newer one at nearby Fort Marcy Park. Vistas from the old cross include those of the Sangre de Cristo mountain range immediately northeast, the Jemez about 40 miles west, and the Sandias, 50 miles south near Albuquerque.

CULTURAL COMPLEX. *500 N Water St, Las Cruces (88001). Phone 505/541-2155. www.lascruces-culture.org.* Found at the north end of Downtown Mall, includes the **Las Cruces Museum of Fine Art & Culture** and the **Braningan Cultural Center,** which oversees the **Bicentennial Log Cabin Museum.** Developing is a Volunteers Memorial Sculpture Garden, five blocks west of the complex at the Historical Santa Fe Depot in the New Mexico Railroad and Transportation Museum. Call for schedule.

ELEPHANT BUTTE LAKE STATE PARK. *NM 195, Elephant Butte (87935). Phone 505/744-5421.* This 40-mile-long lake was created in 1916 for irrigation; later adapted to hydroelectric power. Swimming, windsurfing, water-skiing, fishing (bass, crappie, pike, catfish), boating (ramp, rentals, slips, mooring, three marinas); hiking, picnicking, playground, concession, restaurant, lodge, camping (hookups), cabins. Open daily. **$$**

✪ **EL RANCHO DE LAS GOLONDRINAS.** *334 Los Pinos Rd, Santa Fe (87505). Phone 505/471-2261. www.golondrinas.org.* This living-history museum is set in a 200-acre rural valley and depicts Spanish colonial life in New Mexico from 1700 to 1900. It was once a stop on El Camino Real and is one of the most historic ranches in the Southwest. Original colonial buildings date from the 18th century, and special festivals and theme weekends offer visitors a glimpse of the music, dance, clothing, crafts, and celebrations of Spanish colonial New Mexico. Open June-Sept Wed-Sun 10 am-4 pm. **$**

FORT SELDEN STATE MONUMENT. *1280 Fort Seldon Rd, Radium Springs (88054). Phone 505/526-8911.* Frontier fort established in 1865. General Douglas MacArthur lived here as a boy (1884-1886) when his father was post commander. Famed Buffalo Soldiers were stationed here. Self-guided, bilingual trail. Visitor center has history exhibits. Picnicking. Open Mon, Wed-Sun; closed winter holidays. **$$**

GADSDEN MUSEUM. *2 miles SW on W Barker Rd, Las Cruces (88005). Phone 505/526-6293.* Native American and Civil War artifacts; paintings; hand-painted china; Santo collection; history of the Gadsden Purchase. Open daily; closed holidays. **$**

GEORGIA O'KEEFFE MUSEUM. *217 Johnson St, Santa Fe (87501). Phone 505/946-1000. www.okeeffemuseum.org.* One of the most important American artists of the 20th century, Georgia O'Keeffe lived and worked at Ghost Ranch near Abiqui for much of her career, drawing inspiration from the colors and forms of the surrounding desert environment. This museum houses the world's largest permanent collection of her artwork and is also dedicated to the study of American Modernism (1890-present), displaying special exhibits of many of her contemporaries. Open July-Oct, daily; Nov-June closed Wed. **$$**

GERONIMO SPRINGS MUSEUM. *211 Main St, Truth or Consequences (87901). Phone 505/894-6600.* Exhibits of Mimbres pottery, fossils, and photographs, as well as articles on local history. Ralph Edwards Room, Apache Room, Hispanic Room, and log cabin. Open Mon-Sat; closed Jan 1, Thanksgiving, Dec 25. **$**

HYDE MEMORIAL STATE PARK. *740 Hyde Park Rd, Santa Fe (87501). Phone 505/983-7175.* Perched 8,500 feet up in the Sangre de Cristo Mountains near the Santa Fe Ski Basin; used as base camp for backpackers and skiers in the Santa Fe National Forests. Cross-country skiing, rentals, picnicking (shelters), playground, concession, camping (electric hookups). Open daily. **$$**

⊞ **INDIAN MARKET.** *125 E Palace Ave, Santa Fe (87501). Phone 505/983-5220. www.swaia.org.* Each year in late August, the Santa Fe Indian Market attracts a swarm of national and international buyers and collectors to the largest and oldest Native American arts show and market in the world. Over 1,200 artists from over 100 North American tribes participate in the show, with around 600 outdoor booths set up in the middle of the ancient Santa Fe Plaza. The market is a great opportunity to meet the artists and buy directly from them instead of going through the usual galleries and other middlemen. Quality of work is stressed, as all sale items are strictly screened for quality and authenticity. Numerous outdoor booths sell food, and the event draws an estimated 100,000 visitors to Santa Fe during the weekend, so make your lodging reservations well in advance.

INDIAN PUEBLO CULTURAL CENTER. *2401 12th St NW, Albuquerque (87192). Phone 505/843-7270. www.indianpueblo.org.* Owned and operated by the 19 Pueblos of New Mexico. Exhibits in the museum tell the story of the Pueblo culture; Pueblo Gallery showcasing handcrafted art; Native American dance and craft demonstrations (weekends). Restaurant. Open daily; closed holidays. **$**

INSTITUTE OF AMERICAN INDIAN ARTS MUSEUM. *108 Cathedral Pl, Santa Fe (87501). Phone 505/983-8900. www.iaiancad.org.* The Institute of American Indian Arts, established in 1962, runs a college in south Santa Fe in addition to a museum just off the Plaza. The museum is the only one in the country dedicated solely to collecting and exhibiting contemporary Native American art, much of it produced by the staff and faculty of the college. Inside, you can view educational films, exhibits of contemporary artists, and outdoor sculptures in an enclosed courtyard. Open June-Sept, Mon-Sat 9 am-5 pm, Sun from 10 am; Oct-May, Mon-Sat 10 am-5 pm, Sun from noon. **$$**

INVITATIONAL ANTIQUE INDIAN ART SHOW. *201 W Marcy, Santa Fe (87501). Phone 505/984-6760.* Sweeney Center. Largest show of its kind in the country. Pre-1935 items; attracts dealers, collectors, museums. Held for two days in mid-Aug.

JONSON GALLERY. *1909 Las Lomas NE, Albuquerque (87131). Phone 505/277-4967. www.unm.edu/˜jonsong/.* This gallery, owned by the University of New Mexico and part of its art museums, houses the archives and work of modernist painter Raymond Jonson (1891-1982) and a few works by his contemporaries. Also has exhibitions on the arts in New Mexico. Open Tues 9 am-8 pm, Wed-Fri 9 am-4 pm; closed Mon, weekends, holidays. **FREE**

LENSIC PERFORMING ARTS CENTER. *211 W San Francisco St, Santa Fe (87501). Phone 505/988-7050. www.lensic.com.* The Lensic Theater is one of Santa Fe's historical

and architectural gems, recently reopened after a full restoration completed in 2001. The structure was first built in 1931 in a Moorish/Spanish Renaissance style and has always been Santa Fe's premiere theater space, having played host to celebrities such as Roy Rogers and Judy Garland over the years. Since reopening, it has provided a constantly changing schedule of quality theater, symphony, and performing arts events.

LORETTO CHAPEL. *207 Old Santa Fe Trl, Santa Fe (87501). Phone 505/984-7971. www.lorettochapel.com.* The Loretto Chapel was built in 1873 and is one of the few non-adobe-style buildings in downtown Santa Fe. Modeled after St. Chapelle cathedral in Paris, it was the first Gothic building built west of the Mississippi. The chapel itself is not particularly impressive, but what draws countless tourists is the miraculous stairway, a 22-feet-high spiral wooden staircase built without any nails or central supports that seems to defy engineering logic. According to legend, the stairway was put together with wooden pegs. It makes two complete 360-degree turns and has 33 steps. Open Mon-Sat 9 am-5 pm, Sun 10:30 am-5 pm; closed Dec 25.

MAXWELL MUSEUM OF ANTHROPOLOGY. *University Blvd and Central Ave, Albuquerque (87131). Phone 505/277-4405. www.unm.edu/~maxwell/.* Permanent and changing exhibits of early man and Native American cultures with an emphasis on the Southwest. Open Tues-Fri 9 am-4 pm, Sat 10 am-4 pm; closed Sun, Mon, holidays. **FREE**

MESILLA. *4100 Dripping Spring Rd, Las Cruces (88011). Phone 505/647-9698. www.oldmesilla.org.* Historic village that briefly served as the Confederate capital of the Territory of Arizona. Billy the Kid stood trial for murder here and escaped. La Mesilla consists of the original plaza and surrounding adobe buildings. There are numerous specialty shops, restaurants, art galleries, and museums.

MINERAL MUSEUM. *801 Leroy Pl, Socorro (87801). Phone 505/835-5154.* More than 12,000 mineral specimens from around the world. Free rock-hounding and prospecting information. Open Mon-Sat. **FREE**

MOUNTAIN MAN RENDEZVOUS AND FESTIVAL. *105 W Palace Ave, Santa Fe (87504). Phone 505/476-5100. www.festivalofthewest.com/mountainman.html.* In early August, costumed mountain men ride into town on horseback for the Museum of New Mexico's annual buffalo roast, part of a large gathering of trappers and traders from the pre-1840 wilderness. Participants sell primitive equipment, tools, and trinkets and compete in period survival skills, such as knife and tomahawk throwing, muzzleloader rifle shooting, cannon firing, storytelling, and foot racing.

MUSEUM OF FINE ARTS. *107 W Palace Ave, Santa Fe (87501). Phone 505/476-5072. www.museumofnewmexico.org.* Designed by Isaac Hamilton Rapp in 1917, the museum is one of Santa Fe's earliest Pueblo revival structures and its oldest art museum. It contains over 20,000 holdings, with an emphasis on Southwest regional art and the artists of Santa Fe and Taos from the early 20th century. The St. Francis Auditorium inside the museum also presents lectures, musical events, plays, and various other performances. Open Tues-Sun 10 am-5 pm. **$$$**

MUSEUM OF GEOLOGY AND INSTITUTE OF METEORITICS METEORITE MUSEUM. *200 Yale Blvd NE, Albuquerque (87106). Phone 505/277-4204.* The Museum of Geology contains numerous samples of ancient plants, minerals, rocks, and animals. The Meteorite Museum has a major collection of more than 550 meteorites. Both museums are part of the University of New Mexico. Open Mon-Fri 9 am-4 pm; closed weekends, holidays. **FREE**

MUSEUM OF INDIAN ARTS AND CULTURE. *710 Camino Lejo, Santa Fe (87505). Phone 505/476-1250. www.miaclab.org/indexfl.html.* When the Spanish arrived in the Southwest in the 16th century, they found many sprawling towns and villages that they referred to as Pueblos, a name that is still used to identify American Indian communities in New Mexico today. The Museum of Indian Arts and Culture houses an extensive collection of historic and contemporary Pueblo art from throughout the Southwest. One of the highlights of the museum is an excellent interpretive section, where you can encounter native Pueblo cultures from the viewpoint and narrative of modern-day Pueblo natives and exhibit designers. The museum itself is housed in a large, adobe-style building that blends architecturally into the surroundings; the museum also houses many outstanding examples of Pueblo textiles, pottery, jewelry, contemporary paintings, and other rotating exhibits. An adjacent building houses the **Laboratory of Anthropology,** which contains an extensive library and supports continuing research into Southwestern archeology and cultural studies. Open Tues-Sun; closed Mon, holidays. **$$**

MUSEUM OF INTERNATIONAL FOLK ART. *706 Camino Lejo, Santa Fe (87502). Phone 505/476-1200. www.moifa.org.* The Museum of International Folk Art, which first opened in 1953, contains more than 120,000 objects, billing itself as the world's largest folk museum dedicated to the study of traditional cultural art. Much of the massive collection was acquired when the late Italian immigrant, architect/designer Alexander Girard donated his 106,000-object collection of toys, figurines, figurative ceramics, miniatures, and religious/ceremonial art, which he had collected from more than 100 countries around the world. In addition to the collection in the Girard wing, you'll also find a large collection of Hispanic art in the Hispanic Heritage Wing, as well as costumes and folk art from many cultures in the Neutrogena Collection. Several smaller collections and major temporary exhibits add to a rich museum experience that can easily take several hours to explore. Two museum shops offer a wide variety of folk-oriented books, clothing, and jewelry to choose from. Open Tues-Sun; closed Mon, holidays. **$$**

NATIONAL ATOMIC MUSEUM. *1905 Mountain Rd NW, Albuquerque (87104). Phone 505/245-2137. www.atomicmuseum.com.* This nuclear energy science center, the nation's only such museum, features exhibits depicting the history of the atomic age, including the Manhattan Project, the Cold War, and the development of nuclear medicine. Replicas of Little Boy and Fat Man, the world's first two atomic weapons deployed in Japan in World War II, fascinate visitors, as do the museum's outdoor exhibits of rockets, missiles, and B-52 and B-29 aircraft. Guided tours and audiovisual presentations are also offered. Open daily 9 am-5 pm; closed holidays. **$**

NATIONAL RADIO ASTRONOMY OBSERVATORY. *1003 Lopez Ville Rd, Socorro (87801). Phone 505/835-7000. www.nrao.edu.* The VLA (very large array) radio telescope consists of 27 separate antennas situated along three arms of railroad track. Self-guided walking tour of grounds and visitor center. Open daily. **FREE**

NEW MEXICO ARTS & CRAFTS FAIR. *5500 San Mateo NE, Albuquerque (87109). Phone 505/884-9043. www.nmartsandcraftsfair.org.* Held at the New Mexico State Fairgrounds. Exhibits and demonstrations by craftsworkers representing Spanish, Native American, and other North American cultures. Artists sell their wares, which range from paintings to sculpture to jewelry. Held the last weekend in June.

NEW MEXICO FARM AND RANCH HERITAGE MUSEUM. *4100 Dripping Springs Rd, Las Cruces (88011). Phone 505/522-4100. museums.state.nm.us/frm/frm.html.* This interactive 47-acre museum brings to life Mexico's 3,000-year history and its farming and ranching life. Hands-on exhibits include plowing, blacksmithing, and cow milking. Outdoor animal and plant life. Open Tues-Sun; closed holidays. **$$**

NEW MEXICO MUSEUM OF NATURAL HISTORY AND SCIENCE. *1801 Mountain Rd NW, Albuquerque (87104). Phone 505/841-2800. museums.state.nm.us/nmmnh/nmmnh.html.* Fans of dinosaurs, fossils, volcanoes, and the like will love this museum, with exhibits on botany, geology, paleontology, and zoology. The LodeStar Astronomy Center gives museum-goers a view of the heavens in its observatory. Also on site are a naturalist center, the Extreme Screen DynaTheater, and a café. Open daily 9 am-5 pm; closed holidays. **$**

NEW MEXICO STATE UNIVERSITY. *University Ave, Las Cruces (88005). Phone 505/646-3221. www.nmsu.edu.* Built in 1888, the university now enrolls 15,500 students. On the 950-acre campus are a history museum (open Tues-Sun; free), an art gallery, and an 18-hole public golf course.

OLDEST HOUSE. *De Vargas St and Old Santa Fe Trl, Santa Fe (87501).* Believed to be pre-Spanish; Oldest House was built by Native Americans more than 800 years ago.

OLD SAN MIGUEL MISSION. *403 El Camino Real NW, Socorro (87801). Phone 505/835-1620.* Restored; south wall was part of the original 1598 mission. Carved ceiling beams and corbels; walls are 5 feet thick. Artifacts are on display in the church office (building south of church, Mon-Fri). Open daily. **FREE**

★ OLD TOWN ALBUQUERQUE. *Old Town and Romero rds, Albuquerque (87102).* The original settlement is one block north of Central Ave, the city's main street, at Rio Grande Blvd. Old Town Plaza retains a lovely Spanish flavor with many interesting shops and restaurants.

PALACE OF THE GOVERNORS. *105 Palace Ave, Santa Fe (87501). Phone 505/476-5100. www.palaceofthegovernors.org.* Built in 1610, this is the oldest public building in continuous use in the US. It was the seat of government in New Mexico for more than 300 years. Lew Wallace, governor of the territory (1878-1881), wrote part of *Ben Hur* here in 1880. It is now a major museum of Southwestern history. The Palace, Museum of Fine Arts, Museum of Indian Arts and Culture, Museum of International Folk Art, and state monuments all make up the Museum of New Mexico. Open Tues-Sun 10 am-5 pm; closed holidays. **$$**

PECOS NATIONAL HISTORICAL PARK. *US 25, Santa Fe (87501). Phone 505/757-6414. www.nps.gov/peco/.* The ruins of Pecos Pueblo lie on a mesa along the Santa Fe Trail that served as a strategic trade route and crossroads between Pueblo and Plains Indian cultures. At its peak, the Pueblo housed a community of as many as 2,000 people, and was occupied for nearly 500 years. When the Spanish arrived, it became an important missionary outpost that continued to be occupied until the 1800s, when its last inhabitants relocated to Jemez Pueblo. Ruins of the original multi-story structures survive in the form of large stone walls and several ceremonial kivas that have been restored. The largest ruins are of two Spanish missionary churches that were destroyed in the Pueblo revolt of 1680. An easy 1.25-mile hike and self-guided tour allows you to explore the ruins at you own pace. The visitor center includes historical exhibits and shows an introductory film covering the area's history. Open daily 8 am-5 pm; closed Dec 25. **$$**

❖ **PETROGLYPH NATIONAL MONUMENT.**
6900 Unser Blvd, Albuquerque (87120). Phone 505/899-0205. www.nps.gov/petr/. This park contains concentrated groups of rock drawings believed to have been carved on lava formations by ancestors of the Pueblo. Three hiking trails wind along the 17-mile escarpment. Open daily 8 am-5 pm; closed Jan 1, Thanksgiving, Dec 25. **$**

RIO GRANDE NATURE CENTER STATE PARK.
2901 Candelaria Rd NW, Albuquerque (87107). Phone 505/344-7240. A glass-enclosed observation room overlooks a 3-acre pond that is home to birds and other wildlife. Interpretive displays on the wildlife of the bosque (cottonwood groves) along the Rio Grande, 2 miles of nature trails. Guided hikes, hands-on activities. Open daily 8 am-5 pm; closed Jan 1, Thanksgiving, Dec 25. **$**

SALINAS PUEBLO MISSIONS NATIONAL MONUMENT. *Approx 75 miles SE of Albuquerque via I-40, NM 337, Socorro (87801). Phone 505/847-2290. www.nps.gov/sapu/.* This monument was established to explore European-Native American contact and the resulting cultural changes. The stabilized ruins of the massive 17th-century missions are basically unaltered, preserving the original design and construction. All three units are open and feature wayside exhibits, trails, and picnic areas (open daily; closed January 1, December 25). Monument Headquarters, one block west of NM 55 on US 60 in Mountainair, has an audiovisual presentation and an exhibit depicting the Salinas story. Open daily; closed January 1, December 25.

SAN ILDEFONSO PUEBLO. *NM 502, Santa Fe (87501). Phone 505/455-3549. www.newmexico.org/culture/pueblo_sanildefonso.html.* This pueblo (population 447) is famous for its beautiful surroundings and its black, red, and polychrome pottery, made famous by Maria Poveka Martinez. A photography permit may be purchased at the visitor center. Various festivals take place here throughout the year. The circular structure with the staircase leading up

to its rim is a kiva, or ceremonial chamber. There are two shops in the Pueblo plaza, and a tribal museum adjoins the governor's office. One-half mile west is a fishing lake. Open daily; closed winter weekends; visitors must register at the visitor center. **$$**

SAN MIGUEL MISSION. *401 Old Santa Fe Trl, Santa Fe (87501). Phone 505/983-3974. www.sdc.org/~smiguel/.* Built in the early 1600s, this is the oldest church in the US still in use. Construction was overseen by Fray Alonso de Benavidez, along with a group of Tlaxcalan Indians from Mexico who did most of the work. The original adobe still remains beneath the stucco walls, and the interior has been restored along with Santa Fe's oldest wooden reredos (altar screen). Church services are still held on Sundays. Open daily; closed holidays. **FREE**

SANTA FE CHILDREN'S MUSEUM. *1050 Old Pecos Trl, Santa Fe (87505). Phone 505/989-8359. www.santafechildrensmuseum.org.* Happy activity fills a creative space that absorbs the attention of children of all ages. Hands-on exhibits invite kids to make magnetic structures, route water streams, create paintings, illustrate cartoon movies, discover plants on a greenhouse scavenger hunt, scale an 18-foot-high climbing wall, use an old-fashioned pitcher pump, and weave beads and fabric on a loom. Local artists and scientists make appearances to teach kids in playful, inventive ways. Especially interesting are regularly scheduled events, like Music Under the Big Top and Ice Cream Sunday. Open Wed-Sat 10 am-5 pm, Sun noon-5 pm; closed Mon, Tues, Dec 25. **$**

SANTA FE NATIONAL FOREST. *1474 Radio Rd, Santa Fe (87501). Phone 505/438-7840; toll-free 800/280-2267. www.fs.fed.us/r3/sfe/.* This forest consists of over 1 1/2 million acres. Fishing is excellent in the Pecos and Jemez rivers and tributary streams. Hiking trails are close to unusual geologic formations. There are hot springs in the Jemez Mountains. Four wilderness areas within the forest total more than 300,000 acres. Campgrounds are provided by the Forest Service at more than 40 locations. There are user fees for many areas.

★ SANTA FE PLAZA. *100 Old Santa Fe Trl, Santa Fe (87501). www.santafeinformation.com.* The Santa Fe Plaza, steeped in a rich history, has been a focal point for commerce and social activities in Santa Fe since the early 17th century. The area is marked by a central tree-lined park surrounded by some of Santa Fe's most important historical landmarks, many of which survive from Spanish colonial times. The most important landmark is the **Palace of the Governors,** which was the original seat of local government and is the oldest public building in the US still in use. Native American artists from nearby Pueblos sell handmade artwork in front of the Palace and at various museums, shops, and dining establishments surround the Plaza, making it the top tourist destination in Santa Fe. Numerous festivals and activities are held in the Plaza throughout the year, including the **Spanish Market** and **Indian Market.**

SANTA FE RODEO. *2801 W Rodeo Rd, Santa Fe (87502). Phone 505/471-4300. www.rodeosantafe.org.* The Santa Fe Rodeo offers the chance to see real live cowboys and bucking broncos in action at the outdoor rodeo fairgrounds. Various professional competitions and public exhibitions open to the public are put on during the brief summer season. Rodeo events generally happen during evening and weekend matinee hours. A downtown rodeo parade takes place in mid-June at the start of the season. **$$$$**

SANTA FE SOUTHERN RAILWAY. *410 Guadalupe St, Santa Fe (87501). Phone 505/989-8600. sfsr.com.* Made famous by the 1940s swing tune "Atchison, Topeka & Santa Fe," a small part of this historical rail line continues as the Santa Fe Southern Railway, which still carries freight and tourists between Santa Fe and nearby Lamy, an 18-mile trip. The start of the route is housed in

the old **Santa Fe Depot,** where you can view vintage railcars and shop for gifts and memorabilia in the original mission-style train depot. Several scenic train rides in authentically restored vintage cars are offered to the public, following the original high desert route to and from Lamy. The rides cater to tourists and range from short scenic roundtrips to longer outings that include picnics, BBQs, and various holiday-themed events, such as the Halloween Highball Train and New Year's Eve Party Train.

★ SANTA FE WINE AND CHILE FIESTA. *551 W Cordova Rd, Santa Fe (87505). Phone 505/438-8060. www.santafewineandchile.org.* Begun in 1991, this wildly popular festival honoring the best in food and drink brings in some 2,000 appreciative fans from around the state and across the country for four days of noshing and sipping on the last weekend in September. Roughly 50 local restaurants and 90 wineries from around the globe team up with a half-dozen or so of America's top celebrity chefs and cookbook authors to present a culinary extravaganza in a variety of venues around town. Wine seminars, cooking demonstrations, special vintners' lunches and dinners, and the gastronomic circus called the Grand Tasting, staged in mammoth tents on the Santa Fe Opera grounds, fill a palate-thrilling schedule. **$$$$**

SANTUARIO DE GUADALUPE. *100 Guadalupe St, Santa Fe (87501). Phone 505/988-2027.* Built in 1781 and the oldest shrine in America dedicated to Our Lady of Guadalupe, the Santuario has been converted into an art and history museum specializing in religious art and iconography. The holdings include a large collection of Northern New Mexican santos (carved wooden saints) and paintings in the Italian Renaissance and Mexican baroque styles. A famous rendering of Our Lady of Guadalupe by renowned Mexican artist Jose de Alzibar is also on display. Open Mon-Fri 9 am-4 pm; May-Oct: Mon-Sat 9 am-4 pm; closed Sun, holidays. **FREE**

SENA PLAZA AND PRINCE PLAZA. *Washington and Palace aves, Santa Fe (87501).* Small shops, formerly old houses, built behind portals and around central patios.

SHIDONI BRONZE FOUNDRY AND GALLERY. *1508 Bishop's Lodge Rd, Santa Fe (87501). Phone 505/988-8001. www.shidoni.com.* A fantastic resource for art collectors and sculptors, Shidoni consists of a bronze foundry, art gallery, and outdoor sculpture garden set in an 8-acre apple orchard 5 miles north of Santa Fe. Artists from around the country come to work at Shidoni's 14,000-square-foot foundry, which is open to the general public for self-guided tours. Explore the lovely sculpture garden during daylight hours or shop for works of bronze and metal in the adjacent gallery. Open Mon-Sat; closed Sun, Thanksgiving, Dec 25.

SKI SANTA FE. *Hyde Park Rd (Hwy 475), Santa Fe (87501). Phone 505/982-4429. www.skisantafe.com.* World-class skiing and snowboarding in the majestic Sangre de Cristo Mountains is only a 20-minute drive from the downtown Santa Fe Plaza. Ski Santa Fe is a family-owned resort catering to skiers and snowboarders of all levels, from beginning to expert. In addition to breathtaking views of the city below, the 12,053-foot summit offers six lifts and 44 runs (20 percent easy, 40 percent more difficult, 40 percent most difficult), with a total of 660 acres of terrain. The longest run is 3 miles, and the mountain offers a vertical drop of 1,700 feet. The average yearly snowfall is 225 inches. A PSIA-certified ski school offers group and private lessons for adults and children, and there are restaurants, rental shops, and a clothing boutique on site. The Chipmunk Corner offers activities and lessons for children ages 4-9. Open late Nov-early Apr, daily. **$$$$**

SPANISH MARKET. *750 Camino Lejo, Santa Fe (87501). Phone 505/983-4038. www.spanishmarket.org.* The rich and colorful Hispanic art traditions of northern New Mexico are celebrated twice a year during Spanish Market, the oldest and largest exhibition and sale of traditional Hispanic art in the US. The smaller winter market in December is held indoors in the Sweeney Convention Center (201 W Marcy St), while the larger summer market occupies the entire Santa Fe Plaza for one weekend in July. During the market, as many as 300 vendors sell and display santos (carved saints), hide paintings, textiles, furniture, jewelry, tinwork, basketry, pottery, bonework, and other locally produced handicrafts reflecting the unique and deeply religious traditional art that still flourishes in this part of New Mexico. Sponsored by the Spanish Colonial Arts Society.

STATE CAPITOL. *Old Santa Fe Trl and Pasco de Peralta, Santa Fe (87501). Phone 505/986-4589.* This unique building, in modified Territorial style, is round and intended to resemble a Zia sun symbol. Self-guided tours. Open Memorial Day-Labor Day, daily; rest of year, Mon-Sat; closed holidays. **FREE**

TELEPHONE PIONEER MUSEUM. *110 4th St NW, Albuquerque (87102). Phone 505/842-2937.* Displays trace the development of the telephone from 1876 to the present. More than 400 types of telephones, plus switchboards, early equipment, and old telephone directories, are available for viewing. Open Mon-Fri 10 am-2 pm; weekends by appointment; closed holidays. **$**

★ **TESUQUE PUEBLO FLEA MARKET.** *Next to the Santa Fe Opera, Santa Fe (87501). Phone 505/995-8626. www.tesuquepuebloflea market.com.* At the Tesuque Pueblo outdoor flea market, you'll find hundreds of vendors offering antiques, gems, jewelry, pottery, rugs, and world folk art of all descriptions at very competitive prices. Plan on devoting a couple of hours to browse all the various treasures and myriad of vendor booths stretching for several acres. Even if you don't buy anything, it's a browser's paradise well worth the 15-minute drive from Santa Fe. Open mid-Mar-Dec, Thurs-Sun.

**THE WHEELWRIGHT MUSEUM OF THE
AMERICAN INDIAN.** *704 Camino Lejo, Santa Fe
(87505). Phone 505/982-4636; toll-free 800/607-
4636. www.wheelwright.org.* Founded in 1937
by Mary Cabot Wheelwright and Navajo
singer/medicine man Hastiin Klah to help
preserve Navajo art and traditions, the
Wheelwright now devotes itself to hosting major
exhibits of Native American artists from tribes
throughout North America. The Case Trading
Post in the basement sells pottery, jewelry,
textiles, books, prints, and other gift items.
Open Mon-Sat 10 am-5 pm, Sun 1-5 pm; closed
holidays. **FREE**

WHITE SANDS MISSILE RANGE. *US 70, Las
Cruces (88005). Phone 505/678-1134.* Missiles
and related equipment are tested here. The
actual range is closed to the public; visitors
are welcome at the outdoor missile park and
museum. Open daily; closed holidays. **FREE**

WHOLE ENCHILADA FIESTA. *Downtown Mall.
Main and Las Cruces sts, Las Cruces (88005).
Phone 505/524-6832.* Street dancing, entertainment, crafts, and food, including the world's
largest enchilada. Held the last weekend in Sept.

ZOZOBRA FESTIVAL. *490 Washington Ave, Santa
Fe (87501).* Each year on the Thursday before
Labor Day, the Kiwanis Club of Santa Fe hosts
the burning of Zozobra, a 50-foot effigy of Old
Man Gloom, whose passing away is designed to
dispel the hardships and travails of the previous
year. As part of the Fiestas celebration, Zozobra
started in 1924 when a local artist conceived a
ritual based on a Yaqui Indian celebration from
Mexico. Over the years, Zozobra caught on and
the crowd sizes have grown, making Zozobra
Santa Fe's largest, most colorful, and most spectacular festival. Lasting for several hours, as
many as 60,000 visitors crowd into a large
grassy field in Fort Marcy Park to listen to live
bands, watch spectacular fireworks displays,
and cheer the ritual burning. Fiestas celebrations continue during the Labor Day weekend,
with all day booths and activities setup in the
nearby Plaza. **$$$**

PLACES TO STAY

If you choose to include an overnight stay in
your trip along this Byway, Mobil Travel Guide
recommends the following lodgings.

Albuquerque

★ **BEST WESTERN WINROCK INN.** *18 NE
Winrock Ctr, Albuquerque (87110). Phone 505/
883-5252; toll-free 800/780-7234. www.bestwestern
.com.* 173 rooms, 2 story. Complimentary break-
fast buffet. Check-out noon. TV. Pool. ¢
🅳🔽〰

★★★ **CASAS DE SUENOS OLD TOWN BED
AND BREAKFAST INN.** *310 Rio Grande Blvd SW,
Albuquerque (87102). Phone 505/247-4560; toll-
free 800/242-8987. www.casasdesuenos.com.*
Situated in the valley of the Sandia Mountains
just three blocks from the historic Old Town
area, this inn features the art of local talents.
Beautiful guest rooms offer private baths, private
entrances, and VCRs. Enjoy breakfast in the
sunny garden room. 17 rooms. Children over 12
years only. Complimentary full breakfast. Check-
out 11 am, check-in 3 pm. TV; cable (premium).
In-room modem link. Totally nonsmoking. ¢
🅳🔽

★ **CLUBHOUSE INN ALBUQUERQUE.** *1315
Menaul Blvd NE, Albuquerque (87107). Phone
505/345-0010; toll-free 800/258-2466. www.
clubhouseinn.com.* 137 rooms, 2 story.
Complimentary breakfast buffet. Check-out
noon. TV; cable (premium). Pool, whirlpool. ¢
🅳🔽�〰

★★ **COURTYARD BY MARRIOTT ALBUQUERQUE
AIRPORT.** *1920 S Yale Blvd, Albuquerque (87106).
Phone 505/843-6600; toll-free 800/321-2211.
www.courtyard.com.* 150 rooms, 4 story. Check-
out noon. TV; cable (premium). In-room
modem link. Restaurant, bar. Room service.
In-house fitness room. Indoor pool, whirlpool.
Downhill, cross-country ski 15 miles. Free
airport transportation. **$**
✈🧍🅳🛗🔽〰

★★**PLAZA INN.** *900 Medical Arts NE, Albuquerque (87102). Phone 505/243-5693; toll-free 800/237-1307. www.plazainnabq.com.* 120 rooms, 5 story. Pet accepted; fee. Check-out noon. TV. Laundry services. Restaurant, bar. In-house fitness room. Health club privileges. Indoor pool, whirlpools. Downhill ski 14 miles. Free airport transportation. ¢

🛏D📶🍽️🏊🏊

★★★**SHERATON OLD TOWN HOTEL.** *800 Rio Grande Blvd NW, Albuquerque (87104). Phone 505/843-6300; toll-free 800/237-2133. www.sheraton.com.* With its large, open lobby and tiled floors, this hotel offers a casual yet elegant environment. Located in historic Old Town across from the New Mexico Museum of Natural History, it is close to over 200 specialty stores. All guest rooms feature furniture hand-made by local artists. 188 rooms, 11 story. Check-out noon. TV; cable (premium). In-room modem link. Restaurant, bar. In-house fitness room. Pool, whirlpool, poolside service. Business center. $

🏊🛏🏊🏊D

Algodones

★**HACIENDA VARGAS B&B.** *431 Hwy 313 Historical El Camino Real, Algodones (87001). Phone 505/867-9115; toll-free 800/261-0006. www.haciendavargas.com.* 7 rooms. No room phones. Complimentary full breakfast. Check-out 11 am, check-in 4 pm. Totally nonsmoking. ¢

📶🏊

Bernalillo

★★★**LA HACIENDA GRANDE.** *21 Baros Ln, Bernalillo (87004). Phone 505/867-1887; toll-free 800/353-1887. www.lahaciendagrande.com.* Cathedral ceilings, beautiful views, and an open-air center courtyard grace this bed-and-breakfast, a hacienda built in the 1750s. 6 rooms. Pet accepted. Complimentary full breakfast. Check-out 11 am, check-in 4-6 pm. TV; cable (premium), VCR available (movies). Downhill,

cross-country ski 15 miles. Concierge. Totally nonsmoking. $

📶🏊🍽️

Las Cruces

★**DAY'S END LODGE.** *755 N Valley Dr, Las Cruces (88005). Phone 505/524-7753.* 32 rooms, 2 story. Complimentary continental breakfast. Check-out 11 am. TV; cable (premium). Pool. ¢

D📶🏊

★**FAIRFIELD INN.** *2101 Summit Ct, Las Cruces (88011). Phone 505/522-6840; toll-free 800/228-2800. www.fairfieldinn.com.* 78 rooms, 3 story. Complimentary continental breakfast. Check-out noon. TV; cable (premium), VCR available. Coin laundry. In-house fitness room. Pool. ¢

🏊D📶SC🏊

★★★**HILTON.** *705 S Telshor Blvd, Las Cruces (88011). Phone 505/522-4300; toll-free 800/445-8667. www.hilton.com.* This hotel is just minutes from New Mexico State University, NASA, the White Sands Missile Range, and Historic Old Mesilla. Activities such as golfing, bowling, horseback riding, and fishing are just minutes away. 203 rooms, 7 story. Pet accepted; fee. Check-out 1 pm. TV; VCR available (movies). In-room modem link. Restaurant, bar; entertainment. Room service. In-house fitness room. Health club privileges. Pool, whirlpool, poolside service. Free airport transportation. Overlooks a valley. ¢

🏊D📶🍽️SC🏊

★★**HOLIDAY INN.** *201 E University Ave, Las Cruces (88005). Phone 505/526-4411; toll-free 800/465-4329. www.holiday-inn.com.* 114 rooms, 2 story. Pet accepted; fee. Check-out noon. TV; cable (premium). Restaurant, bar. Room service. In-house fitness room. Game room. Indoor pool, children's pool. Free airport transportation. The enclosed courtyard re-creates a Mexican plaza. ¢

D📶🍽️SC🏊🏊

★★LUNDEEN INN OF THE ARTS. *618 S Alameda Blvd, Las Cruces (88005). Phone 505/526-3326; toll-free 888/526-3326. www.innofthearts.com.* 21 rooms, 2 story. Pet accepted, some restrictions; fee. Complimentary full breakfast. Check-out 11 am, check-in 4 pm. TV in sitting room; cable (premium), VCR available. Lawn games. Built in 1890; antique furnishings. Art gallery; each room named for an artist. ¢

Mesilla

★★MESON DE MESILLA RESORT HOTEL. *1803 Avenida Demesilla, Mesilla (88046). Phone 505/525-9212; toll-free 800/732-6025. www.mesondemesilla.com.* 15 rooms, 2 story. Pet accepted; fee. Complimentary full breakfast. Check-out 11 am, check-in 1 pm. TV; cable (premium). Restaurant, bar. Pool. Scenic views. Totally nonsmoking. ¢

Santa Fe

★★★ADOBE ABODE. *202 Chapelle St, Santa Fe (87501). Phone 505/983-3133. www.adobeabode .com.* Built in 1905 as officer quarters for Fort Marcy, this hotel offers guests a unique stay in finely decorated rooms. Visitors enjoy the complimentary sherry and Santa Fe cookies in the afternoon. 6 rooms. Complimentary full breakfast. Check-out 11 am, check-in 2 pm. TV; cable (premium). $-$$

★★EL REY INN. *1862 Cerrillos Rd, Santa Fe (87502). Phone 505/982-1931; toll-free 800/521-1349. www.elreyinnsantafe.com.* 86 rooms, 1-2 story. Complimentary continental breakfast. Check-out noon. TV; cable (premium). Some fireplaces. Pool, whirlpool. Sauna. Five minutes from the Plaza. $

★★HOTEL PLAZA REAL. *125 Washington Ave, Santa Fe (87501). Phone 505/988-4900.* 56 rooms, 3 story. Check-out noon. TV; cable (premium). In-room modem link. Restaurant, bar. Downhill, cross-country ski 15 miles. Concierge. Territorial-style architecture; fireplaces, handcrafted Southwestern furniture. $$

★★★★INN OF THE ANASAZI. *113 Washington Ave, Santa Fe (87501). Phone 505/988-3030; toll-free 800/688-8100. www.innoftheanasazi.com.* Native American, Hispanic, and cowboy cultures collide at the Inn of the Anasazi, where a masterful blend of New Mexican legacies results in a stunning and unusual lodging. The true spirit of Santa Fe is captured here, where enormous handcrafted doors open to a world of authentic artwork, carvings, and textiles synonymous with the Southwest. The lobby sets a sense of place for arriving guests with its rough-hewn tables, leather furnishings, unique objects, and huge cactus plants in terracotta pots. Located just off the historic Plaza, the inn was designed to resemble the traditional dwellings of the Anasazi. The region's integrity is maintained in the guest rooms, where fireplaces and four-poster beds reside under ceilings of vigas and latillas, and guests discover toiletries made locally with native cedar extract. 59 rooms, 3 story. Pet accepted; fee. Check-out noon. TV; cable (premium), VCR available. Restaurant. In-house fitness room. Health club privileges. Massage. Downhill ski 13 miles, cross-country ski 7 miles. Valet parking available. Concierge. $$

★★★INN OF THE GOVERNORS. *101 W Alameda, Santa Fe (87501). Phone 505/982-4333; toll-free 800/234-4534. www.innofthegovernors.com.* Guests will enjoy relaxing at the piano bar or around the heated outdoor pool. You can venture into town for shopping, hiking, and fine restaurants and even take in an opera or visit the museums. 100 rooms, 2-3 story. Complimentary continental breakfast. Check-out noon, check-in 4 pm. TV; cable (premium). In-room modem link. Some fireplaces. Restaurant, bar; entertainment. Room service. Pool. Downhill, cross-country ski 14 miles. Concierge. $

★**LUXURY INN.** *3752 Cerrillos Rd, Santa Fe (87505). Phone 505/473-0567; toll-free 800/647-1346.* 51 rooms, 2 story. Complimentary continental breakfast. Check-out 11 am. TV; cable (premium). Pool, whirlpool. ¢

★**PARK INN AND SUITES.** *2907 Cerrillos Rd, Santa Fe (87505). Phone 505/471-3000.* 101 rooms, 2 story. Pet accepted; fee. TV; cable (premium). Restaurant, bar. Game room. Pool. $

★★**QUALITY INN.** *3011 Cerrillos Rd, Santa Fe (87505). Phone 505/471-1211; toll-free 800/228-5151. www.qualityinn.com.* 99 rooms, 2 story. Pet accepted, some restrictions; fee. Check-out noon. TV; cable (premium). Restaurant. Room service. Pool. Airport transportation. ¢

Socorro

★**DAYS INN.** *507 N California Ave, Socorro (87801). Phone 505/835-0230; toll-free 800/ DAYS-INN. www.daysinn.com.* 42 rooms, 2 story. Pet accepted; fee. Check-out 11 am, check-in 3 pm. TV; cable (premium). Restaurant. Room service. Pool. ¢

★**SAN MIGUEL MOTEL.** *916 California Ave NE, Socorro (87801). Phone 505/835-0211; toll-free 800/548-7938.* 40 rooms. Complimentary continental breakfast. Check-out noon. TV; cable (premium). Pool. ¢

Truth or Consequences

★**ACE LODGE AND MOTEL.** *1302 N Date St, Truth or Consequences (87901). Phone 505/894-2151.* 38 rooms. Pet accepted; fee. Check-out 11 am. TV. Restaurant, bar. Pool. Airport transportation. ¢

★**BEST WESTERN HOT SPRINGS MOTOR INN.** *2270 N Date St, Truth or Consequences (87901). Phone 505/894-6665; toll-free 800/780-7234. www.bestwestern.com.* 40 rooms. Check-out noon. TV; cable (premium). Pool. ¢

PLACES TO EAT

A long day of driving is sure to make you hungry. At the end of your journey, take a table at one of the following restaurants.

Albuquerque

★**THE 4TH STREET CAFÉ.** *109 4th St NW, Albuquerque (87102). Phone 505/243-1093.* American, Mexican menu. Closed Sat, Sun; major holidays. Breakfast, lunch. Children's menu. Casual attire. Outdoor seating. $

★**ASSETS GRILL & BREWERY.** *6910 Montgomery Blvd NE, Albuquerque (87109). Phone 505/889-6400.* American menu. Closed Sun; major holidays. Lunch, dinner. Bar. Children's menu. Casual attire. Outdoor seating. $$

★★**BARRY'S OASIS.** *445 Osuna, Albuquerque (87109). Phone 505/884-2324.* Greek, Mediterranean menu. Closed Thanksgiving, Dec 25. Lunch, dinner. Bar. Children's menu. Outdoor seating. $$

★**CERVANTES.** *5801 Gibson SE, Albuquerque (87108). Phone 505/262-2253.* Mexican menu. Closed major holidays. Lunch, dinner. Bar. Casual attire. Outdoor seating. $

★★**CHEF DU JOUR.** *119 San Pasquale SW, Albuquerque (87104). Phone 505/247-8998.* Eclectic/International menu. Menu changes weekly. Closed Sun; major holidays. Lunch, dinner (Fri, Sat). Outdoor seating. Totally nonsmoking. $

★★★**LE CAFÉ MICHE.** *1431 Wyoming Blvd NE, Albuquerque (87112). Phone 505/299-6088. www.lecafemiche.com.* Although the food is a bit old-fashioned—think veal Orloff and chicken cordon bleu—this romantic, candlelit restaurant remains a favorite because of the welcoming ambience and attentive service. French country menu. Closed Sun, Mon (lunch only); major holidays. Lunch, dinner. Totally nonsmoking. **$$$**
D

★★★**SCALO.** *3500 Central Ave SE, Albuquerque (87106). Phone 505/255-8782.* Chef Enrique Guerrero has taken over the kitchen of this northern Italian grill, and he has brought back favorites such as chicken cooked under a brick. Italian menu. Closed most major holidays. Lunch, dinner. Bar. Outdoor seating. Dining areas on several levels. **$$**
D

Bernalillo

★★★**PRAIRIE STAR.** *288 Prairie Star Rd, Bernalillo (87004). Phone 505/867-3327. www.santaanagolf.com.* This casual fine-dining restaurant in the Santa Ana Golf Club has stunning views of the Sandias. Among the kitchen's specialties is game. Continental menu. Closed Mon; Dec 25-Jan 1. Dinner. Bar. **$$**
D

★**RANGE CAFÉ AND BAKERY.** *925 Camino del Pueblo, Bernalillo (87004). Phone 505/867-1700. www.rangecafe.com.* Closed Thanksgiving, Dec 25. Breakfast, lunch, dinner. Bar. Children's menu. Totally nonsmoking. **$$**
D

Las Cruces

★★**CATTLE BARON.** *790 S Telshor, Las Cruces (88011). Phone 505/522-7533.* Closed Thanksgiving, Dec 25. Lunch, dinner. Bar. Children's menu. **$$**
D

★★★**MESON DE MESILLA.** *1803 Avenida de Mesilla, Las Cruces (88005). Phone 505/525-9212. www.mesondemesilla.com.* This romantic restaurant in an adobe-style bed-and-breakfast is a haven of sophisticated dining. The Swiss-trained chef combines continental cuisine with Italian and Southwestern accents to create unusual and delicious menus. Continental menu. Closed Mon; Jan 1, Dec 25. Dinner, Sun brunch. Bar. Guitarist (weekends). **$$$**

Mesilla

★★★**DOUBLE EAGLE.** *308 Calle Guadalupe, Mesilla (88004). Phone 505/523-6700. www.doubleeagledining.com.* This historic restaurant in a 150-year-old house is filled with antiques. The continental menu features beef, seafood, poultry, and game. Lunch, dinner, Sun brunch. Bar. Restored adobe house (1848); Victorian decor, antiques. Outdoor seating. Fountain on patio. **$$**
D

★**EL COMEDOR.** *2190 Avenida de Mesilla, Mesilla (88005). Phone 505/524-7002.* Southwestern menu. Closed Jan 1, Thanksgiving, Dec 25. Breakfast, lunch, dinner. **$**

Santa Fe

★★★**THE ANASAZI.** *113 Washington Ave, Santa Fe (87501). Phone 505/988-3236. www.innoftheanasazi.com.* The creators of memorable cuisine at this Plaza mainstay like to point out that the Navajo definition of Anasazi has come to embody an ancient wisdom that is synonymous with the art of living harmoniously and peacefully with the environment. That philosophy is translated in the colorful Native American weavings, petroglyph-inspired art upon the walls of beautiful rock, and mesmerizing fires that crackle and warm the rooms within this dining favorite. Executive chef Tom Kerpon devotes himself to inventive uses of locally grown, organic products, from cactus and sage to chiles and corn. Contemporary Southwestern menu. Menu changes seasonally. Breakfast, lunch, dinner, Sun brunch. Bar. Classical guitarist (brunch). Children's menu. Casual attire. $$$

D

★★★**COYOTE CAFÉ.** *132 W Water St, Santa Fe (87501). Phone 505/983-1615. www.coyote-cafe.com.* Famed cookbook author and pioneer of Southwestern cuisine Mark Miller has enjoyed nothing but success at this bastion of trendy dining found just a block off the Plaza. Although the menu changes seasonally, patrons are assured of finding a whimsical mingling of the cuisines of New Mexico, Mexico, Cuba, and Spain in all manner of meats, fish, and vegetables, served in inventive dishes. Don't miss the house drink special, a margarita del Maguey. Whether seated in the main dining room (try for a window-side table overlooking the street) or on the festive rooftop Cantina, be sure to relax and soak up the setting, decorated by magnificent folk art and artistic lighting fixtures. New Mexican menu. Dinner. Bar/cantina (May-Oct). Casual attire. Outdoor seating. $$$

D

★**EL COMEDOR.** *727 Cerrillos Rd, Santa Fe (87501). Phone 505/989-7575.* Southwestern menu. Closed Thanksgiving, Dec 25. Breakfast, lunch, dinner. Children's menu. Casual attire. Outdoor seating. $$

D

★**EL FAROL.** *808 Canyon Rd, Santa Fe (87501). Phone 505/983-9912.* Mexican menu. Closed major holidays. Lunch, dinner. Bar. Casual attire. Outdoor seating. $

D

★★★★**GERONIMO.** *724 Canyon Rd, Santa Fe (87501). Phone 505/982-1500. www. geronimorestaurant.com.* Housed in a restored 250-year-old landmark adobe, Geronimo (the name of the restaurant is an ode to the hacienda's original owner, Geronimo Lopez) offers robust Southwestern-spiked global fusion fare in a stunning and cozy space. Owners Cliff Skoglund and Chris Harvey treat each guest like family, and this is a nice family to be a part of. Geronimo is inviting and warm, with a wood-burning, cove-style fireplace; eggshell walls; sheer curtains; tall, rich chocolate- and garnet-leather seating; and local Native American-style sculpture and artwork decorating the walls. It feels like a Georgia O'Keefe painting come to life. It's not just the serene and stylish space that earns Geronimo points with its regulars. The food is remarkable, fusing the distinct culinary influences of Asia, the Southwest, and the Mediterranean. Vibrant flavors, bright colors, and top-notch seasonal regional ingredients come together in perfect harmony. While Geronimo is a great place for dinner, it is also a perfect spot to take a break from gallery hopping around lunchtime. When it's warm outside, sit on the patio for prime Canyon Rd people-watching. Global menu. Lunch, dinner. Bar. Casual attire. Outdoor seating. $$$

D

★★**LITTLE ANITA'S.** *2811 Cerrillos Rd, Santa Fe (87501). Phone 505/473-4505.* Mexican menu. Closed Dec 25. Dinner. Children's menu. Casual attire. $$

D SC

★★**MAÑANA.** *101 W Alameda, Santa Fe (87501). Phone 505/982-4333.* Southwestern/ Californian menu. Breakfast, lunch, dinner. Bar. Piano. Casual attire. Outdoor seating. $$

★★★**THE OLD HOUSE RESTAURANT.** *309 W San Francisco St, Santa Fe (87501). Phone 505/988-4455. www.eldoradohotel.com.* Supping on the culinary genius of chef Martin Rios produces a sensation much like that of falling in love—sweet, seductive, and intensely pleasurable. Taking time to prepare every element in the most fastidious fashion, Rios is known for making all sauces from stock reductions and finishing with butter and cream, and for introducing unexpected flavors in otherwise everyday items. Witness his roasted pork tenderloin, accompanied by sweet potatoes pureed with oranges that he has preserved for nine days, and his duck confit and foie gras in puff pastry with pistachios and cherry-celery compote. Take just a moment from swooning over chilled sweet corn soup and lobster soup with lobster tempura and osetra caviar to enjoy the candlelit stucco room, which is adorned with Mexican folk art and bold, oversized paintings in what is part of one of the city's oldest buildings. Contemporary American menu. Closed Thanksgiving, Dec 25. Dinner. Bar. Children's menu. Casual attire. Valet parking available. **$$$**

D

★★**OLD MEXICO GRILL.** *2434 Cerrillos Rd, Santa Fe (87501). Phone 505/473-0338.* Mexican menu. Closed Labor Day, Thanksgiving, Dec 25. Lunch, dinner. Bar. Casual attire. **$$**

D **SC**

★**PLAZA.** *54 Lincoln Ave, Santa Fe (87501). Phone 505/982-1664.* Continental menu. Closed Thanksgiving, Dec 25. Breakfast, lunch, dinner. Children's menu. Century-old building with many original fixtures; stamped-tin ceiling; photos of early Santa Fe. Casual attire. **$$**

★★★**SANTACAFE.** *231 Washington Ave, Santa Fe (87501). Phone 505/984-1788. www.santacafe.com.* Situated a block from the Plaza in the restored Padre Gallegos House, which was built by a colorful priest and politician from 1857 to 1862, Santacafe has been lauded by the *New York Times* for memorable works in globally influenced fish and meats.

Simple but exquisite dishes include a salad of blood oranges and grapefruit with fennel and celeriac remoullade, shrimp-spinach dumplings in a tahini sauce, filet mignon with persillade and green chile mashed potatoes, and roasted free-range chicken with quinoa and a cranberry-chipotle chutney. Patio seating in warmer weather is divine. American menu. Lunch, dinner. Bar. Landscaped courtyard. Casual attire. Outdoor seating. **$$$**

D

★★**VANESSIE OF SANTA FE.** *434 W San Francisco St, Santa Fe (87501). Phone 505/982-9966.* Continental menu. Closed Easter, Thanksgiving, Dec 25. Dinner. Bar. Piano. Children's menu. Casual attire. **$$$**

D

Truth or Consequences

★★**LOS ARCOS STEAK HOUSE.** *1400 N Date St, Truth or Consequences (87901). Phone 505/894-6200.* Steak menu. Closed Thanksgiving, Dec 25. Dinner. Bar. **$$$**

D

Historic Route 66
❊ NEW MEXICO

Quick Facts

LENGTH: 604 miles.

TIME TO ALLOW: 16 hours.

BEST TIME TO DRIVE: Year-round; high seasons are summer and winter.

BYWAY TRAVEL INFORMATION: New Mexico Route 66 Association: 800/766-4405; New Mexico Department of Tourism: 800/545-2070; Byway local Web site: www.rt66nm.org.

SPECIAL CONSIDERATIONS: In areas of higher altitude, sweaters and jackets are recommended, even in warmer months.

BICYCLE/PEDESTRIAN FACILITIES: Historic Route 66 sometimes parallels I-40, but parts of it are now the same road. In places where the two roads become one, biking is neither encouraged nor particularly safe.

Many of the early curiosities that made Route 66 intriguing to travelers have fallen victim to interstate highways, but you can still see much of the route's character if you leave the beaten path, both around Albuquerque and on other parts of Historic Route 66. On Albuquerque's eastern edge, you can pick up parts of Route 66 at Tijeras Canyon, where a serene and rural atmosphere allows you to leave the big city behind. Other parts of Historic Route 66 lead you to quaint and historic sites, enabling you to catch a glimpse into the past and get a taste for what life was like a few decades ago.

THE BYWAY STORY

Historic Route 66 tells archaeological, cultural, historical, natural, recreational, and scenic stories that make it a unique and treasured Byway.

Archaeological

Petroglyph National Monument along Albuquerque's West Mesa gives you the chance to see amazing images carved by native people and early Spanish settlers. With five volcanic cones, hundreds of archaeological sites, and an estimated 25,000 images carved by the native Pueblos and early Spanish settlers, the monument protects part of the early culture and history of the area for generations to come.

Covering a 17-mile stretch, the Petroglyph National Monument allows the past to come alive; images on the rocks tell the stories of natives and settlers in carvings of animals, people, spirals, stars, and geometric shapes. Perhaps the most famous symbol found at the Petroglyph National Monument is that of Kokopelli, the hump-backed flute player, which is still used as a symbol in modern Pueblo art.

Although no one knows the exact dates the carvings were made, archaeologists have compared the petroglyphs with other artwork of a known date. Some carvings are thought the have been created between AD 1300 and AD 1650; others are closer to 3,000 years old. The most recent are thought to have been created by Spanish settlers during the Spanish colonial period.

Cultural

Abandoned pueblos and museums featuring ancient artwork and dress provide Byway travelers with reminders of the early Native American and Spanish culture that thrived centuries before Europeans reached the continent. The Apache, the Navajo, and some nomadic tribes all inhabited the desert land—some lived in permanent mud-brick settlements near waterways that were called pueblos when first encountered by Spaniards. The word pueblo also refers to an Indian culture that is unique to the Southwest and not to a particular tribe. Although they share many common elements, each pueblo has an independent government, and its own social order, religious practices, and language.

The Pueblo people are further distinguished by their unique art. Each tribe's jewelry, pottery, weavings, and other art have a different style. Black-on-black matte pottery, for example, is unique to the San Ildefonso pueblo. Geometric black and white pots are particular to the Acoma. Other non-Pueblo Indians, such as the Navaho and Apaches, are known for their unique and beautiful artwork as well: the Navajos for their weaving and silverwork; the Apaches for their basket weaving. All native artwork has influenced the architecture and art of the Southwest.

Many tribes have cultural centers, where contemporary artists' work can be viewed and purchased. Museums along the Byway also display ancient artifacts, such as pottery and dress, that brings past cultures a little closer. Visitors are also often allowed on tribal land to tour trading posts, cultural centers, and shops.

Spanish conquest is also much engrained in the early New Mexico's culture. Explorers from Spain in search of riches happened upon the New Mexico area in the early 1540s. Although they didn't find their sought-after gold, they did find thousands of potential Catholic converts: the native people of the area. By 1680, Spanish priests had set up more than 80 missions in the area. Although much of the colonization was peaceful, the Spanish culture and Catholic religion imposed on some tribes led to the Pueblo Revolt of 1680. Indians from all over the area overthrew the settlers, burned churches, and killed priests. The Spanish returned 12 years later and were more attuned to native cultures and religions.

Today's culture is a blend of the Spanish and Native American cultures: Catholicism and indigenous religions, along with festivals and architecture that reflect both cultures. Spanish and Native American art, architecture, and music meshed to create a blend that today is known simply as Southwestern. Mariachi music, pottery, and adobe buildings are cultural reflections of the Southwest that result from a fascinating mixture of many civilizations.

Historical

When incumbent governor A. T. Hannett lost the 1926 New Mexico gubernatorial election to Richard Dillon, he was infuriated over the loss and what he felt was a betrayal by his own party. So he exited with a flamboyant farewell gesture, sending orders to E. B. Bail, the district highway engineer, to assemble all road-building equipment north of US 60 and cut a new road between Santa Rosa and Moriarty before the year (and Hannett's term) ended. Historic Route 66 as we know it today was about to be created.

Prior to building Route 66, a road meandered northeast from Santa Rosa to Romeroville near Las Vegas and then joined US 85. From Santa Fe, it descended La Bajada Hill and continued south through Albuquerque to Los Lunas before heading west toward Gallup. The distance from Santa Rosa to Albuquerque during that time was 195 miles.

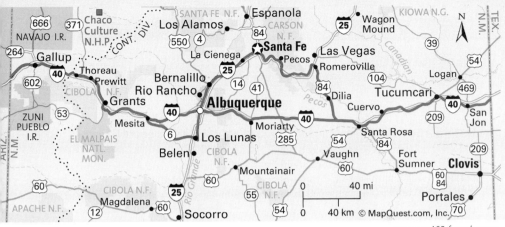

see page A23 for color map

Hannett, in his 1964 book *Sagebrush Lawyer,* recounts that he conceived of the idea of a shorter route by laying a ruler on the map between Santa Rosa and Gallup and saying to a meeting of highway engineers, "Gentlemen, this will be our new highway." Of course, the idea was protested not only by chamber of commerce members in Santa Fe (who led a fight to enlarge and straighten the northern route), but also by delegations from the small towns along US 60, a highway that passed through Vaughn, Encino, Mountainair, and Socorro before heading north to Albuquerque. Business leaders in those towns knew that US 60 would have to compete with the new road, but Hannett prevailed, because the new short-cut would almost halve the distance from Santa Rosa to Albuquerque.

Plunging ahead, Bail, the district highway engineer, realized the near impossibility of the order. Assembling equipment and organizing road crews would take the rest of November, which meant that the actual construction of 69 miles had to be accomplished in just 31 days. The new cutoff would connect the road 7 miles west of Santa Rosa to an existing highway from Moriarty on into Duke City, reducing the distance from 195 miles to 114.

Bail's account of the adventure, first published in 1952 and later appended in *Sagebrush Lawyer,* credits the road crews with marshaling the motley collection of surplus World War I Caterpillars, tractors, and graders "in the late stages of dissolution." They did battle against the blowing snow and dense piñon forests. Irate citizens along the southern and northern routes, upset by the impact that reduced traffic would have on their vital tourist business, tried to sabotage the project. Workers found sugar in gas tanks and sand in their engines. Bail brought in blankets so that the men could sleep next to their equipment at night.

Ironically, no one troubled with the most logical way to put a hitch in the project—by fighting it with a lawsuit. Bail writes, "The one weapon which could have effectively stopped the work was, strangely enough, never used. We tore down fences and cut across pastures without let or hindrance. One property owner threatened us with the law and, so far as memory served, he was the only one in the entire 69 miles to indicate such resistance."

The road was not quite completed by the end of the year, so immediately after taking the oath of office on January 1, 1927, the new governor, Richard Dillon, dispatched an engineer from Santa Fe to halt the venture. However, inclement weather prevented his arrival at the job site before January 3. By then "Hannett's Joke" was complete, and cars drove across the new road. (Hannett denied that his method for accomplishing the project originated as a joke. "I was wide awake to the possibilities of a transcontinental road which would eventually attract a large amount of commercial and tourist trade," he said in *Sagebrush Lawyer.*)

Hannett, whose home base had been Gallup, moved to Albuquerque, practiced law from an office in the Sunshine Building, and wrote a daily column for the *Albuquerque Journal.* Although no monument credits him with the golden thread that helped Albuquerque develop into a metropolitan center, one of the city's streets is named Hannett.

New Mexico

Natural

The Historic Route 66 Scenic Byway is full of natural caves and geological formations. Located throughout the desert, these caves are in unspoiled condition and are open to visitors.

One of the most fascinating natural formations is La Ventana, a large natural arch in the sandstone bluffs on the east side of El Malpais Natural Monument and Conservation Area near Grants. Established in 1987, this monument preserves 114,277 acres, of which 109,260 acres are federal lands. El Malpais means "the badlands," but contrary to its name, this unique area holds many surprises. Volcanic features such as lava flows, cinder cones, pressure ridges, and complex lava tube systems dominate the landscape. Sandstone bluffs and mesas border the eastern side, providing access to vast wilderness.

Another famous and exciting place to visit in El Malpais is the Ice Cave and Bandara Volcano. Nicknamed the Land of Fire and Ice, the two features offer contrasting phenomena: an ancient lava trail winding toward an ice cave on one fork and an erupted volcano on the other. In the ice cave, layers of blue-green ice are up to 20 feet thick and sit in part of a collapsed lava tube, and the temperature never rises above 31 degrees. The Bandara Volcano is 800 feet deep and erupted over 10,000 years ago, leaving a 23-mile lava flow.

Recreational

New Mexico is a land of diversity in culture, climate, and landscape. Evidence of this diversity is everywhere, making the area surrounding the Historic Route 66 the perfect place to find any type of recreation imaginable.

No trip to the area would be complete without dining in one of the authentic Mexican restaurants. Famous for its fiery-hot chili peppers, New Mexican cuisine is an adventure in itself. Mexican food is not all you will find in such a diverse area, however: traditional Native American, Asian, Greek, French, Middle Eastern, and every other conceivable cuisine is available, along with many vegetarian restaurants.

The climate of central New Mexico makes outdoor recreation possible year-round. Summers lend themselves to hiking, camping, biking, and fishing, while New Mexico's winters delight both downhill and cross-country skiers with trails and runs across the state.

The Sandia Mountains, located near Albuquerque, provide exciting recreational opportunities. Travelers enjoy hiking and biking beginner to advanced trails in the summer and skiing the 200 acres of terrain of the Sandia Peak Ski Area in the winter. The ski area's tramway whisks you and your skis or bike to the top of the mountain year-round—just one reason the Sandia Mountains are an excellent place for outdoor adventure.

The geography of the area is unlike any other place. Lush forests, clear lakes, and sporadic mountains break up the desert landscape. Natural caves and rock formations in El Malpais Natural Monument and Conservation Area are open for tourists to view. Erupted volcanoes, bat caves, and sandstone cliffs and mesas dot the beautiful area, providing a truly rare chance to see one of the world's most fascinating regions.

If urban entertainment is what you are looking for, New Mexico has that, too. You may want to catch a symphony, attend a hockey game, or shop in unique outdoor markets. The nightlife heats up as the temperatures cool down after dark. Dance clubs, bars, and live music venues around the larger cities come alive at night.

Scenic

Route 66 is unique in that it embodies plains, grasslands, vistas, mountains, deserts, and virtually every kind of terrain available in New Mexico. The beautiful and varied desert landscape along the Byway, coupled with unique Southwestern architecture, provides an exceptionally scenic drive. The sunsets and sunrises on the Byway are spectacular, and you can see for miles in any direction in most places along the route.

Historic Route 66 is a truly exceptional visual experience. Orange rock dotted with green plantlife rests dramatically against a turquoise-blue sky in summer, creating a postcard-like desert scene. Yet, a few miles down the road, a forest surrounds a bright blue lake, with a waterfall cascading down the dark rock. You'll often find this contrast in this unique geological area: six of the seven life zones identified on Earth are found in New Mexico.

As you approach cities, you'll notice that the architecture of the cities also embodies Southwestern flavor. The stucco and brick buildings are often colorful and particular to the Art Deco style of the 1950s. This style is apparent in the downtown shops, outdoor markets, and residential areas. Even new construction keeps the traditional style alive with colorful buildings of stucco and landscape of cacti and yucca.

HIGHLIGHTS

Because Historic Route 66 is more than 600 miles long, the following must-see tour of the Byway is split into two sections: one starting west of Grants and heading westward into Gallup; the other starting east of Tucumcari and heading westward into Santa Rose.

Western Must-See Tour

• The first stop along this section is just south of McCarty's, off of Exit 96. The **Acoma Sky Pueblo** offers a unique view worth seeing—a city atop a 400-foot mesa. The people of the Acoma Pueblo ask that visitors respect the posted warnings and signs and be respectful of residents. Always ask permission to take photos. Also, if you are fortunate to visit on a celebration day or during a dance, remember that dances are prayers and require concentration. Please do not talk to the dancers, walk on the dance plaza, or applaud when a dance ends.

• The next stop along Route 66 is **El Malpais National Monument** near Grants. The Monument can serve as a central post while visiting several other sites, including **La Ventana Natural Arch, Ice Cave and Bandera Volcano, Inscription Rock,** and **Historic Sands Motel.**

• North of Grants, **Bluewater Lake State Park** offers a relaxing afternoon of hiking and fishing. The **Casamero Pueblo Ruins** near County Road 19 offer a unique view of the area's history. Casamero Pueblo was first recorded by an archaeologist in the mid 1960s. A portion of the site and many smaller sites were reported to have been vandalized prior to this time. Between 1966 and 1975, most of Casamero Pueblo was excavated by archaeologists. In 1976 and 1977, they stabilized the ruins to help prevent deterioration of the walls. Interpretive signs were placed at the site describing the cultural history of the Chacoan Anasazi and the features present at Casamero. The Bureau of Land Management restabilized Casamero Pueblo in 1986, replacing eroded mortar and loose stones. The Casamero Pueblo Ruins is fenced to keep livestock and vehicles from disturbing the site. A parking lot is provided along McKinley County Road 19 for visitors.

• The **Route 66 Drive-In** in Gallup makes a great stop for lunch in keeping with the theme of the drive. Don't forget the **Red Rock Museum** at **Red Rock State Park,** just east of Gallup. Also, while in Gallup, finish your trip along western Route 66 by inquiring about ongoing activities at the Gallup-McKinley County Chamber of Commerce on Montoya Street.

Eastern Must-See Tour

• The modern Route 66 is essentially Interstate 40, although it detours slightly through Tucumcari and Santa Rosa. This section caused quite a lot of trouble back in the early days of Route 66, when the road was narrow and dangerous. This 40-mile stretch of road

heading into Tucumcari was poorly maintained and was full of potholes. Driving long hours through this flat countryside often caused motorists to doze off; hitting an unexpected pothole would cause them to lose control. Many people died in collisions on this narrow road. In fact, some of the older residents in the area will tell you that there were "only six inches and a cigarette paper between you and death on 66." Today, I-40 is wider, safer, and well maintained.

- Once in Tucumcari, take exit 335 into town. Historic Route 66 continues along Tucumcari Blvd. While in Tucumcari, you can easily spend the day shopping or visiting the **Blue Swallow Motel** (the oldest motel in town and one of the most famous along Route 66), **Mesalands Dinosaur Museum,** and **Tucumcari Historical Museum.**

- At the end of Tucumcari Blvd, you can choose one of two routes. This tour takes you north on Route 54 toward Conchas home to **Conchas Lake State Park,** one of New Mexico's largest lakes. The park offers a wide variety of water activities, but onshore exploring offers the potential of finding ancient rock formations and Indian dwellings.

- As you drive south along State Highway 129 toward Newkirk, you'll notice mountains in the distance off to the north. They are home to the **Santa Fe Trail.** Route 66 later follows this trail from Romeroville to Pecos. As you rejoin Route 66 at Newkirk, you may want to take advantage of the rest stop found at the junction. The next nearest public facilities aren't until Santa Rosa.

- Heading farther east along I-40, you pass through **Cuervo,** and head on to **Santa Rosa,** where many activities await you. The **Route 66 Auto Museum** is a must-stop for anyone taking in the true spirit of Route 66. The more adventurous will most likely enjoy a dip at **Blue Hole,** an 81-foot deep clear, natural artesian spring famous for its scuba diving opportunities. A stop at nearby **Santa Rosa Lake State Park** and **Sumner Lake State Park** will give the recreationally minded plenty of choices.

THINGS TO SEE AND DO

Driving along Historic Route 66 will certainly keep your senses engaged, but if you yearn to get out of the car and stretch your legs, or if you'd like to make a mini-vacation out of your trip, check out these attractions along the route.

ACOMA PUEBLO. *NM 23, Grants (87020). Phone toll-free 800/747-0181. www.puebloofacoma.org.* The oldest continuously inhabited pueblo in North America provides a glimpse into well-preserved Native American culture. Tours daily from 8 am. **$$**

ALBUQUERQUE BIOLOGICAL PARK. *903 Tenth St SW, Albuquerque (87102). Phone 505/764-6200. www.cabq.gov/biopark/.* This biological park consists of the **Albuquerque Aquarium,** the **Rio Grande Botanic Garden,** and the **Rio Grande Zoo.** The aquarium features a shark tank, eel tunnel, and shrimp boat. The botanic gardens display formal walled gardens and a glass conservatory. The zoo exhibits include koalas, polar bears, sea lions, and shows. Open daily 9 am-5 pm, until 6 pm in summer; closed Jan 1, Thanksgiving, Dec 25. **$$**

ALBUQUERQUE INTERNATIONAL BALLOON FIESTA. *401 Alameda Pl NE, Albuquerque (87103). Phone 505/821-1000. www.aibf.org.* As many as 100,000 people attend this annual event, the largest of its kind in the world, that fills Albuquerque's blue skies with rainbows of color. Attendees can catch their own balloon rides from **Rainbow Ryders, Inc.** (phone 505/823-1111). Held the first Sat in Oct through the following Sun.

ALBUQUERQUE MUSEUM. *2000 Mountain Rd NW, Albuquerque (87103). Phone 505/243-7255. www.cabq.gov/museum/.* Regional museum of art and history; traveling exhibits; solar-heated building. Across the street from the New Mexico Museum of Natural History and Science. Open Tues-Sun 9 am-5 pm; closed Mon, holidays. **$$**

ATALAYA MOUNTAIN HIKING TRAIL. *Camino Cruz Blanca, Santa Fe (87507).* The Atalaya Mountain Trail, accessible from the parking lot at St. John's College, is one of the most popular and easily accessible hiking trails in Santa Fe. Hikers have the option of taking the longer route (Trail 174), which is approximately 7 miles roundtrip, or parking farther up near the Ponderosa Ridge development and doing a 4.6-mile loop (Trail 170), instead. Both trials eventually join and take you toward the top of Atalaya mountain, a 9,121 feet peak. The first few miles of the trail are relatively easy but become increasingly steep and strenuous as you near the summit of Atalaya Mountain. Hikers who make it to the top are afforded great views of the Rio Grande valley and city below. **FREE**

BILLY THE KID MUSEUM. *1601 E Sumner Ave, Fort Sumner (88435). Phone 505/355-2380. www.billythekidmuseumfortsumner.com.* Contains 60,000 items, including relics of the Old West, Billy the Kid, and Old Fort Sumner. On display is a rifle once owned by Billy the Kid. Open daily; closed the first two weekends Jan, major holidays. **$**

BLUEWATER LAKE STATE PARK. *NM 412, Grants (87020). Phone 505/876-2391. www.emnrd.state.nm.us/nmparks/.* Rolling hills studded with piñon and juniper trees encircle the Bluewater Reservoir. Swimming, water-skiing, fishing (trout, catfish), boating (ramps), picnicking, camping (electrical hookups). Open daily. **$$**

CASAMERO PUEBLO RUINS. *20 miles west of Grants via I-25 and NM 19. Phone 505/761-8700.* Casamero Pueblo was occupied by the Chacoan Anasazi between AD 1000 and 1125 as a community building that served a number of nearby farmsteads. It was used for social and religious activities aimed at uniting individual families into a cohesive community. Casamero is included on the World Heritage List.

CATHEDRAL OF ST. FRANCIS. *Santa Fe (87501). Phone 505/982-5619.* French Romanesque cathedral built in 1869 under the direction of Archbishop Lamy, who served as the prototype for Bishop Latour in Willa Cather's *Death Comes for the Archbishop*. La Conquistadora Chapel, said to be the country's oldest Marian shrine, is here. Tours (summer). Open daily.

CROSS OF THE MARTYRS. *Paseo de la Loma, Santa Fe (87504). Phone 505/983-2567 (the Historic Santa Fe Foundation).* An ideal destination for history buffs and anyone looking for a sensational city view, this large hilltop cross weighing 76 tons and standing 25 feet tall honors the memory of more than 20 Franciscan priests and numerous Spanish colonists who were killed during the 1680 Pueblo Revolt against Spanish dominion. Dedicated in 1920, this cross shouldn't be confused with the newer one at nearby Fort Marcy Park. Vistas from the old cross include those of the Sangre de Cristo mountain range immediately northeast, the Jemez about 40 miles west, and the Sandias, 50 miles south near Albuquerque.

CULTURAL CENTER. *201 US 66 E, Gallup (87301). Phone 505/863-4131. www.southwestindian.com/swIndian/welcome.nsf/subjects/GCC.* Located in a restored historic railroad station; ceremonial gallery, storyteller museum, Indian dances (Memorial Day-Labor Day, evenings), kiva cinema, visitor center, gift shop, and café. Open summer, Mon-Sat; winter, Mon-Fri. **FREE**

EL MALPAIS NATIONAL MONUMENT AND NATIONAL CONSERVATION AREA. *11000 Ice Cave Rd, Grants (87020). Phone 505/783-4774. www.nps.gov/elma/.* These two areas total 376,000 acres of volcanic formations and sandstone canyons. Monument features splatter cones and a 17-mile-long system of lava tubes. The conservation area, which surrounds the monument, includes **La Ventana Natural Arch,** one of the state's largest freestanding natural arches; Cebolla and West Malpais wildernesses; and numerous Anasazi ruins. **The Sandstone Bluffs Overlook,** off NM 117, offers an excellent view of lava-filled valley and the surrounding area. Facilities include hiking, bicycling, scenic drives, primitive camping (acquire Backcountry Permit at Information Center or Ranger Station). The lava is rough; caution is advised. Most lava tubes are accessible only by hiking trails; check with the Information Center in Grants before attempting any hikes. The monument and conservation area are open daily. Information Center and visitor facility on NM 117, open daily; closed Jan 1, Thanksgiving, Dec 25. **FREE**

✪ **EL RANCHO DE LAS GOLONDRINAS.** *334 Los Pinos Rd, Santa Fe (87505). Phone 505/471-2261. www.golondrias.org.* This living-history museum is set in a 200-acre rural valley and depicts Spanish colonial life in New Mexico from 1700 to 1900. It was once a stop on El Camino Real and is one of the most historic ranches in the Southwest. The original colonial buildings date from the 18th century, and special festivals and theme weekends offer visitors a glimpse of the music, dance, clothing, crafts, and celebrations of Spanish colonial New Mexico. Open June-Sept Wed-Sun 10 am-4 pm. **$**

FINE ARTS CENTER. *Stanford Dr and Central Ave, Albuquerque (87102). Phone 505/277-4001.* Houses the **University Art Museum,** which features more than 23,000 pieces in its collection (Tues-Fri, also Sun afternoons; free); the **Fine Arts Library,** which contains the Southwest Music Archives; the **Rodey Theatre;** and the 2,094-seat **Popejoy Hall,** home of the New Mexico Symphony Orchestra and host of the Best of Broadway International Theatre seasons of plays, dance, and music (phone 505/277-2111).

GEORGIA O'KEEFFE MUSEUM. *217 Johnson St, Santa Fe (87501). Phone 505/946-1000. www.okeeffemuseum.org.* One of the most important American artists of the 20th century, Georgia O'Keeffe lived and worked at Ghost Ranch near Abiqui for much of her career, drawing inspiration from the colors and forms of the surrounding desert environment. This museum houses the world's largest permanent collection of her artwork and is also dedicated to the study of American modernism (1890-present), displaying special exhibits of many of her contemporaries. Open July-Oct, daily; Nov-June closed Wed. **$$**

GRZELACHOWSKI TERRITORIAL HOUSE. *Santa Rosa (88435). Phone 505/472-5320.* The store and mercantile were built in 1800; this house was visited frequently by Billy the Kid. Grzelachowski had a major role in the Civil War battle at Glorieta Pass. Open daily, mid-morning-early evening; closed holidays. **FREE**

HYDE MEMORIAL STATE PARK. *740 Hyde Park Rd, Santa Fe (87501). Phone 505/983-7175.* Perched 8,500 feet up in the Sangre de Cristo Mountains near the Santa Fe Ski Basin; used as base camp for backpackers and skiers in the Santa Fe National Forests. Cross-country skiing, rentals, picnicking (shelters), playground, concession, camping (electric hookups). Open daily. **$$**

ICE CAVE AND BANDERA VOLCANO. *Highway 53, 28 miles south west of Grants. Phone toll-free 888-ICE-CAVE. www.icecaves.com.* Excellent example of volcanic activity; hike on lava trails. The ice cave is part of a collapsed lava tube; the temperature never rises above 31 degrees, but reflected sunlight creates beautiful scenery. A historic trading post displays and sells artifacts and Native American artwork. Open daily 8 am-1 hour before sunset. **$$**

 INDIAN MARKET. *125 E Palace Ave, Santa Fe (87501). Phone 505/983-5220. www.swaia.org.* Each year in late August, the Santa Fe Indian Market attracts a swarm of national and international buyers and collectors to the largest and oldest Native American arts show and market in the world. Over 1,200 artists from over 100 North American tribes participate in the show, with around 600 outdoor booths set up in the middle of the ancient Santa Fe Plaza. The market is a great opportunity to meet the artists and buy directly from them instead of going through the usual galleries and other middle-men. Quality of work is stressed, as all sale items are strictly screened for quality and authenticity. Numerous outdoor booths sell food, and the event draws an estimated 100,000 visitors to Santa Fe during the weekend, so make your lodging reservations well in advance.

INDIAN PUEBLO CULTURAL CENTER. *2401 12th St NW, Albuquerque (87192). Phone 505/843-7270; toll-free 800/766-4405. www.indianpueblo.org.* Owned and operated by the 19 Pueblos of New Mexico. Exhibits in the museum tell the story of the Pueblo culture; Pueblo Gallery showcasing handcrafted art; Native American dance and craft demonstrations (weekends). Restaurant. Open daily; closed holidays. **$**

INSCRIPTION ROCK (EL MORRO NATIONAL MONUMENT). *NM 53, Gallup (87301). Phone 505/783-4226.* Here, on the ancient trail taken by the Conquistadores from Santa Fe to Zuni, is the towering cliff that served as the guest book of New Mexico. Don Juan de Oñate carved his name here in 1605; others followed him in 1629 and 1632. Don Diego de Vargas, re-conqueror of New Mexico after the Pueblo Revolt of 1680, registered his passing in 1692, and scores of other Spaniards and Americans added their names to the cliff at later dates. The rock is pale buff Zuni sandstone. The cliff, 200 feet high, has pueblo ruins on its top; pre-Columbian petroglyphs. Visitor center and museum (open daily; closed January 1, December 25; free). Trail (fee), picnic facilities. Primitive camping (fee).

INSTITUTE OF AMERICAN INDIAN ARTS MUSEUM. *108 Cathedral Pl, Santa Fe (87501). Phone 505/983-8900. www.iaiancad.org.* The Institute of American Indian Arts, established in 1962, runs a college in south Santa Fe in addition to a museum just off the Plaza. The museum is the only one in the country dedicated solely to collecting and exhibiting contemporary Native American art, much of it produced by the staff and faculty of the college. Inside, you can view educational films, exhibits of contemporary artists, and outdoor sculptures in an enclosed courtyard. Open June-Sept: Mon-Sat 9 am-5 pm, Sun from 10 am; Oct-May: Mon-Sat 10 am-5 pm, Sun from noon. **$$**

INTER-TRIBAL INDIAN CEREMONIAL. *226 W Coal Ave, Gallup (87301). Phone 505/722-3839.* Red Rock State Park. A major Native American festival; more than 50 tribes from the US, Canada, and Mexico participate in parades, rodeos, games, contests, dances, arts and crafts sales. Second week in Aug.

INVITATIONAL ANTIQUE INDIAN ART SHOW. *201 W Marcy, Santa Fe (87501). Phone 505/984-6760.* Sweeney Center. Largest show of its kind in the country. Pre-1935 items; attracts dealers, collectors, museums. Two days in mid-Aug.

JONSON GALLERY. *1909 Las Lomas NE, Albuquerque (87131). Phone 505/277-4967. www.unm.edu/~jonsong/.* This gallery, owned by the University of New Mexico and part of its art museums, houses the archives and work of modernist painter Raymond Jonson (1891-1982) and a few works by his contemporaries. The gallery also has exhibitions on the arts in New Mexico. Open Tues 9 am-8 pm, Wed-Fri 9 am-4 pm; closed Mon, weekends, holidays. **FREE**

LAGUNA PUEBLO. *Grants (87020). Phone 505/552-6654.* This is one of the 19 pueblos located in the state of New Mexico. The people at Laguna Pueblo (population approximately 7,000) speak the Keresan language. The pueblo consists of six villages: Encinal, Laguna, Mesita, Paguate, Paraje, and Seama. These villages are located along the western boundary of the pueblo. The Laguna Pueblo people sell their arts and crafts on the reservation; items such as Indian belts, pottery, jewelry, baskets, paintings, Indian kilts, and moccasins can be purchased. Visitors are welcomed to the pueblo throughout the year and may encounter various religious observances, some of which are open to the public. However, questions concerning social and religious ceremonies should be directed to the governor of the pueblo. As a general rule, photographs, sketches, and tape recordings of pueblo ceremonials are strictly forbidden. Therefore, it is most important that visitors observe these restrictions and first obtain permission from the governor of the pueblo before engaging in such activities. Fiestas and dances are held throughout the year.

LENSIC PERFORMING ARTS CENTER. *211 W San Francisco St, Santa Fe (87501). Phone 505/988-7050. www.lensic.com.* The Lensic Theater is one of Santa Fe's historical and archi-tectural gems, recently reopened after a full restoration completed in 2001. The structure was first built in 1931 in a Moorish/Spanish Renaissance style and has always been Santa Fe's premiere theater space, having played host to celebrities such as Roy Rogers and Judy Garland over the years. Since reopening, it has provided a constantly changing schedule of quality theater, symphony, and performing arts events.

LORETTO CHAPEL. *207 Old Santa Fe Trl, Santa Fe (87501). Phone 505/984-7971. www.lorettochapel.com.* The Loretto Chapel was built in 1873 and is one of the few non-adobe-style buildings in downtown Santa Fe. Modeled after St. Chapelle cathedral in Paris, it was the first Gothic building built west of the Mississippi. The chapel itself is not particularly impressive, but what draws countless tourists is the miraculous stairway, a 22-feet-high spiral wooden staircase built without any nails or central supports that seems to defy engineering logic. According to legend, the stairway was put together with wooden pegs. It makes two 360-degree turns and has 33 steps. Open Mon-Sat 9 am-5 pm, Sun 10:30 am-5 pm; closed Dec 25.

MAXWELL MUSEUM OF ANTHROPOLOGY. *University Blvd and Central Ave, Albuquerque (87131). Phone 505/277-4405. www.unm.edu/˜maxwell/.* Permanent and changing exhibits of early man and Native American cultures with an emphasis on the Southwest. Open Tues-Fri 9 am-4 pm, Sat 10 am-4 pm; closed Sun, Mon, holidays. **FREE**

MOUNTAIN MAN RENDEZVOUS AND FESTIVAL. *105 W Palace Ave, Santa Fe (87504). Phone 505/476-5100. www.festivalofthewest.com/ mountainman.html.* In early August, costumed mountain men ride into town on horseback for the Museum of New Mexico's annual buffalo roast, part of a large gathering of trappers and traders from the pre-1840 wilderness. Participants sell primitive equipment, tools, and trinkets and compete in period survival skills such as knife and tomahawk throwing, muzzle-loader rifle shooting, cannon firing, storytelling, and foot racing.

MUSEUM OF FINE ARTS. *107 W Palace Ave, Santa Fe (87501). Phone 505/476-5072. www.museumofnewmexico.org.* Designed by Isaac Hamilton Rapp in 1917, the museum is one of Santa Fe's earliest Pueblo revival structures and its oldest art museum. It contains over 20,000 holdings, with an emphasis on Southwest regional art and the artists of Santa Fe and Taos from the early 20th century. The St. Francis Auditorium inside the museum also presents lectures, musical events, plays, and various other performances. Open Tues-Sun 10 am-5 pm. **$$$**

MUSEUM OF GEOLOGY AND INSTITUTE OF METEORITICS METEORITE MUSEUM. *200 Yale Blvd NE, Albuquerque (87106). Phone 505/277-4204.* The Museum of Geology contains numerous samples of ancient plants, minerals, rocks, and animals. The Meteorite Museum has a major collection of more than 550 meteorites. Both museums are part of the University of New Mexico. Open Mon-Fri 9 am-4 pm; closed weekends, holidays. **FREE**

MUSEUM OF INDIAN ARTS AND CULTURE. *710 Camino Lejo, Santa Fe (87505). Phone 505/476-1250. www.miaclab.org/indexfl.html.* When the Spanish arrived in the Southwest in the 16th century, they found many sprawling towns and villages that they referred to as pueblos, a name that is still used to identify American Indian communities in New Mexico today. The Museum of Indian Arts and Culture houses an extensive collection of historic and contemporary Pueblo art from throughout the Southwest. One of the highlights of the museum is an excellent interpretive section, where you can encounter native Pueblo cultures from the viewpoint and narrative of modern-day Pueblo natives and exhibit designers. The museum itself is housed in a large, adobe-style building that blends architecturally into the surroundings; the museum also houses many outstanding examples of Pueblo textiles, pottery, jewelry, contemporary paintings, and other rotating exhibits. An adjacent building houses the **Laboratory of Anthropology,** which contains an extensive library and supports continuing research into Southwestern archeology and cultural studies. Open Tues-Sun; closed Mon, holidays. **$$**

MUSEUM OF INTERNATIONAL FOLK ART. *706 Camino Lejo, Santa Fe (87502). Phone 505/476-1200. www.moifa.org.* The Museum of International Folk Art, which first opened in 1953, contains more than 120,000 objects, billing itself as the world's largest folk museum dedicated to the study of traditional cultural art. Much of the massive collection was acquired when the late Italian immigrant, architect/designer Alexander Girard donated his 106,000-object collection of toys, figurines, figurative ceramics, miniatures, and religious/ceremonial art, which he had collected from more than 100 countries around the world. In addition to the collection in the Girard wing, you'll also find a large collection of Hispanic art in the Hispanic Heritage Wing, as well as costumes and folk art from many cultures in the Neutrogena Collection. Several smaller collections and major temporary exhibits add to a rich museum experience that can easily take several hours to explore. Two museum shops offer a wide variety of folk-oriented books, clothing, and jewelry to choose from. Open Tues-Sun; closed Mon, holidays. **$$**

NATIONAL ATOMIC MUSEUM. *1905 Mountain Rd NW, Albuquerque (87104). Phone 505/245-2137.* This nuclear energy science center, the nation's only such museum, features exhibits depicting the history of the atomic age, including the Manhattan Project, the Cold War, and the development of nuclear medicine. Replicas of Little Boy and Fat Man, the world's first two atomic weapons deployed in Japan in World War II, fascinate visitors, as do the museum's outdoor exhibits of rockets, missiles, and B-52 and B-29 aircraft. Guided tours and audiovisual presentations are also offered. Open daily 9 am-5 pm; closed holidays. **$**

NEW MEXICO MINING MUSEUM. *100 N Iron St, Grants (87020). Phone 505/287-4802; toll-free 800/748-2142.* Only underground uranium mining museum in the world. Indian artifacts and relics; native mineral display. Open Mon-Sat. **$$**

NEW MEXICO MUSEUM OF NATURAL HISTORY AND SCIENCE. *1801 Mountain Rd NW, Albuquerque (87104). Phone 505/841-2800.* Fans of dinosaurs, fossils, volcanoes, and the like will love this museum, with exhibits on botany, geology, paleontology, and zoology. The LodeStar Astronomy Center gives museum-goers a view of the heavens in its observatory. Also on site are a naturalist center, the Extreme Screen DynaTheater, and a café. Open daily 9 am-5 pm; closed holidays. **$**

OLD FORT DAYS. *Santa Rosa (88435).* Held in downtown Santa Rosa, Fort Sumner, and the County Fairgrounds. Includes a parade, rodeo, bank robbery, barbecue, contests, and exhibits. Held the second week in June.

OLDEST HOUSE. *De Vargas St and Old Santa Fe Trl, Santa Fe (87501).* Believed to be pre-Spanish, Oldest House was built by Native Americans more than 800 years ago.

⚒ **OLD TOWN ALBUQUERQUE.** *Old Town and Romero rds, Albuquerque (87102).* The original settlement is one block north of Central Ave, the city's main street, at Rio Grande Blvd. Old Town Plaza retains a lovely Spanish flavor with many interesting shops and restaurants.

PALACE OF THE GOVERNORS. *105 Palace Ave, Santa Fe (87501). Phone 505/476-5100. www.palaceofthegovernors.org.* Built in 1610, this is the oldest public building in continuous use in the US. It was the seat of government in New Mexico for more than 300 years. Lew Wallace, governor of the territory (1878-1881), wrote part of *Ben Hur* here in 1880. It is now a major museum of Southwestern history. The Palace, Museum of Fine Arts, Museum of Indian Arts and Culture, Museum of International Folk Art, and state monuments all make up the Museum of New Mexico. Open Tues-Sun 10 am-5 pm; closed holidays. **$$**

PECOS NATIONAL HISTORICAL PARK. *US 25, Santa Fe (87501). Phone 505/757-6414.* The ruins of Pecos Pueblo lie on a mesa along the Santa Fe Trail that served as a strategic trade route and crossroads between Pueblo and Plains Indian cultures. At its peak, the pueblo housed a community of as many as 2,000 people, and was occupied for nearly 500 years. When the Spanish arrived, it became an important missionary outpost that continued to be occupied until the 1800s, when its last inhabitants relocated to Jemez Pueblo. Ruins of the original multi-story structures survive in the form of large stone walls and several ceremonial kivas that have been restored. The largest ruins are of two Spanish missionary churches that were destroyed in the Pueblo Revolt of 1680. An easy 1.25-mile hike and self-guided tour allows you to explore the ruins at you own pace. The visitor center includes historical exhibits and shows an intro-ductory film covering the area's history. Open daily 8 am-5 pm; closed Dec 25. **$$**

⚒ **PETROGLYPH NATIONAL MONUMENT.** *6900 Unser Blvd, Albuquerque (87120). Phone 505/899-0205.* This park contains concentrated groups of rock drawings believed to have been carved on lava formations by ancestors of the pueblo. Three hiking trails wind along the 17-mile escarpment. Open daily 8 am-5 pm; closed Jan 1, Thanksgiving, Dec 25. **$**

PUERTA DE LUNA. *10 miles S on NM 91, Santa Rosa (88435). Phone 505/472-3763.* Founded in approximately 1862, this Spanish-American town of 250 people practices old customs in living and working.

RED ROCK BALLOON RALLY. *Red Rock State Park, Gallup (87301). Phone 505/722-6274.* Contact Convention and Visitors Bureau for more information. Held the first weekend in Dec.

RED ROCK MUSEUM. *300 W Historic 66 Ave, Gallup (87301). Phone 505/863-1337.* Hopi, Navajo, and Zuni artifacts; gift shop. Open summer, Mon-Sat; winter, Mon-Fri; closed winter holidays. **FREE**

RED ROCK STATE PARK. *Gallup (87301). Phone 505/722-3839.* Desert setting with massive red sandstone buttes. Nature trail, boarding stable. Picnicking, concession, camping (hookups; fee). Interpretive displays, auditorium/convention center, 7,000-seat arena; site of **Inter-Tribal Indian Ceremonial** and rodeos. **FREE**

ROUTE 66 AUTO MUSEUM. *I-40 exit 277, Santa Rosa (88435). Phone 505/472-1966.* Vintage car museum, plus exhibits of Route 66 signs, memorabilia, and toys. Snack bar; gift shop. Open daily 8 am-8 pm. **$**

ROUTE 66 FESTIVAL. *404 W Tumcari Blvd, Tucumcari (88401).* Rodeo, car show, parade, arts and crafts, and entertainment. July.

SANDIA PEAK AERIAL TRAMWAY. *10 Tramway Loop NE, Albuquerque (87122). Phone 505/856-7325.www.sandiapeak.com.* From the base at 6,559 feet, the tram travels almost 3 miles up the west slope of the Sandia Mountains to 10,378 feet, with amazing 11,000-square-mile views. Hiking trail, restaurant at summit, and Mexican grill at base. Open daily 9 am-9 pm in summer, shorter hours rest of year; closed 2 weeks in Apr and 2 weeks in Oct. **$$$$**

SANDIA PEAK SKI AREA. *10 Tramway Loop NE, Albuquerque (87122). Phone 505/242-9133. www. sandiapeak.com.* The ski area has four double chairlifts, surface lift; patrol, school, rentals, snowmaking, café, restaurant, bar. An aerial tramway on the west side of the mountain meets lifts at the top. Longest run is over 2 1/2 miles; vertical drop 1,700 feet. Open mid-Dec-Mar, daily. Chairlift also operates July-Labor Day (Fri-Sun; fee). **$$$$**

SAN ILDEFONSO PUEBLO. *NM 502, Santa Fe (87501). Phone 505/455-3549. www.newmexico .org/culture/pueblo_sanildefonso.html.* This pueblo (population 447) is famous for its beautiful surroundings and its black, red, and polychrome pottery, made famous by Maria Poveka Martinez. A photography permit may be purchased at the visitor center. Various festivals take place here throughout the year. The

circular structure with the staircase leading up to its rim is a kiva, or ceremonial chamber. There are two shops in the pueblo plaza, and a tribal museum adjoins the governor's office. One-half mile west is a fishing lake. Open daily; closed winter weekends; visitors must register at the visitor center. **$$**

SAN MIGUEL MISSION. *401 Old Santa Fe Trl, Santa Fe (87501). Phone 505/983-3974. www.sdc.org/~smiguel/.* Built in the early 1600s, this is the oldest church in the US still in use. Construction was overseen by Fray Alonso de Benavidez, along with a group of Tlaxcalan Indians from Mexico who did most of the work. The original adobe still remains beneath the stucco walls, and the interior has been restored along with Santa Fe's oldest wooden reredos (altar screen). Church services are still held on Sundays. Open daily; closed holidays. **FREE**

SANTA FE CHILDREN'S MUSEUM. *1050 Old Pecos Trl, Santa Fe (87505). Phone 505/989-8359. www.santafechildrensmuseum.org.* Happy activity fills a creative space that absorbs the attention of children of all ages. Hands-on exhibits invite kids to make magnetic structures, route water streams, create paintings, illustrate cartoon movies, discover plants on a greenhouse scavenger hunt, scale an 18-foot-high climbing wall, use an old-fashioned pitcher pump, and weave beads and fabric on a loom. Local artists and scientists make appearances to teach kids in playful, inventive ways. Especially interesting are regularly scheduled events, like Music Under the Big Top and Ice Cream Sunday. Open Wed-Sat 10 am-5 pm, Sun noon-5 pm; closed Mon, Tues, Dec 25. **$**

SANTA FE NATIONAL FOREST. *1474 Radio Rd, Santa Fe (87501). Phone 505/438-7840; toll-free 800/280-2267. www.fs.fed.us/r3/sfe/.* This forest consists of over 1 1/2 million acres. Fishing is excellent in the Pecos and Jemez rivers and tributary streams. Hiking trails are close to unusual geologic formations. There are hot springs in the Jemez Mountains. Four wilderness areas within the forest total more than 300,000 acres. Campgrounds are provided by the Forest Service at more than 40 locations. There are user fees for many areas.

✪ **SANTA FE PLAZA.** *100 Old Santa Fe Trl, Santa Fe (87501). www.santafeinformation.com.* The Santa Fe Plaza, steeped in a rich history, has been a focal point for commerce and social activities in Santa Fe since the early 17th century. The area is marked by a central tree-lined park surrounded by some of Santa Fe's most important historical landmarks, many of which survive from Spanish colonial times. The most important landmark is the **Palace of the Governors,** which was the original seat of local government and is the oldest public building in the US still in use. Native American artists from nearby pueblos sell handmade artwork in front of the Palace and at various museums, shops, and dining establishments surround the Plaza, making it the top tourist destination in Santa Fe. Numerous festivals and activities are held in the Plaza throughout the year, including the **Spanish Market** and **Indian Market.**

SANTA FE RODEO. *2801 W Rodeo Rd, Santa Fe (87502). Phone 505/471-4300. www.rodeosantafe.org.* The Santa Fe Rodeo offers the chance to see real live cowboys and bucking broncos in action at the outdoor rodeo fairgrounds. Various professional competitions and public exhibitions open to the public are put on during the brief summer season. Rodeo events generally happen during evening and weekend matinee hours. A downtown rodeo parade takes place in mid June at the start of the season. **$$$$**

SANTA FE SOUTHERN RAILWAY. *410 Guadalupe St, Santa Fe (87501). Phone 505/989-8600. sfsr.com.* Made famous by the 1940s swing tune "Atchison, Topeka & Santa Fe," a small part of this historical rail line continues as the Santa Fe Southern Railway, which still carries freight and tourists between Santa Fe and nearby Lamy, an 18-mile trip. The start of the route is housed in the old **Santa Fe Depot,** where you can view vintage railcars and shop for gifts and memorabilia in the original mission-style train depot. Several scenic train rides in authentically restored vintage cars are offered to the public, following the original high desert route to and from Lamy. The rides cater to tourists and range from short scenic roundtrips to longer outings that include picnics, BBQs, and various holiday-themed events, such as the Halloween Highball Train and New Year's Eve Party Train.

✪ **SANTA FE WINE AND CHILE FIESTA.** *551 W Cordova Rd, Santa Fe (87505). Phone 505/438-8060. www.santafewineandchile.org.* Begun in 1991, this wildly popular festival honoring the best in food and drink brings in some 2,000 appreciative fans from around the state and across the country for four days of noshing and sipping on the last weekend in September. Roughly 50 local restaurants and 90 wineries from around the globe team up with a half-dozen or so of America's top celebrity chefs and cookbook authors to present a culinary extravaganza in a variety of venues around town. Wine seminars, cooking demonstrations, special vintners' lunches and dinners, and the gastronomic circus called the Grand Tasting, staged in mammoth tents on the Santa Fe Opera grounds, fill a palate-thrilling schedule. **$$$$**

SANTUARIO DE GUADALUPE. *100 Guadalupe St, Santa Fe (87501). Phone 505/988-2027.* Built in 1781 and the oldest shrine in America dedicated to Our Lady of Guadalupe, the Santuario has been converted into an art and history museum specializing in religious art and iconography. The holdings include a large collection of Northern New Mexican santos (carved wooden saints) and paintings in the Italian Renaissance and Mexican baroque styles. A famous rendering of Our Lady of Guadalupe by renowned Mexican artist Jose de Alzibar is also on display. Open Mon-Fri 9 am-4 pm; May-Oct: Mon-Sat 9 am-4 pm; closed Sun, holidays. **FREE**

SENA PLAZA AND PRINCE PLAZA. *Washington and Palace aves, Santa Fe (87501).* Small shops, formerly old houses, built behind portals and around central patios.

SHIDONI BRONZE FOUNDRY AND GALLERY. *1508 Bishop's Lodge Rd, Santa Fe (87501). Phone 505/988-8001. www.shidoni.com.* A fantastic resource for art collectors and sculptors, Shidoni consists of a bronze foundry, art gallery, and outdoor sculpture garden set in an 8-acre apple orchard 5 miles north of Santa Fe. Artists from around the country come to work at Shidoni's 14,000-square-foot foundry, which is open to the general public for self-guided tours. Explore the lovely sculpture garden during daylight hours or shop for works of bronze and metal in the adjacent gallery. Open Mon-Sat; closed Sun, Thanksgiving, Dec 25.

SKI SANTA FE. *Hyde Park Rd (Hwy 475), Santa Fe (87501). Phone 505/982-4429. www.skisantafe.com* World-class skiing and snowboarding in the majestic Sangre de Cristo Mountains is only a 20-minute drive from the downtown Santa Fe Plaza. Ski Santa Fe is a family-owned resort catering to skiers and snowboarders of all levels, from beginning to expert. In addition to breathtaking views of the city below, the 12,053-foot summit offers six lifts and 44 runs (20 percent easy, 40 percent more difficult, 40 percent most difficult), with a total of 660 acres of terrain. The longest run is 3 miles, and the mountain offers a vertical drop of 1,700 feet. The average yearly snowfall is 225 inches. A PSIA-certified ski school offers group and private lessons for adults and children, and there are restaurants, rental shops, and a clothing boutique on site. The Chipmunk Corner offers activities and lessons for children ages 4-9. Open late Nov-early Apr, daily. **$$$$**

SPANISH MARKET. *750 Camino Lejo, Santa Fe (87501). Phone 505/983-4038. www.spanishmarket .org.* The rich and colorful Hispanic art traditions of Northern New Mexico are celebrated twice a year during Spanish Market, the oldest and largest exhibition and sale of traditional Hispanic art in the US. The smaller winter market in December is held indoors in the Sweeney Convention Center (201 W Marcy St), while the larger summer market occupies the entire Santa Fe Plaza for one weekend in July. During the market, as many as 300 vendors sell and display santos (carved saints), hide paintings, textiles, furniture, jewelry, tinwork, basketry, pottery, bone work, and other locally produced handicrafts reflecting the unique and deeply religious traditional art that still flourishes in this part of New Mexico. Sponsored by the Spanish Colonial Arts Society.

STATE CAPITOL. *Old Santa Fe Trl and Pasco de Peralta, Santa Fe (87501). Phone 505/986-4589.* This unique building, in modified Territorial style, is round and intended to resemble a Zia sun symbol. Self-guided tours. Open Memorial Day-Labor Day, daily; rest of year, Mon-Sat; closed holidays. **FREE**

TELEPHONE PIONEER MUSEUM. *110 4th St NW, Albuquerque (87102). Phone 505/842-2937.* Displays trace the development of the telephone from 1876 to the present. More than 400 types of telephones, plus switchboards, early equipment, and old telephone directories, are available for viewing. Open Mon-Fri 10 am-2 pm; weekends by appointment; closed holidays. **$**

✪ **TESUQUE PUEBLO FLEA MARKET.** *Next to the Santa Fe Opera, Santa Fe (87501). Phone 505/995-8626. www.tesuquepuebloof leamarket.com.* At the Tesuque Pueblo outdoor flea market, you'll find hundreds of vendors offering antiques, gems, jewelry, pottery, rugs, and world folk art of all descriptions at very competitive prices. Plan on devoting a couple of hours to browse all the various treasures and myriad of vendor booths stretching for several acres. Even if you don't buy anything, it's a browser's paradise well worth the 15-minute drive from Santa Fe. Open mid-Mar-Dec, Thurs-Sun.

TRES LAGUNAS. *1/4 mile N of Rte 66, E end of town, Santa Rosa (88435).* Fishing, hiking, and nine-hole golf (fee).

TUCUMCARI HISTORICAL MUSEUM. *416 S Adams St, Tucumcari (88401). Phone 505/461-4201. www.cityoftucumcari.com/museum/.* Western Americana; Native American artifacts; gems, minerals, rocks, and fossils; restored fire truck and caboose. Open Tues-Sat 8 am-5 pm, until 6 pm in summer. $

THE WHEELWRIGHT MUSEUM OF THE AMERICAN INDIAN. *704 Camino Lejo, Santa Fe (87505). Phone 505/982-4636; toll-free 800/607-4636. www.wheelwright.org.* Founded in 1937 by Mary Cabot Wheelwright and Navajo singer/medicine man Hastiin Klah to help preserve Navajo art and traditions, the Wheelwright now devotes itself to hosting major exhibits of Native American artists from tribes throughout North America. The Case Trading Post in the basement sells pottery, jewelry, textiles, books, prints, and other gift items. Open Mon-Sat 10 am-5 pm, Sun 1-5 pm; closed holidays. **FREE**

ZOZOBRA FESTIVAL. *490 Washington Ave, Santa Fe (87501).* Each year on the Thursday before Labor Day, the Kiwanis Club of Santa Fe hosts the burning of Zozobra, a 50-foot effigy of Old Man Gloom, whose passing away is designed to dispel the hardships and travails of the previous year. As part of the Fiestas celebration, Zozobra started in 1924 when a local artist conceived a ritual based on a Yaqui Indian celebration from Mexico. Over the years, Zozobra caught on and the crowd sizes have grown, making Zozobra Santa Fe's largest, most colorful, and most spectacular festival. Lasting for several hours, as many as 60,000 visitors crowd into a large grassy field in Fort Marcy Park to listen to live bands, watch spectacular fireworks displays, and cheer the ritual burning. Fiestas celebrations continue during the Labor Day weekend, with all-day booths and activities set up in the nearby Plaza. $$$

PLACES TO STAY

If you choose to include an overnight stay in your trip along this Byway, Mobil Travel Guide recommends the following lodgings.

Albuquerque

★★★ **BRITTANIA W. E. MAUGER ESTATE B&B.** *701 Roma Ave NW, Albuquerque (87102). Phone 505/242-8755; toll-free 800/719-9189. www.maugerbb.com.* "Mi casa es su casa!" is the mantra of this warm bed-and-breakfast located near the business district and Old Town. The guest suites in this restored Queen Anne house offer fresh flowers, antique furniture, and data ports with ISDN Internet connections. 10 rooms (shower only), 3 story. Pet accepted, some restrictions; fee. Complimentary full breakfast. Check-out 11 am, check-in 4-6 pm. TV; cable (premium), VCR available. In-room modem link. Downhill, cross-country ski 12 miles. Sun porch. $

⬛🛍🐾🎿

★★★ **DOUBLETREE HOTEL.** *201 Marquette NW, Albuquerque (87102). Phone 505/247-3344; toll-free 888/223-4113. www.doubletreealbuquerque.com.* Connected to the Albuquerque Convention Center, this hotel is located in the heart of downtown. Many suites offer views of the Sandia Mountains. 295 rooms, 15 story. Check-out noon. TV; cable (premium). Restaurant, bar. In-house fitness room. Health club privileges. Outdoor pool. Downhill ski 15 miles. $

🧍 D 🐾 ➤SC ➤ 🌊

★★ **THE HOTEL BLUE.** *717 NW Central Ave, Albuquerque (87102). Phone 505/294-2400; toll-free 877/878-4868. www.thehotelblue.com.* 135 rooms, 6 story. Complimentary continental breakfast. Check-out noon. TV; cable (premium). In-room modem link. Restaurant, bar. Room service. In-house fitness room. Pool. Airport transportation. ¢

🧍 🌊

★ **HOWARD JOHNSON EXPRESS INN.** *411 Mcknight Ave NW, Albuquerque (87102). Phone 505/242-5228. www.hojo.com.* 100 rooms, 4 story. Complimentary continental breakfast. Check-out noon. TV; cable (premium). Pool, whirlpool. ¢

★★★ **HYATT REGENCY.** *30 Tijeras NW, Albuquerque (87102). Phone 505/842-1234.* Adjacent to the convention center, this hotel is centrally located near Old Town and the Rio Grande Zoo. 395 rooms, 20 story. Check-out noon. TV; cable (premium). Restaurant, bar; entertainment. In-house fitness room, sauna. Health club privileges. Pool, poolside service. Valet parking available. Concierge. $$

★★ **LA POSADA DE ALBUQUERQUE.** *125 2nd St NW, Albuquerque (87102). Phone 505/242-9090; toll-free 800/777-5732. www.laposada-abq.com.* 114 rooms, 10 story. Check-out noon. TV; cable (premium). Restaurant, bar. Downhill ski 15 miles. $

★★ **PLAZA INN.** *900 Medical Arts NE, Albuquerque (87102). Phone 505/243-5693; toll-free 800/237-1307. www.plazainnabq.com.* 120 rooms, 5 story. Pet accepted; fee. Check-out noon. TV. Laundry services. Restaurant, bar. In-house fitness room. Health club privileges. Indoor pool, whirlpools. Downhill ski 14 miles. Free airport transportation. $

Bernalillo

★★★ **LA HACIENDA GRANDE.** *21 Baros Ln, Bernalillo (87004). Phone 505/867-1887; toll-free 800/353-1887. www.lahaciendagrande.com.* Cathedral ceilings, beautiful views, and an open-air center courtyard grace this bed-and-breakfast, a Spanish hacienda built in the 1750s. 6 rooms. Pet accepted. Complimentary full breakfast. Check-out 11 am, check-in 4-6 pm.

TV; cable (premium), VCR available (movies). Downhill, cross-country ski 15 miles. Concierge. Totally nonsmoking. $

Gallup

★ **BEST WESTERN ROYAL HOLIDAY MOTEL.** *1903 W US 66, Gallup (87301). Phone 505/722-4900. www.bestwestern.com.* 50 rooms, 2 story. Complimentary continental breakfast. Check-out 11 am. TV; cable (premium). Indoor pool, whirlpool. ¢

★★ **EL RANCHO.** *1000 E US 66, Gallup (87301). Phone 505/863-9311; toll-free 800/543-6351.* 78 rooms, 2 story. Pet accepted, some restrictions; fee. Complimentary continental breakfast. Check-out 11 am. TV; cable (premium). Laundry services. Pool. ¢

Grants

★★ **BEST WESTERN INN & SUITES.** *1501 E Santa Fe Ave, Grants (87020). Phone 505/287-7901; toll-free 800/780-7234. www.bestwestern.com.* 126 rooms, 2 story. Pet accepted, some restrictions; fee. Check-out noon. TV; cable (premium). Laundry services. Restaurant, bar. Room service. Sauna. Game room. Indoor pool, whirlpool. ¢

Santa Fe

★★★ **ALEXANDER'S INN.** *529 E Palace Ave, Santa Fe (87501). Phone 505/986-1431; toll-free 888/321-5123. www.alexanders-inn.com.* Only a short walk to shopping, restaurants, and galleries, this inn, built in 1903, maintains a quiet and peaceful atmosphere. The rooms are elegant, with hardwood floors and stained-glass windows or lace curtains. 16 rooms, 2 story. Pet accepted; fee. Complimentary continental breakfast. Check-out 11 am, check-in by arrangement. TV; VCR available. Whirlpool. Cross-country ski

10 miles. Concierge. Five rooms in renovated house built in 1903. Totally nonsmoking. **$**

★★ **DANCING GROUND OF THE SUN.** *711 Paseo De Peralta, Santa Fe (87501). Phone 505/986-9797; toll-free 800/745-9910. www. dancingground.com.* 5 casitas, 5 rooms, 2 story. Complimentary continental breakfast. Check-out 11 am, check-in 3-6 pm. TV. Concierge. Totally nonsmoking. **$**

★★★ **FORT MARCY SUITES.** *320 Artist Rd, Santa Fe (87501). Phone 505/982-6636; toll-free 800/745-9910. www.territorialinn.com.* This charming Victorian home is located one block from the historic Plaza. Eight rooms offer private baths, and all feature queen-size beds, alarm clocks, telephones, voice mail, and cable television. Relax in the rose garden or in the hot tub. 10 rooms, 1 with shower only, 2 share bath, 2 story. Children over 10 years only. Complimentary continental breakfast. Check-out 11 am, check-in 3 pm. TV; cable (premium). Some fireplaces. Downhill, cross-country ski 15 miles. The house (circa 1895) blends New Mexico's stone and adobe architecture with pitched roof, Victorian-style interior; sitting room, antiques; garden and tree-shaded lawns more typical of buildings in the East. **$**

★★★ **HOTEL ST. FRANCIS.** *210 Don Gaspar Ave, Santa Fe (87501). Phone 505/983-5700; toll-free 800/529-5700. www.territorialinn.com.* Part of the Historic Inns of America, this hotel was built in 1880 and then rebuilt in 1923 after a fire in 1922. Each room has a high ceiling and original windows, and some rooms have mountain views. The inn is one block from the historic Plaza and close to museums, shops, and galleries. Afternoon tea service is available. 83 rooms, 3 story. Check-out 11 am. TV. In-room modem link. Restaurant, bar. Room service. Downhill ski 15 miles. Concierge. **$**

★★★★ **INN OF THE ANASAZI.** *113 Washington Ave, Santa Fe (87501). Phone 505/988-3030; toll-free 800/688-8100. www.innoftheanasazi.com.* Native American, Hispanic, and cowboy cultures collide at the Inn of the Anasazi, where a masterful blend of New Mexican legacies results in a stunning and unusual lodging. The true spirit of Santa Fe is captured here, where enormous handcrafted doors open to a world of authentic artwork, carvings, and textiles synonymous with the Southwest. The lobby sets a sense of place for arriving guests with its rough-hewn tables, leather furnishings, unique objects, and huge cactus plants in terracotta pots. Located just off the historic Plaza, the inn was designed to resemble the traditional dwellings of the Anasazi. The region's integrity is maintained in the guest rooms, where fireplaces and four-poster beds reside under ceilings of vigas and latillas, and guests discover toiletries made locally with native cedar extract. 59 rooms, 3 story. Pet accepted; fee. Valet parking available. Check-out noon. TV; cable (premium), VCR available. Restaurant. In-house fitness room. Health club privileges. Massage. Downhill ski 13 miles, cross-country ski 7 miles. Concierge. **$$**

★★★ **LA POSADA DE SANTA FE RESORT AND SPA.** *330 E Palace Ave, Santa Fe (87501). Phone 505/986-0000; toll-free 800/727-5276. www.laposadadesantafe.com.* Scattered over six beautifully landscaped acres, this hotel resembles a pueblo with its many cottages, secluded patios, and bubbling fountains. The handsome public rooms in the historic Stabb House have been lovingly restored. 119 rooms, 1-2 story. Check-out noon. TV; cable (premium). Many fireplaces. Restaurant, bar. Room service. Pool, poolside service. Downhill, cross-country ski 15 miles. Concierge. Adobe casitas surround this Victorian/Second Empire Staab mansion (1882); guest rooms are either Pueblo Revival or Victorian in style. **$$**

★★ PUEBLO BONITO BED AND BREAKFAST INN. *138 W Manhattan Ave, Santa Fe (87501). Phone 505/984-8001; toll-free 800/461-4599. www.pueblobonitoinn.com.* 18 rooms, 1-2 story. No A/C. Complimentary buffet breakfast. Check-out noon, check-in 2 pm. TV. Fireplaces. **$**

★★ RADISSON SANTA FE. *750 N St Francis Dr, Santa Fe (87501). Phone 505/992-5800; toll-free 800/333-3333. www.radisson.com.* This beautifully landscaped hilltop hotel is centrally located near the city's major attractions. Guests enjoy the large swimming pool and hot tub as well as complimentary access to the next-door Santa Fe Spa. One- and two-bedroom condos offer kiva fireplaces and full kitchens. 141 rooms, 2 story. Check-out noon. TV; cable (premium). Restaurant, bar; entertainment. Room service. Pool, poolside service. **$**

Santa Rosa

★ HOLIDAY INN EXPRESS. *3202 Will Rogers Dr, Santa Rosa (88435). Phone 505/472-5411. www.holiday-inn.com.* 67 rooms, 2 story. Check-out 10 am. TV. Pool. **¢**

★ LA QUINTA INN. *1701 Will Rogers Dr, Santa Rosa (88435). Phone 505/472-4800; toll-free 888/298-2054. www.laquinta.com.* 60 rooms, 2 story. Pet accepted. Complimentary continental breakfast. TV; VCR available (movies). In-room modem link. Indoor pool, whirlpool. **¢**

Tucumcari

★ COUNTRY INN. *1302 W Tucumcari Blvd, Tucumcari (88401). Phone 505/461-3140.* 57 rooms, 2 story. Pet accepted, some restrictions; fee. Complimentary continental breakfast. Check-out noon. TV; cable (premium). Pool. **¢**

★★ HOLIDAY INN. *3716 E Tucumcari Blvd, Tucumcari (88401). Phone 505/461-3780; toll-free 800/335-3780. www.holiday-inn.com.* 100 rooms, 2 story. Pet accepted, some restrictions; fee. Check-out noon. TV. In-room modem link. Restaurant, bar. Room service. In-house fitness room. Pool, whirlpool. **¢**

★ SUPER 8. *4001 E Tucumcari Blvd, Tucumcari (88401). Phone 505/461-4444; toll-free 800/800-8000. www.super8.com.* 63 rooms, 2 story. Check-out 11 am. TV. Indoor pool. **¢**

PLACES TO EAT

A long day of driving is sure to make you hungry. At the end of your journey, take a table at one of the following restaurants.

Albuquerque

★★★ THE ARTICHOKE CAFÉ. *424 Central St, Albuquerque (87102). Phone 505/243-0200. www.artichokecafe.com.* A perennial favorite among the area's white-tablecloth restaurants, this pleasant eatery has beautiful fresh flowers and a menu that leans toward Italy. Closed Sun; Jan 1, Thanksgiving, Dec 25. Lunch, dinner. Children's menu. Outdoor seating. **$$**

★★ CONRAD'S DOWNTOWN. *125 2nd St NW, Albuquerque (87102). Phone 505/242-9090.* Southwestern menu. Breakfast, lunch, dinner. Bar. Guitarist Fri, Sat evenings. Valet parking available. **$$**

★ LA HACIENDA DINING ROOM. *302 San Felipe NW, Albuquerque (87104). Phone 505/243-3131.* Mexican, American menu. Closed Thanksgiving, Dec 25. Lunch, dinner. Bar. Entertainment Wed-Sun. Children's menu. Outdoor seating, Mexican décor in an old hacienda; antiques, Native American art. **$$**

New Mexico

★ **M AND J.** *403 2nd St SW, Albuquerque (87102). Phone 505/242-4890.* Mexican menu. Closed Sun; major holidays. Lunch, dinner. Children's menu. $
D SC

★ **ROUTE 66 DINER.** ☺ *1405 Central Ave NE, Albuquerque (87106). Phone 505/247-1421.* Closed major holidays. Breakfast, lunch, dinner. Children's menu. Outdoor seating. $
D

★★★ **SCALO.** *3500 Central Ave SE, Albuquerque (87106). Phone 505/255-8782.* Chef Enrique Guerrero has taken over the kitchen of this northern Italian grill, and he has brought back favorites such as chicken cooked under a brick. Italian menu. Closed most major holidays. Lunch, dinner. Bar. Outdoor seating. Dining areas on several levels. $$
D

Bernalillo

★★★ **PRAIRIE STAR.** *288 Prairie Star Rd, Bernalillo (87004). Phone 505/867-3327. www.santaanagolf.com.* This casual fine-dining restaurant in the Santa Ana Golf Club has stunning views of the Sandias. Among the kitchen's specialties is game. Continental menu. Closed Mon; Dec 25-Jan 1. Dinner. Bar. $$
D

★ **RANGE CAFÉ AND BAKERY.** *925 Camino del Pueblo, Bernalillo (87004). Phone 505/867-1700. www.rangecafe.com.* Closed Thanksgiving, Dec 25. Breakfast, lunch, dinner. Bar. Children's menu. Totally nonsmoking. $$
D

Gallup

★ **EARL'S.** *1400 E US 66, Gallup (87301). Phone 505/863-4201.* Mexican, American menu. Closed most major holidays. Breakfast, lunch, dinner. Children's menu. Casual attire. $
D

★ **RANCH KITCHEN.** ☺ *3001 W US 66, Gallup (87301). Phone 505/722-2537.* Mexican, American menu. Closed Dec 24-25, Easter. Breakfast, lunch, dinner. Children's menu. $$
D SC

Santa Fe

★★★ **THE ANASAZI.** *113 Washington Ave, Santa Fe (87501). Phone 505/988-3236. www.innoftheanasazi.com.* The creators of memorable cuisine at this Plaza mainstay like to point out that the Navajo definition of Anasazi has come to embody an ancient wisdom that is synonymous with the art of living harmoniously and peacefully with the environment. That philosophy is translated in the colorful Native American weavings, petroglyph-inspired art upon the walls of beautiful rock, and mesmerizing fires that crackle and warm the rooms within this dining favorite. Executive chef Tom Kerpon devotes himself to inventive uses of locally grown, organic products, from cactus and sage to chiles and corn. Contemporary Southwestern menu. Menu changes seasonally. Breakfast, lunch, dinner, Sun brunch. Bar. Classical guitarist (brunch). Children's menu. Casual attire. $$$
D

★ **THE BURRITO COMPANY.** *111 Washington Ave, Santa Fe (87501). Phone 505/982-4453.* Mexican menu. Closed Dec 25. Breakfast, lunch, dinner. Children's menu. $
D

★★ **CORN DANCE CAFÉ.** *1501 Paseo de Peralta, Santa Fe (87501). Phone 505/982-1200. www.hotelsantafe.com.* Native American menu. Lunch, dinner. Bar. Casual attire. Outdoor seating. Totally nonsmoking. $$$
D

★★★ **COYOTE CAFÉ.** *132 W Water St, Santa Fe (87501). Phone 505/983-1615. www.coyote-cafe.com.* Famed cookbook author and pioneer of Southwestern cuisine Mark Miller has enjoyed nothing but success at this bastion of trendy dining found just a block off the Plaza. Although the menu changes seasonally, patrons are assured of finding a whimsical mingling of the cuisines of New Mexico, Mexico, Cuba, and Spain in all manner of meats, fish, and vegetables, served in inventive dishes. Don't miss the house drink special, a margarita del Maguey. Whether seated in the main dining room (try for a window-side table overlooking the street) or on the festive rooftop Cantina, be sure to relax and soak up the setting, decorated by magnificent folk art and artistic lighting fixtures. New Mexican menu. Dinner. Bar/cantina (May-Oct). Casual attire. Outdoor seating. $$$

D

★ **EL FAROL.** *808 Canyon Rd, Santa Fe (87501). Phone 505/983-9912.* Mexican menu. Closed major holidays. Lunch, dinner. Bar. Casual attire. Outdoor seating. $

D

★★★★ **GERONIMO.** *724 Canyon Rd, Santa Fe (87501). Phone 505/982-1500. www.geronimorestaurant.com.* Housed in a restored 250-year-old landmark adobe, Geronimo (the name of the restaurant is an ode to the hacienda's original owner, Geronimo Lopez) offers robust Southwestern-spiked global fusion fare in a stunning and cozy space. Owners Cliff Skoglund and Chris Harvey treat each guest like family, and this is a nice family to be a part of. Geronimo is inviting and warm, with a wood-burning cove-style fireplace; eggshell walls; sheer curtains; tall, rich chocolate- and garnet-leather seating; and local Native American-style sculpture and artwork decorating the walls. It feels like a Georgia O'Keeffe painting come to life. It's not just the serene and stylish space that earns Geronimo points with its regulars. The food is remarkable, fusing the distinct culinary influences of Asia, the Southwest, and the Mediterranean. Vibrant flavors, bright colors, and top-notch seasonal regional ingredients come together in perfect harmony. While Geronimo is a great place for dinner, it is also a perfect spot to take a break from gallery hopping around lunchtime. When it's warm outside, sit on the patio for prime Canyon Road people-watching. Global menu. Lunch, dinner. Bar. Casual attire. Outdoor seating. $$$

D

★★ **MAÑANA.** *101 W Alameda, Santa Fe (87501). Phone 505/982-4333.* Southwestern, Californian menu. Breakfast, lunch, dinner. Bar. Piano. Casual attire. Outdoor seating. $$

★ **PLAZA.** *54 Lincoln Ave, Santa Fe (87501). Phone 505/982-1664.* Continental menu. Closed Thanksgiving, Dec 25. Breakfast, lunch, dinner. Children's menu. A century-old building with many original fixtures; stamped-tin ceiling; photos of early Santa Fe. Casual attire. $$

★★★ **RISTRA.** *548 Agua Fria, Santa Fe (87501). Phone 505/982-8608. www.ristrarestaurant.com.* Barely off the beaten path in a quiet neighborhood a short drive from the Plaza, this graceful Victorian adobe home provides a departure from typical Santa Fe in both setting and cuisine (although you'll find Southwestern elements in both). Diners gaze out of enormous windows at stands of evergreens while tucking into appetizers such as grilled foie gras and black Mediterranean mussels swept with mint and chipotle. Fresh, seasonal ingredients are the key to the kitchen's successes, and a wine list of 100 French and California vintages keeps local and visiting diners happy. French, Southwestern menu. Dinner. Three intimate dining rooms. Outdoor seating. $$$

D

★ **SHED AND LA CHOZA.** *113 1/2 E Palace Ave, Santa Fe (87501). Phone 505/982-9030. www.sfshed.com.* New Mexican menu. Closed Sun; major holidays. Lunch, dinner. Children's menu. Casual attire. Outdoor seating. Totally nonsmoking. $

D

Jemez Mountain Trail
✳ NEW MEXICO

Quick Facts

LENGTH: 132 miles.

TIME TO ALLOW: 3 hours.

BEST TIME TO DRIVE: Spring and summer; summer is the high season.

BYWAY TRAVEL INFORMATION: Jemez Springs Visitor Information: 505/829-9155.

SPECIAL CONSIDERATIONS: Highway 126 is not paved and is generally closed in the winter due to snow. Bicycles, pedestrians, and passenger vehicles are accommodated according to the various types of roadways. Different sections of the trail have various accessibility and safety issues. Highway 44 is traveled by heavy, high-speed traffic, usually at 65 mph. There are shoulders along the entire two-lane stretch of the highway, but it is not generally considered safe for pedestrians or bicycles. Highway 4 winds through the mountains and is traveled at lower speeds of around 35 mph. Highway 126 is maintained in the summer by the Forest Service and can accommodate all traffic except commercial truck traffic. Travelers should be aware of several fire precautions. Please be a responsible camper. Extinguish all fires completely and be aware of official fire hazard warnings. Call any US Forest Service Office for hazard updates.

BICYCLE/PEDESTRIAN FACILITIES: Highway 4 is used heavily by cyclists and pedestrians. The other roads making up this Byway are not safe for cyclists.

North of Albuquerque, at the unspoiled village of San Ysidro (at the junction of NM 44 and NM 4), quietly begins one of New Mexico's most spectacular scenic drives: the Jemez (pronounced HAY-mez or HAY-mus) Mountain Trail. San Ysidro, in the Upper Sonoran desert terrain, is a village where you can find the work of local artisans and view the restored Spanish adobe church.

Jemez Pueblo, about 5 miles from San Ysidro, is located at the gateway of the majestic Cañon de San Diego. There are over 3,000 tribal members, most of whom reside in a single Puebloan village known as walatowa—the Towa word meaning "this is the place." Enjoy traditional Jemez foods and arts and crafts available at roadside stands in the beautiful Red Rocks area. Jemez Pueblo also offers recreation areas where you can picnic, fish, and enjoy the great outdoors.

A leisurely day trip along the Byway takes you past fantastic geologic formations; ancient Indian ruins and Indian pueblos; and reminders of the area's logging, mining, and ranching heritage. Approximately 65 miles of the Byway wind through the Santa Fe National Forest, and 40 miles of this land is in the Jemez National Recreation Area, where you'll find many opportunities for hiking, fishing, camping, and, in the winter, cross-country skiing. The Jemez Mountains are also famous for natural hot springs.

This picturesque trail is also just a short jaunt from the city of Los Alamos and the Bandelier National Monument.

THE BYWAY STORY

The Jemez Mountain Trail tells cultural, historical, natural, recreational, and scenic stories that make it a unique and treasured Byway.

Cultural

The greater Santa Fe area is extremely culturally diverse due to strong Native American and Spanish influences.

The earliest inhabitants, the Pueblo Indians, greatly impacted the architecture and art that in turn impacted the architecture and art of the Spanish settlers who moved into the area. Today's Southwestern flavor is a blend of both colorful cultures. Of the 19 Native American communities located in New Mexico, eight are in the greater Santa Fe area. All eight are Pueblo Indian tribes, and their communities are referred to as pueblos. Many of these pueblos were established centuries ago—the Taos Pueblo, for example, is thought to have been continuously occupied for close to 1,000 years. Each pueblo has its own tribal government, traditions, and ceremonies and is a sovereign and separate entity. The pueblos typically welcome visitors, especially during specific dances and feast days that are open to the public.

A people of great faith, the early Spanish settlers arrived in 1607 with scores of Catholic priests. The gloriously well-preserved adobe mission churches that dot the greater Santa Fe landscape, along with Spanish-settled villages and Indian Pueblos, are a testament to the strong role of religion in this region. Just as the Spanish created houses of worship from an adobe mix of mud and straw, they built villages and towns in the same architectural fashion. The energy-efficient earthen structures fit into their high desert home in every way—keeping the heat in during the winter and out in the summer—while the low-slung, flat-roofed buildings blended naturally into the land.

Like adobe architecture, art forms practiced by early Spanish settlers were shaped largely from resources they found in their natural environment. Using native aspen and pine, paints derived from natural pigments, and other local materials, they created utilitarian goods and religious objects to adorn their homes and churches. At first, the work echoed the traditional artworks and motifs they had carried with them to the New World from Mexico and Spain. But in time, native artisans developed styles and techniques that were unique to New Mexico alone. Ranging from santos (carved images of saints), furniture, and textiles to works in tin, iron, silver, and straw, the art of the Spanish colonial era remains the art of many Santa Fe-area families who have practiced the traditional techniques for generations. Meanwhile, other contemporary area artists have carried the artistic legacy of their ancestors to new levels of excellence by working in more modern media, including sculpture, photography, painting, jewelry, and literature that reflect the ongoing evolution of Hispanic arts and culture. Today, their works are also collected and exhibited by museums, galleries, and private collectors worldwide, giving the art of New Mexicans a well-deserved place in the world of fine art.

Historical

Jemez State Monument and Bandelier National Monument are special places to discover more about the history of the Jemez Mountain Trail area. Both monuments have exhibits and self-guided tours. Ranger-guided tours are also given upon request. Currently, more than 500,000 people visit these monuments every year.

Natural

You'll find many natural wonders along the Jemez Mountain Trail. The Jemez Mountains are unique from the southern Rockies to the east in that the Jemez are of volcanic upbringing. In fact, the history of the Jemez goes back 1 million years to the eruption of a volcano many times the size of Mount St. Helens that created an area of mountains, mesas, and canyons the size of a small eastern state.

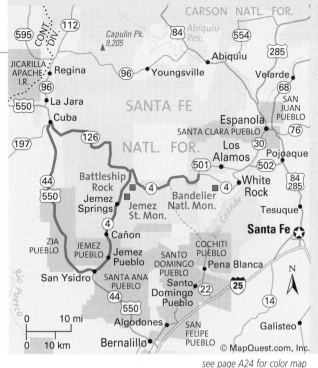

see page A24 for color map

Dominating the western half of the Santa Fe National Forest, the Jemez Mountains resemble a wagon wheel on a topographic map. The hub is formed by the giant Valles Caldera (a crater formed by the volcano's violent explosion), and the spokes are formed by the mesas built of volcanic tuft. Elevations in the Jemez Mountains range from 6,000 feet to 11,000 feet at the top of Redondo Peak in the middle of the caldera. One of the unique legacies of the volcano are the Swiss cheese-like rock cliffs and strange cone-shaped tent rocks that decorate numerous canyons.

The volcanic history of the Jemez Mountains also gives it a colorful heritage. From the red rock country on its lower edges to the deep greens of the forests in its high country, the Jemez Mountains offer some of the greatest natural diversity on Earth. Fortunately, examples of most of it can be viewed or easily accessed from this Byway, the only paved highway that traverses these mountains.

As you travel past San Ysidro along the Jemez Mountain Trail, you pass the towering volcanic plug of Cabezon (meaning big head), which is famous in Navajo folklore. The volcano has a trail leading to its 8,000-foot summit. In addition, 1 mile north of the State Monument at Soda Dam is an unusual geological formation where, over thousands of years, minerals from a natural spring have created a dam that blocks the Jemez River. The river pours through a hole in the dam, forming a waterfall. Soda Dam has become one of the most popular swimming holes in the Jemez Mountains. Also along the Byway is Battleship Rock, a sheer cliff that rises suddenly above the river like the prow of a ship. A few miles past Battleship Rock is the parking lot for Spence Hot Springs, an accessible and scenic place for a long soak in hot mineral waters.

Recreational

The Jemez Mountain Trail offers all sorts of outdoor recreation. Travelers enjoy hiking trails of varying degrees of difficulty, biking trails, fishing, and several camping locations. The unique geological features also allow for outdoor adventures—you can visit caves and tunnels.

Hiking trails are for everyone. For the adventurous, Battleship Rock in the Jemez Mountains provides challenging terrain and an intriguing landscape—the trail is covered in shiny, black obsidian created from volcanic eruptions 5 million years ago. Families can enjoy the Las Conchas Trail, which provides an easy walk to picnic sites and beautiful Southwestern scenery.

If you enjoy biking, the Jemez Mountain Trail provides several trails for all skill levels. Advanced bikers may want to explore Guacamalla and Paliza Canyons, a steep terrain that offers excellent views of green meadows from the top.

Fishing fanatics can enjoy the calm waters located in the San Pedro Parks Wilderness, where cutthroat trout are found in large numbers. Close by, the Holy Ghost and Dragonfly reservoirs provide popular fishing

Laboratory for its work and historic role in the Manhattan Project and the development of the atomic bomb. The **Bradbury Science Museum** offers a great deal of information and fun for everyone.

- After a visit to the museum travel east along State Highway 502, and follow the signs to **Valle Grande,** the remains of a volcano that erupted 1.4 million years ago. Natural hot springs and plenty of recreational opportunities abound in the area.

- After Valle Grande, continue north to Highway 126. This road, all the way to **Cuba,** is not paved but is well traveled. Use discretion, however, when deciding whether to travel this portion of the road: it may be rough in spots and not appropriate for passenger cars. A four-wheel-drive vehicle is recommended for better safety.

- After a rest in Cuba, travel south along Highway 44. A quick detour off of the Byway heading west on the 197 will take you to **Cabezon,** a ghost town that was a flourishing city until the 1940s. Back on Highway 44, head south through the national forest and down toward the many unique Indian Pueblos. The **Zia and Jemez Pueblos** have wonderful opportunities for learning and adventure. To find out more, stop at the **Walatowa Visitor's Center.** (Note that the Jemez Pueblo is not open to the public, except for on festival days.)

- The **Jemez State Monument** is a perfect getaway in the late afternoon and is highlighted by a dip in the **Spence Hot Springs.** Don't forget other wonderful sites that are farther off the Byway.

- **Bandelier National Monument,** near the **Rio Grande,** is a wonderful place to see the ruins of many cliff houses and pueblo-style dwellings of 13th-century Pueblo Indians. A little to the north of Los Alamos, in **Abiquiu,** a cluster of fantastic museums at **Ghost Ranch** is a trip not to be missed.

and water recreation spots. Just a little farther down the Byway, you can catch warm-water fish, such as catfish, crappie, bass, bluegill, and perch at Cochiti Lake. Another fishing area is the Sandia Lakes Recreation Area located on the Sandia Indian Reservation. Several ponds are stocked with trout and other varieties of fish.

If you wish to camp close by the Byway, the Santa Fe National Forest/Jemez National Recreation Area gives you a chance to camp out by rivers and hiking trails. Campgrounds along the Byway include Las Conchas and Jemez Falls (both close to the Jemez River), Redondo (the largest), and San Antonio (an excellent fishing spot offering handicapped-accessible sites).

Scenic

In all seasons, the Jemez Mountains offer some of the most magnificent scenery in the state of New Mexico. Visitors enjoy escaping to a quieter, more relaxing way of life, even if it is only for a day or a weekend.

HIGHLIGHTS

As you travel the Jemez Mountain Trail, consider using the following itinerary.

- Your trip through the Jemez Mountains begins in **Los Alamos,** New Mexico, famous as the home of the **Los Alamos National**

THINGS TO SEE AND DO

Driving along the Jemez Mountain Trail will certainly keep your senses engaged, but if you yearn to get out of the car and stretch your legs, or if you'd like to make a mini-vacation out of your trip, check out these attractions along the route.

BANDELIER NATIONAL MONUMENT.
Los Alamos (87554). Phone 505/672-0343. www.nps.gov/band/. A major portion of this 32,000-acre area is designated wilderness. The most accessible part is in Frijoles Canyon, which features cave dwellings carved out of the soft volcanic turf and houses built out from the cliffs. There is also a great circular pueblo ruin on the floor of the canyon. These houses and caves were occupied from about AD 1150-1550; depletion of resources forced the residents to abandon the area. Some of the modern pueblos along the Rio Grande are related to the prehistoric Anasazi people of the canyon and the surrounding mesa country. There is a paved 1-mile self-guided trail to walk and view these sites. The monument is named after Adolph Bandelier, ethnologist and author of the novel *The Delight Makers,* which used Frijoles Canyon as its locale. There are 70 miles of trails (free permits required for overnight trips; no pets allowed on the trails). Visitor center with exhibits depicting the culture of the Pueblo region (open daily; closed Jan 1, Dec 25), ranger-guided tours (summer), campfire programs (open Memorial Day-Labor Day). Campground (Mar-Nov, daily) with tent and trailer sites (fee; no showers, hookups, or reservations); grills, tables, and water. **$$$**

BRADBURY SCIENCE MUSEUM.
15th St and Central Ave, Los Alamos (87554). Phone 505/667-4444. Displays artifacts relating to the history of the laboratory and the atomic bomb. Exhibits on modern nuclear weapons; life sciences; materials sciences; computers; particle accelerators; geothermal, fusion, and fission energy sources. Open daily; closed holidays. **FREE**

FULLER LODGE ART CENTER AND GALLERY.
2132 Central Ave, Los Alamos (87554). Phone 505/662-9331. www.artfulnm.org. On the ground floor of Fuller Lodge's west wing. The historic log building provides a setting for changing exhibits and features the arts and crafts of northern New Mexico. Open Mon-Sat 10 am-4 pm; closed holidays. **FREE**

JEMEZ STATE MONUMENT.
18160 State Rd 4, Jemez Springs (87025). Phone 505/829-3530. This stabilized Spanish mission (1621) was built by Franciscan missionaries next to a prehistoric pueblo. Self-guided bilingual trail. The visitor center has anthropology and archaeology exhibits. Picnicking. Open daily; closed holidays. **$$**

LOS ALAMOS HISTORICAL MUSEUM.
1921 Juniper, Los Alamos (87544). Phone 505/662-4493 or 662-6272. Artifacts, photos, and other material trace local history from prehistoric times to the present times; exhibit on the Manhattan Project. Open Mon-Sat 10 am-4 pm, Sun 1-4 pm; closed holidays. **FREE**

PAJARITO MOUNTAIN SKI AREA.
Camp May Rd, Los Alamos (87544). Phone 505/662-5725. www.skipajarito.com. Pajarito Mountain is run by the Los Alamos Ski club and is situated near the town of Los Alamos and the ancient volcanic caldera at Valle Grande. Despite being a small resort (280 acres), it offers some excellent, challenging terrain, making it a well-kept secret for local ski buffs. The nearby National Labs attract a diverse group of PhDs and scientists, ensuring interesting conversations on the lifts. Open Fri-Sun, 9 am-4 pm. **$$$$**

SANTA FE NATIONAL FOREST.
1474 Radio Rd, Santa Fe (87501). Phone 505/438-7840; toll-free 800/280-2267 (reservations). www.fs.fed.us/r3/sfe/. This forest consists of over 1 1/2 million acres. Fishing is excellent in the Pecos and Jemez rivers and tributary streams. Hiking trails are close to unusual geologic formations. You'll find hot springs in the Jemez Mountains. Four wilderness

areas within the forest total more than 300,000 acres. Campgrounds are provided by the Forest Service at more than 40 locations.

PLACES TO STAY

If you choose to include an overnight stay in your trip along this Byway, Mobil Travel Guide recommends the following lodgings.

Jemez Springs

★★ **DANCING BEAR BED & BREAKFAST.** *314 San Diego Dr, Jemez Springs (87025). Phone toll-free 800/422-3271. www. dancingbearbandb.com.* 4 rooms, 2 story. Beautifully situated along the Jemez River. Known for gourmet breakfasts. $

★ **JEMEZ MOUNTAIN INN.** *PO Box 28, Hwy 4, Jemez Springs (87025). Phone toll-free 888/819-1075. www.jemezmtninn.com.* 6 rooms, 2 story. Check-out 11 am, check-in 3 pm. Located within walking distance of local restaurants, sights, and attractions. $

★★★ **RIVERDANCER BED AND BREAKFAST.** *16445 Hwy 4, Jemez Springs (87025). Phone 505/829-3262.* Located near the village of Jemez Springs, the beauty of this 5-acre property is the natural landscaping. Guests are treated to a relaxing and refreshing getaway. Enjoy Jemez Falls, natural hot springs, and hot air ballooning. 6 rooms. Complimentary full breakfast. Check-out 11 am, check-in 3-7 pm. TV; cable (premium), VCR available (movies). Massage. Concierge service. On river. Totally nonsmoking. $

La Cueva

★ **ELK MOUNTAIN LODGE.** *37485 Hwy 126, La Cueva (87025). Phone toll-free 800/815-2859. www.elkmountainlodge.cc.* 4 rooms, 2 story. Featuring spacious, private rooms with private entrances and two Jacuzzi tubs. $$

Los Alamos

★★ **BEST WESTERN HILLTOP HOUSE HOTEL.** *400 Trinity Dr at Central, Los Alamos (87544). Phone 505/662-2441. www.bestwestern.com.* 98 rooms, 3 story. Pet accepted, some restrictions. Complimentary breakfast. Check-out 11 am. TV; cable (premium). In-room modem link. Laundry services. Restaurant. Room service. In-house fitness room, massage, sauna. Indoor pool, whirlpool. Downhill, cross-country ski 10 miles. Airport transportation. $

★ **LOS ALAMOS INN.** *2201 Trinity Dr, Los Alamos (87544). Phone 505/662-7211.* 116 rooms, 2-3 story. Complimentary breakfast. Check-out 12:30 pm. TV. Restaurant, bar. Pool, whirlpool. ¢

★ **RENATA'S ORANGE STREET BED AND BREAKFAST.** *3496 Orange St, Los Alamos (87544). Phone 505/662-2651.* 8 rooms, 4 with bath, 2 story. Children over age 5 only. Complimentary full breakfast. Check-out 11 am, check-in 4-7 pm. TV in sitting room. Room service. Downhill, cross-country ski 8 miles. Lawn games. Airport transportation. Concierge service. Totally nonsmoking. $

PLACES TO EAT

A long day of driving is sure to make you hungry. At the end of your journey, take a table at any of the following restaurants.

Jemez Springs

★★ **CONSETTA'S.** *16351 Hwy 4, Jemez Springs (87025). Phone 505/829-4455.* Italian menu. Closed Mon-Tues. Lunch, dinner. A local favorite for freshly prepared Italian cuisine. $

★★ **THE LAUGHING LIZARD INN & CAFÉ.**
PO Box 263, Jemez Springs (87025). Phone
505/829-3108. www.thelaughinglizard.com.
Southwestern menu. Breakfast, lunch, dinner.
Featuring distinctive regional cuisine in a coun-
try setting. **$**

★ **LOS OJOS RESTAURANT & SALOON.**
17596 Hwy 4, Jemez Springs (87025). Phone
505/829-3547. Mexican menu. Lunch, dinner.
Known for its excellent Mexican food and the
only full-service bar in Jemez Springs. **$**

Los Alamos

★★**BLUE WINDOW BISTRO.** *813 Central Ave,*
Los Alamos (87544). Phone 505/662-6305.
Continental menu. Closed Sun; Jan 1,
Thanksgiving, Dec 25. Lunch, dinner.
Children's menu. Totally nonsmoking. **$$**
D SC

★★ **KATHERINE'S FINE DINING.** *121 Longview,*
White Rock (87545). Phone 505/672-9661.
American menu. Closed Sun, Mon. Lunch,
dinner. Upscale restaurant not far from the
Byway featuring progressive American cuisine.
$$

Santa Fe Trail

❋ NEW MEXICO

Part of a multistate Byway; see also CO.

Quick Facts

LENGTH: 381 miles.

TIME TO ALLOW: 8 hours.

BEST TIME TO DRIVE: Early spring through late fall.

BICYCLE/PEDESTRIAN FACILITIES: Sidewalks and bicycle trails are available in some of the communities along the Byway.

The Santa Fe Trail was the first of America's great trans-Mississippi routes. The trail, including the Mountain and Cimarron routes, traversed more than 1,200 miles from Franklin, Missouri, to Santa Fe, New Mexico. From 1821 to 1880, it was an important two-way avenue for commerce and cultural exchange among Spanish, Indian, and American cultures.

The area around the Santa Fe Trail boasts more than 20 historic districts and more than 30 individual sites that are recorded on the National Register of Historic Places. Most of these sites are directly related to the Santa Fe Trail.

THE BYWAY STORY

The Santa Fe Trail tells archaeological, cultural, historical, natural, recreational, and scenic stories that make it a unique and treasured Byway.

Archaeological

The Santa Fe Trail offers many archaeological sites, including some that include early excavations. From 1915 to 1927, Pecos was the subject of one of the first organized excavations of a Southwestern ruin. Pioneer American archaeologist Alfred V. Kidder analyzed the stratigraphy (the sequence in which the archaeological remains of the pueblo were deposited). He noted changes in the artifacts, especially the pottery, from the lower, older layers of occupation through the upper, younger layers. Kidder used the relative ages of the pottery remains to establish relative dates of occupation at Pecos. Based on that information, he and his colleagues devised the Pecos Classification, a sequence of eight prehistoric cultural periods that applied to sites throughout the Southwest.

In 1965, Congress and the president authorized the establishment of Pecos National Monument. In the summer of 1966, National Park Service archaeologists began excavation of the church and convent; their findings not only cast new light on the history of the Southwest but also substantiated reports of 17th-century writers whose words had been held suspect.

Both the church and the convent were puzzling. The 17th-century ecclesiastics had described the church as being large, splendid, magnificent, and of unusual design, but the remaining adobe walls are of a church that had none of those characteristics. Other mission churches in New Mexico had obviously been much grander. Most historians had thought that the early accounts were exaggerated to gain added civil and religious support of missionary efforts in the remote and impoverished frontier province of New Mexico. However, it was discovered that the convent was much larger than those usually associated with a church of modest size.

In the summer of 1967, the project archaeologist discovered stone foundations resting on bedrock and fragments of burned adobe walls. Under and around the ruins of the known church, further excavations uncovered the foundations of an earlier church that was nearly 170 feet long, 90 feet wide at the transept, and 39 feet wide inside the nave. The building was typical of the fortress churches of Mexico. It had bastioned nave walls and subsidiary chapels in thick-walled, cruciform-like (that is, cross-shaped) arms near the sanctuary. Only 18 such structures were known in the Americas until the Pecos find, and none was north of Mexico City.

It is now clear that the large church and convent were constructed in the 1620s and later destroyed during the Pueblo Revolt of 1680. The convent was then reconstructed, and a new church was built following the Reconquest, probably in the early 1700s.

The archaeological survey now in progress is designed to locate small sites showing evidence of activities on which the Pecos livelihood was based. Evidence of agriculture field systems, including check dams, farming terraces, and overnight houses, has been uncovered. Rock art and hunting camps have also been identified, including Apache tipi ring sites that verify historical reports of Apache encampments for trade with the Pecos people. Some evidence suggests that the Pecos area may have been at least a marginal site for human occupation for several thousand years.

Recent excavations have uncovered two large semi-subterranean houses on the grassy flats south and west of monument headquarters. These pithouses, the first to be reported from the Upper Pecos River area, were built in the 9th century. They were probably part of a village that may have been occupied on a seasonal basis. The architecture is similar to that of both the Anasazi people of the Rio Grande Valley and the Mogollon of southern New Mexico.

Cultural

The Santa Fe Trail was the first trail of commerce between the Southwest and the United States. From 1821 to 1880, the Santa Fe Trail was an important two-way avenue for commerce and cultural exchange among Spanish, Native American, and American cultures. While traveling along the Byway, you can see evidence of this abounding culture in many of the events and activities.

Historical

The Santa Fe Trail was the first of America's great Trans-Mississippi routes. The trail, including the Mountain and Cimarron routes, crossed over 1,200 miles from Franklin, Missouri, to Santa Fe, New Mexico. The trail played a critical role in the westward expansion of the United States and fostered an exchange among Spanish, Native American, and American cultures. The Santa Fe Trail was the first international trade route, carrying needed materials from Missouri to northern Mexico and taking back silver, furs, mules, and wood to Missouri.

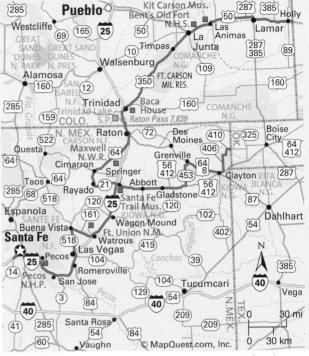

see page A11 for color map

As early as the 1700s, Pueblo and Plains Indian trade fairs at Pecos and Taos introduced Spanish residents to native products. Yet trade between New Mexico and other settlements throughout the West was banned because New Mexico was a colony of Spain and could trade only with the mother country. Beginning in 1810 and succeeding in 1821, uprisings in Mexico gave New Mexico freedom to trade with anyone. November 16, 1821, is recognized as the start of legal international trade between New Mexico and the United States; this date also marks the beginning of the Santa Fe Trail.

The Santa Fe Trail passed through the territories and ranges of many Indian tribes, including the Pawnee, Arapaho, Cheyenne, Comanche, and the Kiowa, so Indian traders used it as a commercial route. After the Mexican War (1846-1848), the Jicarillas, Comanches, Kiowas, and other tribes became increasingly threatened by the traffic on the trail. With the American promise to the people of New Mexico to subdue the various Indian tribes, an intermittent war began that ended in the mid-1870s. The Indian tribes of New Mexico were then confined to reservations.

After the Mexican War (and with New Mexico a US Territory), the Santa Fe Trail became mainly a military road. It supplied goods to the large contingent of troops in the Southwest, and mercantile goods were still carried into New Mexico and Old Mexico. After the Civil War, railroads began laying tracks to the West. By 1879, the first locomotive reached Las Vegas, New Mexico, and in 1880, the railroad reached Lamy (basically the Santa Fe Depot), essentially ending wagon traffic across the 900 miles of plains.

Visitors to New Mexico can still see the most extensive remains of the trail. Historic sites and landmarks found along the trail include Raton Pass, Rabbit Ears, Cimarron, Rayado, Ocate Gap, Fort Union, McNees Crossing, Point of Rocks, the Rock Crossing of the Canadian, Wagon Mound, Watrous (La Junta), Las Vegas, Tecolote, San Miguel del Vado, San Jose del Vado, Pecos, and Santa Fe.

Natural

The Santa Fe Trail offers an array of flora and fauna. Vegetation ranges from small pockets of tall grass prairies to the buffalo and blue grama grass found on the short grass plains east of the Sangre de Cristo Mountains. South and east of Las Vegas, the trail enters the piñon pine and juniper vegetation zones as the elevation increases in the mountains. Antelopes, coyotes, elks, and bears are prevalent in the area. Bird life is profuse, including small mountain bluebirds, hawks, bald eagles, and golden eagles. Many species of reptiles also inhabit the area, including the famous prairie rattlesnake and the much larger and feared western diamondback rattlesnake.

From its eastern-most point at Old Franklin, Missouri, the trail traveled west to Cimarron, Kansas, where it split into two routes. The original trail, the Cimarron Route, headed southwest across Colorado, Oklahoma, and New Mexico. The Mountain Route headed west into Colorado, and then went south to New

Mexico across the rugged Raton Pass. The routes joined again at Watrous, New Mexico. Today, travelers can follow the trail through three national grasslands: Cimarron, Kiowa, and Comanche.

The Cimarron National Grassland near Elkhart, Kansas, contains 23 miles of the trail's Cimarron Route, the longest trail segment on public land. A 19-mile companion trail, a mowed swath across the prairie, parallels the actual trail route. It was constructed for non-motorized traffic. Two trailheads provide drinking water, rest room facilities, vehicle and trailer parking, stock unloading facilities, and ramps for mounting and dismounting horses. Point of Rocks, a large outcropping of rock that rises above the prairie, was visible for long distances from both directions along the trail, so it acted as a landmark and guide for travelers. The panoramic view of the Cimarron River Valley from Point of Rocks was excellent for seeing other travelers or game. Today, you can drive to the top to enjoy this view. A short distance east of Point of Rocks is Middle Springs, a small oasis on the prairie where water rises from an ever-flowing artesian spring. It was the only reliable watering spot for 30 miles each way along the trail. Today, the spring is home to tall trees and brushy undergrowth that attract migrating birds. However, during the Santa Fe Trail days, the spring was probably a treeless and muddy waterhole, trodden and stirred by buffalo, livestock, and trail travelers. This welcome resting spot along the trail now has a picnic area and walking trail for your enjoyment.

The winding ribbon of the Cimarron Route crosses the Kiowa National Grassland (part of the Kiowa and Rita Blanca National Grasslands) 15 miles north of Clayton, New Mexico, off Highway 406. Time, weather, and erosion have not erased the deep wagon ruts stretching across 2 miles of the Kiowa National Grassland. You can almost hear the rumble of freight wagons, the cracking of bullwhips, the thunder of buffalo, and the quiet conversations in Spanish and English by the campfires that took place here. You can also experience the stark isolation of prairie travel and glimpse the subtle prairie tapestry that was savored by countless trail travelers. You can step back in time and enjoy virtually the same prairie vistas and unspoiled beauty that travelers experienced more than 100 years ago. The trail across the Kiowa National Grassland lies between McNees Crossing and Turkey Creek, both resting and watering areas for weary travelers. Rabbit Ears Mountain and Round Mound can be seen looming to the west.

The Mountain Route of the trail coursed northwest after splitting from the main trail at Cimarron, Kansas. Along its length, the Mountain Route unraveled the Aubry Cutoff a few miles east of the Kansas/Colorado line, and the Granada-Fort Union Road just west of the state line. Segments of these two branches can be seen on the southern portion of the Comanche National Grassland; remnants of Springfield, and portions of the Granada-Fort Union Road can be seen near Kim.

As it continued its westward path, the Mountain Route curved to the north, tracing what is now Route 50. Here, the changing horizon from plains to mountains was a major milestone on the journey, surely causing great excitement among the travelers. The mountains may have also produced apprehension as travelers anticipated having to climb over rugged Raton Pass with heavily laden wagons. Today, trail travelers can turn south at La Junta on

Highway 350 to the Sierra Vista Overlook on the northern portion of the Comanche National Grassland. Here, you can experience the same feelings as the early travelers did as you view the mountains to the west. You can also stop for a picnic at Timpas farther south on Highway 350 or continue on to Iron Spring, the first reliable water source after leaving the comforts of Bents Fort, which later became the site of a stage station. Good trail ruts can be found here today.

Recreational

You'll find many recreational activities along the Santa Fe Trail, including fishing, camping, skiing, mountain biking, and hiking. Several state parks and recreational areas are located in northeastern New Mexico. As a matter of fact, outdoor recreation is one of the top four reasons people visit New Mexico.

Scenic

The Santa Fe Trail has some spectacular and rugged scenery. For example, amid the surrounding Fort Union Ranch at Fort Union National Monument, wagon ruts can be seen in the distance. These and other wagon ruts were worn into the landscape of northeastern New Mexico over 150 years ago. Nearby, travelers visit Fort La Junta (built in 1851) and the 1863 fort and supply depot.

There are also many different plants found along the Santa Fe Trail. For example, the flowering plants along the trail are the result of volcanic activity from long ago. Also, 6 miles of the Santa Fe National Forest embrace the trail between the villages of Glorieta (atop the 7,432-foot-high Glorieta Pass) and Canoncito. Stands of tall ponderosa pine, golden aspen, auburn scruboak, ubiquitous piñon pine (the state tree of New Mexico), and juniper are all found here.

HIGHLIGHTS

This Santa Fe Trail tour begins in Santa Fe and heads east over to Clayton, near the borders of Texas and Oklahoma. With a little backtracking, the trail goes north and enters Colorado over the Raton Pass. Full of scenic, natural, and historical treasures, the Byway offers numerous opportunities for both learning and recreation.

- Your first stop will be at **Pecos National Historic Park,** where you'll want to spend some time learning about the ruins of a 14th century Indian pueblo and two 17th century Franciscan missions that crown a fortress-like hill in the verdant Pecos River Valley.

- Your next stop should be in **Las Vegas.** No, not *that* Las Vegas. Las Vegas, New Mexico, has a fantastic wildlife refuge and is worth stopping at to explore the half-mile trail.

- Going north, still on I-25, you'll pass **Buena Vista** and come into **Fort Union National Monument.** The remains of this star-shaped fort are a fantastic sight.

- The **Santa Fe Trail Museum** should be your next stop as you approach the town of **Springer,** and the major highway junction. Enjoy the **Kiowa National Grassland** as you drive east to the border and the town of **Clayton.** While here, don't forget to stop and enjoy **Clayton Lake State Park,** a great place to camp for the evening.

- Next, leaving the Byway for a few miles, take Highway 64 up to **Raton** for a fun experience at the **Sugarite Canyon State Park.** Then, back on the Byway, hop on Highway 64 going south through Cimarron. This drive is fantastic and takes you through the **Cimarron Canyon State Park.** At this point, you may choose to head over to **Taos** and enjoy the museums and ghost towns there, or head back to Santa Fe.

New Mexico

❋ *Santa Fe Trail*

THINGS TO SEE AND DO

Driving along the Santa Fe Trail will certainly keep your senses engaged, but if you yearn to get out of the car and stretch your legs, or if you'd like to make a mini-vacation out of your trip, check out these attractions along the route.

ATALAYA MOUNTAIN HIKING TRAIL. *Camino Cruz Blanca, Santa Fe (87507).* The Atalaya Mountain Trail, accessible from the parking lot at St. John's College, is one of the most popular and easily accessible hiking trails in Santa Fe. Hikers have the option of taking the longer route (Trail 174), which is approximately 7 miles roundtrip, or parking farther up near the Ponderosa Ridge development and doing a 4.6-mile loop (Trail 170), instead. Both trials eventually join and take you toward the top of Atalaya mountain, a 9,121-foot peak. The first few miles of the trail are relatively easy but become increasingly steep and strenuous as you near the summit of Atalaya Mountain. Hikers who make it to the top are afforded great views of the Rio Grande valley and city below.

CAPULIN VOLCANO NATIONAL MONUMENT. *Raton (88740). Phone 505/278-2201.* A dormant volcano that last erupted approximately 10,000 years ago. The strikingly symmetrical cinder cone rises more than 1,500 feet from plains, with a crater 1 mile in circumference and 415 feet deep. Visitors can spiral completely around the mountain on paved road to the rim (open daily); five states can be seen on clear days. Picnic area. Visitor center with exhibits of geology, flora, and fauna of the area (open daily; closed January 1, December 25). Uniformed personnel on duty at the crater rim (summer only). **$$**

CATHEDRAL OF ST. FRANCIS. *Santa Fe (87501). Phone 505/982-5619.* French Romanesque cathedral built in 1869 under the direction of Archbishop Lamy, who served as the prototype for Bishop Latour in Willa Cather's *Death Comes for the Archbishop.* La Conquistadora Chapel, said to be the country's oldest Marian shrine, is here. Tours (summer). Open daily.

CITY OF LAS VEGAS MUSEUM AND ROUGH RIDERS' MEMORIAL COLLECTION. *727 Grand Ave, Las Vegas (88701). Phone 505/425-8726.* Artifacts and memorabilia from the Spanish-American War and turn-of-the-century northern New Mexico life. Open May-Oct, daily; Nov-Apr, Mon-Fri. **FREE**

CROSS OF THE MARTYRS. *Paseo de la Loma, Santa Fe (87504). Phone 505/983-2567.* An ideal destination for history buffs and anyone looking for a sensational city view, this large, hilltop cross weighing 76 tons and standing 25 feet tall honors the memory of more than 20 Franciscan priests and numerous Spanish colonists who were killed during the 1680 Pueblo Revolt against Spanish dominion. Dedicated in 1920, this cross shouldn't be confused with the newer one at nearby Fort Marcy Park. Vistas from the old cross include those of the Sangre de Cristo mountain range immediately northeast, the Jemez about 40 miles west, and the Sandias, 50 miles south near Albuquerque.

◪ EL RANCHO DE LAS GOLONDRINAS. *334 Los Pinos Rd, Santa Fe (87505). Phone 505/471-2261. www.golondrinas.org.* This living-history museum is set in a 200-acre rural valley and depicts Spanish colonial life in New Mexico from 1700 to 1900. It was once a stop on El Camino Real and is one of the most historic ranches in the Southwest. Original colonial buildings date from the 18th century, and special festivals and theme weekends offer visitors a glimpse of the music, dance, clothing, crafts, and celebrations of Spanish colonial New Mexico. Open June-Sept Wed-Sun 10 am-4 pm. **$**

FORT UNION NATIONAL MONUMENT. *NM 161, Las Vegas (88701). Phone 505/425-8025. www.nps.gov/foun/.* Established at this key defensive point on the Santa Fe Trail in 1851, the third and last fort built here was the largest post in the Southwest and the supply center for nearly 50 other forts in the area. It was abandoned by the military in 1891; 100 acres of adobe ruins remain. Self-guided trail with audio stations, living-history programs featuring costumed demonstrations (summer). A visitor center depicts the fort's history and displays artifacts. Open daily; closed Jan 1, Thanksgiving, Dec 25. **$$**

GEORGIA O'KEEFFE MUSEUM. *217 Johnson St, Santa Fe (87501). Phone 505/946-1000. www.okeeffemuseum.org.* One of the most important American artists of the 20th century, Georgia O'Keeffe lived and worked at Ghost Ranch near Abiqui for much of her career, drawing inspiration from the colors and forms of the surrounding desert environment. This museum houses the world's largest permanent collection of her artwork and is also dedicated to the study of American Modernism (1890-present), displaying special exhibits of many of her contemporaries. Open daily 10 am-5 pm, Fri until 8 pm; Nov-June closed Wed; closed holidays. **$$**

HYDE MEMORIAL STATE PARK. *740 Hyde Park Rd, Santa Fe (87501). Phone 505/983-7175.* Perched 8,500 feet up in the Sangre de Cristo Mountains near the Santa Fe Ski Basin; used as base camp for backpackers and skiers in the Santa Fe National Forests. Cross-country skiing, rentals, picnicking (shelters), playground, concession, camping (electric hookups). Open daily. **$$**

⭐ **INDIAN MARKET.** *125 E Palace Ave, Santa Fe (85701). Phone 505/983-5220. www.swaia.org.* Each year in late August the Santa Fe Indian Market attracts a swarm of national and international buyers and collectors to the largest and oldest Native American arts show and market in the world. More than 1,200 artists from over 100 North American tribes participate in the show, with around 600 outdoor booths set up in the middle of the ancient Santa Fe Plaza. The market is a great opportunity to meet the artists and buy directly from them instead of going through the usual galleries and other middle-men. Quality of work is stressed, as all sale items are strictly screened for quality and authenticity.

Numerous outdoor booths sell food, and the event draws an estimated 100,000 visitors to Santa Fe during the weekend, so make your lodging reservations well in advance.

INSTITUTE OF AMERICAN INDIAN ARTS MUSEUM. *108 Cathedral Pl, Santa Fe (87501). Phone 505/983-8900. www.iaiancad.org.* The Institute of American Indian Arts, established in 1962, runs a college in south Santa Fe in addition to a museum just off the Plaza. The museum is the only one in the country dedicated solely to collecting and exhibiting contemporary Native American art, much of it produced by the staff and faculty of the college. Inside you can view educational films, exhibits of contemporary artists, and outdoor sculptures in an enclosed courtyard. Open June-Sept, Mon-Sat 9 am-5 pm, Sun from 10 am; Oct-May, Mon-Sat 10 am-5 pm, Sun from noon. **$$**

INVITATIONAL ANTIQUE INDIAN ART SHOW. *201 W Marcy, Santa Fe (87501). Phone 505/984-6760.* Sweeney Center. Largest show of its kind in the country. Pre-1935 items; attracts dealers, collectors, museums. Phone 505/984-6760. Two days in mid-Aug.

LA FONDA HOTEL. *100 E San Francisco St, Santa Fe (87501).* A longtime center of Santa Fe social life. Former meeting place of trappers, pioneers, merchants, soldiers, and politicians; known as the Inn at the End of the Trail.

LAS VEGAS NATIONAL WILDLIFE REFUGE. *NM 281, Las Vegas (88701). Phone 505/425-3581.* Nature trail, observation of wildlife, including migratory water fowl. Hunting for dove (permit required), Canada geese (permit required, limited drawing); user's fee for hunts. Open daily; some areas Mon-Fri. **FREE**

LENSIC PERFORMING ARTS CENTER. *211 W San Francisco St, Santa Fe (87501). Phone 505/988-7050. www.lensic.com.* The Lensic Theater is one of Santa Fe's historical and architectural gems, recently reopened after a full restoration completed in 2001. The structure was first built in 1931 in a Moorish/Spanish Renaissance style and has always been Santa Fe's premiere theater space, having played host to celebrities such as Roy Rogers and Judy Garland over the years. Since reopening, it has provided a constantly changing schedule of quality theater, symphony, and performing arts events.

LORETTO CHAPEL. *207 Old Santa Fe Trl, Santa Fe (87501). Phone 505/984-7971.* The Loretto Chapel was built in 1873 and is one of the few non-adobe-style buildings in downtown Santa Fe. Modeled after St. Chapelle cathedral in Paris, it was the first Gothic building built west of the Mississippi. The chapel itself is not particularly impressive, but what draws countless tourists is the miraculous stairway, a 22-feet-high spiral wooden staircase built without any nails or central supports that seems to defy engineering logic. According to legend, the stairway was put together with wooden pegs. It makes two 360-degree turns and has 33 steps. Open Mon-Sat 9 am-5 pm, Sun 10:30 am-5 pm; closed Dec 25.

MAVERICK CLUB RODEO. *Maverick Club Arena, Cimarron (87714). Phone 505/376-2417.* Rodeo for working cowboys. Parade, dance. Held July 4.

MORPHY LAKE STATE PARK. *NM 94, Las Vegas (88701). Phone 505/387-2328.* Towering ponderosa pines surround 15-acre mountain lake in **Carson National Forest.** Primitive use area. Fishing (trout), restricted boating (oars or electric motors only; ramp); winter sports, primitive camping. Accessible to backpackers; four-wheel-drive vehicle advisable. No drinking water is available. Open daily. $$

MOUNTAIN MAN RENDEZVOUS AND FESTIVAL. *105 W Palace Ave, Santa Fe (87504). Phone 505/476-5100. www.festivalofthewest.com/ mountainman.html.* In early August, costumed mountain men ride into town on horseback for the Museum of New Mexico's annual buffalo roast, part of a large gathering of trappers and traders from the pre-1840 wilderness. Participants sell primitive equipment, tools,

and trinkets and compete in period survival skills such as knife and tomahawk throwing, muzzleloader rifle shooting, cannon firing, storytelling, and foot racing.

MUSEUM OF FINE ARTS. *107 W Palace Ave, Santa Fe (87501). Phone 505/476-5072. www.museumofnewmexico.org.* Designed by Isaac Hamilton Rapp in 1917, this museum is one of Santa Fe's earliest Pueblo revival structures and its oldest art museum. It contains more than 20,000 holdings, with an emphasis on Southwest regional art and the artists of Santa Fe and Taos from the early 20th century. The St. Francis Auditorium inside the museum also presents lectures, musical events, plays, and various other performances. Open Tues-Sun 10 am-5 pm; closed holidays. $$$

MUSEUM OF INDIAN ARTS AND CULTURE. *710 Camino Lejo, Santa Fe (87505). Phone 505/476-1250. www.miaclab.org.* When the Spanish arrived in the Southwest in the 16th century, they found many sprawling towns and villages that they referred to as pueblos, a name that is still used to identify American Indian communities in New Mexico today. The Museum of Indian Arts and Culture houses an extensive collection of historic and contemporary Pueblo art from throughout the Southwest. One of the highlights of the museum is an excellent interpretive section, where you can encounter native Pueblo cultures from the viewpoint and narrative of modern-day Pueblo natives and exhibit designers. The museum itself is housed in a large, adobe-style building that blends architecturally into the surroundings; the museum also houses many outstanding examples of Pueblo textiles, pottery, jewelry, contemporary paintings, and other rotating exhibits. An adjacent building houses the **Laboratory of Anthropology,** which contains an extensive library and supports continuing research into Southwestern archeology and cultural studies. Open Tues-Sun 10 am-5 pm; closed holidays. $$

MUSEUM OF INTERNATIONAL FOLK ART. *706 Camino Lejo, Santa Fe (87502). Phone 505/476-1200. www.moifa.org.* The Museum of International Folk Art, which first opened in 1953, contains more than 120,000 objects, billing itself as the world's largest folk museum dedicated to the study of traditional cultural art. Much of the massive collection was acquired when the late Italian immigrant, architect/designer Alexander Girard donated his 106,000-object collection of toys, figurines, figurative ceramics, miniatures, and religious/ceremonial art, which he had collected from more than 100 countries around the world. In addition to the collection in the Girard wing, you'll also find a large collection of Hispanic art in the Hispanic Heritage Wing, as well as costumes and folk art from many cultures in the Neutrogena Collection. Several smaller collections and major temporary exhibits add to a rich museum experience that can easily take several hours to explore. Two museum shops offer a wide variety of folk-oriented books, clothing, and jewelry to choose from. Open Tues-Sun 10 am-5 pm; closed holidays. **$$**

OLD AZTEC MILL MUSEUM. *Cimarron (87714). Phone 505/376-2913.* Built as gristmill in 1864. Chuckwagon, mill wheels, and local historical items. Open Memorial Day-Labor Day, Fri-Wed; early May and late Sept, weekends. **$**

OLDEST HOUSE. *De Vargas St and Old Santa Fe Trl, Santa Fe (87501).* Believed to be pre-Spanish; Oldest House was built by Native Americans more than 800 years ago.

PALACE OF THE GOVERNORS. *105 Palace Ave, Santa Fe (87501). Phone 505/476-5100. www.palaceofthegovernors.com.* Built in 1610, this is the oldest public building in continuous use in the US. It was the seat of government in New Mexico for more than 300 years. Lew Wallace, governor of the territory (1878-1881), wrote part of *Ben Hur* here in 1880. It is now a major museum of Southwestern history. The Palace, Museum of Fine Arts, Museum of Indian Arts

and Culture, Museum of International Folk Art, and state monuments all make up the Museum of New Mexico. Open Tues-Sun 10 am-5 pm; closed holidays. **$$**

PECOS NATIONAL HISTORICAL PARK. *US 25, Santa Fe (87501). Phone 505/757-6414. www.nps.gov/peco/.* The ruins of Pecos Pueblo lie on a mesa along the Santa Fe Trail that served as a strategic trade route and crossroads between Pueblo and Plains Indian cultures. At its peak, the pueblo housed a community of as many as 2,000 people, and was occupied for nearly 500 years. When the Spanish arrived, it became an important missionary outpost that continued to be occupied until the 1800s, when its last inhabitants relocated to Jemez Pueblo. Ruins of the original multi-story structures survive in the form of large stone walls and several ceremonial kivas that have been restored. The largest ruins are of two Spanish missionary churches that were destroyed in the Pueblo revolt of 1680. An easy 1.25-mile hike and self-guided tour allows you to explore the ruins at you own pace. The visitor center includes historical exhibits and shows an introductory film covering the area's history. Open daily 8 am-5 pm; closed Dec 25. **$$**

RATON MUSEUM. *218 S 1st St, Raton (88740). Phone 505/445-8979.* Collections relating to the Native American, Hispanic, ranch, railroad, and mining cultures in New Mexico. Open Memorial Day-Labor Day, Tues-Sat; rest of year, Wed-Sat or by appointment; closed holidays. **FREE**

SAN ILDEFONSO PUEBLO. *NM 502, Santa Fe (87501). Phone 505/455-2273.* This pueblo (population 447) is famous for its beautiful surroundings and its black, red, and polychrome pottery, made famous by Maria Poveka Martinez. A photography permit may be purchased at the visitor center. Various festivals take place here throughout the year. The circular structure with the staircase leading up to its rim is a kiva, or ceremonial chamber. There are two shops in the Pueblo plaza, and a tribal museum adjoins the governor's office. One-half mile west is a fishing lake. Open daily; closed winter weekends; visitors must register at the visitor center. **$$**

SAN MIGUEL MISSION. *401 Old Santa Fe Trl, Santa Fe (87501). Phone 505/983-3974. www.sdc.org/~smiguel/.* Built in the early 1600s, this is the oldest church in the US still in use. Construction was overseen by Fray Alonso de Benavidez, along with a group of Tlaxcalan Indians from Mexico who did most of the work. The original adobe still remains beneath the stucco walls, and the interior has been restored along with Santa Fe's oldest wooden reredos (altar screen). Church services are still held on Sundays. Open daily; closed holidays. **FREE**

SANTA FE CHILDREN'S MUSEUM. *1050 Old Pecos Trl, Santa Fe (87505). Phone 505/989-8359. www.santafechildrensmuseum.org.* Happy activity fills a creative space that absorbs the attention of children of all ages. Hands-on exhibits invite kids to make magnetic structures, route water streams, create paintings, illustrate cartoon movies, discover plants on a greenhouse scavenger hunt, scale an 18-foot-high climbing wall, use an old-fashioned pitcher pump, and weave beads and fabric on a loom. Local artists and scientists make appearances to teach kids in playful, inventive ways. Especially interesting are regularly scheduled events, like Music Under the Big Top and Ice Cream Sunday. Open Wed-Sat 10 am-5 pm, Sun noon-5 pm; closed Mon, Tues, Dec 25. **$**

SANTA FE NATIONAL FOREST. *1474 Radio Rd, Santa Fe (87501). Phone 505/438-7840; toll-free 800/280-2267 (reservations).* This forest consists of over 1 1/2 million acres. Fishing is excellent in the Pecos and Jemez rivers and tributary streams. Hiking trails are close to unusual geologic formations. There are hot springs in the Jemez Mountains. Four wilderness areas within the forest total more than 300,000 acres. Campgrounds are provided by the Forest Service at more than 40 locations.

⭐ **SANTA FE PLAZA.** *100 Old Santa Fe Trl, Santa Fe (87501). www.santafeinformation.com.* The Santa Fe Plaza, steeped in a rich history, has been a focal point for commerce and social activities in Santa Fe since the early 17th century. The area is marked by a central tree-lined park surrounded by some of Santa Fe's most important historical landmarks, many of which survive from Spanish colonial times. The most important landmark is the **Palace of the Governors,** which was the original seat of local government and is the oldest public building in the US still in use. Native American artists from nearby pueblos sell handmade artwork in front of the Palace and at various museums, shops, and dining establishments surround the Plaza, making it the top tourist destination in Santa Fe. Numerous festivals and activities are held in the Plaza throughout the year, including the **Spanish Market** and **Indian Market.**

SANTA FE RODEO. *2801 W Rodeo Rd, Santa Fe (87502). Phone 505/471-4300. www.rodeosantafe .org.* The Santa Fe Rodeo offers the chance to see real live cowboys and bucking broncos in action at the outdoor rodeo fairgrounds. Various professional competitions and public exhibitions open to the public are put on during the brief summer season. Rodeo events generally happen during evening and weekend matinee hours. A downtown rodeo parade takes place in mid June at the start of the season. **$$$$**

SANTA FE SOUTHERN RAILWAY. *410 Guadalupe St, Santa Fe (87501). Phone 505/989-8600. sfsr.com.* Made famous by the 1940s swing tune "Atchison, Topeka & Santa Fe," a small part of this historical rail line continues as the Santa Fe Southern Railway, which still carries freight and tourists between Santa Fe and nearby Lamy, an 18-mile trip. The start of the route is housed in the old **Santa Fe Depot,** where you can view vintage railcars and shop for gifts and memorabilia in the original mission-style train depot. Several scenic train rides in authentically restored vintage cars are offered to the public, following the original high desert route to and from Lamy. The rides cater to tourists and range from short scenic roundtrips to longer outings that include picnics, BBQs, and various holiday-themed events, such as the Halloween Highball Train and New Year's Eve Party Train.

SANTA FE TRAIL MUSEUM. *614 Maxwell Ave, Springer (87747). Phone 505/483-2682.* The Santa Fe Trail Museum displays artifacts and exhibits about pioneer life on and around the trail from 1880-1949. Open daily 9 am-4 pm, summer only. **$**

⭐ **SANTA FE WINE AND CHILE FIESTA.** *551 W Cordova Rd, Santa Fe (87505). Phone 505/438-8060. www.santafewineandchile.org.* Begun in 1991, this wildly popular festival honoring the best in food and drink brings in some 2,000 appreciative fans from around the state and across the country for four days of noshing and sipping on the last weekend in September. Roughly 50 local restaurants and 90 wineries from around the globe team up with a half-dozen or so of America's top celebrity chefs and cookbook authors to present a culinary extravaganza in a variety of venues around town. Wine seminars, cooking demonstrations, special vintners' lunches and dinners, and the gastronomic circus called the Grand Tasting, staged in mammoth tents on the Santa Fe Opera grounds, fill a palate-thrilling schedule. **$$$$**

SANTUARIO DE GUADALUPE. *100 Guadalupe St, Santa Fe (87501). Phone 505/988-2027.* Built in 1781 and the oldest shrine in America dedicated to Our Lady of Guadalupe, the Santuario has been converted into an art and history museum specializing in religious art and iconography. The holdings include a large collection of Northern New Mexican santos (carved wooden saints) and paintings in the Italian Renaissance and Mexican baroque styles. A famous rendering of Our Lady of Guadalupe by renowned Mexican artist Jose de Alzibar is also on display. Open Mon-Fri 9 am-4 pm; May-Oct, also open Sat; closed holidays. **FREE**

SENA PLAZA AND PRINCE PLAZA. *Washington and Palace aves, Santa Fe (87501).* Small shops, formerly old houses, built behind portals and around central patios.

SHIDONI BRONZE FOUNDRY AND GALLERY. *1508 Bishop's Lodge Rd, Santa Fe (87501). Phone 505/988-8001. www.shidoni.com.* A fantastic resource for art collectors and sculptors, Shidoni consists of a bronze foundry, art gallery, and outdoor sculpture garden set in an 8-acre apple orchard 5 miles north of Santa Fe. Artists from around the country come to work at Shidoni's 14,000-square-foot foundry, which is open to the general public for self-guided tours. Explore the lovely sculpture garden during daylight hours or shop for works of bronze and metal in the adjacent gallery. Open Mon-Sat; closed Sun, Thanksgiving, Dec 25.

SKI SANTA FE. *Hyde Park Rd (Hwy 475), Santa Fe (87501). Phone 505/982-4429. www.skisantafe.com.* World-class skiing and snowboarding in the majestic Sangre de Cristo Mountains is only a 20-minute drive from the downtown Santa Fe Plaza. Ski Santa Fe is a family-owned resort catering to skiers and snowboarders of all levels, from beginning to expert. In addition to breathtaking views of the city below, the 12,053-foot summit offers six lifts and 44 runs (20 percent easy, 40 percent more difficult, 40 percent most difficult), with a total of 660 acres of terrain. The longest run is 3 miles, and the mountain offers a vertical drop of 1,700 feet. The average yearly snowfall is 225 inches. A PSIA-certified ski school offers group and private lessons for adults and children, and there are restaurants, rental shops, and a clothing boutique on site. The Chipmunk Corner offers activities and lessons for children ages 4-9. Open late Nov-early Apr, daily. **$$$$**

SPANISH MARKET. *750 Camino Lejo, Santa Fe (87505). Phone 505/983-4038. www.spanishmarket.org.* The rich and colorful Hispanic art traditions of Northern New Mexico are celebrated twice a year during

Spanish Market, the oldest and largest exhibition and sale of traditional Hispanic art in the US. The smaller winter market in December is held indoors in the Sweeney Convention Center (201 W Marcy St), while the larger summer market occupies the entire Santa Fe Plaza for one weekend in July. During the market, as many as 300 vendors sell and display santos (carved saints), hide paintings, textiles, furniture, jewelry, tinwork, basketry, pottery, bone work, and other locally produced handicrafts reflecting the unique and deeply religious traditional art that still flourishes in this part of New Mexico. Sponsored by the Spanish Colonial Arts Society.

STATE CAPITOL. *Old Santa Fe Trl and Pasco de Peralta, Santa Fe (87501). Phone 505/986-4589.* This unique building, in modified Territorial style, is round and intended to resemble a Zia sun symbol. Self-guided tours. Open Memorial Day-Labor Day, daily; rest of year, Mon-Sat; closed holidays. **FREE**

STORRIE LAKE STATE PARK. *NM 518, Las Vegas (88701). Phone 505/425-7278.* Swimming, water-skiing, fishing, boating (ramp), windsurfing, picnicking, playground, camping (hookups). Open daily. **$$**

SUGARITE CANYON STATE PARK. *Sugarite Canyon, Raton (88740). Phone 505/445-5607.* This park contains 3,500 acres and offers fishing, ice fishing, boating (oars or electric motors only), and tubing; seasonal bow hunting for deer and turkey, cross-country skiing, ice skating, riding trails (no rentals), picnicking, and camping (fee). Visitor center open May-Sept, daily; rest of year by appointment. **$$**

✪ **TESUQUE PUEBLO FLEA MARKET.** *Next to the Santa Fe Opera, Santa Fe (87501). Phone 505/995-8626. www.tesuquepueblofleamarket.com.* At the Tesuque Pueblo outdoor flea market, you'll find hundreds of vendors offering antiques, gems, jewelry, pottery, rugs, and world folk art of all descriptions at very competitive prices. Plan on devoting a couple of hours to browse all the various treasures and myriad of vendor booths stretching for several acres. Even if you don't buy anything, it's a browser's paradise well worth the 15-minute drive from Santa Fe. Open mid-Mar-Dec, Thurs-Sun.

THE WHEELWRIGHT MUSEUM OF THE AMERICAN INDIAN. *704 Camino Lejo, Santa Fe (87505). Phone 505/982-4636; toll-free 800/607-4636. www.wheelwright.org.* Founded in 1937 by Mary Cabot Wheelwright and Navajo singer/medicine man Hastiin Klah to help preserve Navajo art and traditions, the Wheelwright now devotes itself to hosting major exhibits of Native American artists from tribes throughout North America. The Case Trading Post in the basement sells pottery, jewelry, textiles, books, prints, and other gift items. Open Mon-Sat 10 am-5 pm, Sun 1-5 pm; closed holidays. **FREE**

ZOZOBRA FESTIVAL. *490 Washington Ave, Santa Fe (87501).* Each year on the Thursday before Labor Day, the Kiwanis Club of Santa Fe hosts the burning of Zozobra, a 50-foot effigy of Old Man Gloom, whose passing away is designed to dispel the hardships and travails of the previous year. As part of the Fiestas celebration, Zozobra started in 1924 when a local artist conceived a ritual based on a Yaqui Indian celebration from Mexico. Over the years, Zozobra caught on and the crowd sizes have grown, making Zozobra Santa Fe's largest, most colorful, and most spectacular festival. Lasting for several hours, as many as 60,000 visitors crowd into a large grassy field in Fort Marcy Park to listen to live bands, watch spectacular fireworks displays, and cheer the ritual burning. Fiestas celebrations continue during the Labor Day weekend, with all day booths and activities setup in the nearby Plaza. Held the Thurs before Labor Day. **$$$**

PLACES TO STAY

If you choose to include an overnight stay in your trip along this Byway, Mobil Travel Guide recommends the following lodgings.

Cimarron

★★★CASA DEL GAVILAN. *Hwy 21 S, Cimarron (87714). Phone 505/376-2246; toll-free 800-GAVILAN. www.casadelgavilan.com.* Peace and tranquility are the most appreciated features of this inn. Guests can relax in the library or on the porch while sipping tea or wine. More adventurous guests can go hiking in the trails behind the inn. 5 rooms. No A/C. No room phones. Complimentary full breakfast. Check-out 11 am, check-in 3 pm. Southwestern adobe built in 1912. Totally nonsmoking. ¢
D⚹⬛

Las Vegas (New Mexico)

★BUDGET INN. *1216 N Grand Ave, Las Vegas (87701). Phone 505/425-9357.* 45 rooms, 2 story. Pet accepted, some restrictions; fee. Check-out 11 am. TV; cable (premium). ¢
⬛⬛⬛⬛

★COMFORT INN. *2500 N Grand Ave, Las Vegas (87701). Phone 505/425-1100; toll-free 800/228-5150. www.comfortinn.com.* 101 rooms, 2 story. Complimentary continental breakfast. Check-out 11 am. TV; cable (premium). Indoor pool, whirlpool. ¢
D⬛⬛⬛

★★INN ON THE SANTA FE TRAIL. *1133 Grand Ave, Las Vegas (87701). Phone 505/425-6791; toll-free 888/448-8438. www.innonthesantafetrail.com.* 42 rooms. Pet accepted; fee. Complimentary continental breakfast. Check-out 11 am. TV; cable (premium). In-room modem link. Pool, whirlpool. Lawn games. ¢
D⬛SC⬛

★★PLAZA HOTEL. *230 Plaza, Las Vegas (87701). Phone 505/425-3591; toll-free 800/328-1882. www.plazahotel-nm.com.* 37 rooms, 3 story. Pet accepted; fee. Check-out 11 am. TV; cable (premium). Restaurant, bar. Cross-country ski 5 miles. Historic hotel built in 1882 in the Victorian Italianate-bracketed style; interior renovated; period furnishings, antiques. ¢
D⬛⬛SC

Raton

★★BEST WESTERN SANDS. *300 Clayton Rd, Raton (87740). Phone 505/445-2737; toll-free 800/780-7234. www.bestwestern.com.* 50 rooms. Check-out 11 am. TV; cable (premium). In-room modem link. Restaurant. Pool, whirlpool. ¢
D⬛⬛

★BUDGET HOST MELODY LANE. *136 Canyon Dr, Raton (87740). Phone 505/445-3655; toll-free 800/283-4678. www.budgethost.com.* 27 rooms. Pet accepted, some restrictions; fee. Check-out 11 am. TV; cable (premium). Continental breakfast. ¢
D⬛⬛SC⬛

Santa Fe

★★★ELDORADO HOTEL. *309 W San Francisco, Santa Fe (87501). Phone 505/988-4455; toll-free 800/286-6755. www.eldoradohotel.com.* The Eldorado Hotel's imposing Pueblo Revival-style building is one of Santa Fe's largest and most important landmarks. Its lobby and interiors are lavishly decorated with more than a quarter million dollars of original Southwest art. The Lobby Lounge serves drinks and is a great spot for snacking, people watching, and enjoying live entertainment. Sunday brunch is served in the cozy Eldorado Court; it was voted best brunch by the residents of Santa Fe. 219 rooms, 5 story. Pet accepted; fee. Garage parking, fee. Check-out noon. TV; cable (premium), VCR available (movies). In-room modem link. Restaurant, bar; entertainment. In-house fitness room, massage, sauna. Rooftop pool, whirlpool, poolside service. Cross-country ski 7 miles. Business center. Concierge. $$$

⚐ 🏃 🧍 D ⬛ ➤ SC ⬛

★**GARRETTS DESERT INN.** *311 Old Santa Fe Trl, Santa Fe (87501). Phone 505/982-1851; toll-free 800/888-2145.* 82 rooms, 2 story. Check-out noon. TV; cable (premium). Restaurant, bar. Pool. $

⬛

★★★**HOTEL SANTA FE.** *1501 Paseo De Peralta, Santa Fe (87501). Phone 505/982-1200; toll-free 800/825-9876. www.hotelsantafe.com.* This hotel features such extras as storytelling in front of the kiva fireplace, ceremonial dances, and pottery/paintings. Guests can also relax in the swimming pool or whirlpool or with a massage. 129 rooms, 3 story. Check-out noon. TV; cable (premium). Restaurant, bar; entertainment Fri, Sat. Pool, whirlpool. Downhill, cross-country ski 10 miles. Airport transportation. Concierge. Pueblo Revival architecture; original art by Native Americans. A Native American enterprise. $$

D ⬛ ⬛ ➤ ⬛

★★★**INN AT LORETTO.** *211 Old Santa Fe Trl, Santa Fe (87501). Phone 505/988-5531; toll-free 800/727-5331. www.hotelloretto.com.* Built in 1975, this hotel offers guests a heated outdoor pool, 12 specialty shops, and galleries. Guests can also enjoy skiing, hiking, tennis, and horseback riding. 140 rooms, 4 story. Check-out noon. TV; cable (premium). Guest laundry. Restaurant, bar; entertainment. Room service. Massage. Pool, poolside service. Downhill, cross-country ski 15 miles. Concierge. Adobe building. $$$

⚐ D ✦ ⬛ ➤ ⬛

★★★★**INN OF THE ANASAZI.** *113 Washington Ave, Santa Fe (87501). Phone 505/988-3030; toll-free 800/688-8100. www.innoftheanasazi.com.* Native American, Hispanic, and cowboy cultures

collide at the Inn of the Anasazi, where a masterful blend of New Mexican legacies results in a stunning and unusual lodging. The true spirit of Santa Fe is captured here, where enormous handcrafted doors open to a world of authentic artwork, carvings, and textiles synonymous with the Southwest. The lobby sets a sense of place for arriving guests with its rough-hewn tables, leather furnishings, unique objects, and huge cactus plants in terracotta pots. Located just off the historic Plaza, the inn was designed to resemble the traditional dwellings of the Anasazi. The region's integrity is maintained in the guest rooms, where fireplaces and four-poster beds reside under ceilings of vigas and latillas, and guests discover toiletries made locally with native cedar extract. 59 rooms, 3 story. Pet accepted; fee. Valet parking available. Check-out noon. TV; cable (premium), VCR available. Restaurant. In-house fitness room. Massage. Health club privileges. Downhill ski 13 miles, cross-country ski 7 miles. Concierge. $$

D ⬛ ➤ ⬛ 🧍

★★**RADISSON SANTA FE.** *750 N St Francis Dr, Santa Fe (87501). Phone 505/992-5800; toll-free 800/333-3333. www.radisson.com.* This beautifully landscaped hilltop hotel is centrally located near the city's major attractions. Guests enjoy the large swimming pool and hot tub as well as complimentary access to the next-door Santa Fe Spa. One- and two-bedroom condos offer kiva fireplaces and full kitchens. 141 rooms, 2 story. Check-out noon. TV; cable (premium). Restaurant, bar; entertainment. Room service. Pool, poolside service. $

★★**VILLAS DE SANTA FE.** *400 Griffin St, Santa Fe (87501). Phone 505/988-3000; toll-free 800/869-6790. www.sunterra.com.* 100 rooms, 4 story. Complimentary breakfast buffet. Check-out noon. TV; cable (premium). In-room modem link. In-house fitness room. Pool, whirlpools. Concierge. $$

🧍 ⚐ D ✦ ⬛ SC ⬛

PLACES TO EAT

A long day of driving is sure to make you hungry. At the end of your journey, take a table at one of the following restaurants.

Las Vegas (New Mexico)

★EL RIALTO. *141 Bridge St, Las Vegas (87701). Phone 505/454-0037.* American, Mexican menu. Closed Sun; major holidays. Lunch, dinner. Bar. Children's menu. Historic building (1890s); antiques. $$
D

★PINOS TRUCK STOP. *1901 N Grand Ave, Las Vegas (87701). Phone 505/454-1944.* American, Mexican menu. Closed Thanksgiving, Dec 25. Breakfast, lunch, dinner. Children's menu. $$
D SC

Raton

★★PAPPAS' SWEET SHOP. *1201 S 2nd St, Raton (87740). Phone 505/445-9811.* Closed Sun; most major holidays. Lunch, dinner. Bar. Children's menu. $
D

Santa Fe

★★★THE ANASAZI. *113 Washington Ave, Santa Fe (87501). Phone 505/988-3236. www. innoftheanasazi.com.* The creators of memorable cuisine at this Plaza mainstay like to point out that the Navajo definition of Anasazi has come to embody an ancient wisdom that is synonymous with the art of living harmoniously and peacefully with the environment. That philosophy is translated in the colorful Native American weavings, petroglyph-inspired art upon the walls of beautiful rock, and mesmerizing fires that crackle and warm the rooms within this dining favorite. Executive chef Tom Kerpon devotes himself to inventive uses of locally grown, organic products, from cactus and sage to chiles and corn. Contemporary Southwestern menu. Menu changes seasonally. Breakfast, lunch, dinner, Sun brunch. Bar. Classical guitarist (brunch). Children's menu. Casual attire. $$$
D

★★★COYOTE CAFÉ. *132 W Water St, Santa Fe (87501). Phone 505/983-1615. www.coyote-cafe.com.* Famed cookbook author and pioneer of Southwestern cuisine Mark Miller has enjoyed nothing but success at this bastion of trendy dining found just a block off the Plaza. Although the menu changes seasonally, patrons are assured of finding a whimsical mingling of the cuisines of New Mexico, Mexico, Cuba, and Spain in all manner of meats, fish, and vegetables, served in inventive dishes. Don't miss the house drink special, a margarita del Maguey. Whether seated in the main dining room (try for a window-side table overlooking the street) or on the festive rooftop Cantina, be sure to relax and soak up the setting, decorated by magnificent folk art and artistic lighting fixtures. New Mexican menu. Dinner. Bar/cantina (May-Oct). Casual attire. Outdoor seating. $$$
D

★EL FAROL. *808 Canyon Rd, Santa Fe (87501). Phone 505/983-9912.* Mexican menu. Closed major holidays. Lunch, dinner. Bar. Casual attire. Outdoor seating. $
D

★★EL MESON-LA COCINA DE ESPANA. *213 Washington Ave, Santa Fe (87501). Phone 505/983-6756.* Spanish menu. Closed Sun, Mon; also Jan 1, Thanksgiving, Dec 25. Lunch, dinner. Guitarist weekends. Children's menu. Outdoor seating. Totally nonsmoking. $$
D

★★★★GERONIMO. *724 Canyon Rd, Santa Fe (87501). Phone 505/982-1500. www. geronimorestaurant.com.* Housed in a restored 250-year-old landmark adobe, Geronimo (the name of the restaurant is an ode to the hacienda's original owner, Geronimo Lopez)

offers robust Southwestern-spiked global fusion fare in a stunning and cozy space. Owners Cliff Skoglund and Chris Harvey treat each guest like family, and this is a nice family to be a part of. Geronimo is inviting and warm, with a wood-burning, cove-style fireplace; eggshell walls; sheer curtains; tall, rich chocolate- and garnet-leather seating; and local Native American-style sculpture and artwork decorating the walls. It feels like a Georgia O'Keefe painting come to life. It's not just the serene and stylish space that earns Geronimo points with its regulars. The food is remarkable, fusing the distinct culinary influences of Asia, the Southwest, and the Mediterranean. Vibrant flavors, bright colors, and top-notch seasonal regional ingredients come together in perfect harmony. While Geronimo is a great place for dinner, it is also a perfect spot to take a break from gallery hopping around lunchtime. When it's warm outside, sit on the patio for prime Canyon Road people-watching. Global menu. Lunch, dinner. Bar. Casual attire. Outdoor seating. $$$
D

★GRANT CORNER INN. *122 Grant Ave, Santa Fe (87501). Phone 505/983-6678. www.grantcornerinn.com.* Brunch menu. Children's menu. Guitarist Sun. Colonial-style house built in 1905. Outdoor seating. $$
D

★★MAÑANA. *101 W Alameda, Santa Fe (87501). Phone 505/982-4333.* Southwestern, Californian menu. Breakfast, lunch, dinner. Bar. Piano. Casual attire. Outdoor seating. $$

★★THE PINK ADOBE. *406 Old Santa Fe Trl, Santa Fe (87501). Phone 505/983-7712. www.thepinkadobe.com.* Southwestern, continental menu. Closed major holidays. Lunch, dinner. Bar; entertainment Tues-Thurs, Sat. Children's menu. Historic pink adobe building circa 1700. Casual attire. Outdoor seating. $$
D

★PLAZA. *54 Lincoln Ave, Santa Fe (87501). Phone 505/982-1664.* Continental menu. Closed Thanksgiving, Dec 25. Breakfast, lunch, dinner. Children's menu. Century-old building with many original fixtures; stamped-tin ceiling; photos of early Santa Fe. Casual attire. $$

★SHED AND LA CHOZA. *113 1/2 E Palace Ave, Santa Fe (87501). Phone 505/982-9030. www.sfshed.com.* New Mexican menu. Closed Sun, major holidays. Lunch, dinner. Children's menu. Casual attire. Outdoor seating. Totally nonsmoking. $
D

★★★STAAB HOUSE. *330 E Palace Ave, Santa Fe (87501). Phone 505/986-0000. www.laposadadesantafe.com.* A historic site dating from the late 1800s, the Staab House sits within the famed La Posada Resort & Spa a couple of blocks from the Plaza and has been restored to its Victorian-era elegance. Regulars have become fans of fashionable dining in its Fuego restaurant and delectable margaritas in the Staab House Lounge. Dinner is a particularly appealing brand of Southwestern style, with infusions of regional ingredients in classic dishes. Southwestern menu. Breakfast, lunch, dinner, Sun brunch. Bar. Entertainment (seasonal). Children's menu. Hand-crafted furniture; fireplace. Casual attire. Outdoor seating. $$$
D

Turquoise Trail
✳ NEW MEXICO

Quick Facts

LENGTH: 61 miles.

TIME TO ALLOW: 3 hours.

BEST TIME TO DRIVE: Year-round; high seasons are fall and spring.

BYWAY TRAVEL INFORMATION: Turquoise Trail Association: 888/263-0003; Byway local Web site: www.turquoisetrail.org.

SPECIAL CONSIDERATIONS: If you're venturing into the mountains, take a coat or jacket.

RESTRICTIONS: Snow may cause a chain rule and/or four-wheel drive requirements to be in effect between October and March.

BICYCLE/PEDESTRIAN FACILITIES: There is an interpretive trail that you can hike at the Tijeras Pueblo near Tijeras. Also, keep an eye out for the Balsam Glade Picnic Ground, where unimproved Route 165 leads to a 1-mile trail to Sandia Cave.

B ack roads often lead to glorious scenery and great discovery, and so it is with the Turquoise Trail. When you leave the freeway and venture onto the scenic and historic Turquoise Trail, you get a chance to see 15,000 square miles of central New Mexico from a bird's-eye view atop Sandia Crest, the magnificent summit of the Sandia Mountains that rises 10,678 feet. From here, you can venture into Sandia Crest Wilderness Area while hiking through aspen glades and across flowering meadows, coming upon one spectacular view after another.

You can also drive back in time by visiting the ghost mining towns of Golden, Madrid, and Cerrillos, towns that are now coming alive with arts, crafts, theater, music, museums, and restaurants. In addition, the Museum of Archaeology and Material Culture in Cedar Crest exhibits a 12,000-year timeline that tells the story of North America's earliest inhabitants and goes chronologically through history until the Battle of Wounded Knee in 1890.

All along the way, there is adventure and fun for everyone. To really discover the Land of Enchantment, travel the Turquoise Trail.

THE BYWAY STORY

The Turquoise Trail tells archaeological, cultural, historic, natural, recreational, and scenic stories that make it a unique and treasured Byway.

Archaeological
Over thousands of years, many people have inhabited the area along the Turquoise Trail. Pottery shards, ancient mining quarries, and pueblos are just some of the evidence ancient inhabitants left behind. Prehistoric Indians

relied on many features of the area for their economy, such as the rich deposits of turquoise and local lead, which were used for decoration and glazes in their pottery.

The Tijeras Pueblo, an archaeological site located near the ranger station of the Cibola National Forest, once housed several hundred people. These ancient people lived in the area over 600 years ago. The San Marcos Pueblo offers limited tours (by appointment) and serves as a research site that provides archaeological field experience for students at the University of New Mexico. Many adobe and masonry pueblo structures remain intact at the San Marcos site, and estimates are that the pueblo had between 3,000 and 5,000 rooms. During the 1300s and mid-1400s, the pueblo was also a center for pottery making.

One of the oldest dwellings in the area may be Sandia Cave. Evidence surrounding the cave's earliest occupants remains controversial, but excavations from the cave suggest that people lived in the cave during three different time periods. Pre-Colombian Pueblo-style artifacts; hearths and tools of nomadic hunters; and Folsom spear points used on bison, giant sloths, and horses have all been found in the cave. These artifacts relate the story of a past people and indicate the way in which they lived.

The early pueblo inhabitants of the area surrounding what is known today as Cerrillos Hills Historic Park worked on many turquoise pits, quarries, lead (galena) mines, refining areas, workshops, hearths, and campsites. One of the largest mines is Mount Chalchihuitl. Most of the activity here occurred between AD 1375 and 1500, but grooved axes, mauls, picks, Indian pottery, and campfires are all that is left. The Mina del Tiro, which is thought to be one of the oldest lead mines in the North America, is located on private land nearby. These mines were critically important to the people in the area because they supplied valuable turquoise that allowed decoration of pottery, jewelry, and other items.

Cultural

New Mexico's vibrant history has permeated modern society and left cultural treasures throughout the area. Retaining the flavor of the Southwest, local artisans have saved several of the region's ghost towns and transformed them into artistic communities. Along the Byway, you will find shops and galleries filled with paintings, sculpture, pottery, leather goods, jewelry, furniture, beadwork, toys, art wear, and antiques. Some of the old company stores and houses have also been refurbished as restaurants and bed-and-breakfasts. You will likely want to plan extra time to peruse the cultural offerings of the Turquoise Trail.

Historical

New Mexico's rich mining legacy dates to before the first Spanish conquistadors began exploring the region. Native Americans were the first people who toiled to extract the gold, silver, lead, zinc, and turquoise from the surrounding hills. Indeed, the turquoise found near the Turquoise Trail is considered by some to be the finest in the world. Usually sky blue to light greenish blue, turquoise can also be white, dark blue, jade green, reddish brown, and even violet. In the early 1900s, Tiffany's of New York helped to popularize the shade known as robins' egg blue.

When the Native Americans first began their mining efforts, the mineral deposits were in pure veins. Early digging implements included stone hammers, chisels, and files. After the minerals had been removed from the surrounding rock, the native miners would carry the ore and rock outside the mine in reed baskets or buckets made of hide. Spanish explores estimated that native miners had removed 100,000 tons of rock, based on huge tailing piles and 400-year-old piñon trees growing from the piles.

Although some mining occurred during Spain's (and later Mexico's) ownership of the land, the majority of the mining appears to have been done during the territorial expansion of the United States. Mining communities and camps rapidly sprang up in the area to capitalize on

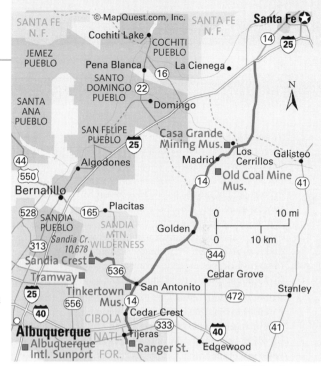

© MapQuest.com, Inc.

see page A25 for color map

the various minerals. Some died out or were absorbed into other communities, depending on the available riches.

Golden, New Mexico, began with humble beginnings during the 1825 gold rush, the first gold rush to occur west of the Mississippi. Here, two mining camps were created to mine placer gold (gold extracted from streams or rivers). In 1880, several mining companies moved into the area and renamed the two camps "Golden" to match their high hopes of developing profitable ventures. However, these hopes faded by 1884, and the population of Golden steadily decreased.

Another popular New Mexico mining community, Cerrillos, hit its peak in the 1880s, due in part to the arrival of the railroad. The early 1880s quickly expanded the local mines, with over 2,000 land claims filed on only a few square miles of land. Soon, Cerrillos swelled to accommodate 21 saloons and 4 hotels. Sadly, prosperity abandoned Cerrillos within the decade. Today, the Cerrillos Hills Historic Park and the immediately adjacent lands contain approximately 45 vertical or near-vertical shafts, with depths exceeding 6 feet.

Madrid, New Mexico, was founded in the oldest coal-mining region of the state and gradually grew to become the center of the coal-mining industry for the region. Under the direction of the superintendent of mines, Oscar Huber, Madrid became a model for other mining towns. Oscar believed that idleness was an enemy to a stable community. His radical views sharply changed mining towns by requiring the miners to participate in the community. Employees were to donate from 50 cents to $1 a month for community causes and were also required to participate in town events such as the Fourth of July celebrations and Christmas light displays. In fact, Madrid became famous for its Christmas light displays. Miners began to light up the winter sky with 150,000 Christmas

lights, powered by 500,000 kilowatt hours of electricity. The power was provided by the company's own coal-fed generators. People from all over the state came to see the light displays and Madrid's annual pageant. The town's Christmas celebrations ended in 1941 with the start of World War II. Eventually, people began choosing natural gas in favor of coal, and the mines near Madrid closed in the early 1950s, causing the town to be abandoned.

Natural

Proud of its natural legacy, New Mexico has preserved many vibrant natural wonders that can be easily accessed along the Turquoise Trail. In the Byway's short length of 61 miles, you're whisked through forests and mountains that are home to a dazzling array of wildlife. Depending on the terrain, you can observe desert wildlife or woodland creatures. Many of these animals make their homes among the juniper, pine, and spruce-fir forests that grow found along the Byway.

But the natural treasures found on the Turquoise Trail began forming millions of years before roads were constructed anywhere in the area. Twenty-four to 34 million years ago, the Cerrillos and Ortiz Mountains along the

191

Turquoise Trail were dikes, or branches, of magma that solidified thousands of feet underground. By the time early Native Americans began to settle these areas, these dikes were exposed and began to crack. This erosion process soon made the area famous for its rich supply of minerals, including gold, silver, lead, zinc, coal, and a wide assortment of turquoise. Today, fossil hunters sift through the outcroppings of shale, hoping to find one of the many fossils of prehistoric life hidden there.

Part of the Byway travels into the Cibola National Forest. Here, the climate varies with elevation, which ranges from 5,000 to over 11,300 feet. Snow can be found in the timberline until June, and some of the higher elevations become very cold at night. During the late summer months, heavy thunderstorms occasionally rumble through higher elevations, dropping the temperature below zero.

The high points of a visit to the Turquoise Trail, however, are Sandia Peak and the Sandia Mountain Wilderness, which offer a view of the sublime. With far-reaching views and cool mountain breezes, you may not want to leave! Long considered sacred by Native American tribes, Sandia Peak and the Sandia Mountain Wilderness provide a welcomed respite with minimal effort for those seeking to escape the woes of civilization.

Recreational

The Turquoise Trail offers many opportunities to enjoy recreation. Both the Sandia Peak Tramway and the Sandia Mountain Wilderness hold adventure and offer a chance to view the outdoors like it has never been seen before.

Built in 1966, the Sandia Peak Tramway is the longest continuous jigback tram in the world, which means it has one car going up while another is coming down, and it has the third longest clear span in the world. The tram is a significant transportation system that brings more than 275,000 people each year from Albuquerque to its 2-mile-high destination on the Turquoise Trail. Visitors experience

an exhilarating ride, breathtaking views, and interesting birds and animals. It is the only place in the United States where visitors traveling on a man-made transportation system are virtually surrounded by a nationally designated wilderness area.

The pristine Sandia Mountain Wilderness is a natural, scenic, and recreational wonder located adjacent to metropolitan Albuquerque. More than 100 miles of recreational trails in the wilderness area offer a wide variety of terrain. Included in the wilderness area are the Sandia Mountains and Sky Island, where a diverse and isolated ecosystem contains different life zones.

Scenic

The Turquoise Trail offers some of the most spectacular scenic views in North America. The scenery on the Turquoise Trail is not only beautiful; it is also incredibly diverse. You can look more than a mile down at what was once the ocean floor millions of years ago, or you can enjoy pristine sights while driving through a variety of ecosystems. You can even look up above at the vastness of the universe as you watch billions upon billions of stars sparkle with no competition from city lights.

Not all of the scenic qualities of the Turquoise Trail are at the top of Sandia Crest, however. The Turquoise Trail offers many miles of unspoiled natural beauty. Its breathtaking scenery and unobstructed views enchant from NM 14 mile 7 to mile 40. Mesas, deserts, and grasslands teem with wildlife and provide a home for horses, cattle, and even an occasional llama or ostrich.

A unique quality of this Byway is the weather. The arid desert climate makes the scenic drive possible in all four seasons. During the summer months on the Byway, you see fast-moving clouds and hundreds of lightning bolts electrifying the sky. In contrast to these wild storms, you may be inspired by the multicolored sunsets in a calm evening sky.

Some of the most enjoyable scenery found along the Byway is man-made. You can view tailings from historic coal mines, representing the only location in the nation where both anthracite and bituminous coal were found. They can also see giant artwork displayed adjacent to the road, the eclectic 1960s town of Madrid, and the Old West town of Cerrillos that inspired movies with its dusty, unpaved roads. The people in Madrid and Cerrillos and their highly visible cultural activities give the Byway some of its outstanding scenic qualities that visitors can enjoy.

HIGHLIGHTS

The best way to truly experience the unique nature of the Turquoise Trail is to stop at the small towns along the Byway and speak with the folks who live there. Here's a sampling of places you may want to stop.

• The first stop along the trail is at the **Sandia Ranger Station** on NM 337. This marks the beginning of the Byway and a nice way to learn the early history of the area. Inquire about road conditions here, as well as special activities that may be planned.

• Between 1948 and 1976, excavations in this area turned up a great amount of archeological remains that helped scientists learn about the **Tijeras Pueblo,** a large tribe believed to exist between AD 1300 and 1600. Many skeletal remains, as well as other objects such as tools, jewelry, corn cobs, and arrow heads are on display at the Maxwell Museum of Anthropology at the University of New Mexico in Albuquerque. The pueblo itself includes 200 rooms, a dozen small buildings, and a kiva. After excavation was finished in the 1970s, the area was covered again with soil to preserve it. A self-guided tour of the area is available.

• Continuing north on 14 out of Tijeras, enjoy the scenery as the road turns from grassland to forest. Turn left on the 536 heading toward Sandia Peak. While at Sandia Peak, be sure to stop at the **Museum of Archaeology and**

Material Culture and the **Tinkertown Museum.** Continue on up the windy road to the **Sandia Peak Tramway.** Take the tramway up the 2.7-mile climb and enjoy the view. After the tram, continue to the highpoint of the road and take a quick tour of the **Sandia Cave.** Don't forget your flashlight!

• Head back down 536 and turn left and continue north on 14. Continue up toward Madrid. Expect to spend some time here enjoying the uniqueness of the town by touring the **Old Coal Mine Museum** and the **Engine House Theatre.** Interesting to note is that this entire town, after being utterly deserted due to a mine shutdown, was advertised for sale in the *Wall Street Journal* in 1954 for a price of $250,000. No one took the offer, but the town has been revived since the 1970s by artisans. A visit here is a real treat.

• Just north of Madrid and before Cerillos, be on the lookout for a unique art display. Animal bones and glass are the tools of artist **Tammy Jean Lange.** No fees are charged here, but a donation box kindly makes a support request. A few miles up the road is **Cerillos,** a town of mostly dirt roads that is a hit for many a passerby. Thomas Edison is reported to have stayed here briefly while conducting studies with the area's minerals. The **Cerrillos Turquoise Mining Museum** run by Todd

Brown is a special feature of the town. Be sure to ask him about the 28-room house that he and his wife built. Don't leave Cerillos without a stop at the **What Not Shop,** a gift shop selling mostly Indian jewelry and crafts.

- Five miles past Cerillos, look for signs pointing to the **Shona Sol Sculpture Garden,** a unique gallery of African sculpture. Finally, make a stop at the **J. W. Eaves Movie Ranch,** home to many famous movies, including *Silverado,* which was shot entirely on site. If you're lucky, the costume lady will show you her Emmy.

THINGS TO SEE AND DO

Driving along the Turquoise Trail will certainly keep your senses engaged, but if you yearn to get out of the car and stretch your legs, or if you'd like to make a mini-vacation out of your trip, check out these attractions along the route.

CERRILLOS TURQUOISE MINING MUSEUM. *17 Waldo St, Cerrillos (87010). Phone 505/438-3008.* If you visit the town of Cerrillos, which was abandoned in the 1920s and in which many scenes of *All the Pretty Horses* were set, stop by the Cerrillos Turquoise Mining Museum, which celebrates the mining legacy of this area with a collection of mineral samples that are breathtaking. Open daily.

CIBOLA NATIONAL FOREST. *2113 Osuna Rd NE, Albuquerque (87113). Phone 505/346-3900.* More than 1 1/2 million acres located throughout central New Mexico. The park includes Mount Taylor (11,301 feet), several mountain ranges, and four wilderness areas: Sandia Mountain, Manzano Mountain, Apache Kid, and Withington. Scenic drives; bighorn sheep in Sandia Mountains. Fishing; hunting, picnicking, and camping (some fees). La Cienega Nature Trail is for the disabled and visually impaired.

MUSEUM OF ARCHAEOLOGY AND MATERIAL CULTURE. *22 Calvary Rd, Cedar Crest (87008). Phone 505/281-2005.* Highlights 12,000 years of Native American history and archaeological artifacts. Turquoise mining exhibit. Open May 1-Nov 1, daily noon-7 pm.

OLD COAL MINE MUSEUM. *2814 Highway 14, Turquoise Trail, Madrid (87010). Phone 505/438-3780.* Restored steam locomotive from coal-mining days. **Engine House Theatre** presents classic, victorian, and western melodramas every weekend throughout the summer. Blacksmith shop, vintage autos and trucks, fire-fighting equipment, medical office equipment, farm equipment, homemaking and carpentry equipment. Open daily, weather permitting.

SANDIA PEAK AERIAL TRAMWAY. *10 Tramway Loop NE, Albuquerque (87122). Phone 505/856-7325.* From the base at 6,559 feet, the tram travels almost 3 miles up the west slope of the Sandia Mountains to 10,378 feet, with amazing 11,000-square-mile views. Hiking trail, restaurant at the summit, and Mexican grill at the base. Open daily 9 am-9 pm in summer, shorter hours rest of year; closed two weeks in Apr and two weeks in Oct. $$$$

SANDIA PEAK SKI AREA. *10 Tramway Loop NE, Albuquerque (87122). Phone 505/242-9133.* The ski area has four double chairlifts, a surface lift; patrol, school, rentals, snowmaking, café, restaurant, and bar. An aerial tramway on the west side of the mountain meets lifts at the top. Longest run over 2 1/2 miles; vertical drop 1,700 feet. Open mid-Dec-Mar, daily. Chairlift also operates July-Labor Day (Fri-Sun; fee). $$$$

SHONA SOL SCULPTURE GARDEN. *Highway 14, Turquoise Trail, Santa Fe (87506). Phone 505/473-5611.* Exhibits some of the world's finest stone sculptors, whose work is also shown around the world. Also features the work of fine Zimbabwean artists. Open weekends 10 am-6 pm. **FREE**

TINKERTOWN MUSEUM. *Turquoise Trail (I-40 exit 175), Sandia Park (87047). Phone 505/281-5233. www.tinkertown.com.* 22-room museum formed from more than 50,000 glass bottles houses miniature wood carvings, many of which are animated, and Western memorabilia. Open daily 9 am-6 pm Apr-Nov. **$**

PLACES TO STAY

If you choose to include an overnight stay in your trip along this Byway, the Mobil Travel Guide recommends the following lodgings.

★ **ELAINE'S, A BED & BREAKFAST.** *PO Box 444, Cedar Crest (87008). Phone 505/281-2467; toll-free 800/821-3092. www.elainesbnb.com.* 5 rooms, 3 story. Set in a beautiful log cabin within easy distance to golfing, hiking, skiing, bird-watching, and more. **$**

★★ **HIGH FEATHER RANCH BED & BREAKFAST.** *29 High Feather Ranch, Cerrillos (87010). Phone 505/424-1333; toll-free 800/757-4410. www.highfeatherranch-bnb.com.* 3 rooms, 1 story. This architecturally stunning ranch features luxurious accommodations and a full gourmet breakfast along 65 private acres. **$$**

PLACES TO EAT

A long day of driving is sure to make you hungry. At the end of your journey, take a table at one of the following restaurants.

★ **THE MINE SHAFT TAVERN.** *2846 Hwy 14, Madrid (87010). Phone 505/473-0743. www.mineshafttavern.com.* American menu. Lunch, dinner. Located in the small town of Madrid, the tavern was built in the 1940s at the old coal mine and has been a local favorite ever since. **$**

★ **KOKOPELLI'S RESTAURANT AND KANTINA.** *12540 N Hwy 14, Sandia Park (81082). Phone 505/286-2691.* American menu. Breakfast, lunch, dinner. Featuring regional American and Southwest cuisines in a family-oriented setting. **$**

★★ **SAN MARCOS CAFÉ.** *3877 Hwy 14, Santa Fe (87505). Phone 505/471-9298.* Southwestern. Breakfast, lunch. Known for its great Southwestern breakfasts and vegetarian cuisine. **$**

Dinosaur Diamond Prehistoric Highway

❋ UTAH

Part of a multistate Byway; see also UT.

Quick Facts

LENGTH: 400 miles.

TIME TO ALLOW: 9 hours to several days.

BEST TIME TO DRIVE: Year-round; high season is summer.

BYWAY TRAVEL INFORMATION: Dinosaurland Travel Board: 800/477-5558; Byway local Web site: www.dinosaurdiamond.org.

SPECIAL CONSIDERATIONS: The mountain passes at Reservation Ridge on US 191 can be treacherous during winter storms. This road is rarely, if ever, officially closed, but sometimes a few hours' delay would be prudent.

RESTRICTIONS: Cleveland-Lloyd Dinosaur Quarry is at the end of 13 miles of gravel road that is accessible to sedans in all weather except deep snow; it is closed during the winter months. The Mill Canyon Dinosaur Trail and Copper Ridge Dinosaur Trackway are reached by a couple of miles of dirt road that is accessible to two-wheel-drive automobiles in good weather but are not advisable for the same vehicles in wet conditions. Dinosaur trackways are difficult if not impossible to see under snow cover.

BICYCLE/PEDESTRIAN FACILITIES: The Dinosaur Diamond Byway includes portions of the interstate (I-70) and various US highways. For this reason, bicycle and foot travel along the route may be prohibited and/or dangerous. However, numerous trails off the Byway delight visitors to the area. The Kokopelli Trail is designed and built for mountain bike travel between Moab and Fruita. Hiking for recreation, solitude, or sightseeing in the area of the Dinosaur Diamond is very popular, however, and you'll find many trails to follow.

The Dinosaur Diamond Prehistoric Highway provides a unique and unparalleled opportunity to experience the thrilling story of dinosaurs and the science and history of discovery behind them. The route combines opportunities to see dinosaur bones still in the ground being excavated and to see dinosaur bones prepared by paleontologists for museums. Museums all along the Byway display both reconstructed skeletons and fleshed-out re-creations of dinosaurs found in the area. In between and sometimes overlapping the dinosaur sites are areas of major archaeological interest. This Byway was occupied by prehistoric Native Americans who saw the area's many rock cliffs as ideal surfaces for their petroglyphs and pictographs. Some of the finest examples and densest concentrations of this rock art in North America are located along or near the Byway.

Along the Byway, you'll find many opportunities to take a breather from the abundance of dinosaur sights and enjoy recreational opportunities. Hiking, camping, mountain biking, fishing, and many other activities can be enjoyed on the acres of public lands in the corridor. River rafting and kayaking suitable for all levels can be arranged on the Green, Yampa, and Colorado rivers. Horseback riding, llama-assisted pack trips, and even mule and goat pack trips can also be arranged through private operators in the area.

Along with unique red, gray, and green rock formations, you can enjoy forested mountain passes, canyons, cliffs, rivers, and plateaus along the Dinosaur Diamond Prehistoric Highway. Wide-open spaces and miles of unobstructed views are the reward for those who travel this Byway.

THE BYWAY STORY

The Dinosaur Diamond Prehistoric Highway tells archaeological, cultural, historical, natural, recreational, and scenic stories that make it a unique and treasured Byway.

Archaeological

The Dinosaur Diamond Prehistoric Highway showcases the archaeological qualities of about 1,000 years ago, when Native American cultures lived and hunted in the area. These cultures maintained their way of life in the desert, and today, remnants of this culture are found along the Byway. The best evidence of these ancient people is the abundance of petroglyphs and pictographs in the area. (Petroglyphs are pictures that are pecked into rock surfaces by using harder rocks, often made into tools; pictographs are pictures painted onto the rocks.)

Ancient Indian petroglyph panels show up on cliff sides and rock surfaces along the Byway, because the sheer rock cliffs and walls served as an ideal place to create this rock art. There are panels in both Utah and Colorado.

Hundreds of rock surfaces in the Moab area display rock art that was created by the Paleo-Indian Fremont and Anasazi cultures. The Golf Course Rock Art site near Moab Golf Course is a large area covered with human and animal figures. Within Arches National Park, Courthouse Wash has both petroglyphs and pictographs on a panel that is 19 feet high and 52 feet long. Also in Arches, Ute rock art may be seen at the Wolfe Ranch near the Delicate Arch Trailhead.

Between Wellington and Myton is Nine Mile Canyon, the greatest concentration of rock art in the world and the premier site of the archaic culture of the Fremont Indians. The canyon also has examples of dwellings that have been untouched for hundreds of years. Nine Mile Canyon is well preserved because of the dry climate and isolation from large population centers. Because of this preservation, the canyon is home to high-quality rock art that

visitors can enjoy, with more than 1,000 sites catalogued to date.

Between Moab and Price are hundreds of additional panels at Thompson Springs, the mouth of Gray Canyon north of Green River, and all through the San Rafael Swell. There are further examples of rock art down in the canyon of the Price River east of Woodside. The Uinta Basin is rife with Fremont rock art in places like Dry Fork Canyon just northwest of Vernal and numerous significant sites in or near Dinosaur National Monument, such as McKee Springs, Cub Creek, and Jones Hole.

Cultural

Because of the isolating nature of living in the desert, many cultural events have sprung up to give people a reason to congregate and enjoy the splendid outdoors. Festivals and events honoring the heritage and natural features of the area give the Byway a cultural flair.

Eastern Utah has been and continues to be the home to many ranches and cattle. In celebration of this culture, rodeos are held periodically throughout the area. In Vernal, the Dinosaur Roundup Rodeo is one of the largest rodeos in the world. In Price, the Black Diamond Stampede Rodeo is held every year. In Vernal, Butch Cassidy Days celebrates the history of the area's most famous outlaws. The San Rafael Swell was a favorite hideout for Butch Cassidy and the Sundance Kid and their gang. The Outlaw Trail went from the wild country of Robber's Roost down by Hanksville, up through the San Rafael Swell and either Nine Mile Canyon or along the canyons of the Green River into the Uintah Basin. It then either continued along the Green or up and over the eastern Uintas to Brown's Park in the tri-state area of Wyoming, Colorado, and Utah. Matt Warner, a former outlaw in the gang, was elected marshal in Price for a number of years. Today, the Outlaw Trail Festival is held every summer in Vernal in honor of these famous outlaws. Josie Morris, an old friend of Cassidy's, built a small

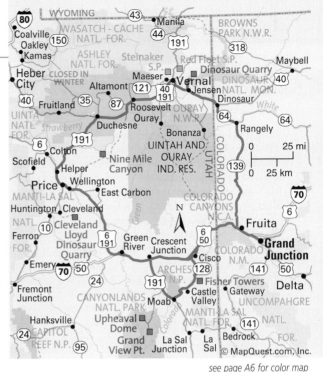

see page A6 for color map

cabin in Cub Creek, part of Dinosaur National Monument. It is preserved and stabilized so that visitors can experience what it's like to rough it in the Old West.

Moab is known as the mountain bike capital of the world, but it is also home to many different festivals and celebrations. Every year in the early spring, participants from all over gather for the Jeep Safari. The slick red rock and warming temperatures in the desert at that time of the year make it a perfect location for extreme driving. If you have more traditional cultural events in mind, the Moab Film Festival showcases the work of independent filmmakers, and Moab hosts an outdoor music festival as well.

Historical

The high mountain desert of eastern Utah has drawn people to the area of the present-day Dinosaur Diamond Prehistoric Highway. Evidences of Native American cultures, such as the Fremont and Ute, can be seen in the rock art along the Byway. The Escalante-Dominguez Expedition, followed by scientific and paleontologic expeditions, undertook early exploration of the area, while Mormon settlers, miners, and immigrants from Europe settled in the area and created a unique and colorful history.

The first recorded venture of Europeans into the area was the Escalante-Dominguez Expedition in 1776. This expedition began in Santa Fe, New Mexico, and attempted to blaze a trail to California in order to access the missions located there; however, their journey was unsuccessful due to the barriers formed by the western Utah deserts. The expedition was led by Father Silvestre Velez de Escalante and Father Francisco Dominguez, accompanied by Captain Bernardo de Miera y Pacheco, a retired military engineer. They explored Canyon Pintado from Douglas Pass toward

what is now Rangely, Colorado, crossed the Green River near Jensen, Utah, and traveled as far west as Spanish Fork before turning back south to return to Santa Fe.

While Escalante and Dominguez came to the area in search of another route west, others have been drawn to eastern Utah because of scientific exploration. Beginning with John C. Fremont in the early 1840s, reports of the majesty of the mountains, the roaring rivers, the expanse and austerity of the deserts, the abundance of game, and the clues to vast mineral resources have enticed adventurers to the intermountain west of the United States. John Wesley Powell, Clarence King, and Ferdinand V. Hayden led extensive geological surveys that helped quantify these resources. Their reports tempted paleontologists with a vast array of undescribed fossils, particularly dinosaurs and prehistoric mammals.

Settlement in the area inevitably brought about great changes to the landscape, such as mining. In the Uintah Basin, gilsonite was the first hydrocarbon to be mined, bringing a small narrow-gauge railroad (the Uintah Railroad) into the southeastern edge of the basin near Dragon. Although several attempts were made to build more railroads into the basin, none was successful. As a result, the Uintah Basin remains one of the largest areas of the US to be undeveloped by railroads. After World War II, petroleum development and phosphate mining became integral to the rural economy. The railroad from Grand Junction, Colorado, to Price, Utah, brought the development of the coal resources in Carbon and Emery counties. As a result of this mining industry, an influx of some 18 different ethnic groups from across southern and eastern Europe and Asia came to work in the mines. This economic development was a great boost to the area.

Natural

The area encompassed by this diamond-shaped Byway is the best place in the world to see dinosaurs in a variety of ways: models and bones on display in museums, bones still in the ground at the sites where they were discovered, bones currently being excavated by paleontologists, and trackways preserved in rocks.

Dinosaurs ruled the Earth long ago. Today, the bones and tracks of these extinct animals can be seen at various sites along the Byway. Many of these sites are located in their natural settings, which makes this Byway one of a kind. Actual dinosaur quarries, which are areas where dinosaur bones are excavated, are along the Byway. You may see dinosaur bones at Mill Canyon Dinosaur Trail or view dinosaur tracks at Copper Ridge Dinosaur Trackway Site, both near Moab. In the Vernal area, you can visit Red Fleet Reservoir State Park, where 190-million-year-old dinosaur tracks are preserved in stony sand dunes along the edge of the lake. Both the Cleveland-Lloyd Dinosaur Quarry near Price and Dinosaur National Monument near Vernal preserve the history of dinosaurs in their natural state.

The only two enclosed dinosaur quarries in America are located on the Dinosaur Diamond: one at Dinosaur National Monument and the other at the Cleveland-Lloyd Dinosaur Quarry. The bones discovered here in 1909 by Earl Douglass date from the Jurassic Period (about 145 million years ago) and were preserved in a riverbed that has been quarried for fossils. Portions of more than 300 individual dinosaurs have been recovered, making the site one of the most prolific dinosaur quarries in the world. The Cleveland-Lloyd Dinosaur Quarry National Natural Landmark has the densest concentration of Jurassic dinosaur bones in the world. The quarry is so dense because about 147 million years ago, dinosaurs were trapped in a muddy bog. Area ranchers found the jumbled remains of these bones, and the quarry has provided dinosaur mounts in more museums around the world than any other in existence. At this quarry, 44 complete Allosaurus specimens have been excavated; appropriately, Utah made the Allosaurus the state fossil in 1988. In nearby Price, dinosaur skeletons, tracks, and fossils are on display at the College of Eastern Utah Prehistory Museum. These exhibits invite visitors to learn more about the history of the area and the effect of the dinosaur on eastern Utah.

Recreational

River rafting is a popular sport to participate in along the Byway. Both calm-water and whitewater trips are available through companies out of Vernal, Moab, and Green River. The whitewater sections can be frightening even to experienced river runners during the high water levels of spring melt, yet some stretches of both the Green and Colorado rivers have flatwater that can be enjoyable in canoes. Grand scenery awaits around every bend in the river. In fact, the Green River in Desolation Canyon has cliffs higher than the Grand Canyon in Arizona.

Hiking opportunities are everywhere along the Byway. The terrain is varied, giving visitors a feel for the many aspects of the landscape along this route. In the mountains, numerous spectacular peaks and lakes are accessible to hikers. The Uinta Mountain Range, the largest east-west mountain range in the 48 contiguous United States, includes the highest point in Utah—Kings Peak—at 13,528 feet. The desert, particularly near Moab, is another popular place to hike and is an entirely different experience from alpine hiking. The red slickrock around Moab provides the perfect surface for hiking while looking for dinosaur trackways or arches. All of the national parks and monuments along the Byway are outstanding places for hiking and camping as well. Outfitters are available all along the Byway for visitors who want guides, horses, or even llamas to help with the load. Hunting and fishing are also popular recreational activities in the area.

Moab has world-famous mountain biking trails to challenge expert riders and lure beginners. The city has quickly become a mountain bikers' paradise, with trails traveling over many miles, often on slickrock. The Slickrock Bike Trail is located east of Moab in the Sand Flats Recreation Area. The Poison Spider Mesa Trail is another popular trail for both jeeps and bikes and is located on the Potash Road. This trail offers spectacular views of the area surrounding Moab and the Colorado River.

Winter sports are also popular along this Byway. Snowshoeing, cross-country skiing, snowmobiling, and ice fishing can be enjoyed in the high country, while hiking (without the summer heat) is a popular activity in the southern desert areas.

Scenic

The Dinosaur Diamond Prehistoric Highway's many scenic views capture the expansive area of land surrounding the Byway. Wide vistas are normal in this desert country, with the horizon stretching on for miles. On hot summer days, the blue sky seems like an endless expanse, and sunsets—going on forever—are magnified because of the open sky. Vistas can include features that are more than 100 miles away.

Canyons with walls of red, green, beige, purple, gray, and white greet you. These scenes are intermingled with forested mountain passes and snowcapped mountains. As you travel winding roads out of canyons, sweeping views

of the valleys below open up before you. Along the northern facet of the Dinosaur Diamond, the Uinta Mountains cut the skyline. Ancient faults and tectonics controlled the development of this maverick mountain range, creating the largest east-west-trending mountain range in the lower 48 states.

The Green River joins the Yampa River in Dinosaur National Monument at Steamboat Rock. The canyon it forms is spectacular whether viewed from the canyon rim or from the river edge. Farther downstream, the river cuts through Split Mountain and then the Gray Tertiary badlands of the Uinta and Green River formations of Desolation Canyon, the main drainage for the Book Cliffs. The Colorado River provides further scenic aspects, meandering through canyons of red rock. The green vegetation near the river contrasts nicely with the sheer red rock cliffs of the canyons, while snowcapped mountain ranges in the distance offer a break in the desert landscape.

THINGS TO SEE AND DO

Driving along the Dinosaur Diamond Prehistoric Highway will certainly keep your senses engaged, but if you yearn to get out of the car and stretch your legs, or if you'd like to make a mini-vacation out of your trip, check out these attractions along the route.

⭐ **ARCHES NATIONAL PARK.** *US 191, Moab (84532). Phone 435/719-2299. www.nps.gov/arch/.* This timeless natural landscape of giant stone arches, pinnacles, spires, fins, and windows was once the bed of an ancient sea. Over time, erosion laid bare the skeletal structure of the Earth, making this 114-square-mile area a spectacular outdoor museum. This wilderness, which contains the greatest density of natural arches in the world, was named a national monument in 1929 and a national park in 1971. More than 2,000 arches have been cataloged, ranging in size from 3 feet wide to the 105-foot-high, 306-foot-wide Landscape Arch. The arches, other rock formations, and views of the Colorado River canyon, with the peaks of the LaSal Mountains in the distance, can be reached by car, but hiking is the best way to explore. Petroglyphs from the primitive peoples who roamed this section of Utah from AD 700 to AD 1200 can be seen at the Delicate Arch trailhead. This is a wildlife sanctuary; no hunting is permitted. Hiking, rock climbing, and camping in isolated sections should not be undertaken unless first reported to a park ranger at the visitor center (check locally for hours). Twenty-four miles of paved roads are open year-round. Graded and dirt roads should not be attempted in wet weather. Devils Garden Campground, 18 miles north of the visitor center off US 191, provides 52 individual and 2 group camp sites (year-round; fee; water available only Mar-mid-Oct). **$$**

ASHLEY NATIONAL FOREST. *US 191, Vernal (84078). Phone 435/789-1181. www.fs.fed.us/r4/ashley/.* The High Uinta Mountains—the only major east-west range in the US—run through the heart of this nearly 1 1/2-million-acre forest. The 1,500-foot-deep **Red Canyon,** the 13,528-foot **Kings Peak,** and **Sheep Creek Geological Area** are here as well. Swimming, fishing, boating (ramps, marinas), whitewater rafting, canoeing; hiking and nature trails, cross-country skiing, snowmobiling, improved or backcountry campgrounds (fee). Visitor centers. **FREE**

CANYONLANDS BY NIGHT. *1861 S Hwy 191, Moab (84532). Phone 435/259-5261. www.canyondlandsbynight.com.* This two-hour boat trip with a sound-and-light presentation highlights the history of the area. Reservations are required; tickets must be purchased at the ticket office. The boat leaves the dock at the bridge, 2 miles north on US 191, at sundown. Open Apr-mid-Oct, daily (weather permitting). **$$$$**

CANYONLANDS FIELD INSTITUTE. *1320 S Hwy 191, Moab (84532). Phone 435/259-7750. canyonlandsfieldinst.org.* Educational seminars and trips featuring geology, natural and cultural history, endangered species, and Southwestern literature. Many programs use Canyonlands and Arches national parks as outdoor classrooms. Open Mon-Fri. **$$$$**

★ **CANYONLANDS NATIONAL PARK.** *2282 S West Resource Blvd, Moab (84532). Phone 435/259-7164. www.nps.gov/cany/.* Spectacular rock formations, canyons, arches, spires, pictograph panels, ancestral Puebloan ruins, and desert flora are the main features of this 337,570-acre area. Set aside by Congress in 1964 as a national park, the area is largely undeveloped. Road conditions vary; primary access roads are paved and maintained, while others are safe only for high-clearance four-wheel-drive vehicles. For backcountry road conditions and information, call 801/259-7164. In the park are the following additional sites:

• **Island in the Sky,** south and west of Dead Horse Point State Park, has **Grand View Point, Upheaval Dome,** and **Green River Overlook.** This section is accessible by car via UT 313 and by four-wheel-drive vehicles and mountain bikes on dirt roads.

• **Needles** has hiking trails and four-wheel-drive roads to **Angel Arch, Chesler Park,** and the confluence of the Green and Colorado rivers. Also here are prehistoric ruins and rock art. This section is accessible by car via UT 211, by four-wheel-drive vehicle on dirt roads, and by mountain bike.

• **Maze** is accessible by hiking or by four-wheel-drive vehicles using unimproved roads. The most remote and least-visited section of the park, this area received its name from the many mazelike canyons. **Horseshoe Canyon,** a separate unit of the park nearby, is accessible via UT 24 and 30 miles of two-wheel-drive dirt road. Roads are usually passable only in mid-March through mid-November.

Canyonlands is excellent for calm-water and whitewater trips down the Green and Colorado rivers. Permits are required for private trips (fee; contact the Reservation Office at 435/259-4351) and commercial trips. Campgrounds (fee), with tent sites, are located at Island in the Sky and at Needles; water is available only at Needles. Visitor centers are in each district and are open daily. **$$**

CLEVELAND-LLOYD DINOSAUR QUARRY. *155 E Main St, Price (84501). Phone 435/637-5060. www.blm.gov/utah/price/quarry.htm.* Since 1928, more than 12,000 dinosaur bones representing at least 70 different animals have been excavated on this site, where you'll also find a visitor center, nature trail, and picnic area. Open Memorial Day-Labor Day, daily; Easter-Memorial Day, weekends only. **FREE**

DAN O'LAURIE CANYON COUNTRY MUSEUM. *118 E Center St, Moab (84532). Phone 435/259-7985. www.grandcountyutah.net/museum/.* Exhibits on the local history, archaeology, geology, uranium, and minerals of the area. Open Mon-Sat afternoons; closed holidays. **$**

DAUGHTERS OF UTAH PIONEERS MUSEUM. *500 W 200 S, Vernal (84078). Phone 435/789-3890.* Relics and artifacts dating from before 1847, when pioneers first settled in Utah; period furniture, quilts, clothing, and dolls; early doctor's, dentist's, and undertaker's instruments; and a restored Little Rock tithing office (1887). Open June through the weekend before Labor Day, Mon-Sat. **FREE**

DEAD HORSE POINT STATE PARK. *313 State Rd, Moab (84532). Phone 435/259-2614. www.utah.com/stateparks/dead_horse.htm.* A promontory rising 2,000 feet above the Colorado River, this island mesa offers views of the LaSal Mountains, Canyonlands National Park, and the Colorado River. Approximately 5,200 acres in region of gorges, cliffs, buttes, and mesas. Visitor center, museum. Picnicking, camping (fee; electricity). RV parking. Open daily. **$**

★ **DINOSAUR NATIONAL MONUMENT/UTAH ENTRANCE.** *4545 E US 40, Vernal (84078). Phone 801/789-8277. www.nps.gov/dino/.* Since 1909, this location has provided more skeletons, skulls, and bones of Jurassic Period dinosaurs than any other dig in the world. The dinosaur site comprises only 80 acres of this 325-square-mile park, which lies at the border of Utah and Colorado. Utah's Dinosaur Quarry section can be entered from the junction of US 40 and UT 149, north of Jensen, 13 miles east of Vernal; approximately 7 miles north on UT 149 is the fossil exhibit. Another 5 miles north is Green River Campground, with 90 tent and trailer sites available mid-May-mid-September. A smaller campground, Rainbow Park, provides a small number of tent sites from May to November. A fee is charged at Green River (water and rest rooms available). Backpacking, hiking, fishing. River rafting on the Green and Yampa rivers, by advance permit from the National Park Service or with concession-operated guided float trips (phone 970/374-2468). Because of snow, some areas of the monument are closed from approximately mid-November to mid-April. **$$**

DINOSAUR QUARRY. *Jensen (84035). Phone 435/789-2115.* Remarkable fossil deposit; exhibit of 150-million-year-old dinosaur remains; and a preparation laboratory on display. Open daily 8 am-4:30 pm; extended hours in summer; closed Jan 1, Thanksgiving, Dec 25.

DINOSAUR ROUNDUP RODEO. *134 W Main St, Vernal (84078). Phone toll-free 800/421-9635. www.vernalrodeo.com.* Held annually in mid-July.

★ **FLAMING GORGE DAM AND NATIONAL RECREATION AREA.** *US 191, Vernal (84078). Phone 435/784-3445. go-utah.com/flaming_gorge_national_recreation_area.* The area surrounds the 91-mile-long Flaming Gorge Reservoir and the 502-foot-high Flaming Gorge Dam. Fishing on the reservoir and river (all year), marinas, boat ramps, water-skiing; lodges, campgrounds (fee). River rafting below the dam. Visitor centers at the dam and at Red Canyon (on a secondary paved road 3 miles off UT 44).

GOBLIN VALLEY STATE PARK. *450 S Green River Blvd, Green River (84540). Phone 435/564-3633.* A mile-wide basin filled with intricately eroded sandstone formations. Hiking, camping (rest rooms, showers). Open daily. **$$**

HOLE 'N THE ROCK. *11037 S Hwy 191, Moab (84532). Phone 435/686-2250.* A 5,000-square-foot dwelling carved into huge sandstone rock. Picnic area with stone tables and benches. Open daily; closed Jan 1, Thanksgiving, Dec 25. **$$**

MANTI-LASAL NATIONAL FOREST. *2290 Resource Blvd, Moab (84532). Phone 435/259-7155. www.fs.fed.us/r4/mantilasal/.* Originally two forests—the Manti in central Utah and the LaSal section in southeastern Utah—now under single supervision. A 1,327,631-acre area partially in Colorado, this forest has among its attractions high mountain scenic drives, deep canyons, riding trails, campsites, winter sports, fishing, and deer and elk hunting. The land of the forest's LaSal division is similar in color and beauty to some parts of the Grand Canyon, but also includes mountains nearing 13,000 feet and pine and spruce forests. Swimming, fishing; hiking, hunting. **FREE**

OURAY NATIONAL WILDLIFE REFUGE. *Vernal (84078). Phone 435/789-0351. ouray.fws.gov.* Waterfowl nesting marshes; desert scenery; self-guided auto tour (limited route during hunting season). Open daily. **FREE**

OUTLAW TRAIL FESTIVAL. *Vernal (84078).* Festivals, sporting events, and theatrical events. Held in late June-mid-Aug.

PACK CREEK RANCH TRAIL RIDES. *LaSal Mountain Loop Rd, Moab (84532). Phone 435/259-5505. www.packcreekranch.com.* Horseback rides, ranging from 1 to 1 1/2 hours, in the foothills of LaSal Mountain. Guided tours for small groups; reservations required. Open Mar-Oct; upon availability. **$$$$**

PREHISTORIC MUSEUM. *College of Eastern Utah, 155 E Main St, Price (84501). Phone 435/637-5060. museum.ceu.edu.* Dinosaur displays, archaeology exhibits; geological specimens. Open Memorial Day-Labor Day, daily; rest of year, Mon-Sat. **FREE**

PRICE CANYON RECREATION AREA. *15 miles N on US 6, then 3 miles W on unnumbered road, Price (84501).* Scenic overlooks; hiking, picnicking, camping (fee). Roads have steep grades. Open May-mid-Oct, daily. **FREE**

RED FLEET STATE PARK. *4335 N US 191, Vernal (84078). Phone 435/789-4432.* Scenic lake highlighted by red rock formations, boating, swimming, fishing; camping. Several hundred well-preserved dinosaur tracks. Open daily. **$$**

RIM TOURS. *1233 S Hwy 191, Moab (84532). Phone 435/259-5223; toll-free 800/626-7335. www.rimtours.com/moab.html.* Guided mountain bike tours in canyon country and the Colorado Rockies. Vehicle support for camping tours. Daily and overnight trips; combination bicycle/river trips available. **$$$$**

SCENIC AIR TOURS. *N Hwy 191, Moab (84532). Phone 435/259-7421 or 435/564-3412.* Flights over Canyonlands National Park and various other tours. Open all year; closed Jan 1, Thanksgiving, Dec 25. **$$$$**

SCOFIELD STATE PARK. *US 6 and UT 96, Price (84501). Phone 435/448-9449.* Utah's highest state park has a 2,800-acre lake that lies at an altitude of 7,616 feet. Fishing, boating (docks, ramps); camping (rest rooms, showers); snowmobiling, ice fishing, and cross-country skiing in winter. Open May-Oct. **$$$**

STEINAKER STATE PARK. *US 191, Vernal (84078). Phone 435/789-4432.* Approximately 2,200 acres on west shore of Steinaker Reservoir. Swimming, water-skiing, fishing, boating (ramp, dock); picnicking, tent and trailer sites (fee). Open Apr-Nov; fishing all year. **$$**

TAG-A-LONG EXPEDITIONS. *452 N Main St, Moab (84078). Phone 435/259-8946; toll-free 800/453-3292. www.tagalong.com.* One- to seven-day whitewater rafting trips on the Green and Colorado rivers; jet boat trips on the Colorado River; jet boat trips and four-wheel-drive tours into Canyonlands National Park; winter four-wheel-drive tours (Nov-Feb). Also Canyon Classics, one-day jet boat trips with cultural performing arts programs. Open Apr-mid-Oct. **$$$$**

UTAH FIELD HOUSE OF NATURAL HISTORY AND DINOSAUR GARDENS. *235 Main St, Vernal (84078). Phone 435/789-3799.* Guarded outside by three life-size cement dinosaurs, this museum has exhibits of fossils, archaeology, life zones, geology, and fluorescent minerals of the region. Adjacent Dinosaur Gardens contain 17 life-size model dinosaurs in natural surroundings. Open daily; closed Jan 1, Thanksgiving, Dec 25. **$**

WESTERN HERITAGE MUSEUM. *328 E 200 S, Vernal (84078). Phone 435/789-7399.* Houses memorabilia from Uintah County's outlaw past as well as other artifacts dealing with a western theme. Includes the Thorne Collection, photographs, and artifacts of the ancient people of Utah. Open Mon-Sat; closed holidays. **FREE**

PLACES TO STAY

If you choose to include an overnight stay in your trip along this Byway, Mobil Travel Guide recommends the following lodgings.

Green River

★ **BEST WESTERN RIVER TERRACE MOTEL.** *880 E Main St, Green River (84525). Phone 435/564-3401; toll-free 800/528-1234. www. bestwestern.com.* 51 rooms, 2-3 story. No elevator. Check-out 11 am. TV; cable (premium). Pool, whirlpool. On river. **¢**

★ **RODEWAY INN WEST WINDS.** *525 E I-70 Business Loop, Green River (84525). Phone 435/564-3421; toll-free 800/228-2000. www.rodeway.com.* 42 rooms, 2 story. Check-out 11 am. TV; cable (premium). Laundry services. Restaurant adjacent. **¢**

Moab

★ **BOWEN MOTEL.** *169 N Main St, Moab (84532). Phone 435/259-7132; toll-free 800/874-5439. www.bowenmotel.com.* 40 rooms, 2 story. Pet accepted, some restrictions; fee. Complimentary continental breakfast. Check-out 11 am, check-in 3 pm. TV; cable (premium). In-room modem link. Totally nonsmoking. **¢**

★★★ **CASTLE VALLEY INN.** *424 Amber Ln, Moab (84532). Phone 435/259-6012; toll-free 888/466-6012. www.castlevalleyinn.com.* Guests will enjoy watching the deer and the variety of birds that come to feed on this inn's property. 5 rooms. Complimentary breakfast. Check-out 11 am, check-in 3-9 pm. Lawn games. **$**

★ **LANDMARK INN.** *168 N Main St, Moab (84532). Phone 435/259-6147; toll-free 800/441-6147. www.moab-utah.com/landmark/motel.htm.* 36 rooms, 2 story. Complimentary continental breakfast. Check-out 11 am, check-in 2 pm. TV; cable (premium). In-room modem link. Restaurant. Pool, children's pool, whirlpool. **¢**

★★ **PACK CREEK RANCH.** *Pack Creek Ranch Rd, Moab (84532). Phone 435/259-5505. www.packcreekranch.com.* 10 rooms. No room phones. Pet accepted, some restrictions; fee. Check-out 11 am, check-in 3 pm. Dining room. Sauna. Pool, whirlpool. Cross-country skiing, hiking. **$$**

�֍ *Dinosaur Diamond Prehistoric Highway*

★★ SUNFLOWER HILL BED AND BREAKFAST.

185 N 300 E, Moab (84532). Phone 435/259-2974; toll-free 800/662-2786. www.sunflowerhill.com. 15 rooms, 2 story. No room phones. Children over 10 years only. Complimentary full breakfast. Check-out 11 am, check-in 3-6 pm. TV; VCR available. Turn-of-the-century adobe farmhouse, cottage amid gardens. Totally nonsmoking. **$**
⊠⌁SC

Price

★ **BEST WESTERN CARRIAGE HOUSE INN.** *590 E Main St, Price (84501). Phone 435/637-5660; toll-free 800/780-7234. www.bestwestern.com.* 41 rooms, 2 story. Complimentary continental breakfast. Check-out noon. TV. Indoor pool, whirlpool. Airport transportation. **¢**
D⊳⌁⊠

★ **GREENWELL INN & CONVENTION CENTER.** *655 E Main St, Price (84501). Phone 435/637-3520; toll-free 800/666-3520. www.castlenet.com/greenwell.* 125 rooms, 1-2 story. Complimentary continental breakfast. Check-out 11 am. TV. Laundry services. In-house fitness room. Health club privileges. Indoor pool. **¢**
⌁⌁D⌁⌁⌁⊠⌁✈

★★ **HOLIDAY INN HOTEL & SUITES.** *838 Westwood Blvd, Price (84501). Phone 435/637-8880; toll-free 800/465-4329. www.holiday-inn.com.* 151 rooms, 2 story. Check-out noon. TV. Restaurant, bar. Room service. In-house fitness room. Health club privileges. Indoor pool. **¢**
⌁D⊠⌁SC⊳✈

Roosevelt

★ **BEST WESTERN INN.** *E Hwy 40, Roosevelt (84066). Phone 435/722-4644; toll-free 800/780-7234. www.bestwestern.com.* 40 rooms, 2 story. Check-out 11 am. TV; cable (premium). In-house fitness room. Pool, whirlpool. **¢**
⌁⌁⌁D⌁⊳⌁

★ **FRONTIER MOTEL.** *75 S 200 E, Roosevelt (98624). Phone 435/722-2201.* 54 rooms. Pet accepted, some restrictions. Check-out 11 am. TV; cable (premium). Restaurant. Pool. **¢**
⌁⌁⌁SC⊳

Vernal

★ **HILLS HOUSE.** *675 W 3300 N, Vernal (84078). Phone 435/789-0700.* 4 rooms, 2 story. Featuring a full breakfast and in-room hot tubs. **$**

★ **LANDMARK INN BED & BREAKFAST.** ⌁ *288 E 100 S, Vernal (84078). Phone 435/781-1800; toll-free 888/738-1800. www.landmark-inn.com.* 11 rooms, 2 story. Complimentary breakfast. This small inn is located in a renovated former Baptist church. **$**
D

★ **THE SAGE MOTEL.** *54 W Main St, Vernal (84078). Phone toll-free 800/760-1442. www.vernalmotels.com.* 26 rooms, 2 story. Classic 1950s roadside motel owned and operated by the same family. **$**

★ **WESTON PLAZA HOTEL.** *1684 W Hwy 40, Vernal (84078). Phone 435/789-9550.* 102 rooms, 3 story. Complimentary continental breakfast. Check-out 11 am. TV; cable (premium). Restaurant, bar; entertainment. Indoor pool, whirlpool. **¢**
⌁D⌁⊠⌁

★ **WESTON'S LAMPLIGHTER INN.** *120 E Main St, Vernal (84078). Phone 435/789-0312.* 167 rooms, 2 story. Check-out 11 am. TV; cable (premium). Restaurant. Pool. **¢**
⊠⌁SC⊳

PLACES TO EAT

A long day of driving is sure to make you hungry. At the end of your journey, take a table at one of the following restaurants.

Green River

★ **TAMARISK.** *870 E Main St, Green River (84525). Phone 435/564-8109.* American menu. Closed Thanksgiving, Dec 25. Buffet: breakfast, lunch, dinner. Children's menu. Country-style café; view of Green River. Totally nonsmoking. **$$**
D

Moab

★ **BANDITOS GRILL.** *467 N Main St, Moab (84532). Phone 435/259-3894.* Mexican menu. Lunch, dinner. Children's menu. Casual attire. Outdoor seating. **$**
D

★★ **CENTER CAFÉ.** *60 N 100 W, Moab (84532). Phone 435/259-4295.* Continental menu. Closed Thanksgiving, Dec 25; Jan. Dinner. Totally nonsmoking. **$$$**
D

★★ **MOAB BREWERY.** *686 South Main St, Moab (84532). Phone 435/259-6333. www. themoabbrewery.com.* American menu. Lunch, dinner. Moab's only on-site microbrewery and restaurant, with a full selection of regional specialties. **$**

★★ **SLICKROCK CAFÉ.** *5 N Main St, Moab (84532). Phone 435/259-8003. www.slickrockcafe .com.* American menu. Breakfast, lunch, dinner. A favorite local spot with adventurous Southwestern-inspired cuisine. **$**

Price

★ **CHINA CITY CAFÉ.** *350 E Main St, Price (84501). Phone 435/637-8211.* Chinese, American menu. Closed Thanksgiving, Dec 25; July. Lunch, dinner. Children's menu. **$$**
D

Vernal

★★ **CURRY MANOR.** *189 S Vernal Ave, Vernal (84078). Phone 435/789-7268.* Indian. Lunch, dinner. A local favorite for authentic Indian cuisine. **$**

★★ **SEVEN ELEVEN CAFÉ.** *77 E Main St, Vernal (84078). Phone 435/789-1170.* American menu. Breakfast, lunch, dinner. Known for its friendly, family-oriented atmosphere and large portions. **$**

The Energy Loop: Huntington and Eccles Canyons Scenic Byways

❋ UTAH

Quick Facts

LENGTH: 86 miles.

TIME TO ALLOW: 1.5 to 4 hours.

BEST TIME TO DRIVE: Summer and fall; summer is the high season.

BYWAY TRAVEL INFORMATION: Castle Country Travel Bureau: toll-free 800/842-0789; Byway local Web site: www.castlecountry.com/byways.htm.

SPECIAL CONSIDERATIONS: Because sections of this Byway climb to altitudes above 10,000 feet, dress warmly during all seasons.

RESTRICTIONS: Certain roads may be closed in winter due to heavy snowfall.

BICYCLE/PEDESTRIAN FACILITIES: Touring and mountain biking experiences are plentiful within minutes of the Byway. In addition, you'll find a variety of hiking and pedestrian trails along stretches of the Byway.

Located in central Utah, the Energy Loop runs through the Manti-LaSal National Forest and offers a firsthand view of Utah's pristine backcountry. The Byway travels through a variety of landscapes that give you a natural perspective on the region, sprinkled with occasional remnants of days gone by.

Situated amid mountainous terrain and pine forests, the Energy Loop runs through Utah's beautiful backyard. Travelers come from miles away to fish the trout-filled waters along the route or to enjoy a picnic in the beautiful forest surroundings. You can also see signs of red rock country.

Deriving its name from the rich coal-mining history of the area, the Energy Loop combines two of Utah's byways: the Huntington Canyon Scenic Byway and the Eccles Canyon Scenic Byway. Along the Byway, you can see early Mormon settlements in Sanpete Valley or visit unique museums in the Byway communities. Towns from Scofield to Huntington revere the days when coal mining was the livelihood of so many of their ancestors. As you pass today's mines, note the harmony between the environment and industrial development.

THE BYWAY STORY

The Energy Loop tells archaeological, cultural, historical, natural, recreational, and scenic stories that make it a unique and treasured Byway.

Archaeological

The Energy Loop and the surrounding areas in central Utah offer an archaeological menagerie for visitors of any knowledge level. As you pass places on the Byway, information kiosks offer stories and facts about the archaeological past of the area. Huntington Reservoir is especially notable for its excavation of the 27-foot mammoth skeleton that was found here in 1988. Other excavations in the area have yielded a short-faced bear, a giant ground sloth, a saber-toothed tiger, and a camel, all from an ice age long ago. Examples and casts of these archaeological finds can be seen in museums on and near the Byway, the most significant being the College of Eastern Utah Prehistoric Museum.

While the Energy Loop is most famous for the mammoth skeleton that was found at the Huntington Reservoir, other treasures await visitors as well. Museums in the area, like the Fairview Museum, the Museum of the San Rafael in Castle Dale, and the College of Eastern Utah Prehistoric Museum, feature artifacts of human inhabitants from the recent past of the pioneers to the more distant past of the Fremont Indian culture. Near the Byway, you can travel through Nine Mile Canyon, a place that has more than 1,000 sites of pictographs and petroglyphs left on the rocks by an ancient people. (Petroglyphs are pictures that are pecked into rock surfaces using harder rocks, often made into tools; pictographs are pictures painted onto the rocks.)

You will also find a tribute to dinosaurs in many of the area museums. Not only have ice-age mammals been found; the area also holds an extensive dinosaur quarry. East of Huntington, the Cleveland-Lloyd Dinosaur Quarry is a place where 145-million-year-old bones and fossils from the Jurassic period are uncovered by paleontologists. The reconstructed skeletons and exhibits in the visitor center and area museums provide a vast amount of information on these creatures of the past. From millions of years ago to just hundreds of years ago, the Energy Loop and its surrounding areas have much to offer in the way of archaeological exploration.

Cultural

Unique cultures have been developing in this area for hundreds of years. Visitors who drive the Byway today can't help but notice buildings and artifacts that point to cultures of the past, yet coal mining and ranching are still very much a part of the lifestyles of the people who live along the Energy Loop now. From early native cultures to settlers from the East, all the cultures that have lived on the land around the Energy Loop have survived rugged territory and left a mark.

The cultural patchwork of the area begins with an ancient culture belonging to a people known as the Fremont Indians. These people moved into the area sometime between AD 300 and 500. Although they were a primitive people, they left behind artifacts of a rich culture in their rock art, baskets, and figurines. The Fremonts usually lived in pit houses made of wood and mud that were entered through an opening in the roof. The weapons and tools of this culture were much different than neighboring Indian cultures, indicating the unique existence of the Fremonts. By the time European settlers reached the area, the Fremont Indian culture had disappeared.

Settlers who came to the area in the early 1800s found an untamed wilderness with many resources. Ranchers found meadows with grass that was perfect for grazing livestock. The ranchers' way of life still continues today in the area. Coal was one of the most important resources found in the area, and as a result, coal-mining towns sprang up all around. The coal-mining culture was a society of hard-working men, women, and children who worked in and around the mines—often at the peril of their own lives. Their story can be found in places like the Scofield Cemetery and several deserted towns. Coal mining, power plants, and hydroelectric power harnessed in the reservoirs are all still present today. These all play a direct part in the name of this Byway—the Energy Loop.

see page A26 for color map

Historical

Few areas in the United States can boast of undiscovered and diverse historical resources the way the area surrounding the Energy Loop can. Travelers along the route see a variety of important historical landmarks, including Native American history, Spanish exploration routes, and the early Mormon settlements that have grown into towns along the Byway. You are in for a diverse historical experience not likely to be matched as you experience the historic coal mining and railroad industries that have deep roots in the area, along with the unique small-town museums in the Byway communities.

Natural

The Energy Loop abounds with natural resources that make it the scenic and productive area that it is. All along the Byway, you see evidence of energy—harnessed or unharnessed—on the Energy Loop. Places like the Skyline Mine and the Huntington Power Plant bring natural fuels to the surface, while canyons and wildflowers bring scenic nature to the surface. With these natural qualities combined, the Wasatch Plateau is a thriving habitat for both wildlife and people.

Through ancient faultlines and geological uplifts, the canyons and valleys along the Byway present a unique topography and beautiful places to pass or stop at. Red rocks of sandstone line the walls of Huntington Canyon, while Eccles Canyon takes drivers through forested ridges and grassy meadows. Because of the thick forests of maple, aspen, and oak, the fall is a colorful time in the canyons of the Energy Loop. As the hundreds of shades of green turn to any number of shades between yellow and red, the Byway acquires a whole new splendor as it hosts a final celebration before the winter.

For the same reasons that this area is rich with prehistoric fossils, it is also rich with coal. The coal in this area was formed nearly 100 million years ago, when plants were covered by land or water. The plant matter was compressed by sediment and hardened into the carbon substance we call coal. Although you may not see any coal, its presence is one of the unique natural qualities of the Byway. The discovery of coal on the Byway was one of the original reasons this area was inhabited and is now appreciated and preserved.

As you drive the Byway, the natural splendor that surrounds the road is impossible to ignore. Streams rush by with trout hiding just near the banks. Mature forests of aspen and pine create a lush habitat for wildlife that lives on the Byway. You may catch a glimpse of a fox or a badger. The wetlands of the Fairview Lakes are the best place on the Byway to observe waterfowl or perhaps a bald eagle. The meadows, streams, and forests all combine to create the perfect habitat for creatures great and small. On the mountaintops, birds of prey circle near the clouds while chipmunks scurry through open fields. And in the spring and early summer, wildflowers dot the road and paint the ridgetops.

※ *The Energy Loop: Huntington and Eccles Canyons Scenic Byways*

Scenic

Wherever the starting point is on the Energy Loop, the road takes travelers through contrasting terrain that changes abruptly. The landscape of the Energy Loop is made up of different areas known as the San Rafael Swell and the Wasatch Plateau. As you drive through these areas, notice the interplay between vegetation and terrain as it creates a scenic view. In some places, mountains are covered in pine and aspen, creating lush, forested canyons. In others, the vegetation is sparse among the red rock formations along the plateaus. Drive the Energy Loop for more than one change of scenery.

Driving through the beautiful stands of mature trees of the Manti-LaSal National Forest, you will notice mountain streams and winding inclines. The shades of light and dark clash directly with the pine and the aspen on the mountaintops of Eccles Canyon. The long grass in the meadows lines the banks of Huntington Creek, with some of the blades dipping down into the scurrying water below. In the distance, you may catch a glimpse of an old log cabin or, perhaps, a bluebird perched on an old fence. Grass and sagebrush appear among the aspen at the tops of the mountains, and a stop at Sanpete Overlook offers a view of the sprawling mountains and valleys beyond overshadowed by clouds.

Tucked away on the corners of the Energy Loop are small communities and historic mining towns. These present a break in the route and an opportunity to drive the streets of the communities to see buildings and cemeteries from days gone by. Many of the towns like Scofield and Fairview offer informational kiosks or museums for exploration. Driving down the streets of one of these quiet communities brings picturesque images.

Recreational

All along the Byway, cars are pulled over, but the drivers are nowhere to be seen unless you check the river. Anglers come from all around to fish for the trout that swim in the waters of the Huntington Creek. Fly fishermen have their pick of cutthroat, brown, and rainbow trout when fishing the streams and rivers on the Byway. Fishing in the six reservoirs along the Byway is also a common recreational activity.

Hiking and biking are also activities worth trying along the Energy Loop. The rocks and cliffs of Huntington Canyon are an enticing invitation to explorers ready to hike along such diverse terrain. Tie Fork Canyon offers a hike among trees and wildflowers of every kind. Joes Valley is a stop that offers options for anglers and hikers. The valley is an excellent place for wildlife spotting or for enjoying the cool mountain air.

Wherever you end up stopping on the Byway, you'll come across several photo opportunities among the wildflowers and scenic overlooks. Capture a picnic or a hike on film. And even if fishing or boating are not options, stop to skip rocks at a reservoir or go wading in a mountain stream. Recreation creates itself in an area as beautiful as that of Huntington and Eccles canyons.

The alluring wilderness begins to appear at the south end of the Byway in a swift transition from pine forested mountains to rocky, red cliffs. Unique yellow and red rock formations with holes, crevasses, and trees scattered throughout are the results of an erratic art form of nature. Some of the rocks appear in vertical slabs wedged together to form a cliff. Others have pockmarks so distinct that, from a distance, they could be mistaken for an archaic language. Scenic turnouts are irresistible for photographing a rock formation against the sky or a river rushing through the canyons.

The scenic qualities of the Energy Loop are diverse and breathtaking. The Byway stretches across the Wasatch Plateau, rising high through steep canyons and down into pristine valleys. As you follow the Byway route, you will be amazed at the constantly changing landscapes that make the drive pleasurable year-round. Castle Valley is located on the eastern side of the Byway at the edge of the dramatic San Rafael Swell near Huntington. This desert valley is gorgeous and in stark contrast with the forested canyons found between Huntington and Fairview.

The Byway makes its way up Huntington Canyon, over a high summit, and down into Fairview Canyon, where you are treated to extraordinary views of mountain slopes and the Sanpete Valley below. Streams, lakes, and reservoirs are abundant on the Byway. At the higher elevations where the Huntington and Eccles Canyons intersect, you'll see U-shaped glacial valleys with rounded peaks and cirques cut by ancient glaciers.

HIGHLIGHTS

Traveling from Fairview, this must-see tour suggests scenic vistas that will make your visit to the Energy Loop a fulfilling one. If you are beginning the tour in Huntington, start at the bottom of this list and work your way up.

• **Electric Lake and Burnout Canyon:** Beginning in Fairview, take UT 31 approximately 10 miles to its junction with Highway 264. Follow 264

for about another 10 miles, and you will come upon a turnout and interpretive signs, along with a view of Burnout Canyon and Electric Lake. Electric Lake was constructed to provide power for the Huntington Power Plant. At the bottom of the lake lay old mines and kilns that were once part of the historic mining town of Connellsville.

• **Scofield:** 12 miles past the Electric Lake Overlook on Highway 264, you will meet with State Highway 96. Travel north for 5 miles to the historic town of Scofield, once the largest town in all of Carbon County. On May 1, 1900, one of the worst mining accidents in US history claimed the lives of hundreds of miners. Visit the old cemetery to see the gravestones of the miners lost on that tragic day. A little farther north, Highway 96 runs beside Scofield State Park and Reservoir, which provides good fishing for trout.

• **Sanpete Valley Overlook:** Leave the Scofield area by heading south on Highway 96, following the road you came in on. Drive back to the junction of Highways 264 and 31 and follow 31 southeast toward the town of Huntington. Approximately 7 miles from the junction, you will find another turnout that shows an impressive view of the Sanpete Valley.

• **Joe's Valley Overlook:** Continue traveling south on UT 31, and you will arrive at another scenic overlook in approximately 8 miles. This turnout provides interpretive signs and a view of Joe's Valley below, a popular recreation area for locals.

THINGS TO SEE AND DO

Driving along the Energy Loop will certainly keep your senses engaged, but if you yearn to get out of the car and stretch your legs, or if you'd like to make a mini-vacation out of your trip, check out these attractions along the route.

CLEVELAND-LLOYD DINOSAUR QUARRY. *155 E Main St, Price (84501). Phone 435/637-5060. www.blm.gov/utah/price/quarry.htm.* Since 1928, more than 12,000 dinosaur bones representing at least 70 different animals have been excavated on this site. Visitor center, nature trail, picnic area. Open Memorial Day-Labor Day, daily; Easter-Memorial Day, weekends only. **FREE**

FAIRVIEW MUSEUM OF HISTORY & ART. *85 North 100 E, Fairview (84629). Phone 435/427-9216. www.sanpete.com/FairviewMuseum.* Paintings, sculpture, and exhibits from Native American and local artists. Life-size replica of the Columbia Mammoth, discovered in 1988. Gift shop. Open Mon-Sat 10 am-6 pm, open until 5 pm in winter.

MANTI-LASAL NATIONAL FOREST. *2290 Resource Blvd, Moab (84532). Phone 435/259-7155. www.fs .fed.us/r4/mantilasal/.* Originally two forests—the Manti in central Utah and the LaSal section in southeastern Utah—they are now under single supervision. A 1,327,631-acre area partially in Colorado, this forest has among its attractions high mountain scenic drives, deep canyons, riding trails, campsites, winter sports, fishing, and deer and elk hunting. The land of the forest's LaSal Division is similar in color and beauty to some parts of the Grand Canyon, but also includes high mountains nearing 13,000 feet and pine and spruce forests. Swimming, fishing; hiking. **FREE**

MUSEUM OF THE SAN RAFAEL. *64 North 100 E, Castle Dale (84513). Phone 435/381-5252 www. museumsanrafael.org.* Dinosaur skeletons, fossils, artifacts from early people who inhabited the area, gemstones and rocks, gallery of artwork. Open Mon-Fri 10 am-4 pm; Sat 1 pm-4 pm.

WESTERN MINING AND RAILROAD MUSEUM. *296 South Main, Helper (84526). Phone 435/472-3009. www.wmrrm.org.* Housed in the old Helper Hotel building (1913-1914), the museum recounts the railroad and mining history of the area. Simulated coal mine, black-smith shop, Butch Cassidy display, recreated mining town, memorabilia, photographs. Gift shop. Open May-Sept 10 am-6 pm Mon-Sat; Oct-Apr 11 am-4 pm Tues-Sat.

PREHISTORIC MUSEUM. *College of Eastern Utah, 155 E Main St, Price (84501). Phone 435/613-5111; toll-free 800/817-9949. museum.ceu.edu.* Dinosaur displays, archaeology exhibits; geological specimens. Open Memorial Day-Labor Day, daily; rest of year, Mon-Sat; closed major holidays. **FREE**

PRICE CANYON RECREATION AREA. *15 miles N on US 6, then 3 miles W on unnumbered road, Price (84501).* Scenic overlooks; hiking, picnicking, camping (fee). Roads have steep grades. Open May-mid-Oct, daily. **FREE**

SCOFIELD STATE PARK. *US 6 and UT 96, Price (84501). Phone 435/448-9449.* Utah's highest state park has a 2,800-acre lake that lies at an altitude of 7,616 feet. Fishing, boating (docks, ramps); camping (rest rooms, showers); snow-mobiling, ice fishing, cross-country skiing in winter. Open May-Oct. **$$**

PLACES TO STAY

If you choose to include an overnight stay in your trip along this Byway, Mobil Travel Guide recommends the following lodgings. Price is about 20 miles from either end of the Byway, to the east.

★ **BEST WESTERN CARRIAGE HOUSE INN.** *590 E Main St, Price (84501). Phone 435/637-5660; toll-free 800/780-7234. www.bestwestern.com.* 41 rooms, 2 story. Complimentary continental breakfast. Check-out noon. TV. Indoor pool, whirlpool. Airport transportation. ¢

[D ☐ ☒]

★ **GREENWELL INN & CONVENTION CENTER.** *655 E Main St, Price (84501). Phone 435/637-3520; toll-free 800/666-3520. www.castlenet.com/ greenwell.* 125 rooms, 1-2 story. Complimentary continental breakfast. Check-out 11 am. TV. Laundry services. In-house fitness room. Health club privileges. Indoor pool. ¢

[⚞ ⚹ D ⚞ ⚞ ⚞ ☒]

★★HOLIDAY INN HOTEL & SUITES. *838 Westwood Blvd, Price (84501). Phone 435/637-8880; toll-free 800/465-4329. www.holiday-inn .com.* 151 rooms, 2 story. Check-out noon. TV. Restaurant, bar. Room service. In-house fitness room. Health club privileges. Indoor pool. ¢

[icons]

PLACES TO EAT

A long day of driving is sure to make you hungry. At the end of your journey, take a table at one of the following restaurants.

Fairview

★ BIRCH CREEK INN. *22130 N 11750 E, Fairview (84629). Phone 435/427-9578.* American menu. Closed Sun. Lunch, dinner. A local favorite with large portions and an inviting atmosphere. $

★ HOME PLATE CAFÉ. *215 N State St, Fairview (84629). Phone 435/427-9300.* American menu. Closed Sun. Lunch, dinner. This restaurant features a baseball-inspired menu of outdoor favorites. $

Huntington

★ CANYON RIM CAFÉ. *505 N Main St, Huntington (84528). Phone 435/687-9040.* American menu. Closed Sun. Lunch, dinner. Local regional cuisine in an attractive family-style setting. $

Price

★ CHINA CITY CAFÉ. *350 E Main St, Price (84501). Phone 435/637-8211.* Chinese, American menu. Closed Thanksgiving, Dec 25; July. Lunch, dinner. Children's menu. $$
[icon]

Flaming Gorge—Uintas Scenic Byway

❋ UTAH

Part of a multistate Byway; see also UT.

Quick Facts

LENGTH: 82 miles.

TIME TO ALLOW: 3 hours.

BEST TIME TO DRIVE: Year-round; high season is summer.

BYWAY TRAVEL INFORMATION: Dinosaurland Travel Board: toll-free 800/477-5558.

SPECIAL CONSIDERATIONS: During the winter, extra care and caution will lengthen the time required to drive from one end of the Byway to the other—it will also lengthen your life span. Because the public lands along the Byway are managed under the Multiple Use Concept, you may have the opportunity to encounter a real western cattle drive along the roadway during the spring and fall months.

RESTRICTIONS: Sections of the mountain highway are occasionally closed due to extreme snowfall during the winter.

BICYCLE/PEDESTRIAN FACILITIES: A growing number of visitors experience this Byway and its surrounding area by utilizing bicycles, motorcycles, ATVs, and hiking trails. Although the Byway can be biked from end to end, stretches exist that require cautious travel. Hundreds of miles of designated trails are easily accessible from the Byway if you're interested in getting out of your vehicle and enjoying the backcountry. The Byway is fortunate to intersect several loop routes that are part of the state-designated Scenic Backways Program. Where appropriate (regarding traveler safety and environmental impact), these loops provide hikers, campers, and mountain bikers with recreational opportunities.

As one of the most aptly named landscapes in the country, Flaming Gorge provides the kind of scenic vistas that refuse to fit in the viewfinder of a camera and must be relived in your memory after you return home. Driving this Byway, you get to watch Flaming Gorge and the Uinta Mountains unfold from several different perspectives.

Outdoor recreation is the biggest attraction for travelers on this Byway. The Flaming Gorge Dam and National Recreation Area, created as a recreational destination, encompasses nearly half of the Byway. The Dinosaur National Monument and Dinosaur Quarry have been among the world's greatest sources for dinosaur skeletons and draw visitors from all over the world. This region has continued to gain popularity as an area where travelers can experience the essence of the West through the existence of world-class rock art and the folklore of early explorers, mountain men, outlaws, and cowboys.

THE BYWAY STORY

The Flaming Gorge—Uintas Scenic Byway tells archaeological, historical, natural, recreational, and scenic stories that make it a unique and treasured Byway.

Archaeological

Beyond its scenic beauty, Flaming Gorge Scenic Byway has pieces of stored ancient history within its grounds and cliff sides. Pictographs and petroglyphs are thought to have been left behind by the Fremont Indians many hundreds of years ago. (Petroglyphs are pictures that are pecked into rock surfaces by using harder rocks, often made into tools; pictographs are pictures painted onto the rocks.) They are

✻ *Flaming Gorge–Uintas Scenic Byway*

evidence that Flaming Gorge has always been an inhabited spot. Ancient rock art can also be found near Dinosaur National Monument on one of the nature trails.

But ancient history goes back further on this Byway, and one of the main reasons people travel to this area is to see the largest quarry of Jurassic dinosaur skeletons in the country. Dinosaur National Monument is a must-see on the Flaming Gorge–Uintas Scenic Byway. Discovered in 1909, the quarry has yielded 11 dinosaur species that were found in the quarry, plus more than 1,600 bones. Here, you can see bones in and out of the quarry and all the places they have to go in between. The exhibits are fascinating, providing a close look at paleontology.

Historical

The route along the Flaming Gorge–Uintas Scenic Byway is rich in history and culture. The first European explorers were Fathers Dominguez and Escalante. Wesley Powell explored the Green River and named many of the Byway's geographic sites, including Flaming Gorge. General William H. Ashley explored the area and established several trading posts. He organized the first Mountain Man Rendezvous in 1825 near Manila.

The Byway parallels the Outlaw Trail that Butch Cassidy and members of the Wild Bunch used. Two turn-of-the-century homesteads on the Byway, Swett Ranch and Jarvies Ranch, are presently managed and interpreted by the Forest Service and Bureau of Land Management. The town of Vernal celebrates Outlaw Days with an outdoor theater depicting sagas of the Wild Bunch, a ride along the Outlaw trail, and other community events. The influence of the Mormon settlers is also evident in the Manila and Vernal areas.

Natural

The Flaming Gorge–Uintas Scenic Byway winds over the eastern flank of the Uinta Mountains and through the Flaming Gorge National Recreation Area, leading you through diverse plant communities that provide a great habitat for more than 390 species of birds, mammals, reptiles, amphibians, and fish. You'll have access to several developed viewing platforms, overlooks, displays, and signs that interpret the different wildlife species, and an outstanding number and variety of wildlife are available for viewing and photography, as well as for hunting and fishing. This Byway is one of the few areas in the US where visitors have the chance to see large herds of deer, elk, moose, and pronghorn antelopes on any given day throughout the year. The seasonal weather changes complement the wildlife migration patterns, which means that you may encounter Rocky Mountain bighorn sheep, river otters, yellow-bellied marmots, Kokanee salmon, red-tailed hawks, mountain bluebirds, golden eagles, bald eagles, and ospreys. Additionally, thousands of sandhill cranes migrate through the Vernal area in April and October each year.

This landscape is the basic setting for the real Jurassic Park, not only for dinosaurs but also for other prehistoric creatures, such as sharks, squids, and turtles. The Utah Field House of Natural History and Dinosaur Gardens serves as an orientation center for the Byway. Dinosaur National Monument features the largest working dinosaur quarry in the world; the world-class displays of dinosaurs and interpretive exhibits provide you with a greater appreciation for the geologic and prehistoric features found along the Byway.

Recreational

Flaming Gorge Reservoir is the most popular recreation spot in Utah. It offers highly developed facilities for camping, hiking, riding, skiing, snowmobiling, and other water-related opportunities on a year-round basis. The visitor centers, gift shops, restaurants, outfitters, guides, boat rentals, and other retailers work together as partners to make this a quality recreational experience. The businesses are set up to easily accommodate visitors for a week or even longer.

see page A27 for color map

Three-hundred seventy-six shoreline miles surround Flaming Gorge Reservoir, creating an angler's paradise. World-record brown trout exceeding 30 pounds and lake trout over 50 pounds have been caught here. People from all over the world visit the Green River for premier blue-ribbon fly-fishing experiences. The nearby High Uintas Wilderness Area (Utah's largest), which offers hundreds of miles of hiking trails and numerous camping sites, also boasts of hundreds of high-elevation lakes that provide outstanding fishing opportunities.

In addition, some local outfitters offer a four-day Jurassic Journey for families with kids 6 to 12 years old. It includes Class II river rafting on the Green River, short hikes to dinosaur country, a visit to a museum, camping, cooking out, and children's activities that help parents vacation, too.

Scenic

One of the most beautiful sights as you drive the Flaming Gorge–Uintas Scenic Byway is to watch the sun as it reflects off the water of the 91-mile Flaming Gorge reservoir. The most famous scenic view of the gorge, however, is of Red Canyon just below the Flaming Gorge Dam. The canyon walls on both sides of the water create an image of a lake clinging to the mountainsides. Half of the Byway follows Flaming Gorge as it curves into the Green River. The red plateaus sloping into Sheep Creek Bay look like abandoned sinking ships as the water laps at the edges.

The mountains that surround the gorge itself are densely forested, providing views of trees that carpet hillsides and scatter across ridges. Traveling through Ashley National Forest, the Byway gives you an excellent opportunity to enjoy the eastern edge of the Uinta mountain range, which is the only major east-west range in the United States. As Utah's tallest mountain range, the Uintas are an inviting sight as the

peaks tower to the sky. The forest is home to wildlife and beautiful scenery consisting of red rocky mountains and majestic peaks. The crags and geological formations along the drive add immensely to the unique views that make Flaming Gorge memorable.

HIGHLIGHTS

While visiting the Flaming Gorge–Uintas Scenic Byway, you can take the following self-guided tour.

• Driving on the Byway from Vernal, you don't want to miss the **Utah Field House of Natural History and Dinosaur Gardens** on the north side of Main Street in the heart of Vernal. See 18 life-sized dinosaurs, as well as artifacts from the Fremont and Ute Indian cultures.

• If you have the time, take a short side trip, following Highway 40 and traveling 20 miles east of Vernal to visit the famous **Dinosaur National Monument.**

• If you're making a quick trip, continue on US 191 to the **Flaming Gorge Dam and Visitor Center,** 6 miles from the Greendale Junction (US 191 and UT 44). There, you'll find picnic sites and other visitor facilities. Be sure to take the guided tour through the dam.

219

- Make a U-turn back on US 191 to travel west on UT 44. If you have time for a longer visit, you could stop at the **Swett Ranch** and partake of pioneer history.

- Continue on your way to the **Red Canyon Overlook and Visitor Center in the Flaming Gorge National Recreation Area,** about 5 miles off of UT 44. The caves and ledges of this scenic wonder offer glimpses into the ancient history of this area.

- If you have some extra time, continue on UT 44 and turn left onto the **Sheep Creek Loop Drive** to see the **Ute Tower.**

THINGS TO SEE AND DO

Driving along the Flaming Gorge–Uintas Scenic Byway will certainly keep your senses engaged, but if you yearn to get out of the car and stretch your legs, or if you'd like to make a mini-vacation out of your trip, check out these attractions along the route.

ASHLEY NATIONAL FOREST. *US 191, Vernal (84078). Phone 435/789-1181. www.fs.fed.us/r4/ ashley/.* The High Uinta Mountains—the only major east-west range in the US—runs through the heart of this nearly 1 1/2-million-acre forest. The 1,500-foot-deep **Red Canyon,** the 13,528-foot **Kings Peak,** and **Sheep Creek Geological Area** are also here. Swimming, fishing, boating (ramps, marinas), whitewater rafting, canoeing;

hiking and nature trails, cross-country skiing, snowmobiling, improved or backcountry campgrounds (fee). Visitor centers. **FREE**

DAUGHTERS OF UTAH PIONEERS MUSEUM. *500 W 200 S, Vernal (84078). Phone 435/789-3890.* Relics and artifacts dating to before 1847, when pioneers first settled in Utah; period furniture, quilts, clothing, and dolls; early doctor's, dentist's, and undertaker's instruments; and a restored Little Rock tithing office (1887). Open June through the weekend before Labor Day, Mon-Sat. **FREE**

✪ **DINOSAUR NATIONAL MONUMENT/UTAH ENTRANCE.** *4545 E US 40, Vernal (84078). Phone 801/789-8277. www.nps.gov/dino/.* Since 1909, this location has provided more skeletons, skulls, and bones of Jurassic Period dinosaurs than any other dig in the world. The dinosaur site comprises only 80 acres of this 325-square-mile park, which lies at the border of Utah and Colorado. Utah's Dinosaur Quarry section can be entered from the junction of US 40 and UT 149, north of Jensen, 13 miles east of Vernal; approximately 7 miles north on UT 149 is the fossil exhibit. Another 5 miles north is Green River Campground, with 90 tent and trailer sites available mid-May to mid-Sept. A smaller campground, Rainbow Park, provides a small number of tent sites from May to Nov. A fee is charged at Green River (water and rest rooms available). Backpacking, hiking, fishing. River rafting on the Green and Yampa rivers, by advance permit from the National Park Service or with concession-operated guided float trips (phone 970/374-2468). Because of snow, some areas of the monument are closed approximately mid-Nov-mid-Apr. **$$**

DINOSAUR QUARRY. *Jensen (84035). Phone 435/789-2115.* Remarkable fossil deposit; exhibit of 150-million-year-old dinosaur remains; preparation laboratory on display. Open daily 8 am-4:30 pm; extended hours in summer; closed Jan 1, Thanksgiving, Dec 25. **$$$**

DINOSAUR ROUNDUP RODEO. *134 W Main St, Vernal (84078).* Phone toll-free 800/421-9635. Held annually in mid-July.

FLAMING GORGE DAM AND NATIONAL RECREATION AREA. *US 191, Vernal (84078). Phone 435/784-3445. go-utah.com/flaming_gorge_national_recreation_area.* The area surrounds the 91-mile-long Flaming Gorge Reservoir and the 502-foot-high Flaming Gorge Dam. Fishing on the reservoir and river (all year), marinas, boat ramps, water-skiing; lodges, campgrounds (fee). River rafting below the dam. Visitor centers at the dam and at Red Canyon (on a secondary paved road 3 miles off of UT 44).

OURAY NATIONAL WILDLIFE REFUGE. *Vernal (84078). Phone 435/789-0351. ouray.fws.gov.* Waterfowl nesting marshes; desert scenery; self-guided auto tour (limited route during hunting season). Open daily. **FREE**

OUTLAW TRAIL FESTIVAL. *Vernal (84078).* Festivals, sporting events, and theatrical events. Held in late June-mid-Aug.

RED FLEET STATE PARK. *4335 N US 191, Vernal (84078). Phone 435/789-4432.* A scenic lake highlighted by red rock formations; boating, swimming, fishing; camping. Several hundred well-preserved dinosaur tracks. Open daily. **$$**

STEINAKER STATE PARK. *US 191, Vernal (84078). Phone 435/789-4432.* Approximately 2,200 acres on the western shore of Steinaker Reservoir. Swimming, water-skiing, fishing, boating (ramp, dock); picnicking, tent and trailer sites (fee). Open Apr-Nov; fishing all year. **$$**

UTAH FIELD HOUSE OF NATURAL HISTORY AND DINOSAUR GARDENS. *235 E Main St, Vernal (84078). Phone 435/789-3799.* Guarded by three life-size cement dinosaurs, this museum has exhibits of fossils, archaeology, life zones, geology, and fluorescent minerals of the region. Adjacent Dinosaur Gardens contain 17 life-size model dinosaurs in natural surroundings. Open daily; closed Jan 1, Thanksgiving, Dec 25. **$**

WESTERN HERITAGE MUSEUM. *328 E 200 S, Vernal (84078). Phone 435/789-7399.* Houses memorabilia from Uintah County's outlaw past as well as other artifacts dealing with a western theme. Includes the Thorne Collection, photographs, and artifacts of the ancient people of Utah. Open Mon-Sat; closed holidays. **FREE**

PLACES TO STAY

If you choose to include an overnight stay in your trip along this Byway, Mobil Travel Guide recommends the following lodgings.

★ **HILLS HOUSE.** *675 W 3300 N, Vernal (84078). Phone 435/789-0700.* 4 rooms, 2 story. Featuring a full breakfast and in-room hot tubs. **$**

★ **LANDMARK INN BED & BREAKFAST.** *288 E 100 S, Vernal (84078). Phone 435/781-1800; toll-free 888/738-1800. www.landmark-inn.com.* 11 rooms, 2 story. This small inn is located in a renovated former Baptist church. **$**

★ **THE SAGE MOTEL.** *54 W Main St, Vernal (84078). Phone toll-free 800/760-1442. www.vernalmotels.com.* 26 rooms, 2 story. A classic 1950s roadside motel owned and operated by the same family. **$**

★ **WESTON PLAZA HOTEL.** *1684 W Hwy 40, Vernal (84078). Phone 435/789-9550.* 102 rooms, 3 story. Check-out 11 am. TV; cable (premium). Restaurant, bar; entertainment. Indoor pool, whirlpool. Continental breakfast. **¢**

★ **WESTON'S LAMPLIGHTER INN.** *120 E Main St, Vernal (84078). Phone 435/789-0312.* 167 rooms, 2 story. Check-out 11 am. TV; cable (premium). Restaurant. Pool. **¢**

❊ *Flaming Gorge–Uintas Scenic Byway*

PLACES TO EAT

A long day of driving is sure to make you hungry. At the end of your journey, take a table at one of the following restaurants.

★★ **CURRY MANOR.** *189 S Vernal Ave, Vernal (84078). Phone 435/789-7268.* Indian menu. Lunch, dinner. A local favorite for authentic Indian cuisine. **$**

★★ **SEVEN ELEVEN CAFÉ.** *77 E Main St, Vernal (84078). Phone 435/789-1170.* American menu. Breakfast, lunch, dinner. Known for its friendly, family-oriented atmosphere and large portions. **$**

A Journey Through Time Scenic Byway

HIGHWAY 12 ✦ UTAH

AN ALL-AMERICAN ROAD

Quick Facts

LENGTH: 124 miles.

TIME TO ALLOW: 1 to 3 days.

BEST TIME TO DRIVE: Spring is the best time of year to explore the lands surrounding Highway 12. High season comes during the summer, when travelers are visiting Bryce Canyon and Capitol Reef. Winter is the off-season, but many travelers find this area to be a winter wonderland, and the Byway is open and maintained year-round.

BYWAY TRAVEL INFORMATION: Garfield County Travel Council: 800/444-6689; Byway travel and tourism Web site: www.brycecanyoncountry.com.

SPECIAL CONSIDERATIONS: Weather can change quickly; thunderstorms are common during the summer. Several stretches of this road are quite isolated and rugged, some with 12 percent grades. The road climbs to 8,000 feet as it crosses Boulder Mountain, rising and falling in steep switchbacks through Escalante Canyons and Boulder Mountain. You'll find several short tunnels in the Red Canyon area. The Aquarius Plateau/ Boulder Mountain segment receives heavy accumulations of winter snow and may be closed temporarily during heavy snowstorms. However, the road is plowed to allow year-round access.

RESTRICTIONS: The Hogsback is high and narrow and can be windy. High-profile vehicles should be prepared.

BICYCLE/PEDESTRIAN FACILITIES: Highway 12 offers a paved bicycle path that allows cyclists to pedal through Red Canyon. Other places along the Byway are suitable for cyclists, although places like the Hogsback have little shoulder space for bicycles.

As you drive the Byway that connects Bryce Canyon National Park and Capitol Reef National Park, you are treated to enticing views and stops, along with a kaleidoscope of color. Byway towns in between offer a flavor of a simple life in the middle of a fantastic wilderness. Historic stops and pullouts provide stories for curious Byway travelers. Ancient ruins and artwork can be found throughout the canyons and rock faces that line this Byway.

At nearly every turn, you have an opportunity to get out of the car and stretch. But stretching is only the beginning. Hiking, horseback riding, and traveling by ATV are irresistible activities that allow you to explore the back roads and trails of this wonderland of sculpted color.

THE BYWAY STORY

Highway 12 tells archaeological, cultural, historical, natural, recreational, and scenic stories that make it a unique and treasured Byway.

Archaeological

Driving this road through some of Utah's most unusual landscapes, the climate and the topography seem all too fantastic for human beings to dwell there. Nevertheless, evidence of ancient civilization is around every corner and within every crevasse of the canyons along Highway 12. The Anasazi, Fremont, and Utes all left their mark on the rugged and challenging land. Their occupation has been preserved in the sandstone of the plateaus and under the sands and soils of the valleys. A thousand years ago, these people made a home of this unique landscape and left evidence of their habitation for visitors, travelers, and archaeologists to see.

Not only was their survival in this wilderness commendable, but the structures that the Anasazi left behind astound travelers and archaeologists alike. As you drive along the base of cliffs and canyons on Highway 12, alcoves high in the rocks hold ancient stone granaries where this hunting and gathering culture would store the food they had collected. The granaries reside in grooves within the cliff side and consist of rocks stacked like bricks with a small hole in the center near the bottom of the structure. Today, we can only guess how the people of so long ago would have reached these heights.

Farther along the Byway, a remarkable display of an excavated Anasazi village is located on the Byway in the community of Boulder. The Anasazi Village State Park Visitor Center is located at the site of a village that once held 200 people. Walls of homes and structures of pit-houses are displayed there as examples of the way these people once lived. Only a few of the structures have been uncovered. The rest remain buried in the ground that surrounds the walkways that take visitors on a tour of the past. Signs of life from so many centuries ago captivate travelers.

One of the most riveting scenes on the Byway is an occasional glimpse of a petroglyph or pictograph. Some of the most impressive examples of this rock art can be seen at Capitol Reef as images of ancient people and animals line the red rock face of nearby Highway 24 and the Fremont River. Pictures and figures were etched on these stone walls all along the Byway and remain as a memorial to this vanished culture. Many of these pictures remain unknown and undiscovered to be found by an alert explorer. While hiking in the mountains of Highway 12, visitors are compelled to treat these drawings and carvings with an utmost solemnity. These pictures of the past are somehow related to us today, and to disturb them is to cause a breach in the connections of these two great periods.

Cultural

Embedded in the rocky precipices of Highway 12 is a conglomeration of cultures—past and present. Over the ages, travelers moving into the area built a home for themselves, incorporating ideas and methods of survival perfected by preceding cultures. The culture that permeates the Byway today is made up of people who hold a deep respect for their predecessors, and towns of the past are now a haven for both travelers and residents on the Byway. Find their heritage and their future in the many festivals and favorite spots all along the Byway.

The cultures of the Fremont Indians and the Anasazi vanished before any cultures surviving today could know them. However, their archaeological remains and artwork enable modern-day experts and visitors to speculate about what these people must have been like. These cultures had a belief system of legends and histories that explained the landforms that surrounded them. One thing is certain: the cultures of the Anasazi, Fremont, and Paiute revered the land of Highway 12 as a special land. Today's cultures feel the same way. Preserving the land and celebrating its natural beauty are common goals for the people who live in communities along the Byway.

Before there was a bridge between the cultures of the future and the past, there was a culture of growth and development. Mormon pioneers established communities over a century ago whose presence today has brought a new collection of stories and histories to tell the story of the Byway. The communities that visitors will observe display the classical elements of a Mormon settlement. People would gather in a town and spread their farms all around the town. This way, an agricultural people developed and preserved a sense of community. This strong sense of community still exists today, and you are invited to partake of it. Thus influences of past cultures are a force that preserves the rural culture of today and passes its spirit onto the travelers who pass this way.

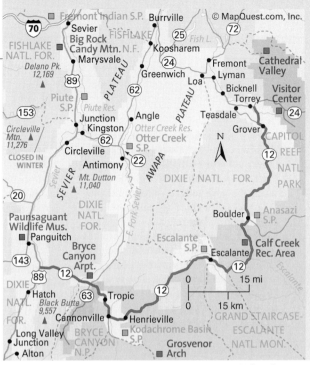

© MapQuest.com, Inc.

see page A28 for color map

Historical

Visitors find a piece of history around every corner along the Journey Through Time. Before Highway 12 became a Scenic Byway, it was a passageway for native tribes, explorers, and pioneers. Their legacy is left behind in the names of prominent places like Powell Point and in places like the historic town of Escalante. Many of the sacred places of the Fremont and Anasazi have been lost and forgotten, but the history that these people left behind is archaeology now. Through the influences of the explorers and the pioneers, lands along the Byway reflect the history of the west to build upon an archaeological and geological history.

The first explorers were Spanish and claimed the land for Spain in 1776. The name of the town Escalante comes from one of the priests who was on the expedition, Silvestre Velez de Escalante. John Wesley Powell more thoroughly explored the land nearly 100 years later in 1869 on a treacherous journey where he lost several of his company. Nearby Lake Powell and Powell Point are now two landmarks that carry his name. By the time he explored the area, Mormon pioneers had already begun to inhabit the region in an attempt to make the desert bloom.

The town of Panguitch was the first place the pioneers attempted to settle. Because of conflicts with the native tribes, they abandoned the settlement until 1871. A string of other towns along the Byway retain a western town appearance with wood storefronts, stone walls, and old-fashioned architecture. In Tropic, visit Ebenezer Bryce's cabin. This rancher/farmer began to utilize the landscape at the mouth of what is now known as Bryce Canyon, one of Utah's most fantastic national parks. The town of Boulder was the last town on the Byway to receive mail by mule. This fertile mountainside is still covered with wooden pioneer fences and old-fashioned barns.

Natural

Landforms along the Highway 12 Scenic Byway inspire visitors with awe and curiosity for the powers of nature. Desertscapes have been preserved to become masterpieces of art that have been tempered with time. Their alluring shapes and curves have a story that begins millions of years ago. That story continues today with the thriving forests and wildlife that live along the Byway. Drive Highway 12 and tour a land carved by water and wind. Layers of rock stacked like giant pancakes pick at the imaginations of travelers. Why is the stone here so colorful? How can the rock formations maintain such unusual shapes? The answers are embedded in layers of color within plateaus and canyon walls that have been decorated with trees and wildlife.

Red Rock Canyon, Bryce Canyon, and Kodachrome Basin offer some of the strangest geological sites that travelers will ever see. The walls of Bryce Canyon are lined with singular, human-like pinnacles that protrude from the rock. So many of them in succession make the canyon look like a crowded stadium. The irregular shapes of the rocks in Bryce Canyon were formed when ancient rivers carved exposed

225

HIGHWAY 12 ✳ *A Journey Through Time Scenic Byway*

layers of the Earth. The meandering of these rivers must have been erratic, for there are thousands of paths through the pinnacles at Bryce Canyon. Red Rock Canyon displays a range of orange and red colors in the rock. Take a hike to discover all the natural arches there. In Kodachrome Basin, evidence of another natural wonder from millions of years ago is in the strange pinnacles of stone. This used to be a geyser basin not unlike the kind found in Yellowstone National Park today. Geologists believe that the towers of stone there are actually fossilized geysers. Their vivid colors are evident from a distance.

Recreational

When Utah's visiting outdoor recreationists get tired of Utah's national parks and other well-known recreation areas, they come to A Journey Through Time Scenic Byway for supreme recreational experiences. Some of the most captivating hikes in Utah are located just off the Byway in the slot canyons of the Grand Staircase or near one of the Byway's state parks. Red Canyon and its accompanying canyons offer trails for hikers, bikers, horseback riders, and ATV enthusiasts. Be ready for an adventure on the slickrock when you travel Highway 12. With trails, backways, and paths, there is an exciting ride ahead whether you are on or off the Byway.

Scenic

Spanning a route of more than 120 miles, Utah's Highway 12 Scenic Byway travels through some of the most diverse and ruggedly beautiful landscapes in the country. The surrounding red rock formations, slickrock canyons, pine and aspen forests, alpine mountains, national and state parks, and quaint rural towns all contribute in making Highway 12 a unique route well worth traveling.

Highway 12 travels from west to east through Garfield County, the home of three national parks, three state parks, and one national recreation area. At the junction of Highway 89, the Byway quickly bisects the beautiful red rock formations of Dixie National Forest's Red Canyon and continues eastward.

Hiking trails, campgrounds, and side roads along the way provide numerous opportunities to further explore the area. Highway 12 ends in Wayne County. The town of Torrey is near the junction, and travelers can take the short drive east along Highway 24 to Capitol Reef National Park, thus adding to the Highway 12 experience.

THINGS TO SEE AND DO

Driving along Highway 12 will certainly keep your senses engaged, but if you yearn to get out of the car and stretch your legs, or if you'd like to make a mini-vacation out of your trip, check out these attractions along the route.

ANASAZI INDIAN VILLAGE STATE PARK. *60 N Highway 12, Boulder (84716). Phone 435/335-7308. www.brycecanyoncountry.com/anasazi.html.* This partially excavated village, believed to have been occupied from 1050 to 1200, is one of the largest ancient communities west of the Colorado River. Fremont and Kayenta Anasazi occupied the area. Museum. Picnicking. Open daily; closed Jan 1, Thanksgiving, Dec 25. $

✪ **BRYCE CANYON NATIONAL PARK.** *UT 63, Panguitch (84764). Phone 435/676-8585. www.nps.gov/brca/.* Bryce Canyon is a 56-square-mile area of colorful, fantastic cliffs created by millions of years of erosion. Towering rocks worn to odd, sculptured shapes stand grouped in striking sequences. The Paiute, who once lived nearby, called this "the place where red rocks stand like men in a bowl-shaped canyon." Although termed a canyon, Bryce is actually a series of breaks in 12 large amphitheaters—some plunging as deep as 1,000 feet into the multicolored limestone. The formations appear to change color as the sunlight strikes from different angles and seem incandescent in the late afternoon. The famous Pink Cliffs were carved from the Claron Formation; shades of red, orange, white, gray, purple, brown, and soft yellow appear in the strata. Park Road follows 17 miles along the eastern edge of the Paunsaugunt Plateau, where the natural amphitheaters are spread out below; plateaus covered with evergreens and valleys filled with sagebrush stretch away into the distance. The visitor center at the entrance station has complete information about the park, including orientation shows, geologic displays, and detailed maps. Open daily; closed Jan 1, Thanksgiving, Dec 25. Lodging is also available Apr-Oct. **$$**

✪ **CAPITOL REEF NATIONAL PARK.** *10 miles E of Richfield on UT 119, then 65 miles SE on UT 24, Loa (84747). Phone 435/425-3791. www.nps.gov/care/.* Capitol Reef, at an elevation ranging from 3,900 to 8,800 feet, is composed of red sandstone cliffs capped with domes of white sandstone. Located in the heart of Utah's slickrock country, the park is actually a 100-mile section of the Waterpocket Fold, an upthrust of sedimentary rock created during the formation of the Rocky Mountains. Pockets in the rocks collect thousands of gallons of water each time it rains. Capitol Reef was so named because the rocks formed a natural barrier to pioneer travel, and the white

sandstone domes resemble the dome of the US Capitol. From 700 to 1350, this 378-square-mile area was the home of an ancient people who grew corn along the Fremont River. Petroglyphs can be seen on some of the sandstone walls. A schoolhouse, farmhouse, and orchards, established by early Mormon settlers, are open to the public in season. The park can be approached from either the east or the west via UT 24, a paved road. A visitor center is located about 7 miles from the west boundary and 8 miles from the east. A 25-mile round-trip scenic drive, some parts unpaved, starts from this point. There are evening programs and guided walks (Memorial Day-Labor Day; free). Three campgrounds are available. Open daily; closed Dec 25. **$**

DIXIE NATIONAL FOREST. *82 N and 100 E, Cedar City (84720). Phone 435/865-3200. www.fs.fed.us/dxnf/.* Camping, picnicking, hiking, mountain biking, winter sports. Open daily. **FREE**

ESCALANTE STATE PARK. *UT 12, Escalante (84736). Phone 435/826-4466.* Petrified forest; mineralized wood, and dinosaur bones. Swimming, fishing, boating (ramps) at reservoir; hiking, bird-watching, picnicking, camping (fee; rest rooms, showers, dump station). Open daily. **$$**

PANGUITCH LAKE. *Phone 435/676-2649.* Located in Dixie National Forest, this 8,000-foot-high lake, which fills a large volcanic basin, is your chance to fish while on the Byway. Resorts, public campgrounds (developed sites, fee), ice fishing, snowmobiling, cross-country skiing.

PAUNSAGAUNT WILDLIFE MUSEUM. *250 E Center St, Panguitch (84759). Phone 435/676-2500 (May 1-Oct 1); 702-877-2664 (Oct 1-May 1). www.brycecanyonwildlifemuseum.com.* More than 400 North American animals in their natural habitats can be viewed here. You can also catch sight of exotic game animals from Africa, India, and Europe. Open May-Sept, daily 9 am-7 pm. **$**

Utah

HIGHWAY 12 ✻ *A Journey Through Time Scenic Byway*

PLACES TO STAY

If you choose to include an overnight stay in your trip along this All-American Road, Mobil Travel Guide recommends the following lodgings.

★★ **BRYCE CANYON LODGE.** *1 Bryce Canyon Lodge, Bryce Canyon (84717). Phone 435/834-5361; toll-free 888/297-2757. www.brycecanyonlodge.com.* 114 units in cabins, motel. Closed Dec-Mar. Check-out 11 am, check-in 4 pm. Coin laundry. Restaurant. Private patios, balconies. Trail rides on mules, horses available. Original 1925 building. **$**
[D] [⚡] [🛏]

★★ **BRYCE CANYON PINES MOTEL.** *Hwy 12, Panguitch (84764). Phone 435/834-5441; toll-free 800/892-7923. www.brycecanyonmotel.com.* 50 rooms, 1-2 story. Check-out 11 am, check-in 2 pm. TV. Heated pool. Restaurant. Some fireplaces, balconies. Early American décor. **¢**
[D] [SC] [🛏]

PLACES TO EAT

A long day of driving is sure to make you hungry. At the end of your journey, try the following restaurant.

★ **FOSTER'S STEAK HOUSE.** *UT 12, Bryce Canyon National Park (84764). Phone 435/834-5227. www.brycecanyoncountry.com/dining.* Steak menu. Breakfast, lunch, dinner. Children's menu. Bakery adjacent. **$$**
[D]

Logan Canyon Scenic Byway

※ UTAH

Quick Facts

LENGTH: 41 miles.

TIME TO ALLOW: 1 hour.

BEST TIME TO DRIVE: Fall; summer is the high season.

BYWAY TRAVEL INFORMATION: Bridgerland Travel Region: 435/752-2161.

SPECIAL CONSIDERATIONS: Logan Canyon Scenic Byway is a two-lane highway. Although the Byway has more passing zones on the upgrade than the downgrade, you'll find only five to eight passing zones.

RESTRICTIONS: Winter weather can be severe in Logan Canyon. The highway patrol may require that vehicles carry tire chains from November through March.

BICYCLE/PEDESTRIAN FACILITIES: Bicycle and pedestrian traffic through the canyon continues to increase as the population grows in Logan and surrounding communities. The Byway consists of roadway shoulders that provide the necessary facilities for bicycle and pedestrian traffic, although in some areas, the shoulders are mostly gravel. Several trail head and bike path entry points are located along the Byway, and several bicycle/pedestrian trails and paths run parallel to the roadway, including Logan River Trails.

Beautiful mountains that tower over the city of Logan and the turquoise waters of Bear Lake captivate visitors and residents year-round. You'll be enchanted by inland seas, a dramatic landscape surrounding this Byway formed by great earthquakes and mountains that tower over the road on both sides. Driving the Logan Canyon Scenic Byway is like entering a new world where the mountains, trees, and river together reveal the undying patterns of nature.

The patterns of the canyon have become intertwined with the patterns of a culture. Once, the land was inhabited only by native tribes of Utah, but as trappers and pioneers entered the region, the land was forever changed. Today, the canyon is recognized as the gem of the surrounding communities. In the summer, the campgrounds are full and the echoes of chattering birds and wind through the trees can be heard throughout. In winter, the stillness of the snow-covered mountainsides lures travelers outdoors for a day of skiing.

Pioneers who made their way here to settle in Cache Valley were the first to make a road through the canyon. Through the determination of the past and the perseverance of today, the beauty of Logan Canyon is accessible as a National Scenic Byway.

THE BYWAY STORY

The Logan Canyon Scenic Byway tells cultural, historical, natural, recreational, and scenic stories that make it a unique and treasured Byway.

✳ *Logan Canyon Scenic Byway*

Cultural

From mountain men to mountain climbers, Logan Canyon has fostered a variety of cultures from its earliest days. As cultures have shifted and evolved over the last few centuries in this corner of northern Utah, memories of the past are still in place, which means you can experience a variety of cultural influences as you visit the Byway. Cultural influences of mountain men and tribal natives still surface from time to time in the now-modern cultures of agriculture and industry.

The Shoshone and Bannock tribes had been living in the areas near Cache Valley and Bear Lake for many years before their lands were forever changed by the coming of fur trappers and, later, settlers. Local tribes still gather to practice beautiful cultural dances and songs; their artwork can be seen in fairs and festivals all through the summer. Mountain men are also honored with festivals and activities.

The coming of the Mormon Pioneers made a significant impact on the culture of the area. Settlers from the Church of Jesus Christ of Latter Day Saints (LDS) developed an agricultural society that still thrives in Cache Valley. The Mormon pioneers also brought with them an appreciation for family and heritage that is still found along the Byway.

Today, because they live so close to a perfect wilderness, most everyone in Cache Valley and Bear Lake has a personal attachment to at least one aspect of Logan Canyon. From exploring nature trails to fishing and canoeing, the skills and pastimes of the first people in Logan Canyon remain with today's residents. Everyone has a niche, and everyone is equally convinced that the value of Logan Canyon is priceless.

You will be delighted as you encounter the cultures of today and celebrate the cultures of yesterday. Summer festivals and year-round information about people and places make every culture along the Byway accessible.

Historical

Although most of the places in Logan Canyon were named in the last 150 years, influences from an earlier past can still be found in places along the Byway. Guinavah-Malibu campground carries the Shoshone word for bird water, which was the earliest name for the Logan River. A mountain man named Jim Bridger gave his name to the region that encompasses the canyon known as Bridgerland. Cache Valley, at the west end of the canyon, was named for the caches that trappers made in the area to store their furs. As Mormon pioneers entered the area in mid-1800s, they established Temple Fork, where they procured the materials they would need to build their temple and tabernacle. And many of the names in the canyon came from the days of the Civilian Conservation Corps (CCC). As these men moved through the canyon, they left a trail of cabins, picnic areas, and campgrounds. Most notable of their achievements is the amphitheater at the Guinavah-Malibu campground.

Stories of highfalutin' families at Tony Grove or an 11-foot-tall bear named Ephraim can be found in places all along the way. These stories are told on Byway markers and at information centers. One of the best places to find out about Logan Canyon history is at Lady Bird Overlook at the mouth of the canyon in Logan, a location that carries history of its own. It was named for President Johnson's wife, Lady Bird Johnson, who initiated the highway beautification plan in the 1960s. At the overlook, you can discover the story of a 1,000-year-old tree and find out why one of the most beautiful spots on the Byway is called China Row.

Logan Canyon was in the land of the Shoshone and the Bannock. Later, Logan Canyon saw the days of the mountain man filled with rendezvous and trapping animals for their fur. When the Mormon pioneers came, the wild land of Logan Canyon was forever changed. Civilization came to the Byway to explore it and discover the wonders of the canyon in the same way that travelers do today. As you pass places along the way,

see page A29 for color map

you might be able to find the stories of Indian tribes, mountain men, pioneers, and farmers who all left their mark in different ways along the Logan Canyon Scenic Byway.

Natural

In Logan Canyon, where a wilderness waits at the doorstep of the Cache Valley community, nature is the one constant that draws people of every age and disposition. Whether they come for a hike in the mountains or to picnic by the riverside, the one unifying appeal is the natural atmosphere that thrives in Logan Canyon. From the moment you reach the mouth of the canyon, you feel an impulse to roll down the window and let the fresh canyon breeze—a mixture of pine, foliage, and the river—fill the car. The canyon is alive with wildflowers, shrubs, and trees of every kind.

Although the mountains seem high, they were once covered with the water of an inland sea called Lake Bonneville. Many of the rock formations that visitors enjoy in the canyon were caused by erosion from Lake Bonneville. Outcroppings, like the one called the China Wall, are simply ancient beaches where the sediment has become solid and provides a perfect place for activities like rock climbing. Just looking up at these mammoth walls of nature is a mesmerizing experience; knowing that they were once ancient beaches makes them even more exotic.

The enchanting Tony Grove Lake, formerly a glacier, is a favorite natural feature in the canyon. Covered with wildflowers in the spring, the shoreline of the lake is partly a mountainside and partly a forest of pine trees. Water has carved numerous caves through the limestone of the canyon, including Logan Cave and Ricks Spring. Other caves in Logan Canyon are not as well known, although backcountry hikers and rock climbers may have the opportunity to stumble across one of them.

The Logan River is the heart of Logan Canyon, its rhythm changing with the seasons. During the spring, the river rages with snow melt runoff, reaching high velocities. In summer, the river slows, fed by delayed runoff from groundwater storage and augmented by the many springs and tributaries that flow into it. The river surface begins to freeze in the fall and by midwinter, the river forms ragged sheets of ice. When the weather is fair, visitors on the shores of Second Dam watch fish jumping and beavers swimming across the water to its dam. In the winter, deer step lightly on the mountainside and pause by the river for a drink. Through its seasons, the Logan River is central to the lives of local residents and wildlife.

Recreational

Logan Canyon recreation is one of the main reasons people come to Cache Valley to visit and to stay. After a short drive into the mountains, you'll find a garden of recreational opportunities—some relaxing and others extreme. From an early morning hike to rock climbing, Logan Canyon is the best place for miles around to unwind.

Logan Canyon's limestone outcroppings are calling for you to climb them. Rock climbers gather from spring through fall to challenge the million-year-old mountainsides. Most of the climbs are bolt-protected sport climbs and are in the 5.10 to 5.12 level of difficulty. In winter, climbers can be found making their way up a frozen waterfall. Another mountainside challenge is offered within the crisp winter air at Beaver Mountain, where skiers and snowboarders gather to test skills of balance and coordination.

Although they might be the most exciting of mountain sports, skiing and climbing aren't the only activities available in Logan Canyon. With 300 miles of hiking trails, Logan Canyon is also a hiker's paradise. Trails lead to every kind of destination, from an ancient juniper tree to a pristine mountain lake. Runners and cyclists especially love the Logan River Trail starting at Red Bridge. On summer mornings, the air is cool and green leaves hang over the trail, creating a scenic place to exercise.

Roads available at Temple Fork and Right Hand Fork provide opportunities for ATVs and motorcyclists to enjoy the exciting back roads of the canyon. During the winter, trailers carrying snowmobiles can be seen entering Logan Canyon. They might be heading to Franklin Basin or the Sinks, where valleys between the trees offer the perfect place to traverse the snow.

When all the snow melts, water sports reach their height in Logan Canyon, whether you are boating or fishing. Logan Canyon is home to the Logan River and Bear Lake, where many travelers take boats and jet skis during the summer for an exhilarating run across its mesmerizing waters. Visitors can also fish for the Bonneville Cisco, which is only found in Bear Lake. The Logan River is famous for fly fishing, but anglers of every kind and age gather at Second and Third Dam to try their luck with a pole. A careful observer will be able to see groups of trout as they gather underneath a bridge nearby, but scuba divers at the east end of Bear Lake have the best view of the local fish. A more secluded setting is found at Tony Grove Lake, where the most popular activity—besides fishing—is canoeing.

Scenic

Logan residents climb the canyon road year-round for recreation, a chance to enjoy the great outdoors, and the pure exhilaration that Logan Canyon scenery provides. They have favorite haunts like Tony Grove Lake, Second Dam, or China Row, where an atmosphere of shady trees, mossy banks, and clear water feeds the imagination. Visitors to Logan Canyon find themselves in an undiscovered wilderness, an enchanted forest, or in the mountains of a distant country. From the mouth of the canyon at First Dam to the captivating overlook at Bear Lake, Logan Canyon scenery draws audiences that come back to see the performance change.

As you begin your ascent to the summit of Logan Canyon Scenic Byway, you'll find yourself overshadowed by the towering mountains, the tops of which are 1 mile above the road. Just below the road, the Logan River flows over a rocky bed through a series of dams. Each dam has its own inviting qualities. Ducks swimming among cattails and reeds set a tranquil scene for anglers at Third Dam and Spring Hollow. A collection of shady picnic tables along the water's edge at Second Dam entices visitors for a lunchtime stop. Later on the drive, the mountains pull apart, revealing grassy meadows on either side of the Byway.

Evergreen pine and juniper intermingled with deciduous maples and aspen provide a contrast of color that makes Logan Canyon a superb road for seeing fall color. Strips of deep red run in the crevasses of the mountainsides where a cluster of maples is growing, making you wish that fall would linger in Logan Canyon. Perhaps one of the best times to enjoy the late fall is just after a rainstorm, when low-lying clouds float just above the road and every tree and leaf displays rich browns, oranges, and reds.

You may have trouble naming the most beautiful scenic highlight on the Byway or even pinpointing what makes the Byway beautiful. It's the way rocky precipices jut out of the mountainside; the way the mountainside slopes upward, taking a forest of trees with it; the way the trees become brilliant red in the fall; and the way the road winds through it all that make Logan Canyon Scenic Byway one of the most enchanting drives in the country.

HIGHLIGHTS

For your own Logan Canyon must-see tour, consider following this itinerary. Note that all mileages are taken from the Logan Ranger Station at the western mouth of the canyon.

- **Mile 2.5—Second Dam:** A favorite spot for local anglers.

- **Mile 5.0—Wind Caves:** This cave is high above the canyon. A 1.5-mile trail provides access. The cave is actually a triple arch formed by wind and water erosion.

- **Mile 12.0—Logan Cave:** This used to be a popular cave to explore, but because of vandalism in 1998, the Forest Service gated and locked the cave entrance. The upside is

that by keeping people out of the cave, the native bat population will likely thrive.

- **Mile 15.4—Ricks Springs:** Despite its name, Ricks Spring is not really a spring; instead, it is a diversion of the Logan River, mixed with a little mountain snowmelt.

- **Mile 19.2—Tony Grove Lake Area:** This worthwhile side trip takes you up a winding road to beautiful Tony Grove Lake.

- **Mile 31.1—Bear Lake Overlook:** On a clear day, Bear Lake sparkles an unusually clear turquoise blue. A display explains the history and geology of the lake and surrounding area.

THINGS TO SEE AND DO

Driving along the Logan Canyon Scenic Byway will certainly keep your senses engaged, but if you yearn to get out of the car and stretch your legs, or if you'd like to make a mini-vacation out of your trip, check out these attractions along the route.

AMERICAN WEST HERITAGE CENTER. *4025 S Hwy 89-91, Wellsville (84321). Phone 435/245-6050; toll-free 800/225-FEST. www.americanwestcenter.org.* An agricultural museum with a typical Mormon family farm of the World War I era; 120 acres of fields, meadows, orchards, and gardens; artifacts and machinery; costumed interpreters; pioneer and Native American crafts fair, art exhibition, antique quilt show; frontier town; medicine man show; log construction; Dutch-oven cooking demonstration. Open Memorial Day-Labor Day, Mon-Sat 10 am-5 pm. $$

BEAR LAKE STATE PARK. *147 W Logan Rd, Garden City (84028). Phone toll-free 800/322-3770.* Covering 71,000 acres on the border of Utah and Idaho, Bear Lake is the state's second-largest freshwater lake. Approximately 20 miles long and 200 feet deep, it offers good fishing for mackinaw, rainbow trout, and the rare Bonneville Cisco. There are boat rentals at several resorts. Three park areas include **State Marina**

on the west shore of the lake, **Rendezvous Beach** on the south shore, and **Eastside** area on the east shore. Swimming, beach, water-skiing, fishing, ice fishing, boating (ramp, dock), sailing; hiking, mountain biking, cross-country skiing, snowmobiling, picnicking, tent and trailer sites (rest rooms, showers, hookups; fee). Open daily. **$$**

BEAVER MOUNTAIN SKI AREA. *Garden City (84028). Phone 435/753-0921. www.skithebeav.com.* Three double chairlifts, two surface lifts; patrol, school, rentals; day lodge, cafeteria. Twenty-two runs; vertical drop 1,600 feet. Half-day rates. Open Dec-early Apr, daily. **$$$$**

DAUGHTERS OF THE UTAH PIONEERS MUSEUM. *160 N Main St, Logan (84321). Phone 435/752-5139.* Exhibits depict Utah's past. Located in the Chamber of Commerce building. Open Mon-Fri. **FREE**

HYRUM STATE PARK. *405 W 300 S, Logan (84321). Phone 435/245-6866.* 450-acre reservoir with beach swimming, water-skiing, fishing, ice fishing, boating (ramp, dock), sailing; picnicking, camping (trailer parking). Open year-round. **$$**

MORMON TABERNACLE. *50 N Main St, Logan (84321). Phone 435/755-5598.* This gray limestone example of an early Mormon building (started in 1865, completed in 1891) seats 1,800 and houses a genealogy library. Open Mon-Fri. **FREE**

MORMON TEMPLE. *175 N 300 E, Logan (84321). Phone 435/752-3611.* The site for this massive castellated limestone structure was chosen by Brigham Young, who broke ground for it in 1877. It was completed in 1884. The grounds are open year-round, but the temple is open only to Mormons.

UTAH STATE UNIVERSITY. *7th N and 7th E sts, Logan (84322). Phone 435/797-1000. www.usu.edu.* Established in 1888, Utah State university now enrolls more than 20,000 students. On campus is the Nora Eccles Harrison Museum of

Art. Open Mon-Fri; closed holidays, also Thanksgiving weekend, Dec 22-Jan 2. **FREE**

WASATCH-CACHE NATIONAL FOREST. *Logan Canyon. 1500 E US 89, Logan (84321). Phone 435/755-3620. www.fs.fed.us/wcnf/.* Fishing, backcountry trails, hunting, winter sports, picnicking, and camping. Fees charged at most recreation sites. Open daily.

WILLOW PARK ZOO. *419 W 700 S, Logan (84321). Phone 435/750-9893. www.ci.logan.ut.us/ parksrec/Willow%20Park%20Zoo/.* A small but attractive zoo with shady grounds and especially good bird-watching of migratory species. Open daily 9 am-dusk; closed Jan 1, Thanksgiving, Dec 25. **$**

PLACES TO STAY

If you choose to include an overnight stay in your trip along this Byway, Mobil Travel Guide recommends the following lodgings.

Logan

★★★**THE ANNIVERSARY INN.** (�־) *169 E Center St, Logan (84321). Phone 435/752-3443; toll-free 800/574-7605. www.anniversaryinn.com.* The guest rooms at this inn are all charmingly unique, each appointed with its own romantic theme. From Jesse James' Hideout to Aphrodite's Court to the Space Odyssey, each room is guaranteed to tickle the senses. 21 rooms. Adults only. Complimentary continental breakfast. Check-out noon, check-in 5 pm. TV; VCR available. Lobby in a historic mansion (1879); Oriental rugs, period furniture. Totally nonsmoking. **$**
◨

★★**BEST WESTERN BAUGH MOTEL.** (�־) *153 S Main St, Logan (84321). Phone 435/752-5220; toll-free 800/462-4154. www.bestwestern.com.* 77 rooms, 1-2 story. Check-out 11 am. TV; cable (premium), VCR available. Fireplaces. Restaurant. Room service. Health club privileges. Pool. **¢**
[D] [SC]

★**COMFORT INN.** *447 N Main St, Logan (84321). Phone 435/752-9141; toll-free 800/228-5150. www.comfortinn.com.* 83 rooms, 2 story. Complimentary continental breakfast. Check-out noon. TV. In-room modem link. In-house fitness room. Indoor pool, whirlpool. ¢

★**DAYS INN.** *364 S Main, Logan (84321). Phone 435/753-5623; toll-free 800/329-7466. www.daysinn.com.* 64 rooms, 2 story. Pet accepted. Complimentary continental breakfast. Check-out 11 am. TV. Laundry services. Indoor pool. ¢

★★★**LOGAN HOUSE INN.** *168 N 100 E, Logan (84321). Phone 435/752-7727; toll-free 800/478-7459. www.loganhouseinn.com.* This historic inn, fully restored with leaded stained-glass windows over the main staircase, was built at the turn of the 20th century. The grounds are landscaped with lilac bushes, evergreens, and maple trees. 6 rooms, 2 story. Complimentary breakfast. Check-out 11 am, check-in 3-5 pm. TV; VCR available. In-room modem link. Fireplaces. Laundry services. Concierge. Totally nonsmoking. $

Millville

★★ **BEAVER CREEK LODGE.** *PO Box 139, Hwy 89, Millville (84326). Phone 435/946-3400; toll-free 800/946-4485. www.beavercreeklodge .com.* 11 rooms, 3 story. Offering many outdoor amenities, from skiing and hiking to snowmobiles. $$

Providence

★★★**PROVIDENCE INN.** *10 S Main, Providence (84332). Phone 435/752-3432; toll-free 800/480-4943. www.providenceinn.com.* As part of the Old Rock Church building, this historic bed-and-breakfast built in 1869 has rooms decorated in various periods: Early American, Victorian, and Georgian. Guests may sit in the parlor and

enjoy the fireplace and selection of reading material or wander the landscaped grounds. 17 rooms, 3 story. Complimentary full breakfast. Check-out 11 am, check-in 4 pm. TV; VCR (movies). In-room modem link. Laundry services. Totally nonsmoking. $

PLACES TO EAT

A long day of driving is sure to make you hungry. At the end of your journey, take a table at one of the following restaurants.

★**BLUEBIRD.** *19 N Main St, Logan (84321). Phone 435/752-3155.* Closed Sun; Thanksgiving, Dec 25. Breakfast, lunch, dinner. Children's menu. Serves old-fashioned sodas at a marble soda fountain. $$

★ **CABIN FEVER CAFÉ.** *180 W 1200 S, Logan (84321). Phone 435/563-4700.* American menu. This is a favorite of Logan residents, providing good food in a comfortable family setting. $

★★ **CAFÉ SABOR.** *600 W Center St, Logan (84321). Phone 435/752-2700.* Mexican menu. This regional Mexican eatery is located in the historic Center Street Depot. $

★ **THE COPPER MILL.** *55 N Main St, Logan (84321). Phone 435/752-0647.* American menu. Lunch, dinner. A local favorite serving family-style food in a comfortable setting. $

★★**GIA'S RESTAURANT AND DELI.** *119 S Main St, Logan (84321). Phone 435/752-8384.* Italian menu. Closed Dec 25. Lunch, dinner. Children's menu. $$

★★ **LE NONNE.** *132 N Main St, Logan (84321). Phone 435/752-9577.* Italian menu. Closed Mon. Located in downtown Logan, this establishment specializes in traditional Italian cuisine. $$

Nebo Loop Scenic Byway

✳ UTAH

Quick Facts

LENGTH: 37 miles.

TIME TO ALLOW: 1 hour.

BEST TIME TO DRIVE: Summer through fall; summer is the high season.

BYWAY TRAVEL INFORMATION: Mountainland Travel Region: 801/229-3800.

SPECIAL CONSIDERATIONS: Most of the route is somewhat narrow and winding. This means that you won't have much opportunity to pass slower vehicles, and speed limits average 30 mph. Plan to sit in the front seat of your vehicle if you are susceptible to carsickness. A 200-foot-long section of the route consists of hairpin curves, so you must slow to about 15 mph in order to get around the 90-degree turns safely.

RESTRICTIONS: Heavy snowfall in the winter necessitates the closure of the Nebo Loop Scenic Byway to passenger vehicles from October to the first of June each year. However, Utah State Park employees groom the road for winter use.

BICYCLE/PEDESTRIAN FACILITIES: This Byway is a popular destination for both road and mountain bikers. The route offers 214 miles of paved and dirt roads, 103 miles of hiking and biking trails, and 71,270 roadless acres for visitors to enjoy. Although a formal bicycle lane has not been designated and the shoulder isn't very wide in most places, cyclists frequently ride the 37-mile loop.

This Byway begins in the quiet community of Payson and ascends back and forth through a canyon of deep, fresh forest that turns to visual fire in the fall. The route continues alongside a cold, rocky creek that drops off into intermittent miniature waterfalls; fishers sit aside this creek in the cool of dusk and let their bait float, listening to a cricket symphony and the fading birds' sonata.

By degrees, the landscape changes into a high-mountain wilderness. Only fields of crisp, bright wildflowers interrupt the thick stands of aspen. Incredibly high overlooks show the Wasatch Mountains sitting loosely below you like a pile of ribbon. From these overlooks, you can also see the Byway's namesake, 11,877-foot Mount Nebo.

This area is so well liked that more than 1 million people visit annually, and a good percentage of them reserve campsites a year in advance to ensure that they get a good spot to relax for a few days. During the summer, most people like to fish at the glass-smooth lakes, such as Payson, or hike on the many trails, such as Loafer Mountain Trail.

THE BYWAY STORY

The Nebo Loop Scenic Byway tells archaeological, cultural, historical, natural, recreational, and scenic stories that make it a unique and treasured Byway.

Archaeological

Archaeological sites in the area show that this valley had one of the largest Native American populations in the Great Basin. In fact, if you had gone to the Byway's Utah Valley Overlook in about AD 1500, you would have seen smoke curling up from several large villages. This Byway now retains two archaeological sites, both of which are associated with Native Americans.

The first, the Nephi Mounds, was an agricultural site used by the Fremont Indians around AD 1300. The Nephi Mounds archaeological site is agriculture in nature, as opposed to most of the mounds in the United States, which are ritualistic or artistic in nature. As one of the primary sites for the Fremont Indian farming, Nephi Mounds was discovered by modern peoples when a farmer uncovered Indian relics in his field.

The second is Walker Flat, a favorite camping spot of the Ute Indians, who liked to spend their summers in these mountains. Walker Flat is also where the Walker War broke out between the Utes and Mormon settlers. The historic Peteeneet Academy displays information about Ute Chief Walker and his followers, the protagonists of the Walker War.

Cultural

Settled by Mormon Pioneers in 1850, the area surrounding the Byway took on the culture of the farmer and the frontiersman, with pieces of the native cultures mixed in. Although towns like Payson and Nephi were established nearby, Mount Nebo and its surrounding landscape were preserved even after a road ran through these backwoods areas; to destroy some of nature's finest work is beyond the culture that still remains on the Nebo Loop today. Proud of their pioneer and native heritage and the legacy of the Nebo Loop, the residents of Payson, Nephi, and surrounding communities enjoy the rivers, lakes, and forests nearby to their fullest extent.

The Byway covers two counties, and as you continue south, the communities become smaller and life becomes simpler. The city now known as Payson was once called Peteetneet, named for Chief Peteetneet of the Ute Tribe. Peteetneet, which means little waters, is now the name of the Academy that exhibits art and museum pieces. Visitors stop at the Peteetneet

Academy on their way to the natural wonders of the Nebo Loop. And like any communities with traditions, the Byway communities host unique festivals throughout the year. Over Labor Day weekend, for example, Payson hosts the Golden Onion Days celebration.

As you drive the Byway, you may want to follow the examples of the local residents and grab your tent and a fishing pole to camp your way along the Nebo Loop. Stop by some of the orchards along the way that have been a main supply of food and income for Nebo's communities for nearly two centuries. By stopping at small communities along the way, you get to see what's in store beyond Mount Nebo.

Historical

The road that became the Nebo Loop had been used for centuries by Native Americans and, later, by explorers and sawmill companies. The road was then built by the Civilian Conservation Corps (CCC) and enhanced by the addition of recreational facilities.

People have inhabited the Byway and its surrounding areas for unrecorded amounts of time. The elusive Fremont Indians made their home here before the Utes, who played a part as settlers arrived in Utah. The Walker War, one of two significant wars between Utah Utes and the Mormon settlers, took place on the northern end of the Byway.

Important explorers, such as Dominques and Escalante (1776), Jedediah Smith (1826), and John C. Fremont (1843), investigated the area and found it attractive. Mountain man Daniel Potts, who came in 1827, said of the Utah Valley, "This is a most beautiful country." The Mormon Battalion also used the road in 1848 on their way back from California and the Mexican War, and the 49ers used it to go west for gold.

Early white settlement is marked by places such as Pete Winward Reservoir. Payson farmers built the Reservoir between 1890 and 1907 with horse teams and drags and named it after the city's first water master. Later, in the mid-1930s, the CCC made significant contributions to the development of the Byway and its components. For example, they built Dry Lake, which was ingeniously filled with water from a canal that was more than a mile away. More importantly, the CCC's rockwork allowed both the paved Byway road and the stream to occupy the narrow space that it does.

The old Loafer Ski Area and the Maple Dell Scout Camp demonstrate the longtime popularity of this Byway for recreation. The Loafer Ski Area was a popular place to relax from 1947 to the mid-1950s. The old slope, whose concrete slab foundations you can still see, had a 930-foot-long towrope and a 284-foot elevation drop. The ski area was rudimentarily furnished: a simple shelter, a toilet, and an outdoor picnic area. The Maple Dell Scout Camp has produced vivid memories for Utah scouts since 1947. Continual improvements have been made at the camp; one of the most notable was construction of a large lodge in 1960, which was made possible by the donations of Mr. Clyde, then the governor of Utah and president of the Boy Scout Council. Later, a dance hall, cottages, and a swimming pool filled with water from a nearby icy spring were added.

By preserving the Nebo Loop as it is today, visitors are able to see this beautiful wilderness as it was 100 or 200 years ago. Its more recent history is preserved in its museums and exhibits and in structures and buildings all along the Byway.

Natural

Named for the tallest peak on the Wasatch mountain range, the Nebo Loop Scenic Byway travels through a variety of terrains and a multitude of natural treasures. From lakes to forests to rocky overlooks, the Nebo Loop displays some of Utah's most beautiful natural settings.

The Byway takes you into the Wasatch mountain range, where you overlook the Utah Valley.

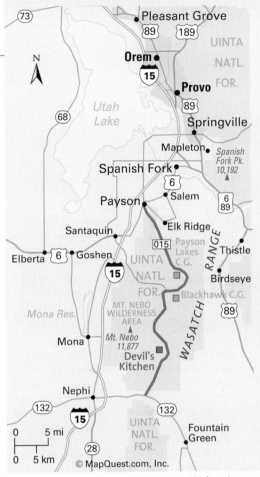

see page A30 for color map

The range was formed from great movements of the Earth's crust and an uplift of sedimentary layers; today, Mount Nebo reaches the height of 11,877 feet above sea level. Viewing the topography from the Byway gives you a sense of Utah's place in the Rocky Mountains.

Some favorite places for travelers on the Byway are Payson Lakes Recreation Area and Devil's Kitchen. Climbing the Byway toward the lakes, you'll pass Payson Creek running through the forest. When you reach the peaceful lakes, you'll find them to be a mountain retreat perfect for fishing, picnicking, or just enjoying the serenity of the gently lapping waters. The Devil's Kitchen has been compared to Bryce Canyon: red rock and strange pillars of rock called hoodoos decorate this part of the Byway. This is where Utah's sandstone sculptures begin.

❋ *Nebo Loop Scenic Byway*

The Byway travels through the Uinta National Forest full of cottonwoods, maples, pines, and aspen. The forest springs up on either side of the road, shading it with millions of leaves. You may also notice the change in plant life as you ascend the Byway—views of sagebrush are soon overtaken by pine and spruce trees. Among the trees live elk, deer, and bobcats. On a very rare occasion, a bear or a cougar comes into view, but these creatures spend time in the most secluded places of the Mount Nebo Wilderness Area.

From lush forests to sandstone basins, the Nebo Loop offers a compact view of some of Utah's unique terrains. Be sure to explore realms of the Nebo Loop Scenic Byway—all created by nature.

Recreational

All the typical outdoor recreational activities can be done here, and some activities, like hunting and horseback riding, that are rarely allowed in other urban forests are allowed here. Nebo Loop is also a popular area for watching wildlife; specific viewpoints have been designated for observing deer, elk, moose, and bears.

Because the Byway is so popular, reservations must be made at least a year in advance for Blackhawk and Payson Lakes campgrounds; the typical weekend occupancy rate is 95 percent during the camping season. Payson Lake is the most popular campground because it offers swimming, canoeing, hiking, fishing, a fully accessible nature trail, and fishing piers for people with disabilities. Blackhawk Campground has the only horse transfer station for people with disabilities in the region that is within an hour of urban populations. Few scenic Byways offer so much recreation while showing so little evidence of use.

Although the Byway attracts more than one million visitors each year, the design of the facilities makes them almost fade into the woods, keeping them fairly invisible to the scenic driver. Payson Lakes Campground illustrates this fact by offering a myriad of recreational activities that remain hidden from the Byway, yet the road is only a few hundred feet away. In the midst of the typical camping experiences is the Mount Nebo Wilderness Area, which offers primitive, roadless recreation for the adventurer. In the winter, Byway recreation includes ice climbing, snowmobiling, snowshoeing, and cross-country skiing.

Scenic

A rare spectrum of crisp, vibrant views is packed into this relatively short Byway, where jagged, frozen mountains are infused with vigorous colors. The diversity spreads across the Byway's flat bottomlands, mid-elevation scrub oak, high alpine fir and aspen, snow-covered peaks, red rock formations, gray sandstone cliffs, and salt flats. Devil's Kitchen typifies this diversity: the short trail to Devil's Kitchen is towered over by dark green pine, but just a short walk later, the green disappears, and the huge red rock spires that are the Kitchen jab into the deep blue sky.

The Byway is an essay in color: wildflowers paint blossom mosaics in the spring and trees explode with color in the fall. If you get up really high, onto one of the Byway's many overlooks, you can view other diverse scenes: the urban sprawl of the Wasatch Front; Utah Lake, the largest body of fresh water in the region; and Mount Nebo, the highest peak in the Wasatch range (11,994 feet).

HIGHLIGHTS

As you travel the Nebo Loop Scenic Byway from the Payson end, consider following this itinerary. If you're starting at the other end, simply read this list from the bottom and work your way up.

- **Mile 0—Peteetneet Academy.** The school was built in 1901 by well-known architect Richard C. Watkins and consists of a three-story building with a bell tower and red sandstone accent on red brick walls. Peteetneet is still used for classes in the fine arts and public meetings and events.

- **Mile 0.8—Maple Dell Scout Camp.** Since 1947, this camp has given scouts a chance to take in vivid scenery and participate in outdoor recreation. In 1960, a large lodge was constructed, along with a dance hall, cottages, and a swimming pool.

- **Miles 7.0 and 7.1—Payson Lakes Day Use Area, Fisherman Entrance.** Payson Lakes has trailer camping and handicapped-accessible sites and features a shoreline nature trail, two beaches, and a universal access pier.

- **Mile 10.2—Blackhawk Campground.** This popular Forest Service campground has group and individual campsites as well as a horse camping facility. The area accommodates equestrian users by featuring tie racks, double-wide camping spurs, and easy access to the trails.

- **Mile 11.5—Beaver Dam Overlook.**

- **Mile 16.2—Santaquin Overlook.**

- **Mile 17.3—Bald Mountain Overlook.**

- **Mile 18.0—Utah Lake Overlook.**

- **Mile 21.9—Nebo Bench Trail (trail head sign).**

- **Mile 22.5—Mount Nebo Overlook.** Much of the geologic base of Mount Nebo is derived from the Oquirrh formation, which includes quartzite, limestone, and sandstone. The multiple advances and retreats of mountain glaciers formed cirque-shaped basins predominantly found in Bald Mountain and Mount Nebo. Many legends are associated with Mount Nebo and its Native American history.

- **Mile 26.6—Devil's Kitchen.** Devil's Kitchen Geologic Area is one of the highlights of the Byway. Eroded layers of red-tinted river gravel and silt form spires and sharp ridges. Visitors viewing this unique feature will marvel at its brilliant contrast to the surrounding mountain greenery. There is a rest room and a handicapped-accessible picnic area.

- **Mile 28.0—Salt Creek Overlook.**

- **Mile 35.2—Junction with Highway 132.** Here you come to the end of the Byway. Nephi is about 10 miles west.

THINGS TO SEE AND DO

Driving along the Nebo Loop Scenic Byway will certainly keep your senses engaged, but if you yearn to get out of the car and stretch your legs, or if you'd like to make a mini-vacation out of your trip, check out these attractions along the route.

GOLDEN ONION DAYS. *Payson (84651).* Includes community theater presentations, 5K and 10K runs, horse races, demolition derby, parade, fireworks, and picnic. Labor Day weekend.

❋ *Nebo Loop Scenic Byway*

MOUNT NEBO. *Payson (84651).* Mount Nebo's (elevation 11,877 feet) three peaks are the highest in the Wasatch range. The Byway travels south through Payson and Santaquin canyons and then climbs 9,000 feet up Mount Nebo, offering a view of **Devil's Kitchen,** a brilliantly colored canyon. This section of the Byway is not recommended for those who dislike heights.

PAYSON LAKES RECREATION AREA. *Phone 801/798-3571.* Fishing, swimming; camping, hiking, backpacking. Located within the Uinta National Forest.

PETEETNEET CULTURAL ARTS CENTER AND MUSEUM. *50 South Peteetneet Blvd. Payson (84651). Phone 801/465-9427.* Named after Ute leader Chief Peteetneet, the center and museum (also called the Peteetneet Academy) is housed in a historic Victorian-style building. Art gallery, photography exhibit, blacksmith shop, visitor's center. Open Mon-Fri 10 am-4 pm.

UINTA NATIONAL FOREST. *88 W and 100 N, Provo (84601). Phone 801/377-5780. www.fs.fed .us/r4/uinta/.* Scenic drives through the 950,000-acre forest; areas include **Provo Canyon, Bridal Veil Falls, Deer Creek Dam and Reservoir, Diamond Fork Canyon, Hobble Creek Canyon,** and **Strawberry Reservoir;** roads give an unsurpassed view of colorful landscapes, canyons, waterfalls. Stream and lake fishing; hunting for deer and elk, camping (fee), picnicking. Reservations accepted.

PLACES TO STAY

If you choose to include an overnight stay in your trip along this Byway, Mobil Travel Guide recommends the following lodgings. Provo is about 15 miles north of Payson, which marks the northern end of the Byway.

★ **CHERRY LANE MOTEL.** *240 E 100 N, Payson (84651). Phone 801/465-2582.* 10 rooms, 1 story. This is a cozy and efficient roadside motel in the classic 1950s model. **$**

★**COMFORT INN.** *830 N Main St, Payson (84651). Phone 801/465-4861; toll-free 800/228-5150. www.comfortinn.com.* 62 rooms, 2 story. Pet accepted; fee. Complimentary continental breakfast. Check-out 11 am. TV; cable (premium). Laundry services. In-house fitness room, sauna. Indoor pool, whirlpool. **¢**

D 🛏 ⬛🐾⛱

★★★ **MARRIOTT PROVO HOTEL AND CONFERENCE CENTER.** *101 W 100 N, Provo (84601). Phone 801/377-4700; toll-free 800/777-7144. www.marriott.com.* Nearby attractions include two shopping malls, as well as the Seven Peaks Water Park and Ice Rink, where the ice hockey competition and practices for the 2002 Winter Olympics were held. 331 rooms, 9 story. Check-out noon. TV; cable (premium). In-room modem link. Restaurant. In-house fitness room, sauna. Pool, whirlpool. Downhill ski 14 miles. Airport transportation. Business center.

🏋 🧗 **D** ⬛⛱

★★★ **SUNDANCE RESORT.** *N Fork Provo Canyon, Sundance (84604). Phone 801/225-4107; toll-free 800/892-1600. www.sundanceresort.com.* This rustic retreat is set amidst the lush wilderness and offers a truly delightful stay. Guests have a choice of mountain cottages to relax in, each a unique blend of elegance and rustic charm. Check-out 11 am, check-in 3 pm. TV; cable (premium), VCR available (free movies). Fireplaces. Dining rooms. Supervised children's activities (June-Sept), ages 6-12. In-house fitness room. Downhill, cross-country ski on site. Concierge. Handmade wooden furniture; Native American art. **$$**

⛷ 🧗 ⛳ 🎿 🏋 ⬛⛱

PLACES TO EAT

A long day of driving is sure to make you hungry. At the end of your journey, take a table at one of the following restaurants.

★★ **DALTON'S FINE DINING.** *20 S 100 W, Payson (84651). Phone 801/465-9182.* American menu. Closed Sun. Lunch, dinner. Featuring upscale regional American cuisine in a refined atmosphere. **$$**

★★ **FOUNDRY GRILL.** *N Fork Provo Canyon, Sundance (84604). Phone 801/223-4220; toll-free 800/892-1600. www.sundanceresort.com.* American menu. Breakfast, lunch, dinner, Sun brunch. Bar. Outdoor seating. Rustic, western décor; fireplace, bare wood floors. Totally nonsmoking. **$$**
[D]

★★★ **THE TREE ROOM.** *N Fork Provo Canyon, Sundance (84604). Phone 801/223-4200; toll-free 800/892-1600. www.sundanceresort.com.* Located at the base of the Sundance ski lift, this restaurant's two-story windows offer stunning views of the rugged mountains and surrounding wilderness. The upscale yet casual room is filled with beautiful displays of American Indian dolls and pottery. The sophisticated new American cuisine includes wild game, steaks, seafood, and herbs and vegetables from the resort's own organic gardens. American menu. Dinner. Bar. Reservations required. Menu changes seasonally. **$$$**
[D]

Beartooth Scenic Byway

❋ WYOMING   AN ALL-AMERICAN ROAD
Part of a multistate Byway; see also MT.

Quick Facts

LENGTH: 69 miles.

TIME TO ALLOW: 3 hours.

BEST TIME TO DRIVE: Early summer mornings.

BYWAY TRAVEL INFORMATION: Shoshone National Forest: 307/527-6921.

SPECIAL CONSIDERATIONS: The alpine climate is rigorous, and severe weather conditions can occur any month of the year. Even during the summer, temperatures range from the 70s on sunny days to below freezing during sudden snowstorms.

RESTRICTIONS: The entire length of the Byway is open from Memorial Day weekend through about mid-October. Snow closes sections of the route during the winter. Check with the local ranger district offices before planning a trip in May or September, because occasional snowstorms can occur during these months.

BICYCLE/PEDESTRIAN FACILITIES: A growing number of visitors experience the Byway and its surrounding areas by bicycle and on foot. You'll find hundreds of miles of designated trails that are easily accessible from the Byway. Although the Byway can be biked from end to end, stretches of the route require cautious travel.

The Beartooth Highway is one of the most spectacular national forest routes on this continent. To many, it is known as "the most beautiful highway in America." From its beginning at the border of the Custer National Forest to its terminus near the northeast entrance to Yellowstone National Park, the Beartooth Highway (US 212) offers you the ultimate high-country experience as it travels through the Custer, Shoshone, and Gallatin national forests.

Since its completion in 1936, the highway has provided millions of visitors a rare opportunity to see the transition from a lush forest ecosystem to alpine tundra in the space of just a few miles. The Beartooth area is one of the highest and most rugged areas in the lower 48 states, with 20 peaks reaching over 12,000 feet in elevation. Glaciers are found on the north flank of nearly every mountain peak that is over 11,500 feet high in these mountains.

THE BYWAY STORY

The Beartooth Scenic Byway tells historical, natural, recreational, and scenic stories that make it a unique and treasured Byway.

Historical

The first recorded travel across the Beartooth Pass area occurred in 1882, when General Sheridan, with a force of 129 soldiers and scouts, 104 horses, and 157 mules, pioneered and marked a route across the mountains from Cooke City to Billings. A year later, a packer named Van Dyke modified the trail and located a route off the Beartooth Plateau into Rock

Creek and Red Lodge. Van Dyke's trail was the only direct route between Red Lodge and Cooke City until the Beartooth Highway was constructed in 1934 and 1935. Remnants of Van Dyke's trail are visible from the Rock Creek Overlook parking lot, appearing as a Z on the mountain between the highway switchbacks about 1/4 mile south of the parking lot.

Doctor Siegfriet and other visionaries from the Bearcreek and Red Lodge communities foresaw, in the early 1900s, the value of a scenic route over the mountains to connect to Yellowstone Park. These men spent many years promoting the construction of a road over the mountains, and even began the construction of a road with hand tools and horse-drawn implements. Other routes were surveyed in the 1920-1925 period, and in 1931, President Hoover signed the "Park Approach Act," which was the forerunner to the funding of the road you now know as the Beartooth Highway. This highway was first opened to public travel on June 12, 1936. The Beartooth Highway was classified as a National Forest Scenic Byway on February 8, 1989.

Natural

A variety of theories exist on the formation of the Beartooth Mountains, but geologists generally agree that the mountains resulted from an uplifting of an Archean block of metamorphic rocks that were eroded, flooded with volcanic lava on the southwest corner, and covered with glaciers. Seventy million years of formation went into making this section of the Rocky Mountains.

The Palisades that stretch along the Beartooth Front were first sedimentary rocks originally deposited as flat-lying beds in an ancient sea. Thrust skyward, they have become conspicuous spires. Pilot and Index Peaks are the remainders of an extensive volcanic field that came into existence 50 million years ago.

Changes are continuing in the present. Yellowstone Park has been an active volcanic center for more than 15 million years. Erosional forces are still at work. Glaciers have shaped the mountains into the range it is today. The glaciers edged their ways down just 10,000 years ago. Younger rocks are the sources of coal that was exploited by the early settlers of Red Lodge.

The Stillwater Complex, a body of igneous magma formed along the northern edge of the mountain range 2.7 million years ago, is one of the rarest and least understood geologic occurrences in the world. It is the site of the only source of the platinum group metals in the Western Hemisphere, mined by Stillwater Mining Company of Nye, Montana.

Recreational

Recreational opportunities are abundant in the area traversed by the Beartooth Scenic Byway. You can cross-country ski on the snowfields in June and July. Play in the snow, hike across the broad plateaus and Forest Service trails (some of which are National Recreation Trails), camp, picnic, and fish for trout in the streams and lakes adjacent to the Byway. You can also view wildflowers, view and photograph wildlife (moose, Rocky Mountain goats, mule deer, black bears, grizzly bears, marmots, and pikas), visit a guest ranch, or take a guided horseback trip from Cooke City. Also, you can bicycle, downhill ski on the headwalls, and photograph nature at its finest. Even when the highway is formally closed to automobiles, snowmobilers may travel the route and enjoy a spectacular winter wonderland.

If you enjoy skiing, each summer in June and July the Red Lodge International Ski Race Camp is conducted on the north side of the East Summit on the Twin Lakes Headwall. This camp, not open to the public for skiing, is for aspiring Olympic-caliber skiers and provides a terrific viewing opportunity.

Scenic

The spire known as the Bears Tooth was carved in the shape of a large tooth by glacial ice gnawing inward and downward against a single high part of a rocky crest. Beartooth Butte is a remnant of sedimentary deposits that once

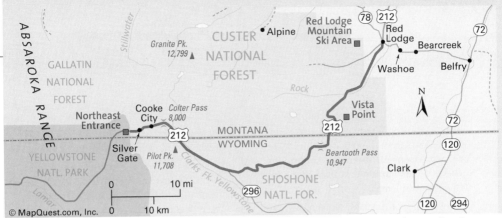

see page A17 for color map

covered the entire Beartooth Plateau. The red-stained rock outcrop near the top of Beartooth Butte was a stream channel some 375 million years ago, so fossils are found in abundance in the rocks of Beartooth Butte.

These treeless areas, near or above the timberline, generally are areas that cannot grow trees. Vegetation is often small, low-growing, and compact—characteristics that are vital to the survival of the plants at this elevation. Wildflowers, often as tiny as a quarter-inch across, create a literal carpet of color during the 45-day or shorter growing season.

On the other hand, the common flowers found below the timberline in wet meadows are Indian paintbrush, monkeyflower, senecio, and buttercups; in drier areas are lupine, beardstongue, arrowleaf balsamroot, and forget-me-nots. The colors and the flowers change weekly as the growing season progresses, but mid-July is generally the optimum for wildflower displays.

Wildlife in the Beartooth country varies from the largest American land mammal, the moose, to the shrew, which is the smallest land mammal. Other animals commonly seen along the highway are mule deer, whitetail deer, elk, marmots (rock chucks), and pine squirrels. Bighorn sheep, Rocky Mountain goats, black bears, and grizzly bears are residents of the area, but none is seen often. Birds include the golden eagle, raven, Clarks nutcracker, Stellars jay, robin, mountain bluebird, finch, hawk, and falcon. Watch for the water ouzel darting in and out of—and walking along the bottoms of—streams.

The snowbanks often remain until August near Beartooth Pass, and remnants of some drifts may remain all summer. A pink color often appears on the snow later in the summer, which is caused by the decay of a microscopic plant that grows on the surface of the snowbank. When the plant dies, it turns red and colors the snow pink.

HIGHLIGHTS

Consider using the following itinerary as you travel the Beartooth Scenic Byway.

- As you come into Red Lodge from the north on US 212, the **Beartooth Plateau** looms over the surrounding prairie foothills as a hulking mass of black, rounded mountains. The plateau, an immense block of metamorphic rock, was heaved up through the Earth's crust about 50 million years ago. Much later, an enormous ice cap smoothed its surface and flowed down into the plateau's side canyons, hollowing them into spacious U-shaped valleys.

- **Red Lodge** is an 1880s coal mining and ranching town lined with turn-of-the-century redbrick storefronts and hotels that cater mainly to skiers and visitors to Yellowstone. Visit the **Beartooth Nature Center,** at the north end of Red Lodge, which exhibits native wildlife.

- The road follows **Rock Creek** into the mountains, winding through grassy hills that soon give way to heavily forested mountains. Rocky outcrops interrupt evergreen forests, and an occasional spire juts over the trees.

Wyoming

❋ Beartooth Scenic Byway

About 13 miles from Red Lodge, the road climbs away from the creek, and suddenly the vista opens up toward the 1,800-foot cliffs that bend around the head of the valley in a tight semicircle.

- After 5 miles of dramatic switchbacks, stop at the **Vista Point scenic overlook.** Here, at 9,200 feet, a short path leads to the tip of a promontory with phenomenal views across Rock Creek Canyon to the high, rolling country of the **Beartooth Plateau.** Signs brief you on the geology, plants, and animals of the area. As you continue on US 212, the trees give out entirely, and you begin crossing a landscape of low, rounded hills covered with grasses, sedges, and lavish wildflowers in summer. Soon, the road cuts back to the rim of the canyon, and from the narrow turnouts, you can see a chain of glacial lakes, including Twin Lakes, 1,000 feet below. Even in July, enough snow accumulates against the headwall here to draw skiers.

- As you pass the ski lift, the **Absaroka Range** breaks over the southwest horizon in a row of jagged volcanic peaks. Wildflower meadows lead to the west summit of **Beartooth Pass,** at an exalted 10,947 feet. From the pass, you descend to a landscape where scattered islands of pine and spruce eke out a living amid knobs of granite and fields of wildflowers. Hundreds of tiny ponds and several small lakes shimmer in glaciated depressions. As you approach the turnoff for Island Lake Campground, two prominent spires of the Absaroka Range swing into view: 11,708-foot Pilot Peak and 11,313-foot Index Peak. Beyond this point, you descend to a forest of lodgepole and whitebark pines toward 10,514-foot Beartooth Butte. Soon, you pass Beartooth Lake, a great picnic spot nestled against the butte's 1,500-foot cliffs.

- When the road breaks out of the trees, look to the left across a deep canyon to see Beartooth Falls cascading through the forest. In another mile, follow the gravel road to **Clay Butte**

Lookout, a fire tower with a smashing view of some of Montana's highest mountains.

- Watch for deer, moose, and elk in the meadows as the road moves down the flank of the plateau to the **Pilot & Index Overlook.** You're looking at the northeastern edge of the Absaroka Range, an eroded mass of lava, ash, and mudflows that began forming 50 million years ago.

- Continue 5 1/2 miles to an unmarked bridge over **Lake Creek** and take the short path back to a powerful waterfall thundering through a narrow chasm. A completely different sort of cascade fans out over a broad ramp of granite in the trees above **Crazy Creek Campground,** 2 1/2 miles farther.

- From here, the road picks up the **Clarks Fork River** and follows it through what is left of a centuries-old forest, much of which fell victim to the great Yellowstone fires of 1988. Soon, the road passes through the tiny tourist crossroads of **Cooke City,** begun as a 19th-century mining camp. In 1877, the Nez Perce Indians retreated through this area on their way to Canada. Four miles beyond, the drive ends at the northeast entrance to Yellowstone National Park.

THINGS TO SEE AND DO

Driving along the Beartooth Scenic Byway will certainly keep your senses engaged, but if you yearn to get out of the car and stretch your legs, or if you'd like to make a mini-vacation out of your trip, check out these attractions along the route.

SHOSHONE NATIONAL FOREST. *808 Meadow Lane Ave, Cody (82414). Phone 307/527-6241. www.fs.fed.us/r2/shoshone/.* This 2,466,586-acre area is one of the largest in the national forest system. The Fitzpatrick, Popo Agie, North Absaroka, Washakie, and a portion of the Absaroka-Beartooth wilderness areas all lie within its boundaries. The forest includes outstanding lakes, streams, big-game herds, mountains, and some of the largest glaciers in the continental United States. Fishing; hunting. Camping.

⭐ YELLOWSTONE NATIONAL PARK. *NE Entrance Rd and Grand Loop Rd, Cody (82190). Phone 307/344-2109. www.nps.gov/yell/.* In 1872, the US Congress set aside more than 3,000 square miles of wilderness in the Wyoming Territory, establishing the world's first national park. More than a century later, Yellowstone boasts a marvelous list of sights, attractions, and facilities: a large freshwater lake, the highest in the nation (7,733 feet); a waterfall almost twice as high as Niagara; a dramatic, 1,200-foot-deep river canyon; and the world's most famous geyser, Old Faithful.

Most of the park has been left in its natural state, preserving the area's beauty and delicate ecological balance. Yellowstone is one of the world's most successful wildlife sanctuaries. Within its boundaries live a variety of species, including grizzly and black bears, elk, deer, pronghorn, and bison—these are wild animals that may look friendly but should not be approached.

The Norris Geyser Basin is 21 miles south of Mammoth Hot Springs. The hottest thermal basin in the world provides a multitude of displays; springs, geysers, mud pots, and steam vents hiss, bubble, and erupt in a showcase of thermal forces at work. The visitor center has self-explanatory exhibits and dioramas (open June-Labor Day, daily). A self-guided trail (2 1/2 miles) offers views of the Porcelain and Back basins from boardwalks (open mid-June-Labor Day). The Museum of the National Park Ranger is also nearby. The area includes more than 1,100 miles of marked foot trails. Some areas may be closed for resource management purposes; inquire at one of the visitor centers in the area before hiking in the backcountry. Guided tours of the wilderness can be made on horseback; horse rentals are available at Mammoth Hot Springs, Roosevelt, and Canyon Village.

Recreational vehicle campsites are available by reservation at Fishing Bridge RV Park (contact TW Recreational Services, Inc, at 307/344-7901 for general information or 307/344-7311 for reservations). During July and August, demand often exceeds supply and many sites are occupied by mid-morning. Overnight vehicle camping or stopping outside designated campgrounds is not permitted. Reservations are required for Bridge Bay, Canyon, Madison, Grant Village, as well as Fishing Bridge RV Park. There are seven additional National Park Service campgrounds at Yellowstone; these are operated on a first-come, first-served basis, so arrive early to secure the site of your choice. Campfires are prohibited except in designated areas or by special permit obtained at ranger stations. Backcountry camping is available by permit only, no more than 48 hours in advance, in person, at ranger stations. Backcountry sites can be reserved for a $15 fee.

Fishing in Yellowstone National Park requires a permit. Rowboats, powerboats, and tackle may be rented at Bridge Bay Marina. Permits are also required for all vessels and must be obtained in person at any of the following locations: South Entrance, Bridge Bay Marina, Mammoth Visitor Center, Grant Village Visitor Center, Lake Ranger Station, and Lewis Lake Campground. Information centers near Yellowstone Lake are located at Fishing Bridge and Grant Village (both open Memorial Day-Labor Day, daily).

At several locations, there are visitor centers, general stores for provisions, service stations, tent and trailer sites, hotels, and lodges. Bus tours run through the park from mid-June to Labor Day (contact Xanterra Parks and Resorts at 307/344-7311).

PLACES TO STAY

If you choose to include an overnight stay in your trip along this All-American Road, Mobil Travel Guide recommends the following lodgings.

★★★ **LAKE YELLOWSTONE HOTEL.** *Yellowstone National Park (82190). Phone 307/344-7311.* This beautiful retreat overlooking Yellowstone Lake was built in 1891. 194 rooms. No A/C. Closed late Sept-late May. Check-out 11 am. Restaurant, bar. **$**

★ **MAMMOTH HOT SPRINGS HOTEL AND CABINS.** *PO Box 165, Yellowstone National Park (82190). Phone 307/344-7311.* 97 rooms, 69 baths, 4 story, 126 cabins. No A/C. Closed Oct-Nov and Mar-Apr. Check-out 11 am. Bar. Cross-country ski on site. **$**

★★ **OLD FAITHFUL INN.** *PO Box 165, Yellowstone National Park (82190). Phone 307/344-7311.* 325 rooms, 246 with bath, 1-4 story. No A/C. Closed mid-Oct-Apr. Check-out 11 am. Restaurant, bar. Many room phones. Historic log structure (1904). Some rooms have a view of Old Faithful. **$**

PLACES TO EAT

A long day of driving is sure to make you hungry. At the end of your journey, try the following restaurant.

★★ **LAKE YELLOWSTONE DINING ROOM.** *Yellowstone National Park (82190). Phone 307/344-7311.* American menu. Closed Oct-May. Breakfast, lunch, dinner. Bar. Children's menu. Totally nonsmoking. **$$**

NOTES

✷ NOTES

NOTES

NOTES

✾ NOTES

✸ NOTES

NOTES

NOTES

NOTES

✳ NOTES